Penguin Education

Thinking and Reasoning

Edited by P. C. Wason and
P. N. Johnson-Laird

Penguin Modern Psychology Readings

General Editor

B. M. Foss

Advisory Board

P. C. Dodwell
Marie Jahoda
S. G. M. Lee
W. M. O'Neil
R. L. Reid
Roger Russell
P. E. Vernon
George Westby

G000058622

Thinking and Reasoning

Selected Readings

Edited by P. C. Wason and
P. N. Johnson-Laird

Penguin Books

Penguin Books Ltd, Harmondsworth,
Middlesex, England
Penguin Books Inc., 7110 Ambassador Road,
Baltimore, Maryland 21207, U.S.A.
Penguin Books Australia Ltd, Ringwood,
Victoria, Australia

First published 1968
Reprinted 1970
This selection copyright © P. C. Wason and
P. N. Johnson-Laird, 1968
Introduction and notes © copyright P. C. Wason and
P. N. Johnson-Laird, 1968

Made and printed in Great Britain by
Cox & Wyman Ltd, London, Reading and Fakenham
Set in Monotype Times Roman

This book is sold subject to the condition that
it shall not, by way of trade or otherwise, be lent,
re-sold, hired out, or otherwise circulated without
the publisher's prior consent in any form of
binding or cover other than that in which it is
published and without a similar condition
including this condition being imposed on the
subsequent purchaser

Contents

Part Three   Inductive Reasoning   131

Part Four   Matching Problems and Conceptual
Thinking   191

Part Five   Information Processing Models and
Computer Simulation   281

Introduction

This book is concerned with directed thinking – the kind of thinking which occurs when someone tries to solve a problem. Many facts about thinking have been discovered but there is no single coherent theory into which they can be integrated. Psychologists who do research on thinking are seldom able to prove each other wrong. On the contrary, they are still demonstrating phenomena and interpreting their findings. Their polemics are reserved for theoretical issues.

The chief difficulty in studying thinking is that it is a private activity which is inaccessible to observation. All that we can observe are the results of thinking rather than the processes which led up to them. Take a man who is given a chess problem to solve – he may just gaze at it and then suddenly announce its solution. The intervening processes between these two events elude our investigation. In the last decade, however, it has been realized that a methodological difficulty is not an excuse for the failure to do research, and there has been a renewed interest in the experimental study of thinking.

Research on thinking has evolved within two main traditions. One tradition has its roots in the Behaviourism of Watson and Hull – a completely objective system which looks for correlations between observable stimuli and responses. Since thinking is not observable, psychologists working in this tradition have been forced into assuming implicit or internal stimuli and responses which mediate the overt response indicating the solution of the problem.

Research in this tradition has been primarily concerned with learning. The emphasis has been placed on trial-and-error with reward stamping in, or reinforcing, the correct response. The organism has been regarded as something passive which learns almost by accident, e.g., the formation of concepts is regarded as a form of discrimination learning in which common elements in different stimuli come to evoke the same response. A typical experiment on problem solving within this tradition is one by Judson, Cofer and Gelfand (1956). They demonstrated that groups of subjects, who first of all learnt lists containing certain words relevant to the solution of a practical problem, subsequently did better in solving the problem than control groups or other groups exposed to lists containing fewer 'key words'. These key words referred to different uses of the problem material, and learning them was assumed to mediate the overt responses which constituted its solution.

The other main tradition has its roots in both the Wurzburg School (1901–13) and in Gestalt psychology. The Wurzburg psychologists were the first to demonstrate the importance of the actual instructions for a task. They criticized the prevailing view that thinking is a progression from one idea to another associated idea, the association having been formed by spatio-temporal contiguity, similarity, etc. Their simple experiments suggested that chains of association were insufficient to explain problem solving. The same stimuli, which on an associationist theory would elicit the same responses, were used in different problems demanding different solutions. Hence they were compelled to postulate a *determining tendency* which guides and controls the process of thinking.

The Gestalt psychologists, on the other hand, emphasized the structure of the problem and the process of re-organization of the perceptual field which leads to insight. This emphasis on perceptual phenomena dominated their research on thinking. Since no clear-cut line can be drawn between perception and cognition the early workers in this field emphasized the perceptual aspect of constructional problems (see Maier, 1) and the structural aspects of practical and mathematical ones (see Duncker, 2).

A more recent development within this tradition has been due to the impact of computer technology. It has been postulated that there are mechanisms in the brain for converting sensory information into a model of the environment, and for utilizing this model in the solution of problems. Such activity, in turn, may involve the transformation of the whole representational system. Thus in this tradition the organism is regarded not as a passive creature which reacts to stimuli in a mechanical way, but as an active, hypothesis-testing system which can modify its own internal structure.

It is difficult to find crucial differences between the predictions which follow from the theoretical notions of these two traditions. But it is, at any rate, evident that psychologists working in the latter tradition have always been much more prepared to postulate complex mechanisms within the brain. It is from this latter tradition that we have chosen the material for this book. It was not feasible to deal with both traditions and hence we have allowed our bias to guide the selection.

The divisions of the book naturally exaggerate the clarity of the boundaries between different conceptual areas. The boundaries we have drawn reflect sometimes a theoretical distinction, sometimes a procedural one, and sometimes merely an aesthetic one. Part One concerns the traditional area of 'problem solving'. Many of the papers in other sections report experiments in which subjects were presented with a problem, e.g., problems in deductive and inductive reasoning. But the term is used here to refer to a wide range of practical, mechanical and mathematical problems which were first studied intensively by the Gestalt psychologists.

Logicians have traditionally distinguished between two types of reasoning – deductive reasoning and inductive reasoning. Deductive inferences are valid by virtue of their form. For example, the following argument is valid whatever sentences are substituted for p and q:

1. if p then q
2. p
   _____
   $\therefore$ q

Inductive inferences, on the other hand, such as the interpolation of a point on a graph, go beyond the given data and there is no criterion for assessing their validity. The truth or falsity of a conclusion is, of course, a different issue from the validity of an inference. Validity means that the conclusion necessarily follows from the premises which may, or may not, be true. Part Two concerns investigations of people's ability to make valid deductive inferences, and Part Three their performance in inductive tasks. As yet there is no clear *psychological* distinction between the two types of inference: people in general are not sufficiently competent in either for a distinction to be made. Work on deductive reasoning has concentrated on the types of error which are commonly made and the reasons for them. Attitudes, prejudices and beliefs, etc., have been shown to have a marked effect on the judgement of validity but this work probably throws more light on personality than it does on thinking. The study of inductive reasoning is facilitated by using games as experimental material. This has two advantages. In games such as chess there is no practical decision procedure, and hence successful performance relies upon more than deductive thinking. Secondly, each move in a game is observable and thus goes some way to externalize the process of thinking.

A study of thinking by Bruner, Goodnow and Austin (1956) was a landmark in the experimental investigation of conceptual

11

thinking. It demonstrated how the attainment of a new concept, e.g., learning to tell German cars from French ones, might be externalized in the laboratory. In a typical task the subject has to select stimuli, one by one, from a whole array, being told each time whether the instance selected was a member of the concept which the experimenter had in mind. As in games, the sequence of choices enables the investigator to make inferences about the particular strategy which the subject had adopted, and to compare this with an 'ideal' strategy.

Part Four has emphasized the less well known British work on matching problems which call for similar conceptual skills. In a matching problem one set of elements: A, B, C, D, has to be matched with another: 1, 2, 3, 4. The subject has to discover, by a process of elimination, the correct matchings from a limited set of information given by the experimenter. Two papers by American authors, however, have been included to illustrate developments in this area since the work of Bruner.

Part Five is largely concerned with the computer simulation of thinking. The development of digital computers has enabled the psychologist to theorize in a new way. He can write his theory in the form of a computer programme which produces an output symbolizing the relevant human behaviour. Conceptual behaviour seems to be dominated by so-called *heuristic methods*, i.e., 'rules of thumb', which do not guarantee solution of a problem but which may be useful as logical short-cuts. Our knowledge of the great variety of different heuristics, and their structural properties, is primarily due to research on simulation. The papers in this section tend to be theoretical rather than empirical, and this is due to the great difficulty of making meaningful comparisons between human and computer performance. A stringent test for this purpose was first proposed by the English mathematician, A. M. Turing (1950). It requires a human being to try to tell the difference between the outputs of a man and a machine. If no difference can be detected, then it is claimed by some workers that the program which controlled the computer is a sufficient explanation of human behaviour. What is really needed, however, is a valid quantitative measure so that the psychologist can tell which (slight) modifications of his program improve the simulation.

Part Six is devoted to the development of thinking in the child. It contains representative papers by two of the most influential thinkers in this field: Piaget and Bruner. It would be wrong, however, to call these investigators and their associates 'child psychologists' or 'educational psychologists' simply because they use children as subjects. Piaget's main concern is with 'genetic epistemology' – a study of the way in which the individual constructs and organizes his knowledge as a function of his age and his society. Similarly, Bruner is concerned with cognitive growth – the way in which human beings learn to represent their experience, and the way in which they are affected by their cultural and linguistic environment.

The readings in this book may all be regarded as studies of how people solve problems. But a more important skill is the ability to *find* problems in the first place – to discover, invent or recognize a problem. Once problems have been formulated, computers are increasingly able to solve them. But the day when computers are able to find worth-while problems is remote. Much research has been done on the personality of creative people, but we still know very little about the processes underlying the creative *act*. The challenge to the psychologist is how to trap invention in the laboratory.

References

BRUNER, J. S., GOODNOW, J. J., and AUSTIN, G. A. (1956), *A study of thinking*, Wiley.

JUDSON, A. J., COFER, C. N., and GELFAND, S. (1956), 'Reasoning as an associative process. II. "Direction" in problem solving as a function of prior reinforcement of relevant responses', *Psycol. Reports*, vol. 2, pp. 501–7.

TURING, A. M. (1950), 'Computing machinery and intelligence', *Mind*, vol. 59, pp. 433–60. Reprinted in Feigenbaum, E. A., and Feldman, J. (eds.), *Computers and thought*, McGraw-Hill, 1963.

Part One PROBLEM SOLVING

The experimental study of problem solving has its origin in the early work of the Gestalt psychologists who used many different kinds of problem, ranging from mechanical puzzles to abstract mathematical problems. A classic paper by Maier (1) demonstrates how the perception of the solution of a problem is like perceiving a hidden figure in a puzzle picture. The Gestalt theorist who was most concerned with the study of thinking was Max Wertheimer (1959). His experimental approach was extended by his pupil, Karl Duncker, from whose monograph we have selected two extracts which epitomize the Gestalt contribution. The first is concerned with the practical problem of destroying a tumour with X-rays without at the same time destroying healthy tissue. The second is about a simple but rather subtle mathematical problem. By modern standards such experiments were often methodologically weak. But the ideas which inspired them have in several instances withstood more refined experimental tests, e.g., Birch and Rabinowitz (3), and Adamson (4). Saugstad and Raaheim (5) present evidence to support their conception of the role played by previous experience in problem solving. Finally, Luchins and Luchins (6) describe a number of experiments which demonstrate how a habitual method of problem solving may lead to one overlooking 'obvious' short-cuts in similar problems.

References

WERTHEIMER, M. (1959), *Productive thinking*, Tavistock.

1 N. R. F. Maier

Reasoning in Humans. II. The Solution of a Problem and its Appearance in Consciousness

Excerpts from N. R. F. Maier, 'Reasoning in humans. II. The solution of a problem and its appearance in consciousness', *J. comp. Psychol*, vol. 12 (1931), pp. 181–94.

Introduction

In an earlier study (3) it was found that experience and its proper selection were not enough to account for the appearance of an original solution. Rather an organizing principle which was called 'direction' was necessary. The present study is concerned with the appearance of the solution and hopes to answer the following questions: (a) does the solution develop from a nucleus or does it appear as a completed whole? (b) what is the conscious experience of an individual just before the solution is found? (c) is the reasoner conscious of the different factors which aid in bringing about the solution?

Method and Procedure

Individual subjects were presented with a problem to which there were several solutions. All but one of the solutions were quite obvious. The difficult solution was the one that was studied because it required originality and was less likely to be linked up with past experience. The simple solutions, however, were not excluded from the experiment. When one was found the subject was asked to find another. The easier solutions thus functioned as (a) a means for encouraging the subject; (b) a period of orientation and adjustment to the situation and the experimenter; and (c) a means of stating the problem without limiting the freedom of the subject.

The experiment was carried on in a large room which contained many objects such as poles, ringstands, clamps, pliers, extension cords, tables and chairs. Two cords were hung from the ceiling, and were of such length that they reached the floor. One hung near a wall, the other from the center of the room. The subject was told, 'Your problem is to tie the ends of those two strings together.' He soon learned that if he held either cord in his hand he could not reach the other. He was then told that he could use or

17

do anything he wished. The experimenter then started his stop-watch without the subject observing it.

When one solution was found the subject was told, 'Now do it a different way.' If he then attempted a modification of his first solution he was told that it really was no different. Thus he soon learned that a solution involving a different principle was desired. When the difficult or test solution was found the experiment ended. If it was not found and the subject insisted that he could find no other way of solving the problem, suggestions or 'helps' were given.

After completing the experiment the subject was asked to report where he got the idea of his last solution and what was in his mind previous to the solution. After a free report, specific questions were asked. During the experiment, when the subject was inactive, he was asked of what he was thinking. When active such questions were unnecessary.

The different types of solutions to the problem were as follows:

Solution 1. One cord was anchored with a large object (such as a chair) placed part way between the cords, while the other cord was brought over to it.

Solution 2. One of the cords was lengthened (with the extension cord, for example) and the other reached with the hand.

Solution 3. While holding one cord the other was pulled in with a pole.

Solution 4. A weight was tied to the cord hanging from the center of the room and then put in motion, thus making it a pendulum. The other cord was then brought near the center and the swinging cord caught as it approached the middle point between the two cords. Solution 4 is the one with which we are concerned in this experiment.

In case the last solution was not found and the subject was ready to give up after having conscientiously worked for at least ten minutes, suggestions or 'helps' were given. (Subjects who were prone to give up were encouraged to continue their efforts.) These hints were as follows:

Hint 1. The experimenter walked about the room, and, in passing the cord which hung from the center of the room, he put it in slight motion a few times. This was done without the subject knowing that a suggestion was being given. The experimenter merely walked to the window and had to pass the cord. It was noted whether or not the moving cord was in the subject's line of vision. If the subject was facing in a different direction, the action was repeated.

Hint 2. In case hint 1 failed to bring about the solution within a few minutes, the subject was handed a pair of pliers and told 'With the aid of this and no other object there is another way of solving the problem.'

In case hint 2 was not followed by the solution, hint 1 was repeated. If it again failed to produce the solution the subject was shown the solution.

The subjects used were graduate and under-graduate men and women students attending the University of Chicago. For the main part of this experiment, sixty-one subjects were used. Others used for testing certain points will be referred to when discussed.

Results

On the basis of their success in solving the problem the subjects may be divided into the following three groups:

1. Those who solved the problem without the aid of 'helps'. There were twenty-four (39·3 per cent) subjects in this group.

2. Those who solved the problem after 'helps' were given. This group contained twenty-three (37·7 per cent) subjects.

3. Those who failed to find solution 4 after the 'helps' had been given. The remaining fourteen (23 per cent) subjects were in this group.

The data obtained from the subjects in group 2 are the most enlightening. Where the subjects in group 1 got the idea of solution 4 can only be known through their introspections. Group 3 did not solve the problem and are therefore of no direct use in our analysis. In group 2, however, the function of the 'helps' can be studied.

Table 1 gives the results of subjects in group 2. In the first column the numbers and sex of the subjects are indicated. In the second column, the solutions which were found by the subject before suggestions were given, are indicated in order. The third column gives in minutes and seconds the time in which the last of these solutions was found (6:15, for example, means six minutes and fifteen seconds). The fourth, fifth, and sixth columns give the time at which the different 'helps' were given. It should be noted that hint 1 was never given until ten minutes had been spent on the problem (except for subject 47) and the subject had had an unproductive period of considerable length after his last solution. In column 7 the time for the first appearance of the idea of solution 4 is given. (Any remark or behavior which indicated that the subject had the idea is regarded as the

Table 1
Subjects who Solved Problem after 'Helps' were given

	1	2	3	4	5	6	7	8	9	10
				Time in minutes and seconds				Number of seconds from last hint to	How solution	Hint 1
Subject		Preliminary solutions	Last solution	Hint 1	Hint 2	Hint 3	Solution 4	solution 4	appeared	reported
5 M.		1, 3, 2	6:00	13:00			13:35	35	W	No
8 M.		1, 2	2:45	13:30			14:10	40	W	No
10 M.		1, 3	4:30	10:00			10:45	45	W	No
14 F.		1, 3	3:30	10:00			11:00	60	P	Yes
18 M.		2, 1, 3	8:30	12:40			13:10	30	W	No
19 F.		3, 1	7:40	11:30			12:00	30	W	No
25 F.		1, 2, 3	9:25	16:00			18:00	120	P	Yes
30 F.		1, 2	5:00	10:30	13:30	19:00	19:40	40	W	No
31 M.		1, 3, 2	6:30	11:30			12:00	30	W	No
32 F.		1, 2, 3	13:40	15:00	17:20		18:00	40	W	No
35 M.		1, 3	5:30	10:10	12:50	14:00	14:30	30	P	Yes
38 M.		1, 2	4:00	10:00			10:20	20	W	Yes

40 F.	3, 1	5:05	10:30		10:50	20	P	No
42 F.	2, 1	4:50	10:15		10:30	15	W	No
43 F.	1, 2	5:40	10:30		13:00	150	P	Yes
44 F.	1, 2, 3	8:00	15:00		15:15	15	P	Yes
45 M.	1, 3, 2	5:30	12:50		13:50	60	W	No
47 F.	1	3:45	9:15		9:40	25	W	No
48 M.	1, 3, 2	5:00	10:00	18:10	18:30	20	W	No
51 M.	1, 3	5:00	11:00		11:25	25	W	No
54 F.	1, 2	6:10	11:10	16:15	12:00	50	P	Yes
59 F.	1, 2, 3	8:20	14:45		15:10	25	W	No
60 F.	1, 3	6:30	12:00		12:40	40	W	No
Average		6:07	11:47			42		
A.D.		1:42	1:37			20.3		

first appearance of the idea.) When the idea of swinging the cord occurred without the idea of attaching a weight, the time given is for the appearance of the idea of swinging the cord providing the subject did fasten a weight to the cord later without suggestions from the experimenter.

Column 8 gives the number of seconds which elapsed between the time that the effective 'help' was given and the appearance of solution 4. It should be noted that this interval of time is usually very short (average 42 seconds).

In some cases the idea of the solution appeared complete, i.e., the idea of the pendulum occurred to the subject. In other cases the idea of swinging the cord and the idea of attaching a weight appeared separately. Such subjects would throw things at the cord; say they wished the wind would blow harder; or speak of some magnetic force which might draw in the cord. A little later the utilization of a weight would occur to them. In column 9, W means that the idea of solution 4 appeared as a whole and P means that it appeared in parts. (This classification was made on the basis of the subjects' behavior and verified by their introspections.)

In column 10, 'yes' means that the subject referred to hint 1 as aiding him in finding the solution. 'No' means that hint 1 was not referred to in the free report of the subject and further questioning did not reveal that it played a part in bringing about the solution. [. . .]

We find two distinct types of experiences among the subjects in group 2. (a) Those who experienced the solution as a whole and (b) those who experienced it in two steps. When the experience was of the first type the swaying of the cord was not reported as having been an aid, except in one case; when it was of the second type the swaying was reported in all but one case. There is thus only one exception to each of these generalizations.

Subjects who experienced the solution as a whole failed to report that hint 1 aided them in finding the solution. Three explanations as to why they did not report it are possible. They are as follows:

1. Hint 1 in reality did not help these subjects to find the solution. The additional time is all that was needed.

2. The subjects for some reason or other did not wish to admit that hint 1 assisted them.

3. Hint 1 was not experienced because the sudden experience of the solution dominated consciousness.

In order to test the first possible explanation these subjects are compared with fifty-five other subjects who were given as much time to solve the problem as they desired. At least thirty minutes of effort was requested before they were permitted to give up. It was found that 80 per cent of those solving the problem (solution 4) solved it within the first ten minutes. Only 20 per cent required more than ten minutes. As hint 1 was given after at least ten minutes had been spent on the problem and as 49 per cent of those solving the problem solved it after hint 1 was given, the effectiveness of hint 1 can hardly be doubted. In fact, we should expect *less* than 20 per cent late solutions if hint 1 is ineffective, because subjects in groups 1 and 2 were often given more than ten minutes before the presentation of hint 1 when they had not shown signs of being unproductive.

A further reason for believing that hint 1 was effective is that the solution was found in an average of forty-two seconds after hint 1 was given.

The second possibility is unlikely for the following reasons:

1. Two 'helps' were tested in order to determine which was the more likely to aid in producing solution 4. The one was that of putting the cord in motion, and was given casually as before. The other consisted of twirling a weight tied to the end of a cord, and the subject's attention was specifically called to it as a possible help. From limited data the first of these 'helps' was found to be far more efficient than the second even though it was not known to be a suggestion and the second was called a suggestion. When, however, both 'helps' were given to a small group of subjects (none of which knew suggestions were being given), three of them solved after the helps were given, all three said the 'twirling' helped them. None however mentioned the swaying of the cord. The twirling of the weight preceded the swaying of the cord by several minutes, but the solution appeared only after the cord was swayed. Thus the subjects gave the wrong 'help' credit for the aid they received.

2. In the four cases in which hint 2 was given (table 1) *it* was referred to in three cases.

3. Subjects who got the solution in two parts did not fail to refer to hint 1 as an aid.

The third possibility, i.e., that hint 1 played an important part in bringing about the solution, yet was not consciously experienced when the solution appeared as a whole, seems to be the most plausible explanation. [. . .]

The reports of subjects in group 1 are in every respect similar to those in group 2 who did not refer to hint 1. On the whole the reports show that the solution appeared suddenly and no development could be noted. The solution was often compared with other situations, but it was never known whether the similarity was seen after the solution to the problem had occurred or whether the recalled situation aided them in solving the problem.

The reports tend to favor a 'trial and error' explanation of reasoning in that the subjects tell about thinking of one thing and trying it out, then thinking of something else and realizing that it would not work, etc. The pendulum solution was just another thing recalled.

Subjects in group 3 and those of group 2 who received hint 2 (pliers given to subject) reported that when they were told the problem could be solved with a pair of pliers, they immediately thought of using them as tongs and wished for nice long ones. Only one subject thought of using them as a weight. Three subjects, however, thought of using them as a weight when hint 1 was repeated.

Reports during and after the experiment showed that there was a great tendency to think of variations of previous solutions. For example, subjects could not rid themselves of the idea of anchoring one or the other of the cords and would apply it in different ways just to be doing something. This tendency was most marked in subjects who had great difficulty with the problem.

When the solution was shown to the subjects who failed, they immediately saw what hint 1 and hint 2 should have done for them, but could not understand why they had not seen it before. They insisted that they were not as stupid as their demonstration would seem to indicate.

The results may be briefly summarized as follows:

1. Usually the solution appeared suddenly and as a complete idea.

2. There was a marked tendency to repeat variations of previous solutions.

3. When suggestions or 'helps' were necessary, the very 'help' which brought about the solution was not consciously experienced except in cases in which the solution appeared in steps.

4. The subjects' reports seemed to satisfy a 'trial and error' theory, but the following discussion will point out that the objective results cannot be interpreted in this manner.

Discussion

Previously it was found (3) that the manner in which one tried to solve a problem (the reasoner's 'direction') was dependent on what one saw the difficulty to be. In the problem used in the present experiment the difficulty may be seen to be any one of the following four:

1. How to make one cord stay in the center while the other cord is reached. Solution 1 overcomes this difficulty.

2. What to do to make the cords long enough to bridge the gap. Solution 2 answers the purpose in this case.

3. What can be done to extend the reach. In this case solution 3 applies.

4. As the one cord cannot be reached while holding the other, one cord must in some way be made to move toward the other. In this case solution 4 is the possibility.

In the first three solutions activity on the part of the subject is necessary – he must use some sort of tool, but in the fourth, something must be put in operation – a principle of a machine must be used. Making the cord do something is unusual, yet it is this type of principle that is involved in most creative work.

Another difficulty in the pendulum solution is that the cord must be transformed into something else. It must be seen as a pendulum rather than as a cord hanging from the ceiling. This change in meaning is a decided source of difficulty.

Making the cord sway (hint 1) is a helpful suggestion because a swaying cord is more nearly a pendulum than a stationary one. Hence the transformation from cord to pendulum is partly made by hint 1. Presenting the subject with pliers is of no benefit so long as the pliers are seen as pliers. They become useful, however, when they are seen as a weight. (The fact that the subjects did tend to see the pliers as pliers was shown from the subjects' behavior and introspections.) The swaying cord plus an object which might be seen as a weight can, however, more easily become a pendulum than a swaying cord without such a selected object. The 'helps' are thus added elements which make the pendulum organization more readily experienced, just as additional points represent the organization of a circle more readily than three points.

That reasoning is characterized by such changes in organization and meaning as we have found is typical of the Gestalt view. Changes in meaning and in organization are experienced suddenly. This characteristic was well brought out by the problem used in the present study.

When we picture the solution of a problem as the sudden combination and organization of elements, it is not at all surprising to find that the very thing which sets off this combination is unexperienced. Before the solution is found there is inharmony. The reasoner cannot quite see the relation of certain things in the room to the solution of the problem. The next experience is that of having an idea. The 'transformation' or 'organization' stage is not experienced in reasoning any more than in reversible perspective. The new organization is suddenly there. It is the dominant experience and covers any factor which just preceded it.

If, however, the solution comes in two steps, as was true for part of the subjects, the case is somewhat different. The results showed that in such cases the suggestion (hint 1) was exaggerated, i.e., subjects conceived the idea of making the cord sway harder. The change from a slight sway of the cord to a violent sway involves no great change in meaning and the idea is in no way complete. True, it has become more nearly a pendulum, but only when the cord swings by itself, and not because of a breeze for example, is it the solution. Because this 'swinging' stage of the solution is tried out for a short period before the application of a weight is seen it is experienced. Enough of this stage is present before the solution is found so as to receive attention and is thus not imbedded in it or covered by it, as in the cases when the solution is experienced as a whole. The transition stage has thus bridged the gap between the experience of the cord hanging from the ceiling and the 'pendulum' idea.

From the above it then seems that arm-chair speculation or experimentation which relies entirely on introspective data can never give a complete picture of the reasoning process. When a solution appears suddenly and completely the very factor which sets it off may be lost to consciousness. Just what factors set off a new organization cannot be known except by means of an objective measure. In the problem used in this study the cord was often swayed by the subjects themselves. Just how often such accidental movements of the cord gave rise to the solution cannot be stated. It is very likely that they often did. This being the case, we can see the very important role which chance plays in problem solving. Yet viewed in this way it is 'trial and error' of quite a different nature. The chance swaying must organize other elements to form the pendulum. This ability to form new organizations depends on the individual. Köhler's ape (2) which put two sticks together by accident and then used them as a long stick with which to reach the food is a good example of chance solutions of this sort.

Because introspective reports are in harmony with a mental 'trial and error' theory the source of these theories is explained, but reasoning remains unexplained. The reports of the subjects in this experiment throw no light on the nature of reasoning. The objective data, though not in harmony with the reports on certain essential points do, however, throw light on the nature of reasoning. That the data from controlled experimentation should be accepted in preference to subjective reports can hardly be questioned.

Further, mental 'trial and error' can hardly be regarded as an explanation. What must be explained is how and why certain ideas appear in consciousness. After the idea is conscious the fundamental process is over. Association (in the usual sense) can explain why some ideas are recalled, but it cannot explain the appearance of other ideas, e.g., original ideas. A problem which is similar to one that was solved in the past may call up a solution by similarity. If it works the explanation is satisfactory. If it does not work, however, such a memory becomes an obstruction. The writer (3), has shown how such past experiences give rise to interfering habits.

A problem which is different from one solved in the past, but which has the same principle involved in the solution, cannot have its solution explained by similarity because there is no similarity until both solutions are known. When the solutions of such problems are explained by the principle of similarity the explanation seems to be nothing other than rationalization. Duncker (1) found no transfer from problem to problem when the solutions were similar and the problems dissimilar.

References

1. DUNCKER, K., 'A qualitative study of productive thinking', *Ped. Sem.* and *J. genet. Psychol.*, vol. 33 (1926), pp. 642–708.
2. KÖHLER, W., *The mentality of apes*, Kegan Paul, 1925, Penguin Books, 1957.
3. MAIER, N. R. F., 'Reasoning in humans. I. On direction' *J. comp. Psychol.*, vol. 10 (1930), pp. 115–43.

2 K. Duncker

On Problem-Solving

Excerpts from K. Duncker, 'On problem-solving', *Psychol. Monogr.*, vol. 58 (1945), whole no. 270, chapters 1 and 3.

The Solution of Practical Problems

Introduction and Formulation of the Problem

A problem arises when a living creature has a goal but does not know how this goal is to be reached. Whenever one cannot go from the given situation to the desired situation simply by action, then there has to be recourse to thinking. (By action we here understand the performance of obvious operations.) Such thinking has the task of devising some action which may mediate between the existing and the desired situations. Thus the 'solution' of a practical problem must fulfil two demands: in the first place, its realization must bring about the goal situation, and in the second place one must be able to arrive at it from the given situation simply through action.

The practical problem whose solution was experimentally studied in greatest detail runs as follows: given a human being with an inoperable stomach tumor, and rays which destroy organic tissue at sufficient intensity, by what procedure can one free him of the tumor by these rays and at the same time avoid destroying the healthy tissue which surrounds it?

Such practical problems, in which one asks, 'How shall I attain . . . ?', are related to certain theoretical problems, in which the question is, 'How, by what means, shall I comprehend . . . ?' In the former case, a problem situation arises through the fact that a goal has no direct connexion with the given reality; in the latter case – in theoretical problems – it arises through the fact that a proposition has no direct connexion with what is given in the premises. As example in the latter field, let us take again the problem with which I experimented in greatest detail: why is it that all six-place numbers of the type *abcabc*, for example 276276, are divisible by thirteen?

It is common to both types of problems that one seeks the ground for an anticipated consequence; in practical problems, the actual ground is sought; in theoretical problems, the logical ground.

In the present investigation the question is: *How does the solution arise from the problem situation? In what ways is the solution of a problem attained?* [. . .]

A Protocol of the Radiation Problem

Let us begin with the radiation problem. Usually the schematic sketch shown in Figure 1 was given with the problem. Thus, it was

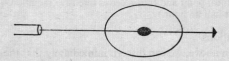

Figure 1

added, somebody had visualized the situation to begin with (cross-section through the body with the tumor in the middle and the radiation apparatus on the left); but obviously this would not do.

From my records I choose that of a solution-process which was particularly rich in typical hunches and therefore also especially long and involved. The average process vacillated less and could be left to run its own course with considerably less guidance.

Protocol

1. Send rays through the esophagus.

2. Desensitize the healthy tissues by means of a chemical injection.

3. Expose the tumor by operating.

4. One ought to decrease the intensity of the rays on their way; for example – would this work? – turn the rays on at full strength only after the tumor has been reached. (Experimenter: False analogy; no injection is in question.)

5. One should swallow something inorganic (which would not allow passage of the rays) to protect the healthy stomach-walls. (*E:* It is not merely the stomach-walls which are to be protected.)

6. Either the rays must enter the body or the tumor must come out. Perhaps one could alter the location of the tumor – but how? Through pressure? No.

7. Introduce a cannula. (*E:* What, in general, does one do when, with any agent, one wishes to produce in a specific place an effect which he wishes to avoid on the way to that place?)

8. (Reply:) One neutralizes the effect on the way. But that is what I have been attempting all the time.

9. Move the tumor toward the exterior. (Compare 6.) (The *E* repeats the problem and emphasizes, '. . . which destroy *at sufficient intensity*'.)

10. The intensity ought to be variable. (Compare 4.)

11. Adaptation of the healthy tissues by previous weak application of the rays. (*E:* How can it be brought about that the rays destroy only the region of the tumor?)

12. (Reply:) I see no more than two possibilities: either to protect the body or to make the rays harmless. (*E:* How could one decrease the intensity of the rays en route? [Compare 4.])

13. (Reply:) Somehow divert ... diffuse rays ... disperse ... stop! Send a broad and weak bundle of rays through a lens in such a way that the tumor lies at the focal point and thus receives intensive radiation.[1] (Total duration about half an hour.)

Impracticable 'Solutions'

In the protocol given above, we can discern immediately that the whole process, from the original setting of the problem to the final solution, appears as a series of more or less concrete proposals. Of course, only the last one, or at least its principle, is practicable. All those preceding are in some respect inadequate to the problem, and therefore the process of solution cannot stop there. But however primitive they may be, this one thing is certain, that they cannot be discussed in terms of meaningless, blind, trial-and-error reactions. Let us take for an example the first proposal: 'Send rays through the esophagus'. Its clear meaning is that the rays should be guided into the stomach by some passage free from tissue. The basis of this proposal is, however, obviously an incorrect representation of the situation inasmuch as the rays are regarded as a sort of fluid, or the esophagus as offering a perfectly straight approach to the stomach, etc. Nevertheless, within the limits of this simplified concept of the situation, the proposal would actually fulfil the demands of the problem. It is therefore genuinely the solution of a problem, although not of the one which was actually presented. With the other proposals, the situation is about the same. The second presupposes that a means – for example, a chemical means – exists for making organic tissue insensitive to the rays. If such a means existed, then everything would be in order, and the solution-process would have already come to an end. The fourth proposal – that the rays be turned on at full strength only when the tumor has been reached – shows again very clearly its derivation from a false analogy, perhaps that

1. This solution is closely related to the best solution: *crossing of several weak bundles of rays at the tumor*, so that the intensity necessary for destruction is attained only here. Incidentally, it is quite true that the rays in question are not deflected by ordinary lenses; but this fact is of no consequence from the viewpoint of the psychology of thinking.

of a syringe which is set in operation only when it has been introduced into the object. The sixth suggestion, finally, treats the body too much as analogous to a rubber ball, which can be deformed without injury. In short, it is evident that such proposals are anything but completely meaningless associations. Merely in the factual situation, they are wrecked on certain components of the situation not yet known or not yet considered by the subject.

Occasionally it is not so much the situation as the demand, whose distortion or simplification makes the proposal practically useless. In the case of the third suggestion, for example ('expose the tumor by operating'), the real reason why radiation was introduced seems to have escaped the subject. An operation is exactly what should be avoided. Similarly in the fifth proposal, the fact is forgotten that not only the healthy stomach-walls must be protected but also all parts of the healthy body which have to be penetrated by the rays.

A remark on principle may here be in order. The psychologist who is investigating, not a store of knowledge, but the genesis of a solution, is not interested primarily in whether a proposal is actually practicable, but only in whether it is formally practicable, that is, practicable in the framework of the subject's given premises. If in planning a project an engineer relies on incorrect formulae or on non-existent material, his project can nevertheless follow from the false premises as intelligently as another from correct premises. One can be a 'psychological equivalent' to the other. In short, we are interested in knowing how a solution develops out of the system of its subjective premises, and how it is fitted to this system.

Classification of Proposals

If one compares the various tentative solutions in the protocol with one another, they fall naturally into certain groups. Proposals 1, 3, 5, 6, 7 and 9 have clearly in common the attempt to *avoid contact between the rays and the healthy tissue*. This goal is attained in quite different ways: in 1, by re-directing the rays over a path naturally free from tissue; in 3, by the removal of the healthy tissue from the original path of the rays by operation; in 5, by interposing a protective wall (which may already have been tacitly implied in 1 and 3); in 6, by translocating the tumor towards the exterior; and in 7, finally, by a combination of 3 and 5. In proposals 2 and 11, the problem is quite differently attacked: the accompanying destruction of healthy tissue is here to be avoided by the *desensitizing or immunizing of this tissue*. A third method is

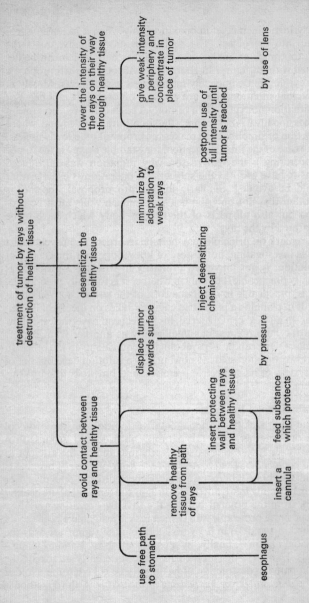

Figure 2

used in 4, perhaps in 8, in 10 and 13: *the reduction of radiation intensity on the way*. As one can see, the process of solution shifts noticeably back and forth between these three methods of approach.

In the interests of clarity, the relationships described are presented graphically in Figure 2. [. . .]

The Process of Solution as Development of the Problem

It may already have become clear that the relationship between superordinate and subordinate properties of a solution has *genetic* significance. *The final form of an individual solution is, in general, not reached by a single step from the original setting of the problem; on the contrary, the principle, the functional value of the solution, typically arises first, and the final form of the solution in question develops only as this principle becomes successively more and more concrete. In other words, the general or 'essential' properties of a solution genetically precede the specific properties; the latter are developed out of the former.* The classification given in Figure 2 presents, thus, a sort of '*family tree*' of the solution of the radiation problem.

The finding of a general property of a solution means each time a *reformulation of the original problem*. Consider for example the fourth proposal in the protocol above. Here it is clearly evident that at first there exists only the very general functional value of the solution: 'one must decrease the intensity of the radiation on the way'. But the decisive reformulation of the original problem is thereby accomplished. No longer, as at the beginning, does the S seek simply a 'means to apply rays to the tumor without also destroying healthy tissue', but already – over and above this – a means to decrease the intensity of the radiation on the way. The formulation of the problem has thus been made sharper, more specific – and the proposal not to turn the rays on at full strength until the tumor has been reached, although certainly wrong, arises only as a solution of this new, reformulated problem. From this same reformulation of the problem there arises, at the end of the whole process, the practicable solution, 'concentration of diffuse rays in the tumor'. With the other proposals in the protocol, the case is similar: the solution-properties found at first, the functional values, *always serve as productive reformulations of the original problem*.

We can accordingly describe a process of solution either as development of the solution or as development of the problem. Every solution-principle found in the process, which is itself not yet ripe for concrete realization, and which therefore fulfils only the first of the two demands given on page 28, functions from then on as reformulation, as sharpening of the original setting of the problem. *It is therefore meaningful to say that what is really done in any solution of problems consists in formulating the problem more productively.*

To sum up: *The final form of a solution is typically attained by way of mediating phases of the process, of which each one, in retrospect, possesses the character of a solution, and, in prospect, that of a problem.*

At the same time it is evident that, generally speaking, a process of solution penetrates only by degrees into the more specific circumstances and possibilities of the given situation. In the phase, 'avoiding contact between rays and healthy tissue', for example, there is still very little reference to the concrete individuality of the situation. The rays function for the time being as 'active agent', the tumor as 'the place to be influenced', and the healthy tissue as 'surrounding region which must be protected'. In the next phase, 'redirection of the rays over a tissue-free path to the stomach', at least the possibility of such a displacement of the rays is already made use of. In the search for a free pathway, the situation is then subjected to an even more precise inspection; as a consequence, such a specific component of the situation as the esophagus enters the solution-process and is used in a sensible manner.

To widen our horizon, let us here demonstrate with a mathematical example how a solution-process typically arrives at the final solution by way of mediation problem- or solution-phases. The original problem is to prove that there is an infinite number of prime numbers (to find 'something from which follows that there exists . . .'). A step which is quite decisive, although subjectively hardly noted, consists in the solution-phase: 'I must prove that for any prime number p there exists a greater one.' This reformulation of the problem sounds quite banal and insignificant. Nevertheless I had Ss who never hit on it. And without this step, the final solution cannot be reached.[2]

A further solution-phase would run as follows: 'To prove the existence of such a prime number, I must try to construct it.' With one of my Ss, I could follow clearly the way in which, to this

2. The solution consists in the construction of the product of all prime numbers from 1 to p and adding to it 1. The resultant number is either itself a prime number, or it is a product of prime numbers greater than p. For, with the exception of the special case of 1, a prime number less than p cannot be contained in a multiple of itself increased by 1 without a remainder. Thus in any case, a prime number greater than p exists. (Q.E.D.)

phase, a further one attached itself as a mere explication: 'One must therefore construct a number greater than p which cannot be represented as a product.' From here on, clearly directed to 'avoiding a product', the S proceeded to construct the product of all numbers from 1 to p and to add 1 – incidentally, without having realized that the resultant number need not be itself a prime number, but may merely contain the desired number as a fraction of itself. [. . .]

'Suggestion from Below'

There exist cases in which the final form of a solution is not reached from above, i.e., not by way of its functional value. This is a commonplace of 'familiar' solutions. If the final solution of a problem is familiar to the S, it certainly need no longer be constructed, but can be reproduced as a whole, as soon as the problem is stated.

More interesting cases exist. We must always remember that a solution has, so to speak, two roots, one in that which is sought and one in that which is given. More precisely, *a solution arises from the claim made on that which is given by that which is sought. But these two components vary greatly in the share they have in the genesis of a solution-phase.* A property of a solution is often very definitely demanded (characterized, hinted at) before it is discovered in what is given; but sometimes it is not. An example from the radiation problem: the esophagus may be discovered because a free path to the stomach is already sought. But it may also happen that, during a relatively vague, planless inspection of what is given in the situation, one 'stumbles on the esophagus'. Then the latter – so to speak, from below – suggests its functional value: 'free path to the stomach'; in other words, the concrete realization precedes the functional value. This sort of thing happens not infrequently; for the analysis of the situation is often relatively planless. Nor is this disadvantageous, when the point is to find new ideas. [. . .]

Right at the beginning of the radiation problem, the E can speak of 'crossing', or can draw a cross, without the S's grasping what that means. (Cf. the solution by crossing a number of weak bundles of rays in the tumor.) If, on the other hand, the S is already of his own accord directed to 'decreasing the intensity on the way', he will understand the suggestion sooner than if his thinking is dominated, for example, by the completely different demand for 'a free path for the rays'. We can formulate the general proposition that a suggestion is the sooner understood or assimilated, the closer it approaches the genealogical line already under development, and, within this line, the nearer it is to the problem-phase then in operation; in short, the more completely it is already anticipated. [. . .]

Learning from Mistakes (Corrective Phases)

As yet we have dealt only with the progress from the superordinate to the subordinate phases (or vice versa), in other words, with progress along a given genealogical line. That this is not the only kind of phase succession is, one should think, sufficiently indicated by the protocol given above. Here the line itself is continually changed, and one way of approach gives way to another. Such a *transition to phases in another line* takes place typically when some tentative solution does not satisfy, or when one makes no further progress in a given direction. *Another* solution, more or less clearly defined, is then looked for. For instance, the first proposal (esophagus) having been recognized as unsatisfactory, quite a radical change in direction takes place. The attempt to avoid contact is completely given up and a means to desensitize tissues is sought in its place. In the third proposal, however, the S has already returned to old tactics, although with a new variation. And such shifting back and forth occurs frequently.

It will be realized that, in the transition to phases in another line, the thought-process may range more or less widely. Every such transition involves a return to an earlier phase of the problem; an earlier task is set anew; a new branching off from an old point in the family tree occurs. Sometimes a S returns to the original setting of the problem, sometimes just to the immediately preceding phase. An example for the latter case: from the ingenious proposal, to apply the rays in adequate amounts by rotation of the body around the tumor as a center, a S made a prompt transition to the neighboring proposal: 'One could also have the radiation apparatus rotate around the body.' Another example: the S who has just realized that the proposal of the esophagus is unsatisfactory may look for another natural approach to the stomach. This would be the most 'direct' transition, that is, the transition which retrogresses least. Or, renouncing the natural approach to the stomach, he looks for another method of avoiding contact. Or, again, he looks for an altogether different way to avoid the destruction of healthy tissue. Therewith, everything which can be given up at all would have been given up; a 'completely different' solution would have to be sought.

In such retrogression, thinking would naturally not be taken back to precisely the point where it had been before. For the failure of a certain solution has at least the result that now one tries '*in another way*'. While remaining in the framework of the old *Problemstellung*, one looks for another starting point. Or again, the original setting may itself be altered *in a definite direction*, because there is the newly added demand: from now on, that property of the unsatisfactory solution must be avoided which makes it incompatible with the given conditions. An example: the fully developed form of our radiation problem is naturally preceded by a stage in which the problem runs only as follows: destroy the tumor with the aid of appropriate rays. The most obvious solution, which consists simply in sending a bundle of sufficiently strong rays through the body into the tumor, appears at once inadequate, since it would clearly have the result of destroying healthy tissue as well. In realization of this, *avoidance of the evil* has to be incorporated *as an additional demand* into the original form of the problem; only in this way does our form of the radiation problem arise (cure . . . without destruction of healthy tissue). [. . .]

Such learning from errors plays as great a role in the solution-process as in everyday life. While the simple realization, *that* something does not work, can lead only to some variation of the old method, the realization of *why* it does not work, the recognition of the *ground of the conflict*, results in a correspondingly definite *variation which corrects* the recognized defect. [. . .]

On Solution-Processes with Mathematical Problems

The '13' Problem

The final solution of a mathematical problem, specifically of a problem in which a proof is demanded, has the form: 'something, not to be proved here, from which the proposition follows.' With such mathematical problems, the solution is typically reached not in one step, but in several successive steps. Here again we are interested chiefly in the heuristic methods which, in view of given conditions, thinking may use in finding the various solution-phases.

I experimented a great deal with the following problem: why are all six-place numbers, of the form 276,276, 591,591, 112,112, divisible by 13? Here a single individual protocol may be given which, aside from a few typical as well as fruitless aberrations, contains the most practicable way of solution:

1. Are the triplets themselves perhaps divisible by 13?

2. Is there perhaps some sort of rule here about the sum of the digits, as there is with divisibility by 9?

3. The thing must follow from a hidden common principle of structure – the first triplet is 10 times the second, 591,591 is 591 multiplied by 11, no: by 101. (*E:* So?) No: by 1001. Is 1001 divisible by 13? (Total duration 14 minutes.)

For the present, let us consider only process 3. It begins with an *analysis of the goal*.[3] For the proposition that all numbers of the type abcabc are divisible by 13 means, on close examination, only that the divisibility by 13 is derivable from a property common to these numbers. The *S* now searches for such a common property, more precisely, for a 'structural property', a common character relevant to divisibility. With this a process of *analysis of the situation*, more exactly of *analysis of premises*, is introduced.

Since what is required is characterized as 'a common character relevant to divisibility', the search is restricted to a limited province. However, there are *S*s who at this point seek only some common character other than that given. Consequently, they are often 'stuck' in the purely visual. They observe, for instance, that the first and the last of any four consecutive digits are equal, which is of course of no further help.

Now the following is important: what is sought is not yet characterized as a 'common divisor', but at most as 'relevant to divisibility'. The relation of ground and consequence which is decisive for the solution: 'if a common divisor of numbers is divisible by *q*, then the numbers themselves are divisible by *q*', enters into the process only after a relatively vague analysis of the situation has already disclosed a part of the 'if' premise, of the 'ground'. In the present case, this premise consists of two parts: (1) such numbers are divisible by 1001, and (2) 1001 is divisible by 13. And only by the discovery of part-premise 1 does the thinking process hit upon the decisive relation of ground and consequence. From this, the second part-premise is then organically derived, as its 'completion' ('Is 1001 perhaps divisible by 13?'). Thus the discoveries of the first and of the second part-premises occur under quite different conditions: the former precedes the decisive proposition, the latter is dictated by this proposition.

To forty-five *S*s (thirty-five in three group experiments, ten in individual experiments), I gave this problem without any aid. The decisive relations were for none of them suggested directly

3. 'Goal' of course does not mean here 'practical goal', but that which is to be comprehended, which is to be proven. Strictly speaking, analysis of the goal is therefore here '*analysis of the proposition*'.

by the problem's goal. Not one single time did the phrase: 'I will just see whether the numbers have any divisor divisible by 13' arise directly from the original problem-setting. If it had, this demand would then have been imposed on a situation as yet un-analysed.[4] On the other hand, every time the common divisor 1001 had been arrived at[5] by a process of analysis of premises – although not necessarily just that described above – the S immediately went on to investigate whether 1001 was divisible by 13. That is, the S experienced this inquiry as still to be made. Thus it becomes indirectly apparent that the decisive ground-consequence relation is now coming into play. Incidentally, all these Ss – at least at the question, 'Why?' – explained their solutions by the existence of this 'familiar' and 'evident' relation.

This result, which will soon prove typical, may be formulated as follows: *The decisive relation which connects solution and goal is here 'suggested from below'. It is suggested by a part of the premise, a part which is found through analysis of presuppositions and of goal.* The rest of the solution is found as '*completion*' of the relation so discovered. In our example, the analysis of premises had the form of a 're-centering' of the material originally given: abcabc=abc × 1001.

Let us here briefly discuss a few proposals which are fruitless, although often produced, and which stemmed chiefly from the fact that the Ss had not yet grasped the generality of the pattern abcabc, and consequently gave too much attention to the concrete examples. Part two of the individual protocol given above on page 38 raises the question of a rule about the sum of the digits. Behind the search for such a rule lies the general knowledge that a relevant relation sometimes exists between the sum of digits and divisibility. The following wild explication of the premises was clearly inspired by the notion of the sum of the digits: '2+7+6=5+9+1=15 [cf. the numerical examples on page 37]. Is this significant?' Of thirteen protocols more closely examined, six referred to this notion of summing digits. The idea in the single protocol mentioned above – that the pairs or triplets which constituted the examples might themselves be divisible[6] by 13 – occurred with the

4. By this I do not mean that some such thing could never occur, e.g., with practised mathematicians. We are interested only in the fact that the other way exists, and that, as is yet to be shown, it is a typical way of finding the solution.

5. Among those forty-five Ss, this happened with all who arrived at the solution, namely with nine. (The thirty-five Ss of the group experiments had only about five minutes for solving the problem.)

6. From this it would of course follow that the whole six-place numbers as well are divisible by 13.

same frequency (namely 6/13). In 2/13 instances, the Ss investigated whether the examples might be powers of 13. In 3/13 instances, the S specialized his model, e.g., he tried 100,100, because, as is quite well known, the general principle of a solution is often more evident in certain particular cases. (Occasionally, such specializations appear also with other problems. In fact, they are often quite sensible and represent a rather general heuristic method.)

Experiments with Various Aids

In order to test the possible effect of certain hunches on the further course of the process, one can use the method of aids in the following way: the experimenter throws such ideas into the process from without, and observes what effects they typically have. With the '13' problem, I carried out group experiments in which six different groups of Ss received different aids during the process:

Aid (a) 'The numbers are divisible by 1001',

Aid (b) '1001 is divisible by 13',

Aid (c) 'If a common divisor of numbers is divisible by 13, then they are all divisible by 13',

Aid (d) 'If a divisor of a number is divisible by p, then the number itself is divisible by p',

Aid (e) 'Different numbers can have in common a divisor which is in turn divisible',

Aid (f) 'Look for a more fundamental common character from which the divisibility by 13 becomes evident'.

A seventh group (control group) received the problem without any aid (w.a.).

In other words, in both a and b a concrete premise of the decisive ground-consequence relation is given as aid; in c this latter itself is given (in a more general form, i.e., still lacking application); in both d and e, an abstract component of the decisive relation (in d by far the more important one) is given; and finally in f the allusion to explication of a more fundamental common character. If one considers these six aids with reference to whether and in what genetic succession they appear spontaneously in a solution-process left to itself, one gets the following result. In forty-five experiments set up *without aids*, the hunch f ('deeper common character') always occurred before all the others; a ('divisible by 1001') always before all except f; and c (the decisive ground-consequence relation) always before b ('1001 divisible by 13'). The variations d and e are probably not to be expected at all as spontaneous phases.

Table 1 contains all the collected data from three group experiments, namely the number of Ss (in percentages) who solved the problem in each of the seven groups.

Table 1

Groups	No. of Ss*	Percentage of Ss who solved the problem
a	22	59
b	10	50
c	13	15
d	22	14
e	10	0
f	13	15
w.a.	26	8

*In one of the three group experiments, the subjects were sixty-three students of the University of Berlin, who took part in a psychology seminar for beginners. In the two other group experiments, last year students of two secondary schools were concerned (fifty-three Ss). In the data which interest us, all three experiments agree.

From Table 1 we may derive two important facts:

1. The premises containing the concrete allusion to 1001 (*a* and *b*) facilitate the solution far more than all the other aids. More particularly: aid *b*, which, as was mentioned, never appears as a spontaneous phase of a solution-process unless preceded by *a*, but which has in common with the latter the concrete allusion to 1001, helps about as much as *a*.

2. The other aids are of practically no help. [. . .]

In these results, it seems to me worth noting that the pertinent general relation (cf. *c* or *d*), given as an aid, is of practically no help. From what was previously said, we knew only that, in the unaided process, it hardly ever arises unless there is some effort to analyse the premises. Now we see that, when artificially 'grafted on', it hardly facilitates the solution, while its concrete premises, containing the reference to 1001, do so to a high degree.

The Real Difficulty in the '13' Problem

The report on the varying efficacy of various aids confirms an inference which, in fact, we might have drawn before: *the real difficulty of the 13 problem is overcome as soon as the common divisor 1001 emerges*. To average subjects, numbers of the type abcabc do not easily look like multiples of 1001, not even if the Ss are expressly urged to search for a common divisor (cf. aids *c, d, e*). Qualitative data confirm very impressively the difficulty of this 'recentering'. For the most part, the *S*s were much surprised when it was finally pointed out to them that the numbers were multiples of 1001 (had the form abc × 1001), which they then certainly had to admit. Before, they had merely applied the customary procedure of long division to the examples.

How firmly the banal structure deriving from mechanical division is impressed on the numbers, is shown as well by the following protocol. By analysis of the goal, a *S* had arrived at this idea, which is not at all bad: 'Doesn't the proposition mean that the remainder from the division of abc by 13, set in the thousand-digit place before abc, must result in a four-place number divisible by 13?' But in spite of very great effort, the *S* got no further. And yet it would have been necessary only to apply this observation to the second triplet as well, and to relate the two remainders. The result would have been a number of the form *roor*, which would at once have revealed its relationship to 1001. But the penetrating realization was not reached that two or more remainders from the division of separate summands of a number together yield a summand of the same number. For the S concerned, the numbers were too 'poor in relational aspects' for this.

If the difficulty depends quite essentially on the fact that, in the structure abcabc as usually conceived, the divisor 1001 is well 'hidden', it follows that the difficulty must decrease with every variation of the illustrative numbers which makes the divisor 1001 more evident and thereby more accessible to an explicatory analysis. Such a variation was suggested to me by an individual experiment which took the following course: 'If the proposition is valid, then any two consecutive numbers of the type abcabc must also be divisible by 13, e.g., 276,276 and 277,277 – and therefore also their difference, 1001. Now this will have to be proved. Is 1001 divisible by 13? – Yes.'

In this process, we are interested in the decisive analytical step. The *S* had seen spontaneously that genuine 'neighbors' exist among numbers of the type abcabc. This view of the situation shows some independence from the usual conception, and is already quite close to the required structure: '276 thousands plus 276 units'. The 'neighbor'-relation points to the constant difference and thus suggests the following relation, which is evident and also well known: 'If a number *a* as well as the difference *a-b* is divisible by *q*, then *b* is also divisible by *q*'. (It is clear that here again the decisive relation is reached only by way of an analysis of goal and of premises.)

Now to this solution-process I owe the following variation of the 13 problem, which was meant to facilitate the discovery of 1001. The text remained just the same except for the three examples. These were no longer '276,276; 591,591; 112,112', but, '276,276; 277,277; 278,278'. The effect (see Table 2) was astounding. The 'neighbor'-relation of the illustrative numbers set the situation-analysis on the trail of the difference 1001, and thus led to the solutions.

Although the numbers in Table 2 appear too small,[7] they are not so, and for the following reasons: according to our former experiments with the old setting and on similar subject-material, 0·4 solutions are to be expected with five subjects, i.e., 0 corresponds entirely to the result to be expected. Furthermore, the fact that in the new setting three out of four Ss solved the problem corresponds to a percentage of solutions which I could otherwise approximate only by the most effective aids (for instance, 'the numbers are divisible by 1001'). But above all, the three Ss actually reached the solution through 1001 as a *difference* between examples, a quite unusual procedure.

Table 2

Examples	Ss	Solutions
276,276⎫ 591,591⎭	5	0
276,276⎫ 277,277⎭	4	3

7. The interaction is significant ($p = 0·048$) on a Fisher-Yates Exact test. (Eds.)

3 H. G. Birch and H. S. Rabinowitz

The Negative Effect of Previous Experience on Productive Thinking

H. G. Birch and H. S. Rabinowitz, 'The negative effect of previous experience on productive thinking', *J. exp. Psychol.*, vol. 41 (1951), pp. 121–5.

The part which is played by past experience in human problem-solving behavior has long been a subject for experiment and discussion. Investigations viewing the evidence from different theoretical vantage points have arrived at diverse conclusions which in some instances identify problem solving with trial-and-error learning (3), in other cases (1, 8) consider past experience in general as providing the raw materials out of which a problem-solving response may be fabricated, and on occasion some investigators have even neglected to consider the question of past experience as essential for a problem-solving theory (9). One of the reasons for the diversity of roles which have been accorded to past experience is that problem solving is by no means a unitary process. Although in all problem solving a solution is arrived at, the processes of behavior whereby the solution is achieved are of several different kinds. Maier (8) has served to clarify this issue by sharpening the often belabored distinction between *reproductive* and *productive thinking*. His discussion was developed in terms of the part which past experience may play in each type of performance. Reproductive thinking, Maier believes, is characterized by the solution of problems by means of the existence of stimulus equivalences in the novel (or problem) situation and in the previously mastered situation. Thus, for him, reproductive thinking and transfer of training are to be considered closely similar if not identical phenomena. *Productive thinking*, however, is not merely the process of arriving at a solution through the direct application of previous learning. In productive thinking past experience is repatterned and restructured to meet current demands, and is thus the counterpart of reasoning as Maier has defined that term (6). In the present study we are concerned with the relation of past experience to the productive thinking process, and not with reproductive thinking.

Probably the studies which have contributed most directly to an understanding of the manner in which the background of past experiences influences the nature of human productive thinking are those of Maier (6, 7) and Duncker (2). Maier, in his examination of the relation between stimulus equivalence and reasoning (8), identified several ways in which past experience may affect problem-solving activities. Problem solving may be facilitated by equivalences which exist in the immediate problem situation and in past experience. Further, as he has shown elsewhere (6), and as Birch (1) has shown for the chimpanzee, the background of past learning represents an essential repertoire of behavior which must be available for restructuring when new situational demands develop. On the other hand, productive thinking is impossible if the individual is chained to the past. The past experience may become a hindrance and an obstacle which blocks productive thinking and reduces behavior to stereotyped and fruitless essays.

It is primarily with this negative effect which may be exercised by past experience that Duncker has dealt in his problem-solving experiments (2). In a series of situations designed to study what he terms 'functional-fixedness', Duncker tried to determine the manner in which the previous utilization of an object for a dissimilar function in the *same problem context* affected its availability in subsequent problem solving, and found that such specific experience made the objects previously utilized in this manner significantly less available as instruments when the problem presented for solution was changed. Two weaknesses in experimental design limit the generality of the inferences which may be drawn from Duncker's results. In the first place, by using the same objective situation for both his 'pre-utilization' experience and for his new problem-solving task, he makes it impossible to determine whether the difficulty in using a previously utilized object for the solution of a new problem derives from the limitation of the functional properties of this object by the prior experience, from the establishment of false problem-solving directions, from the development of attitudes of completion ('over and done with') on the part of the S which effectively remove the already-used object from the field of activity, or from any of a variety of other effects. Secondly, in selecting the different tools which would be available to the Ss in their problem-solving activities, Duncker made no attempt to equate the instruments for different degrees of objective adequacy as tools in solving the problem. Obviously, if the objects in the 'pre-utilization' group are objectively less adequate as tools than are the non pre-utilized materials, the scales are weighted in favor of fewer solutions for the 'pre-utilization' group. In not a few instances Duncker's problem situations may be criticized on these grounds, and the question arises as to whether his results derive as much from the pre-experimental object selection as from the effects of pre-utilization of the materials by the subjects.

To remove these impediments to interpretation of this aspect of the effects of previous experience on problem solving, it is necessary to study the problem under conditions in which the background of prior specific experience is obtained by the Ss in a situation remote from the crucial problem-solving task, and to contrast as problem-solving tools objects whose adequacy as instruments is objectively equal. The design of the present study stems from these considerations.

Subjects and Procedure

Twenty-five students at the City College, New York, were used as Ss in this experiment. These Ss were divided into three groups, a control group and two experimental groups. The control group had six Ss, and the experimental groups contained ten and nine Ss, respectively.

As the crucial problem-solving task in this experiment, all Ss were required to solve the two-cord problem used extensively by Maier (7) in his studies of 'direction' in problem solving. In this problem the S is required to tie together the free ends of two cords which are suspended from the ceiling to the floor of a corridor. The distance between the two cords is such that the S cannot reach one cord if the other is held. In our arrangement the problem could be solved only if the S would tie a weight to the end of one of the strings and thus convert it into a pendulum which could be set swinging and thus be caught on its upswing while the stationary cord was held. The two cords could then be tied together and the problem solved. In our situation only two objects could be utilized as weights. The first of these objects was an electrical switch and the second, an electrical relay. The conditions of pretest training involved the acquisition of differential prior experience with these objects by our Ss. The pretest training was conducted as follows:

Group S contained nine Ss who were given the pretest task of completing an electrical circuit on a 'bread-board' by using a *switch*, which had to be installed if the circuit were to be completed and controllable.

Group R consisted of ten Ss who received pretest training in the completion of an identical circuit by the use of a *relay*, which is essentially a switch.

Group C, the control group, consisted of six engineering students with a wide variety of electrical experience. These Ss were given no pretraining. The Ss in groups R and S had had little or no experience with electrical wiring.

Shortly after having completed the pretesting tasks, the Ss were presented with the two-cord problem and asked to solve it by using the objects lying before them on a table. Only two objects were present, a *switch* and a *relay*, each identical with the ones used in the pretraining period.

Since the two-cord problem is very difficult to solve without the presentation of 'direction'-producing hints, such hints were presented by E nine minutes after the presentation of the problem. The hints consisted in brushing against the string or strings and 'accidentally' setting them swinging. Solutions were always achieved within three minutes after the presentation of hints. All Ss were individually tested. Upon completing the two-cord problem, the Ss were asked why they had chosen either the switch or the relay as the pendulum weight.

Results

The results reported will deal primarily with the nature of the choice of objects made by the Ss in the critical task situation. These data for all groups are shown in Table I. The control group chose equally between the switch and the relay as pendulum weights which might be utilized for the solution of the two-cord problem. These data indicate that for individuals with prior experience which is not heavily weighted in favor of either the switch or the relay, no significant difference exists between the objects in terms of their utility as tools in solving the two-cord problem.

Table 1

Frequency of Choice of Objects in Problem Solution

Group	N	No. Using Relay	No. Using Switch
Control (*C*)	6	3	3
Exper. (*R*)	10	0	10
Exper. (*S*)	9	7	2

The behavior of the Ss who had received specific pre-utilization experience with either the switch or the relay differed in a striking manner from the behavior of the Ss who had not received such experience. Those who had initially been trained to complete an electrical circuit with a relay never utilized this object as the pendulum weight for the solution of the two-cord problem. In every instance the Ss chose the switch, an object not previously manipulated, as the object which was to be converted into a pendulum bob in the solution of the two-cord problem. On the other hand, the Ss who had initially been trained to use a switch for the completion of an electrical circuit preponderantly chose the relay as the pendulum weight in solving the two-cord problem.

If the results on solving the two-cord problem for both the switch and relay pre-utilization groups are combined, it is found that seventeen of the nineteen Ss used that object with which they had had no pre-experimental training as the problem-solving tool. There are less than five chances in one hundred that such results could have occurred as the result of chance fluctuations in responding on the part of the Ss. It may, therefore, be inferred that the nature of the previous specific experiences of the Ss was influential in determining their problem-solving choices.

The replies which the Ss made to the question, 'Why did you use the switch (or relay) as the pendulum weight?' further indicate that the pre-utilization experiences exercised a decisive effect upon their problem-solving efforts. Those Ss who used the switch as the pendulum weight in the two-cord problem offered varying reasons for its superiority over the relay as a pendulum bob. They claimed that it was easier to attach, more compact, etc. The Ss who tended to use the relay as the pendulum bob in solving the two-cord problem proffered equally 'good' reasons for their selection. The relay, they claimed, was easier to attach, heavier, etc. In both groups of Ss individuals became somewhat defensive when queried as to the reasons for their choices, and typically replied by prefacing their answers with the remark, 'Anyone can see that this one is better as a pendulum weight.' A number of Ss even went so far as to say, 'Any *fool* can see that this one is better.' Since these remarks are directed with equal vehemence at either the switch or at the relay, it is clear that the Ss were not advancing objective reasons for their choices, but were, rather, revealing the effects which their prior specific experience was having on their perceptions.

Discussion

Although the present study was designed primarily to explore a neglected aspect of problem-solving behavior, it has some significance for problem-solving theory and provides clarifications for several important questions. In the first place, the results reveal that the question of the role played by past experience in productive thinking cannot receive a uniform answer until the nature of the past experience is clearly understood. Even though this study indicates that prior experience of a specific kind with a potential problem-solving tool effectively prevents this instrument from being used in problem solution, there is little doubt on the basis of other studies (1, 4) that a different kind of experience may enhance the value of an object as a tool in problem solving. Therefore, what appears to be important for problem solving is not that an individual's performance is dependent upon past experience *per se*, but rather that *different kinds* of experience are differentially effective in influencing the content of problem-solving behavior. Our results therefore are in accord with those of Katona (5), who found that *how* and *what* an individual learned and not simply *whether* he learned determined the amount of positive transfer effect that occurred in subsequent learning.

Perhaps the most interesting phase of our results concerns the manner in which the individual's previous experience influenced his perceptions. The pre-utilization experience apparently changed the perceived properties of the object previously used in a different context to such a degree that its problem-solving characteristic could not be readily seen. This change in perception was probably based on the manner in which the previous experience had emphasized the instrument as an *electrical object* and so made for extreme difficulty in perceiving it in terms of its general characteristic of *mass*, which is essential for pendulum construction. The kind of previous experience presented therefore functioned to limit the number of the properties of the object that could be perceived by the *S*.

These results suggest that there are two phenomenally describable kinds of learning that may be important in problem solving. The first variety of learning involves the acquisition by *S* of certain broad, nonspecific, general notions about the properties of the object or method experienced. This was undoubtedly the case in Birch's study of chimpanzee problem solving (1), where young chimpanzees who were initially incapable of using a stick to take distant food into reach manifested this ability after a very short period of play with sticks. It is this general, broad, nonspecific experience which seems to provide the repertoire of experience essential for productive thinking.

A second type of learning involves the acquisition of experiences which convert the initial perception of broad, general properties of an object into perceptions of specific limited functional characteristics. It is this second variety of learning which appears to have occurred in the pre-utilization experiences of the *S*s in our study and to have produced what Duncker (2) refers to as 'functional fixedness' in problem-solving perceptions. Such fixedness limits the range of perceptual organizations capable of being developed by the *S* and so interferes with problem solving.

1. BIRCH, H. G., 'The relation of previous experience to insightful problem-solving', *J. comp. Psychol.*, vol. 38 (1945), pp. 367–83.
2. DUNCKER, K., 'On problem-solving' (trans. L. S. Lees), *Psychol. Monogr.*, 1945, no. 270.
3. GUTHRIE, E. R., and HORTON, G. P., *Cats in a puzzle box*, Rinehart, 1946.
4. JACKSON, T. A., 'Use of the stick as a tool by young chimpanzees', *J. comp. Psychol.*, vol. 34 (1942), pp. 223–35.
5. KATONA, G., *Organizing and memorizing*, Columbia U.P., 1939.
6. MAIER, N. R. F., 'Reasoning in humans. I. On direction', *J. comp. Psychol.*, vol. 11 (1930), pp. 115–43.
7. MAIER, N. R. F., 'Reasoning in humans. II. The solution of a problem and its appearance in consciousness', *J. comp. Psychol.*, vol. 12 (1931), pp. 181–94.
8. MAIER, N. R. F., 'Reasoning in humans. III. The mechanisms of equivalent stimuli and of reasoning', *J. exp. Psychol.*, vol. 35 (1945), pp. 349–60.
9. WERTHEIMER, M., *Productive thinking*, Tavistock, 1959.

4 R. E. Adamson

Functional Fixedness as Related to Problem Solving: A Repetition of Three Experiments

R. E. Adamson, 'Functional fixedness as related to problem solving: a repetition of three experiments', *J. exp. Psychol.*, vol. 44 (1952), pp. 288–91.

The study of problem solving and thinking has been retarded by the lack of agreed-upon theoretical concepts supported by adequate data from experiments. As a part of a larger program concerned with these matters, some of the more promising hypotheses have been assembled, and preliminary experiments undertaken to repeat the demonstrations upon which these hypotheses rest.

One inviting hypothesis is that problem solving may in some instances be delayed through the 'functional fixedness' of solution objects. That is, owing to his previous use of the object in a function dissimilar to that demanded by the present problem, *S* is inhibited in discovering the appropriate new use of the object. This hypothesis was proposed by Duncker (3), who designed ingenious experiments to support it, but carried the experiments through with but fourteen *S*s and under poorly specified experimental conditions. It seemed wise, therefore, to repeat some of his experiments both to substantiate his results, if possible, and to ascertain the efficacy of the problems for use in further investigations. The success of Birch and Rabinowitz (1) in demonstrating functional fixedness in a related experiment encouraged us to hope for positive results.

Procedure

Subjects. – All *S*s taking part in this study were college students from elementary psychology classes. There were fifty-seven *S*s, of whom thirty-five were men, twenty-two women. Twenty-nine *S*s were assigned to the experimental group, twenty-eight to the control group. All *S*s were of proximate ages and had been exposed to little experimentation.

Problems. – Duncker's 'box', 'gimlet', and 'paperclip' problems were presented to each *S* in the order named. In the first of these, the box problem, *S*'s task is to mount three candles vertically on a screen, at a height of about 5 ft., using to accomplish this task any of a large number of objects which are lying before *S* on a table.

Among these objects are three paste-board boxes of varying sizes, five matches, and five thumbtacks, the crucial objects for solution of the problem. The solution is to mount one candle on each box by melting wax on the box and sticking the candle to it, then to tack the boxes to the screen.

The gimlet problem involves suspending three cords from a board attached to an overhead beam. Among the variety of objects available are two screw-hooks and the gimlet itself, the objects from which the cords may be hung.

The paperclip problem consists of first attaching four small black cardboard squares to a large white square, then hanging the large square from an eyelet screwed into the aforementioned beam. Included among the objects lying before S on the table are a number of paperclips. These may be used to attach the small squares to the large one, and one of them, when bent to form a hook, will serve to hang the large square from the eyelet.

Design. – The experimental and control groups were given the same problems to solve. For the experimental group, however, at least one of the solution objects was 'burdened' with a prior function in each problem. Thus, the candles, matches, and tacks for the box problem were placed in the three boxes before they were given to S. Hence, the boxes had for their initial function that of containing, whereas in their solution function they had to be used as supports or platforms. Similarly the gimlet initially had to be used to start holes for the screw-hooks, and in the paperclip problem, the four black squares had to be attached to the white one with paperclips. Duncker referred to the experimental group as the 'after pre-utilization' group.

The control group was given the problems without any pre-utilization. In the case of the box problem, the empty boxes were placed on the table at varying distances from the other crucial solution objects. Holes into which the screw-hooks and the gimlet could be screwed were already drilled into the beam in the case of the gimlet problem; the four black squares were stapled to the white one in the paperclip problem. Thus, none of the crucial objects was used with a function prior to its use as a solution object.

Solution scores were taken as one possible measure of functional fixedness, and time-to-solution constituted another measure. A maximum time of twenty minutes was allowed for solution of each of the problems.

Results

Box problem. – The results of the box problem, presented in Table

1, confirm Duncker's finding that functional fixedness results from
pre-utilization. The performance of the experimental group was
markedly inferior to that of the control with respect both to the
number of solutions obtained and the time required to reach
solution. Prior usage of the boxes as containers inhibited their
being used as platforms.

The chi-square value comparing the two groups on the time
score was obtained by using as a cutting point the median time-to-
solution of the combined groups. All cases for which there was
no solution were assigned to the above-median category. With 1
df, each of the chi squares was highly significant. Since the direction of the difference was predicted, a one-tail test of significance
was employed for both this and the following two problems.

Table 1

Box Problem

Group	n	Number solving	Time-to-solution*
Exper.	29	12 (41%)	7 (24%)
Control	28	24 (86%)	22 (78%)
		$\chi^2 = 12.0\ p = 0.001$	$\chi^2 = 14.8\ p = 0.001$

* Number below median of combined group.

Table 2

Gimlet and Paperclip Problems

Problem and group	n	Mean time-to-solution (sec.)	SD	t'	p*
Gimlet					
Exper.	26	246·6	124·7	3·71	0·001
Control	28	144·0	67·7		
Paperclip					
Exper.	29	107·9	96·0	2·38	0·01
Control	28	63·0	31·5		

* Single-tail test.

Gimlet problem. – Since only three Ss failed to solve this problem,
all from the experimental group, the solution score could not
demonstrate a difference between the experimental and control
groups. Accordingly, only the results from the time measure are
given in Table 2. The three Ss failing to reach solution were not

considered in the analysis of the data, thus reducing the total n to 54 for this experiment.

Since, as shown in Table 2, the variances for the two groups are not homogeneous, the use of t as a test of significance was inappropriate. Instead, t' was employed.[1] The highly significant difference obtained shows clearly the presence of functional fixedness.

Paperclip problem. – The results from the paperclip problem are also shown in Table 2. Since all Ss were able to solve this problem, only time scores are given. As in the first two problems, pre-utilization of the solution objects with a function different from that demanded by the problem resulted in significantly poorer performance by the experimental group.

Reliability of individual performance. – An analysis was made of the performance of the experimental group to determine whether individual achievement on one of the three problems was significantly related to achievement on either of the other two. Chi square was used to test whether individuals scoring below the median in time-to-solution for one of two problems also showed a significant tendency to score below the median for the other. (Since only twelve of twenty-nine Ss solved the box problem, a median time-to-solution could not be obtained; instead, the distribution was dichotomized in terms of solution or no-solution.) A relation significant at the 0·05 level was found between the box problem and the paperclip problem. Neither of the other chi squares was significant. Clearly, achievement on a single problem involving pre-utilization is not a reliable measure of individual susceptibility to functional fixedness.

Discussion

Duncker's study (3), involving these three experiments, used two measures of performance: number of presolutions, and number of solutions. In the present study, the number of pre-solutions was discarded as a measure, because it was found to be overly dependent upon the subjective judgement of E. Number of solutions proved to be a satisfactory measure for only the box problem. Since all Ss solved the paperclip problem, and all but three solved the gimlet problem, no difference between the experimental and

---

1. This technique was suggested by Dr Quinn McNemar. Instead of utilizing one estimate of the population variance, t' incorporates the estimated variances from two populations (2). It is, in consequence, useful in such a situation as the present one, replacing t which assumes homogeneity of variance.

the control groups could be revealed by this measure. It would appear that the *S*s in the present study were more able than those employed by Duncker.

Although the measures previously used by Duncker failed to show functional fixedness in two of the three present experiments, a new measure, time-to-solution, gave positive results in all three experiments. Essentially, then, the present results confirm those obtained by Duncker.

The results of Duncker, of Birch and Rabinowitz, and those obtained in this study afford convincing proof of the existence of functional fixedness. The reality of this phenomenon having been established, two lines of investigation are of immediate interest: (*a*) determination of those conditions which influence the occurrence of functional fixedness, and (*b*) exploration of its relation to other kinds of set in problem solving.

References

1. BIRCH, H. G., and RABINOWITZ, H. S., 'The negative effect of previous experience on productive thinking', *J. exp. Psychol.*, vol. 41 (1951), pp. 121–5.
2. COCHRAN, W. G., and COX, G. M., *Experimental design*, Wiley, 1950.
3. DUNCKER, K., 'On problem-solving', *Psychol. Monogr.*, Vol. 58 (1945) no. 5 (whole no. 270).

5 P. Saugstad and K. Raaheim

Problem-Solving, Past Experience and Availability of Functions

Excerpts from P. Saugstad and K. Raaheim, 'Problem-solving, past experience and availability of functions', *Brit. J. Psychol.*, vol. 51 (1960), part 2, pp. 97–104.

Introduction

[. . .] Thinking must be understood in terms of learning as well as of perception and also in terms of principles for memory. The one-sided approaches to the study of thinking among experimental psychologists may be due to the fact that, during the last generation, the thought processes have relatively seldom been the object of a more direct experimental analysis. Attempts are usually made to account for them in terms of principles derived from studies of simpler situations particularly within learning and perception.

It is a conviction of the writers that not only will an understanding of thinking be increased by a direct experimental attack on problems in this area, but so also will the processes involved in learning and perception. An outline for a framework based upon a more direct attack on problems of problem solving has been presented elsewhere (Saugstad, 1955, 1958) and will be briefly indicated here.

In the hope of making communication more efficient – an overwhelmingly difficult problem in studies in this area – attention is restricted to problem situations involving concrete objects, such as stones, sticks, ropes, balls, iron nails, boxes, pieces of string and implements of various sorts (e.g., pairs of pliers, screwdrivers, hammers). In problem situations of such a concrete nature the solution is attained by the use of definite objects in definite ways and, in the attainment of the solution, the objects may be said to serve definite functions. A concrete problem may now be subjected to a logical analysis in terms of these functions. The solution may be conceived of as the arrangement of a number of functions into some definite sequence. In previous experiments (Saugstad, 1955; Saugstad and Raaheim, 1957), the functions available to an individual have been assessed by the following simple procedure, called an availability test. The individual is presented with one object at a time and asked, according to some specified rules, to list as many functions for this object as possible. This procedure is carried through without any mention of a definite problem situation.

So far, the term 'function' has been used here in its relatively vague every-day meaning. Instead of attempting to lay down a more formal definition at present, it is thought wiser to attempt to clarify the term slowly as the experimental work progresses. To some extent its meaning is implicitly given by the procedure adopted in the first experiment by Saugstad (1955), but to avoid some misunderstandings (Székely, 1958; Saugstad, 1958) some brief comments on certain aspects will be presented.

Functions may be considered as varying in specificity or generality. One may think of a function as something determined by some very specific context or one may have in mind a large variety of situations. For example, I may use a stone in one specific situation to crack one specified nut, or I may use a stone to crack nuts in general in a variety of situations. This wider generality was what Saugstad (1955) had in mind when he designed his first availability test in such a way that the subjects were asked, first, to state a function in a general form and then to give three concrete examples of the function. The procedure followed in the experiments performed thus rests on the assumption that functions may be perceived or conceived of in a more or less general form. The results of the experiments performed within this framework indicate that, under certain circumstances, functions may be relatively independent of the situational context. On the other hand, experiments by Duncker (1945), Adamson (1952), Birch and Rabinowitz (1951) reveal that, under other circumstances, availability of a function may be highly dependent upon the situational context. The degree to which a function is dependent upon the situational context can be clarified only by more systematic empirical research. Attention should be called to the fact that, so far, attempts have been made within this framework to avoid situations which may be conducive of fixation of a function. [. . .]

A number of hypotheses with interesting theoretical implications may be formulated with regard to functions. [. . .] In the experiments performed so far, concentration has been on the following question: will a person who has available the necessary functions for the solution of the problem actually solve this problem? In the exploration of this question the assumption has been made that a function available in the availability test will be available also in the problem situation. Results of the experiments (Saugstad, 1955, 1957; Saugstad and Raaheim, 1957) suggest that the question is to be answered in the affirmative. An individual having available the necessary functions will solve the problem. [. . .]

The problem of whether or not availability of the necessary past experiences is sufficient for solution is of considerable theoretical interest. Mainly based upon Maier's (1930) well-known pendulum problem, Gestalt psychologists (Wertheimer, 1959; Koffka, 1935) and Gestalt-oriented psychologists (Leeper, 1951) have argued that availability of the necessary past experiences is not sufficient for the solution of a problem. In his experiment, Maier demonstrated to a group of subjects what he considered to be the three essential principles for the solution of the pendulum problem. Since only one in a group of subjects after this demonstration solved the pendulum problem, Maier concluded that availability of the necessary past experiences for the solution of a problem was not sufficient for arriving at the solution. A repetition of this experiment by Saugstad (1957) took steps to make sure that subjects had understood the demonstrations, as purported by Maier and as necessitated by his conclusion. It revealed that close to 100 per cent of the subjects having the principles available solved the problem. The principles involved in Maier's demonstrations were abstract and this may be the reason why the demonstrations had little or no effect. It might be thought that a demonstration, by way of concrete objects, of the necessary functions for solution might be more effective. If the subject having received such a demonstration solved the problem, this would be an effective way of showing that an analysis of problem solving in terms of functions reveals an important aspect of problem-solving behaviour. Such a type of experiment will also have some bearing on the problem of the effects of hints and demonstrations in problem solving which has been the subject of a number of investigations (Maier, 1930, 1931, 1933, 1945; Reid, 1951; Battersby, Teuber and Bender, 1953; Marks, 1951; Cofer, 1951).

Experimental

Subjects

All the pupils in one class in a secondary school in Oslo served as subjects. The pupils, males aged 17–18 years, were majoring in mathematics and physics.

The problem

Since the problem has been described in detail by Saugstad and

Raaheim (1957), only a rough outline will be given here. The subject is faced with the task of transferring a number of steel balls from a glass into a metal cylinder. The glass containing the steel balls is placed on a movable wooden frame and the metal cylinder to the side of it. The subject has to keep behind a wooden table, or a chalk line, 260 cm. away from the wooden frame. At his disposal for the solution of the problem the subject has four newspapers of a certain size, a length of string, a pair of pliers, five elastic bands, and one iron nail. The correct solution to the problem consists in bending the nail by the pair of pliers into a hook, attaching the nail to the string and throwing the nail into the wooden frame, making it catch on to the frame, and then pulling in the frame on which the glass of steel balls lies. The newspapers are then to be rolled into tubes, which are inserted into each other to form a continuous passage. The newspapers are held together by the elastic bands. Through this tube the steel balls are directed into the cylinder from behind the table.

Procedure

Demonstration of the critical functions. – Analysis of the problem had previously shown that all subjects giving the function 'hook' for the nail and the function 'tube' for the newspaper, would solve the problem. It was decided to demonstrate only these two functions, called the critical functions. The demonstrations were carried out by reading the following instructions. 'We will now present you with some objects which all may be used in a number of ways. We want you to give us some examples for the use of the objects.' A newspaper rolled into a tube is handed to the subject. 'This object you may use to conduct something through. Could you give some examples?' A nail bent into a hook is handed to the subject. 'This object may be used to catch things with. Could you give some examples?' When the subject had given as an example in answer to the first question: air, or some other gas, water, sand, balls, pebbles, or some other smaller objects, this was considered a satisfactory indication that he had grasped the meaning of the function stated for the newspaper. When the subject had answered the second question with: angle for fishing, to hang things on, as a hook, or to catch on to wood or some softer material, the example was considered an indication that he had grasped the meaning of the function stated for the bent nail. If the subject did not give any of the examples mentioned he was asked to continue until he had met the criterion as stated.

Design. The subjects were first given the demonstrations as described in one room and then immediately led into another room where they were presented with the problem situation. The control group of an experiment previously reported by Saugstad and Raaheim (1957) served as control group for the present study. This group was presented with the problem without any previous demonstrations. The subjects of this group, forty-five pupils from secondary schools in Oslo, had the same characteristics as the subjects in the experimental group. The subjects of both groups were tested individually.

Subjects were allowed 30 minutes on the problem. The demonstrations of the critical functions took from 1 to 3 minutes.

Results

Table 1 shows the number of subjects, in each group, who had solved the problem after 5, 10, 15, 20, 25, or 30 minutes. (The percentage number of solutions is shown in brackets, to the nearest whole per cent.) The figures show that, at every time interval, the subjects who had received the demonstrations were superior to those who had not. Taking 30 minutes as the time limit, solutions were given by nineteen out of the twenty subjects of the experimental group as opposed to only ten out of the forty-five subjects of the control group: this difference is significant at the 1 per cent level (χ^2 corrected for continuity).

Table 1

| Group | No. of solutions | | | | | | Total no. of subjects |
	5 min.	10 min.	15 min.	20 min.	25 min.	30 min.	
Exp.	5 (25)	14 (70)	17 (85)	18 (90)	19 (95)	19 (95)	20
Contr.	0 (0)	0 (0)	3 (7)	7 (16)	9 (20)	10 (22)	45

Only two subjects in the experimental group spent more than 20 minutes on the solution. As noted above the demonstrations took from 1 to 3 minutes. Therefore, the difference in number of solutions between the experimental and the control group cannot be explained in terms of greater familiarity with the material on the part of the subjects in the experimental group.

The results which seem to be highly reproducible, indicate that subjects from the same population as the subjects of this experiment will almost always solve the ball problem when the two critical functions have been demonstrated to them.

Discussion

Almost all the subjects who had the two critical functions demonstrated to them solved the problem. This suggests that an analysis in terms of availability of functions uncovers an important aspect of problem-solving behaviour. By means of this analysis, it appears to be possible, in a simple way, to provide an individual with the part experiences necessary for the solution of a problem. The analysis of a problem situation in terms of functions makes it possible to predict which aspects in a problem situation should be pointed out to the subjects not solving the problem. The present results thus make it possible to formulate, in a tentative manner, the conditions under which a hint will be effective: a hint will be effective to the extent to which it makes available the critical functions for the solution of a problem.

We will from this angle consider some experiments with concrete objects where hints are introduced. Maier (1931) constructed the problem of tying together two ropes which were hung so far apart that, when an individual was holding one, the other could not be reached. To solve this problem, the subject had to make a pendulum out of one of the ropes by tying an object on to it. In this problem situation, it was found effective to give one of the ropes a push. The push may reasonably be said to make available the function served by the rope. Battersby *et al.* (1953) used the same problem situation, but they gave hints by placing objects which suggested the function of a weight to the subject – thus emphasizing another aspect for the construction of the pendulum. Again it is to be expected, as it transpired, that the hint was effective. Cofer (1951) also used the same situation but had his subjects memorize lists of words before they were presented with the problem. More solutions were produced in a group of subjects who had memorized among other words, rope, swing, and pendulum.

The above formulation for the effect of hints may also help to clarify some of Maier's (1945) reasoning around a more recent experiment. We will concentrate on one aspect of this experiment. Maier presented one group with the problem of constructing a hat rack. This was done by making a longer pole out of two shorter ones, and by placing this longer pole between floor and ceiling and clamping them together by a table clamp. The clamp in this construction served as a hat rack. Another group of subjects were placed before the construction after it had been completed and asked to list its possible functions. It was found that there was a proportionally larger number of subjects in the first group who were able to construct the hat rack than there were subjects in the last group who could suggest the function of a hat rack or some similar function. As we understand him, Maier argues that the situations for the two groups were equivalent and that it is strange, therefore, that the results came out as they did. But the two situations are not equivalent and the results are not at all surprising. Evidently, it is difficult to perceive or conceive of the function of a hat rack in the clamp; few subjects in the second group perceived this function. The first group being assigned the task of constructing a hat rack has, *through the instructions*, received a hint that some object may serve as a hat rack. For this reason, a larger proportion of them finds the function of hat rack for the clamp. It is thus seen that the two groups are treated entirely differently in one crucial aspect. The situation for the subjects receiving the instruction to build a hat rack is similar to that of the subjects in Cofer's (1951) experiment who, before they were presented with the problem of tying the two ropes together, had memorized the list containing the critical words, rope, swing, pendulum. In both experiments, the subjects received important verbal hints concerning the critical function for one crucial object in the attainment of the solution to the problem.

In still another of his ingenious experiments Maier (1933) was able to raise the number of solutions in a group of subjects by giving them a lecture on how to solve problems. The results of this experiment are of course very interesting, even if it is difficult to draw any definite conclusions as to what in the lecture had the effect of helping the subjects to find more solutions. According to the present analysis in terms of functions, it is natural to assume that the lecture helped the subjects find more functions than they otherwise would have found. In view of the content of the lecture this interpretation seems reasonable.

The present results also serve as a check on one of the assumptions underlying the conclusion drawn from previous experiments by Saugstad (1955) and Saugstad and Raaheim (1957) that a subject having available the necessary functions in the problem situation will solve the problem. Some of the main assumptions underlying this conclusion have recently been discussed elsewhere by Saugstad and Raaheim (1959). One of these had a bearing on the fact that the availability tests might have a selective effect. The subjects who, according to the availability tests, were credited with the necessary functions might be superior in general intelligence or in some problem-solving ability. Since they were superior in one or both of these respects they might be superior in combining the necessary functions into the correct sequence involving the solution. Thus, there might possibly exist a group of subjects having the necessary functions available in the problem situation, but not being able to combine the functions into the correct sequence. Previous analysis (Saugstad and Raaheim, 1957) makes it probable that there exists *no* such group of subjects. The results of the present experiment give a further check on this assumption. In the experimental group, close to 100 per cent solved the problem as against 20 per cent in the control group. The problem solvers in the first group can, therefore, not reasonably be considered superior to the problem solvers of the second group with regard to a possible problem solving ability or to general intelligence. When almost all subjects of the experimental group solved the problem the reason is most likely that the main determiner of success in problem-solving is availability of functions. However, it should be noted that the combination of the functions for the subjects in the experimental group might be somewhat easier, since the previous demonstrations might have emphasized the two critical functions and thus made easier their combination. Yet it seems safe to conclude that there were still a number of possible functions which might be combined. If the ability to combine functions was an important factor in determining success in problem solving one would expect it to manifest itself in the problem situation of this experiment.

References

ADAMSON, R. E. (1952), 'Functional fixedness as related to problem solving: a repetition of three experiments', *J. exp. Psychol.*, vol. 43, pp. 288–91.

BATTERSBY, W. S., TEUBER, H. L., and BENDER, M. B. (1953), 'Problem-solving behavior in men with frontal or occipital brain injuries', *J. Psychol.*, vol. 35, pp. 329–51.

BIRCH, H. G., and RABINOWITZ, H. S. (1951), 'The negative effect of previous experience on productive thinking', *J. exp. Psychol.*, vol. 41, pp. 121–5.

COFER, C. N. (1951), 'Verbal behavior in relation to reasoning and values', in Guetzkow, H. (ed.), *Groups, leadership and men*, Carnegie Press. (Quoted after Johnson, 1955.)

DUNCKER, K. (1945), 'On problem-solving', *Psychol. Monogr.*, vol. 58, no. 5 (whole no. 270).

JOHNSON, D. M. (1955), *The psychology of thought and judgement*, Harper.

KOFFKA, K. (1935), *Principles of Gestalt psychology*, Harcourt, Brace.

LEEPER, R. (1951), 'Cognitive processes', in Stevens, S.S. (ed.), *Handbook of experimental psychology*, Wiley.

MAIER, N. R. F. (1930), 'Reasoning in humans. I. On direction', *J. comp. Psychol.*, vol. 10, pp. 115–43.

MAIER, N. R. F. (1931), 'Reasoning in humans. II. The solution of a problem and its appearance in consciousness', *J. comp. Psychol.*, vol. 12, pp. 184–94.

MAIER, N. R. F. (1933), 'An aspect of human reasoning', *Brit. J. Psychol.*, vol. 24, pp. 144–55.

MAIER, N. R. F. (1945), 'Reasoning in humans. III. The mechanisms of equivalent stimuli and of reasoning', *J. exp. Psychol.*, vol. 35, pp. 349–60.

MARKS, M. R. (1951), 'Problem solving as a function of the situation', *J. exp. Psychol.*, vol. 41, pp. 74–80.

REID, J. W. (1951), 'An experimental study of "analysis of the goal" in problem-solving', *J. gen. Psychol.*, vol. 44, pp. 51–69.

SAUGSTAD, P. (1955), 'Problem-solving as dependent on availability of functions', *Brit. J. Psychol.*, vol. 46, pp. 191–8.

SAUGSTAD, P. (1957), 'An analysis of Maier's pendulum problem', *J. exp. Psychol.*, vol. 54, pp. 168–79.

SAUGSTAD, P. (1958), 'Problem-solving and availability of functions. A discussion of some theoretical aspects', *Acta Psychol.*, vol. 13, pp. 384–400. *Nord. Psychol.*, vol. 10, pp. 216–32.

SAUGSTAD, P., and RAAHEIM, K. (1957), 'Problem-solving and availability of functions', *Acta Psychol.*, vol. 13, pp. 263–78. *Nord. Psychol.*, vol. 9, pp. 205–20.

SAUGSTAD, P., and RAAHEIM, K. (1959), 'Problem-solving and availability of functions in children', *Acta Psychol.*, vol. 16, pp. 45–58. *Nord. Psychol.*, vol. 11, pp. 45–58.

SZÉKELY, L. (1958), 'Some comments on problem-solving availability and test-magic', *Acta Psychol.*, vol. 14, pp. 152–7. *Nord. Psychol.*, vol. 10, pp. 108–13.

WERTHEIMER, M. (1959), *Productive thinking*, Tavistock.

6   A. S. Luchins and E. H. Luchins

New Experimental Attempts at Preventing Mechanization in Problem Solving

Excerpts from A. S. Luchins and E. H. Luchins, 'New experimental attempts at preventing mechanization in problem solving', *J. gen. Psychol.*, vol. 42 (1950), pp. 279–97.

Introduction

More than a decade ago we began a series of extensive investigations of the possible deleterious effects of habituated behavior (4, 5). We have been concerned with the blinding effects of habit, with what happens when a habit 'ceases to be a tool discriminantly applied but becomes a procrustean bed to which the situation must conform; when, in a word, instead of the individual mastering the habit, the habit masters the individual' (4, p. 93). Specifically, our studies have dealt with the tendency to impute a procedure, repeated in a series of similar tasks, to subsequent problems which possess more direct solutions. This tendency toward mechanization has been taken as evidence of an Einstellung (or a special kind of mental set). Various experimental factors introduced to prevent an Einstellung from developing or to weaken it after it occurred, have on the whole been quite ineffective. The present paper deals with some new experimental attempts to prevent or overcome this Einstellung tendency.

In order to facilitate understanding of the present experimental variations, we shall first briefly describe the original basic experiment upon which they are founded (4, pp. 1–17; 3).

Basic Experiment

The experiment involves volume-measuring problems, in each of which a certain number of empty containers and a supply of fluid are considered to be furnished. By means of these, with the use of pencil and paper, S is to figure out how to obtain a stipulated volume of fluid. The problems, presented at intervals of about $2\frac{1}{2}$ minutes, are given in Table 1.

The first task is for illustrative purposes. If the jars, in the order written, are labeled with the letters a, b, c, respectively, then Problems 2 to 6 are solvable by the formula $b - a - 2c$; e.g., $127 - 21 - (2 \times 3)$ equals $127 - 27$ equals 100 gives the solution of Problem 2. The next two tasks are solvable by this formula and by other simpler ones; $a-c$ and $a+c$, respectively. The ninth problem does not fit the formula $b-a-2c$ but is solved by $a-c$. Problems 10 and 11 are similar to the seventh and eighth.

Table 1
The Tasks

| Problem | Containers given (capacity in quarts) | | | To get |
	a	b	c	
1	29	3		20 quarts
2	21	127	3	100 ,,
3	14	163	25	99 ,,
4	18	43	10	5 ,,
5	9	42	6	21 ,,
6	20	59	4	31 ,,
7	23	49	3	20 ,,
8	15	39	3	18 ,,
9	28	76	3	25 ,,
10	18	48	4	22 ,,
11	14	36	8	6 ,,

Problems 2 through 6 are the Einstellung problems, and Problems 7 through 11, which test their effect, are the test problems or the criticals. The method represented by the formula $b-a-2c$ is called the Einstellung method: the procedures represented by the formulas $a-c$ and $a+c$ are named the direct methods.

Measures of the amount of mechanization or set, the amount of Einstellung effect, are given by the percentage of Einstellung solutions of the first two criticals, trials 7 and 8, (considered as a unit and called C_1C_2); the percentage of Einstellung solutions of the last two criticals, trials 10 and 11, (considered as a unit and called C_3C_4); and the percentage failure of Problem 9. A measure of the amount of recovery from mechanization is given by the increase in direct solutions in C_3C_4 as compared with C_1C_2.

This basic experiment and its variations have been administered by the author to over 9,000 Ss. In computing the results we considered the responses of only those Ss who solved at least the last two Einstellung problems (the two problems immediately preceding the criticals) by the Einstellung method, since we were interested in the effect that such solutions had upon subsequent solutions of the criticals. Most of these Ss showed considerable Einstellung effect. Recovery from mechanization was in general not large for adult groups, and was negligible in most elementary school groups.

Limiting the Amount of Fluid

The Einstellung procedure is more wasteful of fluid than are the direct methods of solution, in the sense that it requires the discarding of a larger volume of fluid. For example, in the second critical – given a 15-quart jar, a 39-quart jar, and a 3-quart jar, obtain 18 quarts of fluid – the Einstellung method necessitates beginning with 39 quarts of which only 18 are actually utilized while 21 quarts are discarded, but the direct method uses only the 18 quarts demanded by the solution.

In an attempt to further the use of the direct procedures in the criticals, we decided to emphasize the need for finding methods of solution which were not wasteful of fluid. Since the search for economical methods would be realistic only if the amount of fluid available was limited, it was decided to alter the basic setup, in which the supply of fluid was well nigh unlimited, and to set the volume available at 539 quarts. This volume suffices to solve all the 10 problems after the introductory one, if *S* employs the Einstellung procedure in the Einstellung problems and the direct methods in all criticals. As was the case when the original setup was administered to elementary school children, the fluid was said to be milk.

After the introductory remarks and the first problem were presented as in the basic experiment, *S*s of the present variation were told:

> You will receive ten more problems. In each, your task will be to measure the amount of milk asked for by a customer, using as measures any or all of the empty containers he gives to you. There is a large tank from which you may take out the milk but, for sanitary reasons, once you put milk in a certain customer's containers you cannot pour it back into the tank or use it for anyone else; you will have to throw away any milk you do not actually give to him, once it is in his containers. The tank contains 539 quarts of milk which will satisfy the orders of all ten customers, if you are careful to use methods which waste as little milk as possible.
>
> When you finish a problem, figure out how much milk there is left in the tank. Write down the amount in the space allowed for the next problem so that you will be able to see whether there is enough milk left with which to solve that problem.

After these instructions, the first Einstellung problem was presented and $2\frac{1}{2}$ minutes allowed for its solution. Then, as in the basic experiment, the two methods of solving this task[1] were illustrated. In addition, in each case the class was shown how to

1. $127 - 21 - (2 \times 3) = 127 - 27 = 100$ and $127 - (9 \times 3) = 127 - 27 = 100$.

determine and record the amount of milk remaining in the tank. The subsequent problems were then presented as in the basic experiment.

It was hoped that the knowledge that he must not needlessly waste the fluid would produce a persistent drive on S's part to search for economical, direct solutions, and that in keeping track of available fluid, S would be reminded of the need for conserving the dwindling supply by utilizing economical procedures. An S who kept account of available fluid and used the Einstellung method in the Einstellung problems and the first two criticals, would find that he was left with only 17 quarts in the tank, insufficient to solve the remaining tasks in the Einstellung manner, and only enough to solve the last problem in the direct way. The repeated failure to use the Einstellung method might help disrupt the mental set and cause recovery in C_4.

Finally, while an S in the basic experiment might be satisfied with solving all the problems but one or a few, Ss in the present variation might feel a deeper sense of failure if unable to do some of the criticals, since the assigned task was to solve each problem so that sufficient fluid would remain for the subsequent ones. For these reasons, it was believed that the present variation might be successful in operating against Einstellung effects.

Experiment 1

The described setup was administered to four classes in the sixth year of a New York City public elementary school. Excluded from consideration are the responses of 20 Ss who did not solve the last two Einstellung problems. Of the remaining 139 Ss, only 33 obeyed instructions and consistently computed and recorded the volume of available fluid; with minor exceptions the computations involved were correct. These 33 showed only 35, 15, and 5 per cent Einstellung solutions[2] of C_1C_2, No. 9, C_3C_4, respectively, while the 106 who failed to keep the record throughout (most of them stopped after the first two or three problems) contributed 81, 76, and 79 per cent Einstellung solutions of these problems. The 30 per cent recovery shown by those who kept track of available fluid contrasts sharply with the 2 per cent made by those who failed to keep the record.

Considering the group as a whole, we find that this experimental variation was not very successful in operating against Einstellung effects; the results fall within the range of responses made by

2. When it simplifies the presentation of data, we shall refer to failures of Problem 9 as Einstellung solutions.

similar sixth year groups which had participated in the basic experiment.

Comments of Ss after the experiment furnished varied explanations for the failure of so many consistently to keep account of available fluid. Some claimed that they required the allotted $2\frac{1}{2}$ minutes for a problem, and did not have time to compute the amount of remaining milk. Others said that they became so engrossed in working on the problems that they forgot the instructions. A few admitted that while they remembered the directions, and even complied with them initially, they did not trouble to keep the record thereafter, since it seemed superfluous and a waste of time; as long as they were able to obtain the correct answers to the problems, they saw no point in determining the contents of the tank.

While those who kept track of the remaining milk showed comparatively little Einstellung, one might ask why they showed any. It was our impression, based on discussions with the Ss, that some of those who did keep the record of the fluid did so in quite mechanical a fashion, without relating the computations to their methods of solution of the problems. They often paid scant attention to the amount of available milk before beginning the next problems, or, in a few cases, ignored this figure if it indicated to them that there was insufficient milk to permit the utilization of their method, reasoning that it was better to 'solve' the remaining problems under these conditions than not to solve them at all, or that perhaps they had erred in their record-keeping.

Experiment 2

Since so many Ss did not keep track of the fluid in the previous experiment, it was decided to vary that setup by reminding the class of this instruction *after every problem*. In addition, those whose records after the second critical revealed that they did not have sufficient fluid with which to solve the three remaining tasks, were given the opportunity to return to the first two criticals and to search for less wasteful solutions. [. . .]

Problems 9, C_3, and C_4, written on the blackboard at the usual $2\frac{1}{2}$ minute intervals, were allowed to remain there for fifteen minutes.

This setup was utilized in two sixth-year classes and resulted in each of the 60 Ss keeping a consistent, fairly accurate account of available fluid. Nonetheless, they showed 80 and 73 per cent Einstellung solutions of C_1C_2 and No. 9, prior to the interruption after the latter task. These results, similar to the range of responses made by sixth-year classes in the basic experiment, hint that the record-keeping *per se* did not induce the use of direct solutions, that there was not, in general, a causal relationship between keeping the record and searching for economical methods. Discussions with the Ss revealed that most of them computed the volume of available milk in a highly mechanical fashion, because they were reminded to do so, but that the computations had little significance to them; previous experiments (4, pp. 60–63) also have indicated that a reiterated instruction of this sort tends to become meaningless to the Ss. In the present experiment many admitted that they actually did not consult the computations before solving the subsequent problem or that they ignored it if it did not support the use of the Einstellung method.

Subsequent to the interruption following the ninth problem, after which Ss had the opportunity to do some of the problems again, the 60 Ss gave only 17, 13, and 13 per cent Einstellung solutions of C_1C_2, No. 9, and C_3C_4, respectively. These differences in results testify to the efficacy of centering Ss, after the ninth task, on the possible lack of fluid, reminding them that wasteful methods might have produced this lack, and giving them another chance to solve some of the problems. The success of the interruption after the ninth task further supports the assumption that an individual tends to persist in the use of a stereotyped mode of response until some dramatic occurrence causes him to start searching for new methods (cf. 1, p. 342).

Experiment 3

In the previous experiment considerable recovery occurred when Ss were given the opportunity to do some of the criticals again. We were interested in matching a similar opportunity against 'speed conditions'. Accordingly, as in previous speed experiments (4, pp. 53–56) Ss were first told that they were being tested to see how quickly they could solve the eleven problems (all of which had already been written on the blackboard), that they must work as quickly as they could, and bring their papers to E as soon as they finished so that he might record the time of completion. At frequent intervals, they were told that they must hurry, that younger children worked faster, etc. In other respects the initial instructions were similar to those of Experiment 1, including the restriction against returning milk to the tank and the direction to compute and record the amount of remaining fluid.

This setup was administered to two sixth-year classes. It was found that only four out of 62 Ss kept a consistent record of the remaining fluid. These four showed no Einstellung effect, while the remaining 58 *S*s gave 100 per cent Einstellung solutions of all criticals. As each of the latter brought over his paper, *E* told him that he had failed to keep tab of the amount of milk remaining in the tank and that because of the wasteful methods he used, he actually had not had enough fluid to do even the ninth problem. He was given another sheet of paper, told to do the problems again, to keep a record, and to pay particular heed to the last five problems.

On their second papers, only 16 of the 58 showed recovery, so that the latter now gave 73 per cent Einstellung solutions of each critical – which, while it differed significantly from the previous 100 per cent, was as large as the Einstellung effects yielded by some sixth-year groups which received the basic setup. It is noteworthy that the 16 *S*s employed the direct solution in every critical while the others never utilized this procedure; they repeated the Einstellung method throughout, even using it in Problem 9 where it did not yield the desired volume of water and did not at all solve the problem. It would seem from the results that a dramatic occurrence which starts one searching for new methods does not necessarily reduce Einstellung effects. A possible explanation for this seems to lie in the subjects' reactions to the situation.

Most of the *S*s who had to do their work over later told us that they were disturbed and humiliated by *E*'s announcement that they had not solved the problems correctly and must do them again, since it meant that in spite of all their hurrying they would now be among the last to finish and might even fail the test. They said that when they attempted to do the problems over, they could not relax and think clearly; they could think of nothing but their failure and the need for speed. Some of these *S*s tended to submit their second papers within a few minutes, often running all the distance to *E* in order to save a few seconds; many were clearly under the influence of the 'speed atmosphere', the effects of which were also seen in strained faces, broken pencil points and occasional tears.

Discussion

It is our impression (corroborated by *S*s comments) that the initial instructions focused some *S*s on the need for conserving the amount of milk through the utilization of economic methods, but that their inability to find a more economical procedure than the Einstellung method in the first few problems led them to abandon their search for other methods as a waste of time, or led them to conclude that the Einstellung procedure was the least wasteful or, in fact, the only method of dealing with these problems. Finally, it could have been that, even though S was initially concerned with discovering more economical methods, the repeated use of the Einstellung method in the Einstellung problems developed in him a mechanical tendency to repeat it, a tendency which swept in its wake any consideration of other methods. Opposed to these Ss were those who paid no heed at all to the need for discovering economical procedures but who from the start fell victim to the Einstellung tendency. In other words, in these experiments as in previous ones, distinctions must be drawn among Einstellung effects (a) which are the result of a conscious generalization, (b) which result from sheer mechanical perseveration, and (c) which initially arise from a generalization but change into mechanical repetition.

We wonder whether the lack of success of the variation employed in Experiment 1 is not in some ways an outcome of the fact that we used arithmetical problems, and that the Ss, elementary school children, had developed certain attitudes and habits toward arithmetic as a result of their schooling. They were accustomed to the use of isolated drill in arithmetic, where in order to 'learn' a method or a formula they practised it in a series of similar problems – a situation quite similar to our experimental setup. They were accustomed to being taught a method and then practising it; to have to discover procedures was not only quite foreign to them in arithmetic but also in most school subjects. [. . .]

Addition of a Fourth Jar

Essentially, the main difference between the basic setup and the present one was the addition in each problem of a fourth jar not required by the Einstellung method. This change was introduced because we had noticed that Ss who participated in the original study often imposed the Einstellung procedure upon a problem without first surveying all the given containers. It appeared that they viewed the problems from the frame of reference of this procedure, since often they immediately selected the largest jar, the center jar, and removed excess fluid from it with the two remaining containers. Maintenance of this frame of reference was strengthened by the original setup since each problem, after the introductory one, consisted of three jars and the Einstellung method demanded just this number. That the tasks in the present variation involved four jars might lessen the likelihood of S rapidly imputing this method to them. Even if set to employ the Einstellung procedure, he would first have to examine the four containers in order to select the ones to utilize; in the course of so doing he might become aware of the direct solution or of other solutions made possible by the addition of the fourth jar.

The content of the superfluous container was given as 89, 43, 27, 37, 22, 15, 16, 37, 16, and 4 quarts in Problems 2–11, respectively. Preliminary experimentation revealed that Einstellung effects were as large as in the basic experiment when the additional jar was consistently placed in the same position with relation to the other containers, particularly when it was always first or always last. It was therefore decided to vary the position of this jar which was presented as the 3rd, 2nd, 4th, 3rd, 4th, 2nd, 1st, 3rd, 4th, and 3rd in Problems 2–11, respectively.

Experiment 1

The variation was administered in two New York City public elementary schools to 148 children in four classes on the sixth-year level, classes similar in composition to sixth-year groups which had participated in the basic experiment. The group as a whole (including those who failed to use the Einstellung method in both of the two problems immediately preceding the criticals) gave from 4 to 11 per cent Einstellung solutions and from 80 to 90 per cent direct solutions of the criticals, quite the reverse of results usually shown by similar groups which participated in the basic experiment. Those 28 Ss who did employ the Einstellung method in both the two problems prior to the criticals gave 28, 7, and 10 per cent Einstellung solutions of C_1C_2, No. 9, and C_3C_4, respectively. This was more Einstellung effect than the group as a whole, but significantly less than that shown by a comparative group of 36 Ss which received the basic setup. It is interesting to compare the 18 per cent recovery from mechanization made by the 28 Ss, with the complete lack of recovery in the comparative group.

Of the 148 Ss who received the four-jar setup, 120 failed to employ the Einstellung method in the last two Einstellung problems. There were 24 Ss who did solve these two problems, but who used another procedure, frequently a roundabout variation of the Einstellung method (e.g., $163 - 25 - 43 - 14 - 25 + 14 + 43 - 14 = 99$), in one or both of them. The remaining 96 Ss, constituting 65 per cent of the entire group, failed to solve these two problems, in contrast to the average 12 per cent failure in the sixth-year public elementary school groups of the basic experiment.

In short, the increase of direct solutions of the criticals was offset by an increase in failures and inefficient solutions of the Einstellung problems.

Experiment 2

The four-jar setup was also administered to 125 high school students in three classes on the third and fourth year levels of the High School of Science in New York City. They constituted a select group with regard to intelligence and to aptitude for mathematics or science. The group as a whole (including those who did not employ the Einstellung method in the two problems prior to the criticals) showed from 11 to 28 per cent Einstellung solutions and from 59 to 74 per cent direct solutions of the criticals, about the reverse of results made by high school groups of the basic experiment. Those 71 Ss who did employ the Einstellung procedure in these two problems gave 46, 19, and 16 per cent Einstellung solutions of C_1C_2, No. 9, and C_3C_4, respectively. This was more Einstellung effect than the group as a whole but significantly less than that made by a comparative group of 42 Ss of the same school which received the basic setup. The 30 per cent recovery from mechanization shown by the 71 Ss compared favorably with the 13 per cent made by the comparative group.

There were 54 Ss receiving the four-jar setup who did not use the Einstellung method in the last two Einstellung problems. Of these, 19 solved these problems but used other methods, usually cumbersome variations of the Einstellung procedure, in one or both of them. The remaining 35 Ss failed to solve at least one of these problems, in contrast to their almost universal solution in high school groups receiving the basic setup.

Thus, in comparison with the basic experiment, the four-jar variation again yielded more direct solutions of the criticals and (although not to as marked a degree as in the elementary school group) more inefficient solutions and failures of the Einstellung problems.

Discussion

In an attempt to understand the nature of solution of the criticals, we questioned the Ss after the experiment. The replies of some of those who employed the direct methods in these problems substantiated the hypothesis raised in the introduction, i.e., while they were examining a problem the direct procedure suddenly confronted them, 'stared them in the face', even though they had previously used the Einstellung method or variation of it. For some this occurred in the first critical, and for others, after their experience with Problem 9.

Those who failed to employ the direct method in any or all of the criticals, either could offer no explanations for their behavior, simply stated that they did not see the direct solutions or that they had become accustomed to the longer solutions, or said that they had learned in the earlier problems to focus on the largest jar or on a subtractive process.

There are several plausible explanations of the inefficient solutions and failures of the Einstellung tasks, explanations rooted both in theoretical considerations and in some Ss' comments. To begin with, many Ss developed a vague idea of beginning with the largest jar[3] and pouring from it, depending on a 'hit and hope' method to obtain the required volume. This resulted frequently in clumsy variations of the Einstellung procedures, involving unnecessary steps which negated each other. Insufficient time to carry out the numerous steps or an error in calculation somewhere along the way contributed to failures, particularly in the elementary school classes.

Moreover, the addition of the fourth jar made the problems look more complicated and actually increased their complexity by increasing the number of possible numerical combinations of the containers. In the basic experiments, S was faced with problems which were less complex both in appearance and in structure, since to use the Einstellung procedure in them required all of the three given containers. In order to employ the Einstellung method in the four-jar variation, S had to discard one, only one, and the proper one oft he containers. In selecting the jar to be filled initially, and in selecting the jars with which to pour ,he might choose the superfluous containers – and err. Nothing in the statement of the problem told how many and which jars should be employed in the solution.

The basic setup had a familiar ring to the Ss because of its similarity to arithmetical isolated drill exercises to which they were well accustomed. To be given problems in which it was necessary to discard one of the givens was an unusual assignment for them. They had been taught to use all the hypotheses given in a problem; indeed, some of the high school students had learned in their geometry classes to check off each hypothesis as they used it, and if any were left unchecked they knew that they had not proceeded

3. Preliminary experiments in which this possibility was ruled out show somewhat smaller percentages of Einstellung effects but greater percentages of failures to solve the Einstellung problems.

correctly. While in natural problem solving situations the selection of facts and hypotheses from the many available ones is an important aspect of the problem solving process, it appeared to be a highly artificial procedure to many of our *S*s because of the nature of their school training. [. . .]

Finally some preliminary experiments indicated that (*a*) when the additional containers were very outstanding, either because of their size or position, the Einstellung effect was large and (*b*) when *S*s received the basic setup followed by the four-jar variation, those who showed large Einstellung effects in the former tended to do so even in the variation – they had learned the Einstellung method so well that no superfluous hypotheses stood in the way of their applying it. [. . .]

Concretizing the Tasks

We hoped that removing the problems from the abstract, symbolic level, and placing the emphasis on manipulation of jars rather than on written computations, might reduce the Einstellung effect. That there were *S*s who regarded the numbers as essentially abstract symbols and who stressed computation involving the numbers, was seen when to the basic setup we added, as a last problem, one of the following: given a 5-quart jar, a 25-quart jar, and a 10-quart jar, get 0 quarts; given a 3-quart jar, a 65-quart jar, and a 29-quart jar, get 3 quarts; given a 4-quart jar, a 67-quart jar, and a 17-quart jar, get 4 quarts. Fifty per cent of a class of college students blithely proceeded to obtain no water through the complicated mechanics of the Einstellung method: $25 - 5 - (2 \times 10) = 0$, quite indicative that this was to them an abstract, arithmetical operation. Thirty per cent of another college class devised an ingenious solution to the second-mentioned problem: $65 - 29 - (11 \times 3) = 3$; in 'eleven times three' they repeatedly filled the 3-quart jar but failed to give the obvious solution to the problem – filling this jar once! Sixty-two per cent of a third college class failed to solve the last-mentioned problem, which required no complicated computations but merely the filling of the 4-quart jar. It seemed that these *S*s did not view the figures as representations of the content of jars.

Finally, many participants in the basic experiment and its variations tended to transfer to the setup school-fostered attitudes toward arithmetic which appeared to favor Einstellung effect. We hoped that the effect of such attitudes would be diminished if in place of mere numbers actual jars were substituted, if the tasks were placed on a concrete level.

Outstanding differences between the basic setup and the one utilized in the present variation were that an actual supply of fluid was furnished, and that corresponding to the order in which the jars had been written in each problem, three containers were set on a table before S, with the corresponding volumes printed in large numerals on the surfaces facing S. The jars were made from used cardboard milk containers of the two-gill, pint, and quart size. These were cut down so that the proportions were roughly similar in appearance to the proportions of the numerals labeled on them. To make the setup appear more realistic to S, the numerals were said to refer to the number of cubic centimeters which constituted the capacity of the jars, rather than to quarts as in the basic experiment.

The experiment was conducted in a classroom containing a sink; the sink faucet served as the source of water and the sink as the receptical for excess water. The setup was administered individually and was, except for the described differences, similar to individually conducted experiments with the corresponding arithmetical problems.

Experiment 1

The experiment was conducted with 26 children of the sixth year of a New York City elementary school but only 22 solved the last two Einstellung problems, and only their results are considered. Pencil and paper were furnished at the outset 'to be used if needed'. All but two of the Ss first calculated the solution of each problem with pencil and paper before manipulating the jars. These two showed no Einstellung effects. The group as a whole gave Einstellung effects within the range of results made by similar groups which received the original setup: 68, 64, and 68 per cent Einstellung solutions of C_1C_2, No. 9, C_3C_4, respectively. Since so many Ss first figured out the solution on paper and then handled the jars in accordance with their calculations, our purpose in introducing the concrete jars was quite effectively defeated.

Experiment 2

Thirty college students, all of whom solved the two tasks prior to the criticals in the Einstellung manner, gave as much Einstellung effect in C_1C_2 as did a similar group in the basic experiment, but showed better results in the remaining criticals. They gave 60, 33, and 33 per cent Einstellung solutions of C_1C_2 No. 9, C_3C_4, respectively. Most of them regarded the entire affair as child's play until they were startled by the unsuccessfulness of their attempt to use the Einstellung method in Problem 9. Many first made some written calculations in each problem. Others quickly generalized the Einstellung method as a rule of solution and as soon as a set of three jars was presented, they rapidly filled the center one and poured from it, once into the container to the left and twice into the container to the right. It seemed that those who carefully examined each set of containers, who treated each problem as possessing individual requirements, and who used written calculations only as a check on their manipulations, showed little or no Einstellung effect.

Experiment 3

When pencil and paper were not provided and were expressly forbidden, 10 sixth-year elementary school pupils were found incapable of solving most of the Einstellung problems. Under these conditions, 20 college students, all of whom solved the two problems prior to the criticals in the Einstellung manner, made 55, 50, and 30 per cent Einstellung solutions of C_1C_2, No. 9, C_3C_4, respectively. Some mentally calculated the arithmetic involved before manipulating the jars, thus putting the problem on a symbolic level. Others generalized the Einstellung method as a rule or formula, or claimed that they caught on to the 'trick' which worked in these problems. Here too, there were differences in results between the foregoing and those who carefully surveyed each set of jars to see what method of solution it suggested.

Discussion

Concretizing the problems did not eliminate the Einstellung phenomenon. It appears that a tendency toward mechanization can occur both on the concrete and abstract levels. Thus the Einstellung tendency is not solely due to the fact that abstract symbols are involved in the basic setup. Of course it could have happened that what we witnessed in this experiment was the development, in the process of manipulating the actual jars, of a motor set, such as that found in weight lifting experiments. It is our impression, however, that this did not occur in most of the cases. The major factor in determining whether or not an Einstellung developed seemed to be the attitude with which S viewed the tasks.

One implication for education is that in teaching mathematics it is not sufficient to make the problems more concrete, more life like. The trend toward concretizing mathematical problems by relating them more closely to everyday activities is in part motivated by the desire to make the subject matter more meaningful to the child; but this need not result in giving the child a better insight into mathematics – he may still repeat blindly certain rules and formulas. What are needed are teaching methods which will lead to understanding of the structural qualities of mathematical concepts and encourage productive thinking. (For a detailed discussion of such teaching methods the reader is referred to 2, 3, and 6.)

References

1. HILGARD, E. R., *Theories of learning*, Appleton-Century-Crofts, 1948.
2. DUNCKER, K., 'On problem-solving', *Psychol. Monogr.*, vol. 58 (1945), no. 270, pp. 1–113.
3. KATONA, G., *Organizing and memorizing*, Columbia U.P., 1939.
4. LUCHINS, A. S., 'Mechanization in problem solving', *Psychol. Monogr.*, vol. 54 (1942), no. 248, pp. 1–95.
5. LUCHINS, A. S., 'Classroom experiments on mental set', *Amer. J. Psychol.*, vol. 59 (1946), pp. 295–8.
6. WERTHEIMER, M., *Productive thinking*, Tavistock, 1959.

Additional References

LUCHINS, A. S., *Proceedings of the symposium on mental set*, International Congress of Psychology, Moscow, 1966.
LUCHINS, A. S., and LUCHINS, E. H., *Rigidity of behavior*, University of Oregon Press, 1959.

Part Two DEDUCTIVE REASONING

The experimental study of deductive reasoning has been mainly concerned with the syllogism – a type of inference first systematically studied by Aristotle. The following is an example. Some Greeks are men, some men are clever, therefore some Greeks are clever. The early work of Woodworth and Sells (1935) appeared to demonstrate that judgements of the validity of an inference are influenced by an 'atmosphere effect' – a global impression that an inference is valid, if it has the same form as its premises. In the above example the two premises have the atmosphere of 'some', and this may lead erroneously to the judgement that the inference is valid. The strength of the atmosphere effect is a controversial matter. Chapman and Chapman (7) dispute its existence, and Henle (8) argues against the conventional view that man is poor at deductive reasoning. It is her view that in a logical task the subject's underlying logical competence is distorted by extraneous performance variables. The *linear* syllogism involves the ordering of terms in a series, e.g., Fred is taller than Bill, John is shorter than Bill, therefore Fred is taller than John. This type of inference has been studied intensively in this country by Sir Cyril Burt (1919) and Ian Hunter (1957). De Soto *et al.* (9) present evidence for the ingenious idea that such inferences are made by constructing a mental picture of the terms arranged in a series. It seems that people prefer to picture evaluative series in a vertical orientation with the 'better' things above the 'worse'. Wason's experiment (10) uses non-syllogistic inference – a topic rather ignored although perhaps more relevant to everyday reasoning – and examines the therapeutic value of self-contradiction on subsequent performance.

References

BURT, C. (1919), 'The development of reasoning in school children', *J. exp. Pedag.*, vol. 5, pp. 68–77, 121–7.

HUNTER, I. M. L. (1957), 'The solving of three-term series problems', *Brit. J. Psychol.*, vol. 48, pp. 286–98.

WOODWORTH, R. S., and SELLS, S. B. (1935), 'An atmosphere effect in formal syllogistic reasoning', *J. exp. Psychol.*, vol. 18, pp. 451–60.

7 L. J. Chapman and J. P. Chapman

Atmosphere Effect Re-examined

Excerpt from L. J. Chapman and J. P. Chapman, 'Atmosphere effect re-examined', *J. exp. Psychol.*, vol. 58 (1959), no. 3, pp. 220–6.

One of the most widely accepted explanations of reasoning error is the 'atmosphere effect' advanced by Woodworth and Sells (1935) and by Sells (1936) to account for patterns of error in syllogistic tasks. The atmosphere effect receives favorable mention in such well-known text-books as those by Underwood (1949) and Woodworth and Schlosberg (1956), and in Stevens' *Handbook* (Miller, 1951).

Although Sells concluded his article with the caution, 'The results obtained, far from possessing finality, are much rather a point of departure for further researches in this field,' such further research has not been done and his conclusions have often been accepted without question.

The present paper will present a re-examination of the atmosphere effect. The design of Sells' study will be scrutinized, a new study will be presented, and inferences will be made concerning the preferred errors in syllogistic reasoning. An attempt will be made to offer an interpretation other than atmosphere effect to explain the error patterns.

We must first define the terms used to describe syllogisms. The terminology is a uniform one, based on long tradition. For details see any introductory logic textbook, such as Cohen and Nagel (1934). The following summary, however, presents sufficient information for purposes of this paper.

There are four forms of categorical propositions used in syllogisms:

Name	Expression	Symbol
Universal affirmative	All S's are P's	A
Universal negative	No S's are P's	E
Particular affirmative	Some S's are P's	I
Particular negative	Some S's are not P's	O

A syllogism consists of three such statements, the first two of which are the premises.

1. The major premise, which states the relation between the middle term and the predicate of the conclusion.

2. The minor premise, which states the relation between the middle term and the subject of the conclusion.

3. The conclusion which is the inferred, or deduced, relation between the minor term and the major term.

The figures of the syllogism are the four possible arrangements of the terms in the major and minor premises, in which S is the subject of the conclusion, P the predicate of the conclusion, and M the middle term.

Fig. I	Fig. II	Fig. III	Fig. IV
M – P	P – M	M – P	P – M (Major premise)
S – M	S – M	M – S	M – S (Minor premise)
S – P	S – P	S – P	S – P (Conclusion)

The mood of a syllogism refers to the combination of three propositions from among the four kinds of categorical propositions, stated in the order of major premise, minor premise, and conclusion. For example, a syllogism of the A I I mood, in the first figure, is as follows:

> All M's are P's.
> Some S's are M's.
> Therefore:
> Some S's are P's.

This is a valid syllogism.

Each of the three propositions of a syllogism could be an A, E, I, or O. Considering the major and minor premises only, there are sixteen such possibilities of combination. Fourteen of these sixteen yield no valid conclusion in one or more of the four figures.

Sells (1936) gave students 169 syllogisms, of which 127 were invalid, and asked them to decide the truth or falsity of each. The Ss could mark each syllogism as 'absolutely true', 'probably true', 'indeterminate', or 'absolutely false'. For purposes of scoring, Sells considered the 'absolutely true' and the 'probably true' to be agreement, and considered the 'indeterminate' and the 'absolutely false' to be disagreement with the item. Using this scoring system, he calculated the percentage of Ss who agreed with the conclusion of each invalid syllogism. He found that error scores were very high, the incorrect agreements running between 2 per cent and 80 per cent. He also found that the type of invalid conclusion which was most often accepted varied a great deal among the different pairs of premises.

He asserted that the pattern of the error preferences could be explained by the atmosphere effect. The atmosphere effect has been formulated in two different ways.

In their original formulation, Woodworth and Sells (1935) describe the atmosphere effect in syllogistic reasoning as a drawing of conclusions on the basis of the global impression of the premises. Thus an affirmative premise, i.e., 'all are' or 'some are' (A or I) produces an affirmative atmosphere, and a negative premise, i.e., 'none are' or 'some are not' (E or O) produces a negative atmosphere. A universal premise ('all are' or 'none are') produces a universal atmosphere, and a particular premise ('some are' or 'some are not') produces a particular atmosphere. Sells presents two subprinciples of atmosphere effect as self-evident. These are: (a) a combination of a universal and a particular premise produces a particular atmosphere; (b) a combination of an affirmative premise with a negative premise creates a negative atmosphere. It should be noted that these rules predict a conclusion for one kind of premise pair which has a wording other than that of either of the premises, i.e., for a universal negative combined with a particular affirmative, they predict a particular negative.

In addition to the atmosphere effect, Woodworth and Sells also used a principle of 'caution' to explain the pattern of error preferences. 'Caution' is a tendency to accept weak and guarded conclusions rather than strong conclusions. This means acceptance of 'some are' conclusions more readily than 'all are' conclusions, and 'some are not' conclusions more readily than 'none are' conclusions.

In a second article, Sells re-formulated the atmosphere effect to incorporate this principle of caution. Thus he states (1936, p. 34) that the conclusions favored by atmosphere for AA premises is A, or the weaker I. Using the revised atmosphere effect he reported 100 per cent success in predicting the preferred errors in all moods. However, Sells does imply in a footnote (1936, p. 36) that the incorporation of caution into atmosphere may not be justified.

Sells found that for the sixteen possible paired combinations of the four kinds of premises, acceptance of I conclusions always exceeded A; acceptance of O conclusions exceeded E in all except one borderline case; and either I or O was the preferred error for all but one of the sixteen. His formulation of atmosphere effect was advanced as accounting for these error preferences.

However, the nature of his test format might be expected to dictate high scores on I or O. If an A answer is accepted (e.g., all A's are B), logically, an I must be also (e.g., some A's are B), and similarly if an E answer is accepted, an O must be also. Therefore, if Ss were self-consistent on Sells' test, all those Ss who regarded an A or E conclusion as acceptable for a given premise pair would, necessarily, also regard as acceptable the I and O conclusions respectively, when these were offered. Thus I or O acceptances should never be smaller than A or E on this true-false format, and would be expected to be larger. Thus it appears that some of Sells' findings might be an artifact of his test format, rather than being attributable to 'atmosphere'.

On the other hand, if these error patterns are primarily accounted for by 'atmosphere', then they ought also to be found in a multiple-choice format in which S is given two premises and can choose from among the various possible conclusions on a single item. This is the method of the present investigation.

There is an additional source of confusion in evaluating Sells' findings. Inspection of his items and their designations reveals that in the designation of the mood for fifty-seven of his invalid syllogisms he differed from the conventional use of the term, although he did not indicate to the reader that he did so. This discrepancy consisted of labeling the mood in terms of the order of presentation of the premises, ignoring the distinction between major and minor premises. He also labeled figure ignoring this distinction in twenty-seven items, and did not clearly indicate this.

Sells (1936, Appendix A) stated that he had used invalid syllogisms in figures and moods which by conventional designation are valid, such as E I O which is valid in all figures. The test items which he listed as invalid were invalid, but were in moods and figures other than those he indicated. This makes it impossible to determine if the error preferences might be related to the logical status of the syllogisms.

Method

Materials. – A syllogism test was constructed which consisted of 42 experimental items and 10 filler items, each containing two premises and five alternative conclusions, e.g.,

> Some L's are K's
> Some K's are M's
> Therefore:
> 1. No M's are L's.
> 2. Some M's are L's.
> 3. Some M's are not L's.
> 4. None of these.
> 5. All M's are L's.

The correct answer for all 42 experimental items was 'none of these'.

Like Sells, we used statements only about letters, in order to avoid the influence of previous knowledge and opinions on error preference. [. . .]

A complete listing of the figures and moods is shown in Table 1.

In addition to the 42 experimental items for which a valid conclusion was not possible, there were 10 items for which a valid conclusion could be reached. These were filler items, included to prevent Ss from discovering that none of the experimental items had a valid conclusion except 'none of these'.

The five alternative conclusions were assigned randomly to the five positions, with the restriction that each alternative appeared equally often in each position.

Instructions. – The instructions gave an example of an AA-first figure syllogism (for which either A or I is a valid conclusion) and specified the task as marking the correct alternative from among the five choices.

In addition, the instructions specified that choosing the alternative, 'none of these', would mean that none of the four other alternatives is correct. Following the lead of Sells, the instructions discussed the meaning of the word 'some', as in the expression 'Some X's are Y's'. The word 'some' was to mean 'at least some' and would not, in itself, necessarily mean that some X's are not Y's.

Subjects. – The *S*s were 222 students in introductory psychology classes at Northwestern University who stated in response to a question that they had not dealt with syllogistic reasoning in a college course.

Results

The percentage of *S*s who chose each alternative is listed for the various combinations of premises and figures in Table 1. As seen there, accuracy scores were very low, the mean accuracy score being 20 per cent. The sheer number of errors may be in part attributed to the fact that students do not expect a test to consist chiefly of problems with no solution. However, this does not predict preference for one wrong solution over another. There was a marked piling up of choices on one of the four erroneous conclusions for all of the kinds of premise pairs except EO and OE, on which the error preference split between two alternatives, O and E. For every item, the distribution of error preference departed from chance ($P < 0.001$), as shown by chi square.

The preferred error varied greatly among the fourteen kinds of pairs of premises. Unfortunately, there is no readily available statistical technique for determining the significance of the differences in error preference between the various items and groups of items. However, for most of the relevant comparisons the differences are so massive and clear-cut that a significance test is not required. For most items, a single erroneous alternative was chosen by a majority of *S*s. Moreover, there is a striking consistency for all items using the same type of premise pair; at the same time there are striking differences among the different kinds, except between those which contain the same proposition forms in differing positions. For example, A I and I A premises yield quite similar results. Pairs of moods containing the same proposition form have, for the most part, the same error preference without regard for which is the major or minor premise; this fact justifies comparison of these results with Sells' even though he did not utilize the distinction.

Table 1

Percentage of Ss Choosing Each Alternative[a]

Item No.	Premises	Fig.	A	E	I	O	N	Item No.	Premises	Fig.	A	E	I	O	N
12	AA	II	83	6	3	1	7	5	II	IV	2	3	68	13	15
17	AA	II	82	5	3	1	9	20	II	III	1	5	63	5	26
39	AA	II	77	5	6	1	10	51	II	III	4	5	64	5	23
4	AE	I	3	81	3	5	8	7	IO	III	1	6	13	48	31
23	AE	III	1	85	0	5	8	34	IO	IV	2	5	11	60	22
41	AE	I	1	82	3	6	7	48	IO	I	2	6	10	55	27
8	AI	II	3	7	75	7	8	22	OI	I	1	4	14	59	21
15	AI	IV	3	3	80	6	8	33	OI	III	1	7	15	52	24
46	AI	IV	10	2	74	6	7	44	OI	IV	1	5	11	55	27
13	IA	I	5	5	78	8	5	29	EE	IV	1	57	4	3	36
19	IA	II	5	11	68	7	9	36	EE	II	3	59	5	5	28
42	IA	I	3	4	83	4	7	40	EE	II	2	47	4	7	40
11	AO	III	2	7	14	61	16	30	EO	I	3	24	10	32	32
24	AO	I	1	2	13	76	8	35	EO	II	1	26	9	32	32
52	AO	IV	1	4	10	74	11	47	EO	III	5	25	6	21	44
25	OA	II	0	7	12	64	16	2	OE	IV	2	28	12	24	34
32	OA	IV	3	4	11	70	12	27	OE	I	3	39	5	19	34
43	OA	I	1	6	7	78	8	50	OE	III	3	41	7	19	30
9	IE	I	1	62	6	13	18	3	OO	III	0	8	10	50	31
26	IE	III	2	59	5	16	19	14	OO	IV	0	5	11	60	24
49	IE	IV	2	48	6	24	20	45	OO	II	1	8	11	45	35

[a] N designates choosing the alternative 'none of these'. The other designations are explained in the text.

Discussion

Let us consider whether the atmosphere effect explains the error preferences shown in Table 1. Taking the formulation as originally advanced by Woodworth and Sells (1935) (i.e., omitting the principle of caution), we find that this set of principles fails to fit the results for I E and O E premises, on both of which the preferred error is E while the predicted error is O. It also does poorly on E O, for which the results show E to be a strong rival of the predicted O.

Sells' (1936) second and final formulation of the atmosphere effect (i.e., including the principle of caution) is even less applicable to the results. Of the fourteen kinds of pairs of premises, it fails to predict not only for the three mentioned above, but also for A A, A E, and E E. It appears that for these five or six kinds of premise pairs, Sells' finding that the particular conclusions were more popular than the universal may be attributable to his true-false test format.

Since the atmosphere predictions are not substantiated, we must look for other principles of explanation. However, we will be able to offer only intuitive evidence for them.

In seeking such hypotheses we should take into account what we already know about reasoning behavior. First of all, it is known from the findings of Wilkins (1928) and of Sells (1936) that many Ss interpret the A and O propositions to mean that the converse is also true. They interpret the statement 'All A's are B's' to mean that 'All B's are A's,' and the statement 'Some A's are not B's' to mean that 'Some B's are not A's'. (Acceptance of the converse is valid for E and I propositions.)

Such interpretations, although logically invalid, often correspond to our experience of reality, and being guided by experience are usually regarded as justifiable procedures. One may realistically accept the converse of many, perhaps most, O propositions about qualities of objects; e.g., some plants are not green, and also some green things are not plants. The reason for this is that when we assert one particular negative about A and B (some A's are not B's), we normally are not in a position to assert the universal affirmative (all B's are A's), that would rule out the converse particular negative (some B's are not A's). In short, 'Some green things are not plants' would be false only if all green things were plants.

The acceptance of the converse of the A propositions is also often appropriate, e.g., all right angles are 90°, also all 90° angles are right angles. Our students' chief exposure to formally presented deductive reasoning had been in introductory mathematics courses in which such reversal of A propositions is usually justified because in that context 'are' means 'are equal to' rather than the syllogistic 'is included in'.

The principle of accepting the converse of A and O propositions would explain the results for all of our six kinds of premise pairs (the first eighteen items of Table 1) that yield a valid syllogistic conclusion in at least one other figure (other than the figures used here).

In the remainder of the items, acceptance of the converse of itself yields no syllogistic conclusion. For these, an additional principle must be found. It is known that conclusions are often reached by probabilistic inference (Cohen and Nagel, 1934; Mill, 1879), and our Ss had no way of knowing that all but strict deductive reasoning is disallowed in the syllogistic game. By one kind of probabilistic inference, S reasons that things that have common qualities or effects are likely to be the same kinds of things, but things that lack common qualities or effects are not likely to be the same. In the syllogism, the available common characteristic is the middle term. Such thinking is not unreasonable; rather it is the reasoning process by which most science progresses. Thus a chemist might reason as follows: 'Yellow and powdery material has often been sulphur. Some of these test tubes have yellow powdery material. Therefore some of these test tubes contain sulphur.' This is an invalid III syllogism of the second figure, yet the conclusion has some probability. The scientist would regard the conclusion as tentative and attempt to check it by other means.

Probabilistic inference, coupled with the acceptance of converses, also explains the errors in the remaining premise pairs. In the case of an I coupled with an O premise in the second figure, e.g., 'Some A's are B's, some C's are not B's,' S reasons that some A's and some C's do not share the common quality of B and therefore some C's are not A's. For O propositions in which the middle term is the subject rather than the predicate, the proposition must be restated to express the converse. Probabilistic inference yields analogous results for the case of an I with an E.

In the case of two E premises such as 'No A's are B's, no C's are B's', the middle term, B, is not shared. Therefore, by probabilistic inference, no C's are A's. Similarly, two O premises yield an O conclusion. However, in the latter case the propositions must, when necessary, be restated in the converse to cast them in the second figure.

The predicted conclusions by probabilistic inference for EO and OE are less clear. For example, 'No A's are B's, some C's are not B's.' Should we conclude that some C's are not A's, or that no C's are A's? As seen in Table 1, Ss split their choices between

these two alternatives, a result which further supports the interpretation that such probabilistic inference was used.

The eighteen items for which only acceptance of the converse
yields a conclusion have a mean accuracy score of 9 per cent, and
those for which probabilistic inference is necessary have a mean
accuracy score of 28 per cent.

We might describe the errors in Table 1, then, in terms of Ss'
regarding as proved something which is merely probable. If so,
they were behaving as fairly reasonable but incautious people.
This corresponds to our impressions gained from everyday observations of undergraduates.

Von Domarus (1944) and more recently Arieti (1955) have
suggested that, in syllogistic reasoning, concluding that two things
are the same because they share a common quality is distinctively
pathological. They say this error is found in schizophrenics but
not in normals. Clearly, the present findings contradict their
suggestion. If those writers are reporting a partially valid clinical
observation, the validity must exist in a greater error tendency
among schizophrenics, or the appearance of the error in contexts
in which normals would not show it. Such a difference of degree
rather than kind would be consistent with other evidence, recently
pointed out by Chapman (1958), that many aspects of the so-
called schizophrenic thinking disorder consist in exacerbations of
normal error tendencies.

The principles advanced here to explain the error preferences
for the fourteen types of premise pairs are intended to deal only
with the main error preferences. There seem to be some other less
important systematic sources of error choice. For example, on
pairs of premises involving two particulars (II, IO, OI, and OO)
one might expect that A and E conclusions would be only random
error. Yet E choices are consistently more frequent than A choices.
This is probably due to the tendency, noted by logic teachers, to
misinterpret a statement of the form 'No A's are B's' to mean that
nothing has been proved.

In addition, in most cases where an I or O proposition is the
preferred error, the other of the two propositions is the second
most preferred error (except for EO and OE premises).

This error pattern might be attributed to the fact that I and O
propositions imply one another except when we are in a position
to assert a contradictory universal. For example, the statement
'Some A's are B's' implies that some A's are not B's unless we can
assert that all A's are B's. In the normal use of particulars, we are
not in a position to assert this stronger universal.

91

The suggestions that we have advanced to explain the error preferences are tentative ones. We have offered one possible solution, but other investigators might prefer a different one.

References

ARIETI, S. (1955), *Interpretation of schizophrenia*, Brunner.

CHAPMAN, L. J. (1958), 'Intrusion of associative responses into schizophrenic conceptual performance', *J. abnorm. soc. Psychol.*, vol. 56, pp. 374–9.

COHEN, M. R., and NAGEL, E. (1934), *An introduction to logic and scientific method*, Harcourt, Brace.

MILL, J. S. (1879), *A system of logic*, Harper.

MILLER, G. A. (1951), 'Speech and language', in Stevens, S. S. (ed.), *Handbook of experimental psychology*, Wiley.

SELLS, S. B. (1936), 'The atmosphere effect: an experimental study of reasoning', *Arch. Psychol.*, *N.Y.*, vol. 29, pp. 3–72.

UNDERWOOD, B. J. (1949), *Experimental psychology*, Appleton-Century-Crofts.

VON DOMARUS, E. (1944), 'The specific laws of logic in schizophrenia', in Kasanin, J. S. (ed.), *Language and thought in schizophrenia*, University of California Press.

WILKINS, M. C. (1928), 'The effect of changed material on ability to do formal syllogistic reasoning', *Arch. Psychol.*, vol. 16, pp. 1–83.

WOODWORTH, R. S., and SCHLOSBERG, H. (1956), *Experimental psychology*, Holt. (Rev. ed.).

WOODWORTH, R. S., and SELLS, S. B. (1935), 'An atmosphere effect in formal syllogistic reasoning', *J. exp. Psychol.*, vol. 18, pp. 451–60.

8 M. Henle

On the Relation Between Logic and Thinking

Excerpt from M. Henle, 'On the relation between logic and thinking',
Psychol. Rev., vol. 69 (1962), pp. 366–78.

The question of whether logic is descriptive of the thinking process, or whether its relation to thinking is normative only, seems to be easily answered. Our reasoning does not, for example, ordinarily follow the syllogistic form; and we do fall into contradictions. On the other hand, logic unquestionably provides criteria by which the validity of reasoning may be evaluated. Logical forms thus do not describe actual thinking, but are concerned with the ideal, with 'how we ought to think'. And yet a problem seems to be concealed beneath this easy solution.

It is interesting to note that a number of the older writers on logic regarded their discipline as the science of thought. It will not be possible here to survey the vast literature, some of which bears only by implication on our problem, but some examples will illustrate this position. Cohen and Nagel (1934) summarize the older view: 'An old tradition defines logic as the science of the laws of thought' (p. 18). Kant (1885) holds that 'logic is a science of the necessary laws of thought, without which no employment of the understanding and the reason takes place' (p. 3). Psychology, on the other hand, supplies only the contingent, not the necessary, rules of thought. John Stuart Mill (1874) likewise views logic as comprising 'the science of reasoning, as well as an art, founded on that science' (p. 18). He continues:

> Whatever has at any time been concluded justly, whatever knowledge has been acquired otherwise than by immediate intuition, depended on the observance of the laws which it is the province of logic to investigate. If the conclusions are just, and the knowledge real, those laws, whether known or not, have been observed (p. 22).

Boole (1854), as a final instance, regards 'the laws of the symbols of Logic' as 'deducible from a consideration of the operations of the mind in reasoning' (pp. 45–6). Boole deduces the law of contradiction, for example, from a fundamental law of thought (pp. 49–51).

More recent writers, on the other hand, have tended to reject the view that the laws of logic are those of the human understanding. Again, only a few illustrations will be given. Cohen (1944) remarks:

That the laws of logic are not the universal laws according to which we do actually think is conclusively shown, not only by the most elementary observation or introspection, but by the very existence of fallacies (pp. 2–3).

A similar point is made by Nagel (1956):

Little need be said in refutation of the view that logical principles formulate the 'inherent necessities of thought' and are generalized descriptions of the operations of minds. Surely the actual occurrence of beliefs in logically incompatible propositions makes nonsense of the claim that the principle of noncontradiction expresses a universal fact of psychology (p. 66).

Regarding the work of Boole referred to above (*An Investigation of the Laws of Thought*), Cohen and Nagel (1934) comment: 'The title is a misnomer' (p. 112). A more extreme statement of this point of view is by Bertrand Russell (1904):

Throughout logic and mathematics, the existence of the human or any other mind is totally irrelevant; mental processes are studied by means of logic, but the subject-matter of logic does not presuppose mental processes, and would be equally true if there were no mental processes (p. 812).

Schiller (1930), too, holds that syllogistic reasoning 'has nothing whatever to do with actual reasoning, and can make nothing of it' (p. 282). He describes the 'Laws of Thought' (laws of identity, contradiction, and excluded middle) as 'verbal conventions' (p. 251).

The changed point of view with regard to the relation between logical principles and the laws of thought seems to be a function of an altered intellectual climate rather than of any fundamental discoveries about the nature of reasoning. It thus seems worthwhile to reopen the question, the more so since it has implications for a number of central issues in the psychology of thinking. First, however, it may be of interest to examine a few more forms in which the present question has been raised.

Discussion of the figures[1] of the syllogism has at times centered on their relevance to actual thinking. J. N. Keynes (1887) cites several writers who reject the fourth figure because they hold that

1. For a description of the figures of the syllogism, see Chapman and Chapman (5). (Eds.)

we do not actually reason in it (pp. 230–1). Kant (1885), indeed, finds all but the first figure both useless and false; the fourth in particular he calls unnatural (pp. 84–90). Keynes, on the other hand, argues for the admission of Figure 4 on the same grounds, namely its relevance to actual thinking: 'It is not actually in frequent use, but reasonings may sometimes not unnaturally fall into it' (p. 232).

Psychologists investigating reasoning processes have tended to underemphasize the role of logic in the thinking of their subjects. To illustrate, Bruner, Goodnow, and Austin (1956) suggest that

much of human reasoning is supported by a kind of thematic process rather than by an abstract logic. The principal feature of this thematic process is its pragmatic rather than its logical structure (p. 104).

Individuals tend to prefer 'empirically reasonable propositions' to logical ones (p. 104). Morgan and Morton (1944) conclude that:

A person is likely to accept a conclusion which expresses his convictions with little regard for the correctness or incorrectness of the inferences involved. Our evidence will indicate that the only circumstance under which we can be relatively sure that the inferences of a person will be logical is when they lead to a conclusion which he has already accepted (p. 39).

Lefford (1946) states that the principles of logical inference 'are techniques which are not the common property of the unsophisticated subject' (p. 144). He goes so far as to distinguish from the logical inference

psychological inferences which may be made by the ordinary person. . . . A psychological inference is not valid or invalid except when judged as a logical inference: psychological inference is purely a fact (p. 145).

Common to all these statements by the psychologists is the assumption that logical principles are irrelevant, if not antithetical, to much actual reasoning.[2] This conclusion is derived from the high incidence of wrong inferences of subjects under test conditions, especially in the case of emotionally relevant material. A different conclusion has been drawn by Von Domarus (1944)

2. A different, but related, position is that represented by Dollard and Miller (1950), who hold that being logical is a learned drive. The child, it is argued, is punished for logical contradictions and absurdities, for illogical and contradictory plans. The result for most people is 'a learned drive to make their explanations and plans seem logical' (p. 120). The implication is, of course, that without this specific training the individual's thinking would not be (or seem) logical.

from observation of errors in the reasoning of schizophrenic patients. This author argues, not that the reasoning of his subjects is unrelated to logic, but rather that it conforms to a logic whose laws are different from those of Aristotelian logic. This is 'para-logic', which excludes the law of contradiction and 'accepts identity based upon identical predicates' (p. 111). This idea has been elaborated by Arieti (1955) who sees the operation of this logic (which he calls paleologic) not only in schizophrenic and primitive thinking, as Von Domarus does, but also in dreams, in some infantile thinking, and in the transference situation in psychoanalysis.

Again it is of interest to find that the earlier writers mentioned above were equally aware of the problem of error, but viewed it in a way that was entirely compatible with their conception of logic as the science of the laws of the mind. 'It is easy to see how truth is possible,' writes Kant (1885, p. 44) 'since in it the understanding acts according to its own essential laws.' Error, however, is difficult to understand since it constitutes 'a form of thought inconsistent with the understanding'. Its source is thus not to be sought in the understanding itself, but rather in the 'unobserved influence of the sensibility on the understanding', the sensibility being that faculty which 'supplies the material for thought'. Boole (1854) likewise considers that 'the phenomena of incorrect reasoning or error . . . are due to the interference of other laws with those laws of which *right* reasoning is the product' (p. 409). He reminds us that 'the laws of correct inference may be violated, but they do not the less truly *exist* on this account' (p. 408). Mill (1874) is still more explicit. Discussing fallacies of ratiocination, he points out that since

the premises are seldom formally set out, . . . it is almost always to a certain degree optional in what manner the suppressed link shall be filled up. . . . [A person] has it almost always in his power to make his syllogism good by introducing a false premise; and hence it is scarcely ever possible decidedly to affirm that any argument involves a bad syllogism (p. 560).

In the case of arguments consisting not of a single syllogism but of a chain of syllogisms, he considers the commonest fallacy of ratiocination to lie in a changing of the premises as the argument proceeds.

Two clearly contrasting alternatives thus present themselves: is logic (or Aristotelian logic) largely irrelevant to the thinking process, or is it concerned with the laws of thinking? Since we will here be concerned only with deductive reasoning, we may reformulate the question more specifically in these terms. But since, as has so often been pointed out, the premises from which we reason are commonly not spelled out, since our inferences so frequently appear as enthymemes,[3] this fact must be taken into consideration. We may ask: if we know the premises – tacit as well as explicit – from which a person reasons, can we put the process in syllogistic form? Do the rules of the syllogism describe processes that the mind follows in deductive reasoning, even when the syllogistic form is not explicitly employed?

It has been shown above that the existence of error had been used as evidence for the irrelevance of logic to the actual thinking process. On the other hand, a different interpretation of error has been suggested. Since the problem of error seems to be a particularly fruitful one in which to join the issues before us, it will be taken as the context for the present discussion. Once more we may reformulate our question as follows: do errors in deductive reasoning mean that the logical process has been violated? As Mill expresses it, does the occurrence of error mean that the syllogism is a bad one? Or can the error be accounted for otherwise? Is it possible that a process that would follow the rules of logic if it were spelled out is discernible even when the reasoning results in error?

The distinction being made here is a familiar one in the psychology of learning and thinking. Thus Koffka (1935, Ch. 12) distinguishes between learning as accomplishment and the learning processes responsible for this accomplishment. Köhler's (1927) distinction between 'good errors' and stupid ones is likewise relevant. Good errors, he points out, 'may, in a certain sense, be absolutely appropriate to the situation' (p. 217) although they solve the problem no more than do stupid ones. Wertheimer (1959), too, distinguishes between solutions obtained by 'blind' procedures and 'fine, genuine solutions'. Again the difference is one of process, since in both cases the result may be the same. In the same way, in connexion with the present problem, we may ask: given contrasting results – correct solutions and errors in deductive reasoning – what can we say about the thinking processes that account for them? Are the processes necessarily different because their effects are different?

Illustrative data that bear on this issue will be presented. They were obtained from forty-six graduate students of psychology

3. 'A syllogism that is incompletely stated, in which one of the premises or the conclusion is tacitly present but not expressed, is called an enthymeme' (Cohen and Nagel, 1934, p. 78).

who were asked to evaluate the logical adequacy of deductions presented in the context of everyday problems. Most of the subjects had no training in formal logic. The material was presented under group conditions, the subjects writing out their judgements and their grounds for making them. Instructions included an explicit statement that the logical adequacy of the arguments was to be judged, not the truth of the statements. [. . .]

The present data will be used only to illustrate the reasoning processes in cases of error; no quantitative results will be presented. As many authors have shown, the incidence of error in deductive reasoning depends on the form of the syllogism and its contents, as well as on instructions to the subjects. Quantitative results would have relevance only to the particular conditions studied here, whereas an inquiry into the nature of the errors obtained might be of more general interest.

Several processes may be distinguished which led to error in dealing with the presented material:

Failure to Accept the Logical Task

More specifically, this means failure to distinguish between a conclusion that is logically valid and one that is factually correct or one with which the subject agrees. This source of error has already been reported by Henle and Michael (1956, p. 124).

A sample syllogism follows, along with responses in which errors occur because of failure to grasp or accept the logical task.

Syllogism 6. A group of women were discussing their household problems. Mrs Shivers broke the ice by saying: 'I'm so glad we're talking about these problems. It's so important to talk about things that are in our minds. We spend so much of our time in the kitchen that of course household problems are in our minds. So it is important to talk about them.' (Does it follow that it is important to talk about them? Give your reasoning.)

Responses: 'The conclusion does not follow. The women must talk about household problems because it is important to talk about their problems, not because the problem is in their minds.'

'No. It is not important to talk about things that are in our minds unless they worry us, which is not the case.'

'No. Just because one spends "so much time" in the kitchen it does not necessarily follow that household problems are "in our minds".'

It should be noted that subjects who failed to accept the logical task frequently gave correct responses that are just as irrelevant to the question of the relation of logic to the thinking process as are the errors just cited. A few examples follow:

'Yes. It could be very important to the individual doing the talking and possibly to some of those listening, because it is important for people to 'get a load off their chest', but not for any other reason, unless in the process one or the other learns something new and of value.'

'Yes. It seems obvious that problems which are in the forefront of one's mind bring more consideration to them and possibly newer aspects when they are discussed with another. Two heads may be better than one.'

'Yes it does. By talking about household problems, a problem can be solved or worked through.'

The errors illustrated here clearly do not demonstrate an inability of the subjects to reason logically, since they have not accepted the logical task. They have evaluated the content of the conclusion, not the logical form of the argument. Richter (1957, p. 341) makes the same distinction, carrying the analysis a step farther. Apart from careless mistakes and those arising from 'imperfections in the classifying operation' – i.e., from an inability to make logical deductions, he describes errors arising from 'a general failure to grasp the concept of "logical validity"' and those arising from the 'the specific inability to differentiate "logical validity" from another attribute of syllogisms,' namely their factual status. To apply to the present data, the factual criterion needs to be interpreted to mean what is believed to be true or reasonable as well as what is known to be true. With Richter's distinction in mind, we may note that no subject failed completely to grasp the logical task. Still, one individual judged on the basis of belief rather than logical validity in the case of nine out of ten syllogisms, and several others judged in this manner with at least half of the syllogisms presented.

Restatement of a Premise or Conclusion so that the Intended Meaning is Changed

In a number of cases examination of the material from which a subject reasoned showed that it differed from that which was originally presented. In such cases the validity of the argument can, of course, be judged only in relation to the syllogism actually employed, not the one intended.

1. In the case of syllogisms in which a conclusion from two particular premises was to be evaluated, the premises were

99

occasionally restated as universals, from which the conclusion followed. The following syllogism permitted this kind of change:

Syllogism 8. Mrs Cooke had studied home economics in college. 'Youth is a time of rapid growth and great demands on energy,' she said.. 'Many youngsters don't get enough vitamins in their daily diet. And since some vitamin deficiencies are dangerous to health, it follows that the health of many of our youngsters is being endangered by inadequate diet.' (Does it follow that the health of many youngsters is being endangered by inadequate diet? Give your reasoning.)

Responses: 'Yes. Youngsters (A) don't get vitamins (B). Not getting vitamins (B) dangerous to health (C). Youngsters (A) in danger of poor health (C).'

'This follows. . . . Youth doesn't get enough vitamins. Vitamins are necessary or bad health results. Therefore youth are endangered. All of these follow logically, and I believe a correct inference has been made.'

2. Other changes were introduced into the premises by subjects whose reasoning was found to be correct even though their answers to the intended problem were wrong. The same syllogism (Syllogism 8) will be used to illustrate.

Responses: 'There is some question about the equivalence of "don't get enough vitamins" and a vitamin deficiency dangerous to health. If one assumes their equivalence, then the conclusion just about manages to follow.'

'Correct if we assume that the youngsters are lacking those vitamins in their diet which endanger health.'

'It seems to follow, assuming that the deficient vitamins are also the vital ones.'

Everyday discussions permit greater scope for such changes in meaning than does the material employed here. Private meanings of terms or idiosyncratic or unconscious equations of concepts may enter in to prevent two people from drawing the same conclusion even though they start ostensibly from the same material.

Omission of a Premise

Occasionally a subject employed only one of the presented premises. The informal manner in which the premises were set out made possible this treatment of the material. Syllogism 6 (see above) will be used to illustrate.

Responses: 'Not correct logically. (*a*) A group of women spend much of their time in the kitchen; (*b*) thus household problems occupy their minds. . . . (*c*) Therefore it is important to talk about them. Mrs Shivers' subjective thinking.'

'Doesn't follow from the preceding statement. Because she spends a lot of time in the kitchen and household problems are on her mind, it doesn't follow that it is important to talk about them.'

In a few cases, indeed, both of the intended premises were omitted by the subject. For example (Syllogism 6):

'No it doesn't follow. The fact that she spends much time in the kitchen has nothing to do with whether or not it is important to talk about the problems.'

It will be seen that in all these cases in which a premise has been omitted, the subject correctly reports that the conclusion does not follow. If we disregard the intended premises and consider only the material actually used in reasoning, the subjects' deductions are seen to be correct.

Slipping in of Additional Premises

Under the present conditions this device was infrequent, but it seems to be more common where premises are stated less completely, and where the issues are of more immediate practical concern, as in everyday discussion. For example, premises may be added that are so commonplace, so much taken for granted, that they escape attention.

Instances of the adding of assumptions to our material follow. Since they are readily understandable, and for the sake of brevity, the responses will be quoted without the presented syllogism.

Responses: 'Without intending sophistry it must be pointed out that the implicit premise is "crime is bad". If this is granted, the conclusion follows that if comics contribute to influence the youth along criminal paths, they should be eliminated.'

'. . . If comic books are an evil influence, then they should be got rid of.' Here the subject is clearly employing an implicit premise that he added to the material presented, namely 'Whatever is an evil influence should be got rid of.'

Again in these cases, wrong answers are obtained by correct reasoning if we consider the syllogism as the subject understood it rather than the one the investigator hoped to present.

When all the above processes have been taken into account, a considerable number of errors remain. Do these represent true fallacies? It is difficult to say since in these cases either no account of the reasoning process is supplied, or an unclear explanation is given, or else the subject merely sets out the premises and conclusion given to him without comment. It might be that many of these errors would have been found on examination to involve processes similar to the ones described above, so that no error in reasoning is involved. On the other hand, the possibility of true fallacies cannot be excluded.

In connexion with the unexplained errors, it is worth noting that almost as many correct responses as errors were unexplained or unclearly explained. The absence of explanation is thus no reason to suspect a reasoning process of being fallacious.

It must also be mentioned that the processes described above as producing apparent errors although the deductive process is correct are by no means viewed as constituting a complete list. They were observed with particular materials and under particular conditions; and it is to be anticipated that further research will expand this list. Chapman and Chapman (1959), for example, have suggested several additional processes by which error is produced in syllogistic reasoning, one of which involves a misunderstanding of the task different from that described here.

Despite the limitations of the present data, they do show clearly that when subjects arrive at apparently invalid conclusions, or when they fail to spot a fallacy, they often do so because they have worked with materials different from those intended or because they have undertaken a task different from the one intended. In such cases, if we consider the materials and task as they were actually understood by individual subjects, we fail to find evidence of faulty reasoning. It must be concluded that the presence of error does not constitute evidence that the laws of logic are irrelevant to actual thinking. The data tend, rather, to support the older conception that these laws are widely discernible in the thinking process.

Discussion

An examination of errors in syllogistic reasoning leads to two conclusions: (*a*) While the possibility of fallacy often cannot be excluded it is, in Mill's words, 'scarcely ever possible decidedly to affirm that any argument involves a bad syllogism.' (*b*) Where error occurs, it need not involve faulty reasoning, but may be a function of the individual's understanding of the task or the materials presented to him. [. . .]

In considering the place of logical inference in everyday life, it is necessary also to take into account what Aristotle (1945) has termed the 'practical syllogism', the case in which the conclusion drawn from the two premises becomes an action. [. . .] If we include, as it seems we must, the practical syllogism in the 'great business of life', that of drawing inferences, it becomes difficult indeed to accept the conclusion that human beings are unable to reason logically. A couple of contemporary examples will suggest how ubiquitous is the practical syllogism in everyday life. 'It is too far to walk to the Public Library; I must take a subway or bus. The Fifth Avenue bus passes the Public Library. I must take the Fifth Avenue bus.' 'I do not want to wear the same dress two days in succession. I wore this dress yesterday; so I do not want to wear this dress today.' It is difficult to see how the individual could cope with the ordinary tasks of life if the practical syllogism embodied techniques which are not, as one author quoted above put it, 'the common property of the unsophisticated subject', if, indeed, it were not a natural mode of functioning of the conscious mind.

Furthermore, if people were unable to reason logically, so that each arrived at different conclusions from the same premises, it is difficult to see how they could understand each other, follow one another's thinking, reach common decisions, and work together.

It might be argued that in the case of the practical syllogism we are dealing not with an implicit logical process, but with a learning process in which each response is cued off by the preceding one. There seem to be at least two grounds for rejecting such an interpretation. (a) There are cases in which the practical syllogism leads to a solution which is genuinely novel for the individual. This is surely so for some of the examples cited above, at least the first time they occur. Indeed, if the responses were habitual ones, the reasoning process would not be necessary. (b) Our data obtained from conventional syllogisms suggest that a logical process often occurs even in cases in which the reasoning seems fallacious. Such data can thus not be interpreted in terms of the 'learned drive' postulated by Dollard and Miller (1950, p. 120) 'to make . . . explanations and plans seem logical.' And since they sometimes lead to novel conclusions (cf. Wertheimer, 1938), they cannot be interpreted as habitual responses. In the interests of parsimony, therefore, a common explanation for the practical syllogism and the verbal one seems preferable. An interpretation in terms of an implicit logical process would fit both kinds of case.

Two further implications of the present data may be mentioned. They suggest an approach to the problem of the influence of needs and attitudes on the reasoning process. For the problem remains: why do motivational influences so often appear to impair thinking?

It is a plausible hypothesis that these influences do not distort the reasoning process, as has frequently been stated or implied – indeed that they do not act at all on the reasoning process – but rather that they affect the materials with which thinking works. Although this is not the place for a detailed analysis, one or two specific effects of this kind may be suggested. (*a*) It may be that a strong attitude toward, or emotional involvement with, particular material is in part responsible for the difficulty which many unsophisticated subjects experience in distinguishing between drawing a conclusion that is logically valid and one that is believed to be correct. Over a wide range of practical situations these two tasks are not in conflict; and the distinction is thus not an easy one. There is evidence that attitudes and emotions may limit the ability to make distinctions (cf. Henle, 1955). If this suggestion is correct, the more personally relevant the material employed, the more difficult it will be to accept the logical task. Such an effect might go a long way toward explaining the report of a number of writers that individuals are unable to reason logically about emotionally toned material. (*b*) An attitude can select from among the possibilities that the material presents, singling out, for example, one among several possible meanings. It may be that such a process is responsible for the changes in the meaning of premises observed in our data. (For possibilities of further analysis of this kind, cf. Henle, 1955).

That motivational processes may act on reasoning in the manner suggested here receives support from a recent study by Kopp (1960), who subjected to a similar analysis reasoning processes related to the delusions of paranoid schizophrenics. His subjects, like the present ones, made errors which were found to lie more in the premises from which the reasoning proceeded than in the actual drawing of inferences.

In this connexion, it would be interesting to analyse Arieti's (1955) examples of 'paleological' thinking in the terms of the present study. Unfortunately, the published data are too scant to permit such an analysis. The examples presented would be fallacies in terms of Aristotelian logic if one could assume that the premises as understood by the subject are the same as those understood by the examiner. That this is the case may be doubted in a number of instances; and the search for an archaic logic thus seems premature. Some examples will be given which seem to call for an analysis different from Arieti's.

Arieti cites the case of a woman who 'needed to identify herself with the Virgin Mary because of the extreme closeness and spiritual kinship she felt for the Virgin Mary' (1955, p. 195). The reasoning process is described as follows: 'The Virgin Mary was a virgin; I am a virgin; therefore, I am the Virgin Mary.' In the absence of additional material, we may only speculate that the proposition 'I am the Virgin Mary' was not a conclusion deduced from the stated premises, but that it belongs rather in the category of revealed truth or intuition, not in that of deductive inference. It seems likely to the present writer that the syllogism quoted above was in the nature of a justification of this intuition to the examiner rather than the grounds for belief in it. The argument itself could be evaluated only in the light of additional information.

Another kind of example of Arieti's (1955) illustrates what he considers to be the propensity of young children 'to indulge in paleologic thinking':

> A girl, three years and nine months old, saw two nuns walking together, and told her mother, 'Mommy, look at the twins!' She thought that the nuns were twins because they were dressed alike. The characteristic of being dressed alike, which twins often have, led to the identification with the nuns (p. 199).

Again a different interpretation suggests itself: rather than viewing it as a deduction, we may take this process more simply as an instance of an inaccurate concept. Arieti also discusses dream symbols as examples of paleologic thinking. It is particularly difficult for the present writer to view such symbols as inferences, as if they were the conclusions of processes of deductive reasoning. They seem, rather, to involve a much more immediate grasping of similarities.

It is amusing to note that Arieti (1955) regards some delusions of identification as instances of paleologic, and describes the 'formal mechanism' by which they are produced in a way that could easily be restated as a valid Aristotelian syllogism:

> If A may be identified with B because they have a common quality, it will be sufficient for me to acquire a quality of the person I want to be identified with, in order to become that person (p. 207).

Further discussion of the problems raised by Arieti must await more complete data.

The present study has implications also for another problem. To label an inference fallacious, as is clear from the analysis of this paper, is to make a statement about the results of reasoning, but not about the process that is responsible for these results. It might be a matter of considerable interest to study systematically and in detail the reasoning involved in various fallacies. It might be found that many fallacies are produced, not by faulty reasoning, but by specific changes in the material as the subject understands it. Some of the syllogisms employed here involved the fallacy of the undistributed middle; here changes of premises from particulars to universals and other changes in the meaning of premises were not uncommon. Two of the arguments presented contained illicit conversions, but no relevant data were obtained since the subjects systematically ignored the conversion and centered their attention on other parts of the material.[4] In connexion with illicit conversions, the discussion of Chapman and Chapman (1959) is of interest; these authors suggest implicit assumptions and changes in meaning that may be involved in the acceptance of such conversions. [. . .]

In conclusion, observations have been presented which are consistent with the view that the rules of the syllogism describe processes that the mind follows in deductive reasoning, even when the syllogistic form is not explicitly employed. A word of caution is necessary at this point. The present observations apply to deductive reasoning only. Even within this category, a very limited number of logical forms has been studied; and the study has been concerned only with the evaluation of presented arguments, not with the construction of arguments of one's own. The investigation needs to be extended before the generality of the conclusion can be assessed. It must also be pointed out that there are many types of thinking to which logical analysis does not apply at all, for example many aspects of free association, fantasy, many creative processes. To apply logical analysis to such processes (for example, Arieti's discussion of dream symbols) is as much an error as to ignore the underlying logical structure of incompletely stated arguments.

References

ARIETI, S. (1955), *Interpretation of schizophrenia*, Brunner.
ARISTOTLE (1945), *Movement of animals* (trans. E. S. Forster), Harvard U.P.
BOOLE, G. (1854), *An investigation of the laws of thought*, Macmillan.
BRUNER, J. S., GOODNOW, J. J., and AUSTIN, G. A. (1956), *A study of thinking*, Wiley.
CHAPMAN, L. J., and CHAPMAN, J. P. (1959), 'Atmosphere effect re-examined', *J. exp. Psychol.*, vol. 58, pp. 220–6.

4. This unexpected finding cannot be attributed to an insensitivity of the subjects to logical processes. Rather the fault lies with the investigator who, in the effort to disguise the formal structure of the syllogism, included irrelevancies that were taken by many subjects as the material for evaluation.

COHEN, M. R. (1944), *A preface to logic*, Holt.

COHEN, M. R., and NAGEL, E. (1934), *An introduction to logic and scientific method*, Harcourt, Brace.

DOLLARD, J., and MILLER, N. E. (1950), *Personality and psychotherapy*, McGraw-Hill.

HENLE, M. (1955), 'Some effects of motivational processes on cognition', *Psychol. Rev.*, vol. 62, pp. 423–32.

HENLE, M., and MICHAEL, M. (1956), 'The influence of attitudes on syllogistic reasoning', *J. soc. Psychol.*, vol. 44, pp. 115–27.

KANT, I. (1885), *Introduction to logic and essay on the mistaken subtilty of the four figures* (trans. T. K. Abbott), Longman's, Green.

KEYNES, J. N. (1887), *Studies and exercises in formal logic*, Macmillan, 2nd ed.

KOFFKA, K. (1935), *Principles of Gestalt psychology*, Harcourt, Brace.

KÖHLER, W. (1927), *The mentality of apes* (trans. E. Winter), Harcourt, Brace, 2nd ed.

KOPP, S. (1960), *Deductive reasoning in paranoid schizophrenics*, Unpublished doctoral dissertation, New School for Social Research.

LEFFORD, A. (1946), 'The influence of emotional subject matter on logical reasoning', *J. gen. Psychol.*, vol. 34, pp. 127–51.

MILL, J. S. (1874), *A system of logic*, Harper, 8th ed.

MORGAN, J. J. B., and MORTON, J. T. (1944), 'The distortion of syllogistic reasoning produced by personal convictions', *J. soc. Psychol.*, vol. 20, pp. 39–59.

NAGEL, E. (1956), *Logic without metaphysics*, Free Press.

RICHTER, M. N., Jr (1957), 'The theoretical interpretation of errors in syllogistic reasoning', *J. Psychol.*, vol. 43, pp. 341–4.

RUSSELL, B. (1904), 'The axiom of infinity', *Hibbert J.*, vol. 2, pp. 809–12.

SCHILLER, F. C. S. (1930), *Logic for use*, Harcourt, Brace.

VON DOMARUS, E. (1944), 'The specific laws of logic in schizophrenia', in Kasanin, J. S. (ed.), *Language and thought in schizophrenia*, University of California Press.

WERTHEIMER, M. (1938), 'The syllogism and productive thinking', in Ellis, W. D. (ed.), *A source book of Gestalt psychology*, Kegan Paul, Trench, Trubner, Selection 23.

WERTHEIMER, M. (1959), *Productive thinking*, Tavistock.

9 C. B. De Soto, M. London and S. Handel

Social Reasoning and Spatial Paralogic

C. B. De Soto, M. London and S. Handel, 'Social reasoning and spatial paralogic', *J. Pers. soc. Psychol.*, vol. 2 (1965), pp. 513–21.

Mickey Mantle tells of an exhibition baseball game in which he and Willie Mays, both superstars, were playing. Unhappily, the two superstars were having a bad day. Finally a leather-lunged fan shouted at Mantle, 'I came to see which of you guys was better, you or Mays. Instead, I'm seeing which is worse!'

Mantle knew he had been insulted. But wherein was the insult? It could be argued that for a rational investigator the two questions would be strictly equivalent. The discovery that A is better than B seems identical to the discovery that B is worse than A. Yet it is clear that the antonyms do not interchange freely, that 'better' somehow connotes general goodness, whereas 'worse' connotes general badness. The words convey more than strictly relational or comparative meaning; they say something about absolute positions.

Such paralogical implications of 'better' and 'worse' have significance beyond their use in taunting ballplayers. Comparisons may be odious, but they abound in people's description of their world, particularly their social world. Statements like 'Lincoln was greater than Washington' and 'Sue is better than Mary' are the very stuff of social reasoning. People have in fact a fateful predilection for linear orderings. They are prone to place elements in linear orderings to the exclusion of other structures and they handle linear orderings more facilely than most other structures (Coombs, Raiffa and Thrall, 1954; De Soto, 1960). But it would be a mistake to dismiss the popularity of linear orderings by saying they are easy or simple. For structures are not intrinsically easy; they are easy only as people's cognitive apparatuses or schemas make them so (De Soto, 1960, 1961; Inhelder and Piaget, 1958; Mandler and Cowan, 1962). People evidently have apparatuses which enable them for the most part to handle linear orderings efficiently. Their apparatuses are not necessarily the logician's, however. On the contrary, anecdotes like Mantle's provide evidence that they are more paralogical than logical. And if there is to be hope of understanding and modifying the predilection for linear orderings, psychology must study the paralogic, not the logic, of linear orderings.

This article reports three investigations of people's thinking about social orderings, the first a rather thorough experimental analysis of their reasoning about orderings formed of the relations 'better' and 'worse', the second a study of tendencies to assign spatial directions to nonspatial ordering relations like 'better' and 'worse', and the third an experimental analysis of reasoning with additional ordering relations, testing predictions derived from the first and second investigations. Throughout, it was taken for granted that people do not always operate as logic machines, and the aim was not to make that negative point – so often made in past research on reasoning – but to uncover the laws or mechanisms that account for their departures from strict logic.

The Paralogic of 'Better' and 'Worse'

Experiment 1

The previous experiments that come closest to an attack on the paralogic of ordering relations are those concerned with what has been called the linear syllogism (Woodworth and Schlosberg, 1954, p. 843). The linear syllogism differs from the traditional syllogistic forms in that the relations between elements are relations of order rather than of inclusion or implication. For example:

Premise 1: Mantle is better than Mays.
Premise 2: Mays is better than Moskowitz.
Conclusion: Mantle is better than Moskowitz.

Experiments in which subjects were given various valid and invalid linear syllogisms to evaluate have established that such syllogisms vary in difficulty. Unfortunately these experiments were not systematic enough to pinpoint the subjects' paralogic. They led to one general conclusion: that a linear syllogism is easy to evaluate when the ordering of the elements is maintained as they are presented in the premises. The example above fulfils this requirement by giving first the man at one extreme (Mantle), then the man in the middle (Mays), and finally the man at the other extreme (Moskowitz). If the premises were switched, or if Premise 1 was modified to read, 'Mays is worse than Mantle', the requirement would be violated and the syllogism should become difficult. This conclusion seems almost self-evident, but the experiment to be reported here demonstrates that it is in fact wrong.

The trouble with the earlier experiments, the reason that they gave misleading results, was that they did not vary systematically and fully the linear syllogisms presented to the subjects, but instead used a small and inadequate sampling of them. Given an ordering of three elements, A, B, and C, with A the best, B in the middle, and C the worst, there are eight ways of presenting the ordering in syllogistic form, eight premise combinations, as shown in Table 1. In the present experiment, all eight were used, along with eight premise combinations which do not yield orderings.

Method. – The syllogisms were printed on cards for presentation to the subjects, with men's first names replacing the letters A, B, and C. Each premise combination was used four times with varied questions of the following forms: 'Is A better than C?' 'Is C better than A?' 'Is A worse than C?' and 'Is C worse than A?' The subjects received the cards in different random orders.

The subjects' task is described well by the instructions given them:

This experiment is concerned with the understanding of the relationships between different people. You will each receive a deck consisting of 64 cards. On each card you will find printed two statements followed by a question. The two statements will give you some information about the relationships among three individuals and the question will ask about the relationship between two of these people. Below the question will be these possible answers: 'Yes', 'No', and '?'. If the answer to the question is 'Yes', circle 'Yes'. If the answer is 'No', circle 'No'. If the question cannot be answered conclusively 'Yes' or 'No' from the information given in the two statements, circle '?'. If you cannot decide which of the three answers is correct, do not circle anything.

You will be given 10 seconds to work on each card. I will say 'Next' every 10 seconds. Each time I say 'Next', turn the top card over and work on it, placing the previous card on another pile, even if you have not circled an answer on it. Do not move on to a new card until you hear me say 'Next'.

When a name is repeated on the same card, it refers to the same person, but when it is repeated on a different card, it refers to a different person.

The subjects in this experiment were 117 Johns Hopkins undergraduates.

Results. – Table 1 presents the percentage of correct answers given by the subjects for the eight premise combinations which yielded true orderings. It is apparent – even without any correction for guessing – that the premise combinations varied quite widely in difficulty. An analysis of variance performed on the data (assigning a correct answer a score of 1 and a wrong answer a score of 0) yielded a significant main effect for premise combinations ($F = 13.45$, $df = 7/812$, $p < 0.001$).

Discussion. – One can reject immediately the classic conclusion about what makes linear syllogisms easy or difficult. According to the classic conclusion, Premise Combinations 1 and 4 should be easy, since both proceed from one extreme to the middle to the other extreme in presenting the elements. All the other combinations should be difficult. Instead, Combination 4, far from being easy, is one of the most difficult combinations, and 5 and 6, which should be difficult, are among the easiest.

Clearly, an altogether different paralogic is required to account for the findings. We would like to propose two paralogical principles that seem helpful. These principles are not new, but their previous application has been to tasks other than reasoning tasks. The first principle is that people learn orderings better in one direction than the other. The second principle is that people end-anchor orderings.

There is less precedent for the first principle than for the second. One hint of it is found in views of rote serial learning which hold that the subject learns by chaining forward from the first item and backward from the last item, but learns better in the forward direction than in the backward direction (Ribback and Underwood, 1950), producing the well-known asymmetry of the serial position curve.

Consider the application of the first principle to the data in Table 1. We propose that the differences among the four premise combinations in the upper half of the table can be well accounted for by this simple statement: people learn an evaluative ordering more readily from better to worse than from worse to better. There are two ways in which this statement applies to a premise combination: within premises and between premises. A premise proceeds from better to worse within when it gives the better element first and the worse element second, as in 'A is better than B'. It proceeds from worse to better within when it gives the worse element first and the better element second, as in 'B is worse than A'. A premise combination proceeds from better to worse between premises when it gives the better pair (A and B) first and the worse pair (B and C) second. It proceeds from worse to better between premises when it gives the worse pair (B and C) first and the better pair (A and B) second.

As indicated in the 'Analysis' column of Table 1, Premise Combination 1 proceeds in the optimal direction uniformly both

111

within and between premises, and it is the easiest of the four upper premise combinations, in accordance with the hypothesis. Premise Combinations 2 and 3 both proceed in the optimal direction in one sense but in the wrong direction in the other sense, and produce intermediate difficulty. Premise Combination 4 proceeds in the wrong direction in both respects and produces the greatest difficulty.

Table 1

Percentage of Correct Answers for Various Premise Combinations Based on 'Better' and 'Worse'

Premise combination	% correct	Analysis
1. A is better than B	60·5	Within premises: better-to-worse
B is better than C		Between premises: better-to-worse
2. B is better than C	52·8	Within premises: better-to-worse
A is better than B		Between premises: worse-to-better
3. B is worse than A	50·0	Within premises: worse-to-better
C is worse than B		Between premises: better-to-worse
4. C is worse than B	42·5	Within premises: worse-to-better
B is worse than A		Between premises: worse-to-better
5. A is better than B	61·8	Within premises: ends-to-middle
C is worse than B		Between premises: better-to-worse
6. C is worse than B	57·0	Within premises: ends-to-middle
A is better than B		Between premises: worse-to-better
7. B is worse than A	41·5	Within premises: middle-to-ends
B is better than C		Between premises: better-to-worse
8. B is better than C	38.3	Within premises: middle-to-ends
B is worse than A		Between premises: worse-to-better

The second principle – that people end-anchor orderings – has long been used by investigators of judgements and ratings, who commonly find that the extreme items of an ordered series of items are judged most consistently and serve as reference points for judgements of other items (Volkmann, 1951). It has also been used by investigators of rote serial learning in accounting for the fact that subjects learn the end items first and best (Feigenbaum and Simon, 1962). More recently, it has been found that even in non-serial learning of an ordering the end items are learned first (De Soto and Bosley, 1962), and it has been proposed that in all cognitive tasks involving orderings, people will tend to end-anchor.

How does this principle apply to a linear syllogism? We have already hypothesized that the order in which elements are given in a premise has significance of one sort; now we hypothesize that it has significance of an additional sort. We hypothesize that it is helpful to the subject if the first element given in the premise is an end element in the ordering, the best or the worst, so that the premise proceeds from an end toward the middle rather than from the middle toward an end. This proposition does not make differential predictions for the first four premise combinations, in each of which one premise combination has the desirable property and one does not. It applies to the second four premise combinations in Table 1. Combinations 5 and 6 possess the desirable property in both premises and are easy. Combinations 7 and 8 lack it in both and are difficult. The first principle also applies partially to these latter four premise combinations. Within premises they are alike in having one premise go from better to worse and one from worse to better. In the between-premises sense, however, they differ. Combinations 5 and 7 give the better pair first, unlike 6 and 8, and should be relatively easier, as they are.

To conclude, the results in Table 1, which can only be called chaotic in the light of the classic statements about linear syllogisms, seem to be quite nicely organized by these two simple paralogical principles.

And these principles may illuminate other phenomena. The first principle implies that 'better' should be the word of choice for interrelating elements more often than 'worse'. This prediction is confirmed by the L count (Thorndike and Lorge, 1944), which shows that 'better' is used 2,354 times in 4.5 million words, while 'worse' is used only 450 times. (It should be noted that a reversed hypothesis – an argument that syllogisms using 'better' are easier than syllogisms using 'worse' *because* 'better' is the more frequent word – would be unable to account for the differences in difficulty between premise combinations like 1 and 2, which use identical words in different arrangements.)

The two principles together imply that the occasion for using the word 'worse' would be to interrelate elements at the bad end of an ordering, and not too far toward the middle of the ordering, just as forward chaining takes up a larger portion of the list than backward chaining in serial learning. The baseball fan who cast Mantle and Mays into the nether world of ball players by asking who was worse rather than who was better can be seen, then, as capitalizing on something more than idiosyncrasies of words.

The Paralogic of Spatial Directions

Questioning of the subjects in Experiment 1 indicated that most of them solved the syllogisms with the aid of imagery. Most commonly, they imagined the men's names as arranged in a vertical ordering, with the best man the highest and the worst man the lowest. 'Better than' was transformed in their thinking into 'above'; 'worse' became 'below'.

The use of spatial imagery in thinking about nonspatial orderings has been noted previously by such diverse introspectionists as Lashley (1961) and Inhelder and Piaget (1958, p. 252). Unfortunately, however, casual introspective observations fail to prove that this imagery plays a key role in such thinking, much less delineate the role. After all, the serious and intensive investigations of imagery by Titchener and his students ended in failure to prove that images are anything more than insignificant concomitants of thinking (Brown, 1958, p. 92).

An alternative approach is to regard images only as clues to the processes of thought and seek independent data bearing on the role of spatial representations in thinking about orderings. Such an attempt was made in the two remaining experiments.

Experiment 2

This experiment was a systematic investigation of people's imputations of spatial directions to 'better' and 'worse' and also to 'has lighter hair than' and 'has darker hair than', the latter pair chosen for having no apparent ties to spatial directions.

Method. – The subjects were given printed statements about the relation between two people, for example, 'Tom is better than Bill', and instructed to write the names of the people in two of four boxes printed on the same sheet of paper. Two boxes were at the ends of a vertical line and two were at the ends of a horizontal line which crossed the vertical one. The subjects were instructed to enter the names in opposite boxes, choosing them as seemed appropriate in consideration of the statement made about the names.

In addition to the four relations mentioned above, four others were included as buffers. Each subject received the eight relations in a different random order with the restriction that 25 subjects received 'better' before 'worse', 25 received 'worse' before 'better', 25 received 'lighter' before 'darker', and 25 received 'darker' before 'lighter'. The subjects were 50 Johns Hopkins undergraduates.

Results. – In the upper half of Table 2 are shown the frequencies with which the subjects imputed the various spatial directions to the various relations when the relations were the first of their kind presented. That is, of the 25 subjects who received 'better' as their first evaluative relation, 23 treated the statement as proceeding downward, placing the first (better) man on top. One treated it as proceeding upward, with the first man on the bottom, and one treated it as proceeding from left to right, with the first man on the left. In contrast, of the 25 subjects who received 'worse' as their first evaluative relation, 19 treated it as proceeding from bottom to top, with the remaining 6 subjects scattering their choices among the other three directions. These data yielded a chi-square of 28·3, significant at the 0·001 level.

Table 2

Frequencies with Which Spatial Directions Were Imputed to Nonspatial Relations

Relation	Imputations when relation was first of its kind			
	Direction			
	Top-to-bottom	Bottom-to-top	Left-to-right	Right-to-left
Better	23	1	1	0
Worse	3	19	2	1
Lighter	12	0	10	3
Darker	5	0	17	3

Relation	Imputations when relation was second of its kind		
	Direction		
	Opposite direction	Same direction	Other axis
Better	20	3	2
Worse	21	1	3
Lighter	9	13	3
Darker	14	8	3

For the hair-color relations, the pattern is altogether different. Both 'lighter' and 'darker' are treated with considerable frequency as top-to-bottom and also left-to-right, and, unlike 'better' and 'worse', are decidedly not ascribed directions opposite to one another. These data yielded a nonsignificant chi-square.

In the lower half of Table 2 are presented results for cases in which each relation was the second of its kind. Here the breakdown of the data is according to how the subject treated this relation relative to his treatment of the first relation of the kind, whether he imputed to it the opposite direction, the same direction, or a direction on the other axis. It is evident that for the evaluative relations the popular response was to impute the opposite direction to the second relation; 41 of the 50 subjects did so. For the hair-color relations, there was a much weaker tendency to do this; 23 of the 50 subjects did so. A correlated-proportions chi-square of 11.57, significant at the 0·001 level, was calculated from these figures.

Discussion. – This experiment provides evidence that evaluative relations are indeed tied to a vertical axis in most people's thinking. 'Better than' proceeds from top to bottom, and 'worse than' from bottom to top, whenever they are presented. Hair-color relations are not so tied, although there were nevertheless some consistencies in the subjects' treatment of them.

Experiment 3

In the older work on linear syllogisms there appears to have been a tacit assumption that ordering relations are homogeneous so far as people's handling of them in a reasoning task is concerned. These earlier experiments did in fact present subjects with syllogisms based on varied ordering relations, for example, 'is fairer [or darker] than', 'is to the left [or right] of', but they did not make comparisons among the different relations. In the present experiment direct comparisons were made of people's performance on linear syllogisms formed of various ordering relations.

An attempt was made, however, to do more than answer the simple question of whether or not varying the relation makes a difference in people's performance. The attempt was predicated on the general hypothesis that in reasoning about orderings of elements people rely on spatial representations or thought-models which they construct in some cognitive space. With the results of Experiments 1 and 2 in hand, it seemed possible to frame some fairly strong predictions based on this hypothesis about the outcome of a further experiment on linear syllogisms.

Consider first syllogisms based on an explicit naming of relative positions on a vertical axis, that is, 'above' and 'below'. If, as we have supposed, subjects are in fact thinking of such relations when ostensibly concerned with 'better' and 'worse', then one might predict they would perform on 'above' and 'below' much as they performed on 'better' and 'worse'. In particular, they should proceed more readily in a downward direction than in an upward one, just as they proceeded more readily in a worseward direction than in a betterward one. Our hypothesis is that worseward *is* downward in their thinking.

Consider next syllogisms based on relations with no intrinsic tie to a spatial axis, such as the hair-color relations. We have not precluded the possibility that in solving such syllogisms subjects will use spatial representations, but we would have to predict that they would not use them in a single fixed way. The results of Experiment 2 imply that whichever name is given first will be placed at the preferred starting point of one of the axes (top of a vertical axis or left end of a horizontal axis), and the following relational term will be transformed, whichever it is – lighter or darker – into 'above' or 'to the left of'. The subject should have no difficulty with this first premise. What then of the second premise? Having already imputed a spatial direction to the relation given in the first premise, he should be able to handle the second premise readily if it uses the same relation. But if it uses the opposite relation, he may be in trouble because, as the results of Experiment 2 clearly imply, he will not readily impute the opposite spatial direction of this new relation. In sum, in contrast to the findings for 'better' and 'worse' and the prediction for 'above' and 'below', the prediction for 'lighter' and 'darker' is that they will be equally difficult, and that syllogisms restricted to one or the other will be relatively easy, but that syllogisms including both will be exceptionally difficult.

Finally, consider syllogisms based explicitly on left-right relations. The results from Experiment 2 indicate that the left end is the preferred starting point for a horizontal ordering, just as is the top end of a vertical ordering. On the basis of this finding, it would seem reasonable to predict that people will proceed from left to right more readily than from right to left in handling horizontal linear syllogisms, that there is a left-right asymmetry corresponding to the above-below asymmetry. In other respects too the results for left-right syllogisms should resemble those for above-below syllogisms for the reason that both are explicitly tied to spatial directions.

Method. – For the comparisons to be made in this experiment, it was considered sufficient to work with the selected premise combinations and questions shown in Table 3, together with eight combinations not yielding orderings. Cards and instructions were prepared closely resembling those of Experiment 1. The subjects were 146 Johns Hopkins undergraduates.

Table 3

Percentage of Correct Answers for Selected Premise Combinations Based on Various Relations

Combination	Better-worse	Relation Above-below	Relation Left-right	Relation Lighter-darker
1.	A is better than B B is better than C Is A better than C? 67·5	A is above B B is above C Is A above C? 65·8	A is to the left of B B is to the left of C Is A to the left of C? 52·0	A has lighter hair than B B has lighter hair than C Does A have lighter hair than C? 63·0
2.	C is worse than B B is worse than A Is C worse than A? 47·0	C is below B B is below A Is C below A? 50·0	C is to the right of B B is to the right of A Is C to the right of A? 38·4	C has darker hair than B B has darker hair than A Does C have darker hair than A? 64·4
3.	A is better than B C is worse than B Is C better than A? 66·7	A is above B C is below B Is C above A? 65·1	C is to the right of B A is to the left of B Is A to the right of C? 45·2	A has lighter hair than B C has darker hair than B Does C have lighter hair than A? 39·7
4.	B is worse than A B is better than C Is C better than A? 35·9	B is below A B is above C Is C above A? 46·6	B is to the left of C B is to the right of A Is A to the right of C? 26·7	B has darker hair than A B has lighter hair than C Does C have lighter hair than A? 24·7

Results. – Table 3 presents, in the better-worse column, data taken from Experiment 1 (the percentages vary somewhat from their counterparts in Table 1 because of the restriction to one question per premise combination), and, in the remaining columns, data obtained from the 146 additional subjects. An analysis of variance performed on the new data yielded a significant Premise Combinations × Relations interaction ($F=9.77$, $df=6/870$, $p<0.001$), clearly disproving the old supposition that ordering relations are homogeneous in reasoning tasks. The specific predictions are confirmed in detail.

As predicted, the better-worse and above-below results are very much alike, with the only sizable discrepancy occurring for Premise Combination 4. In particular, the hypothesis that people will proceed downward more readily than upward in above-below linear syllogisms is confirmed by the difference between Combinations 1 and 2 in the above-below column.

The prediction that syllogisms based on 'lighter' alone or 'darker' alone would be relatively easy – and equally easy – is clearly confirmed, as is the prediction that syllogisms based on mixtures of 'lighter' and 'darker' would be exceptionally difficult.

In the left-right column, the hypothesis that people will proceed from left to right more readily than the reverse is confirmed by a comparison of the percentage correct for Combination 1, which proceeds from left to right both within and between premises, and Combination 2, which proceeds from right to left in both senses. The prediction that the overall pattern of results for this column should resemble that for the above-below column is less clearly substantiated. The results certainly are much more like the above-below results than they are like the lighter-darker results. But the percentages are lower throughout the column – left-right syllogisms seem generally difficult. Unfortunately, Premise Combinations 3 and 4 do not correspond exactly to those in the above-below column; they proceed in the wrong direction between premises, probably reducing these percentages still further.

Discussion. – The confirmation of the several predictions appears to give strong support to the hypothesis that people rely on spatial representations in thinking about orderings. The unpredicted result, the general difficulty of left-right syllogisms, may also support it. Momentary inability to decide which direction is left and which is right is a common failing – certainly more common than ignorance of which way is up and which down. It is a failing that could be expected to impair performance on a left-right syllogism for a subject who used spatial representations, but hardly for a subject who treated left and right simply as verbal opposites.

Spatial Representations and the Ordering Schema

These findings seem helpful in answering earlier questions about how it is that people are so good at giving elements a linear ordering in their thinking, yet so poor at interrelating them in most other ways (De Soto, 1960), and at giving the same set of elements more than one ordering (De Soto, 1961). The earlier answer was that people have an ordering schema, an inner mechanism or procedure for ordering things, and lack schemas for most other ways of interrelating things. This appeal to schemas seemed preferable for a number of reasons to the essentially nonpsychological statement that linear orderings are intrinsically easier than other structurings of elements. But, despite its value as a reminder that inner processes must subserve even – or especially – the accomplishments people find easy, it has the shortcoming of saying nothing about what these inner processes might be like.

Now it can be argued that the inner procedure in thinking about orderings consists primarily in arranging elements on an axis in some cognitive space. We believe this view makes comprehensible a number of otherwise disconnected and inexplicable phenomena.

Predilection for single orderings

The tendency to treat a given set of elements as having only one ordering, with strong aversion to multiple orderings of the set, has been noted as a phenomenon and problem in diverse realms of thought (De Soto, 1961; Sampson, 1963). It was, in fact, originally established as an inductive generalization based on its diverse manifestations. Subsequent experiments pinpointed it as a difficulty in applying the same schema to the same set of elements more than once, rather than as simply the difficulty of handling complex tasks. But even those experiments failed to reveal anything about the internal processes involved.

Now, the explanation of the predilection would run as follows. People are good at thinking of elements as ordered because they can readily arrange them appropriately on an axis – ordinarily the vertical axis – in their cognitive space. But this space is in a sense one-dimensional. It does not provide other axes; even the left-right axis seems relatively unavailable. And the space is certainly not an n-dimensional cartesian coordinate system in which an element can have different values on different dimensions, nor can an element simultaneously occupy different positions on the one axis. Thus if a subject is asked to think of people as ordered by wealth, he can do so readily enough, arranging them on the vertical axis. But he cannot simultaneously arrange them on another axis called 'power', or one called 'prestige'. There is no other axis, no additional way of imposing an ordering on the set of elements.

It is not by chance that 'high' and 'low', and 'above' and 'below', have their tremendous range of metaphorical meanings, nor is it a surprise that they are among the most frequently used words in the language according to the Thorndike-Lorge (1944) count.

Indeed, according to the dictionary definitions of such words as 'high', the tie to the vertical axis we have found for better-worse relations seems to exist for the three major dimensions of meaning reported by Osgood, Suci, and Tannenbaum (1957), good-bad, strong-weak, and fast-slow. The failure of lighter-darker relations to be so tied may be quite exceptional, perhaps occurring because lighter-darker relations are usually used only to contrast, not to order, elements. And when an evaluative component is introduced into lighter-darker relations, it too may quickly become tied to the vertical axis, as in 'high yaller', the lightest-skinned (best) Negro.

Linear order as good figure

Perhaps a more profound problem in thinking than the predilection for single orderings is the evident predilection for linear orderings at the expense of other varieties of organization, such as partial orderings and dominance structures (Coombs *et al.*, 1954; De Soto, 1960; De Soto and Kuethe, 1959; Kuethe, 1962; Wunderlich, Youniss, and De Soto, 1962). It appears that the linear ordering is, by analogy with 'good figures' in perception, a 'good figure' in cognition. Thought tends toward the linear ordering; and the linear ordering is evaluated positively. It is no accident that the generic term for good arrangement in English is *order*: the prototypic example of good arrangement is order in its narrow sense of linear order.

Under the hypothesis that thinking about seemingly abstract orderings depends on spatial representations, one might look for evidence that the spatial representations themselves have 'good figure' properties. One source of such evidence is suggested by Asch's (1958) remarkable finding that 'straight' in English, as well as its equivalent in other languages, universally carries a metaphoric meaning of goodness and propriety, whereas 'crooked' conveys evil and impropriety. We can add that it is good to be

121

'upright' or 'on the level', and bad to be 'oblique', 'slanted', or 'biased'. And other spatial structures which in principle could subserve cognitive organizations have much weaker positive connotations, if not negative ones: it is bad to be cross, or to cross someone, and especially to double-cross someone; it is bad to be square; a love triangle is bad; a vicious circle is bad; it is bad to have a checkered career; or to weave a web of deceit. The *evolutionary tree* – a very apt metaphor for the partial ordering laid down by evolutionary processes – does not have strong negative connotations, but it hardly has the appeal of the seriously misleading *scale of nature* which dominated western thought for so long (Lovejoy, 1960).

It seems probable that the linear ordering, and perhaps also the simple grouping, are pre-eminent good figures in cognition in a way unmatched by any perceptual good figures. If this is so, it is urgent to realize it and seek some understanding of it, for only by knowing our proclivities can we avoid being trapped by them.

References

ASCH, S. E. (1958), 'The metaphor: a psychological inquiry', in Tagiuri, R., and Petrullo, L. (eds.), *Person perception and interpersonal behavior*, Stanford U.P., pp. 86–94.

BROWN, R. (1958), *Words and things*, Free Press.

COOMBS, C. H., RAIFFA, H., and THRALL, R. M. (1954), 'Some views on mathematical models and measurement theory', *Psychol. Rev.*, vol. 61, pp. 132–44.

DE SOTO, C. B. (1960), 'Learning and social structure', *J. abnorm. soc. Psychol.*, vol. 60, pp. 417–21.

DE SOTO, C. B. (19 61), 'The predilection for single orderings', *J. abnorm. soc. Psychol.*, vol. 62, pp. 16–23.

DE SOTO, C. B., and BOSLEY, J. J. (1962), 'The cognitive structure of a social structure', *J. abnorm. soc. Psychol.*, vol. 64, pp. 303–7.

DE SOTO, C. B., and KUETHE, J. L. (1959), 'Subjective probabilities of interpersonal relationships', *J. abnorm. soc. Psychol.*, vol. 59, pp. 290–4.

FEIGENBAUM, E. A., and SIMON, H. A. (1962), 'A theory of the serial position effect', *Brit. J. Psychol.*, vol. 53, pp. 307–20.

INHELDER, B., and PIAGET, J. (1958), *The growth of logical thinking*, Basic Books.

KUETHE, J. L. (1962), 'Social schemas', *J. abnorm. soc. Psychol.*, vol. 64, pp. 31–8.

LASHLEY, K. S. (1961), 'The problem of serial order in behavior', in Saporta, S. (ed.), *Psycholinguistics*, Holt, Rinehart & Winston, pp. 180–98.

LOVEJOY, A. O. (1960), *The great chain of being*, Harper.

MANDLER, G., and COWAN, P. A. (1962), 'Learning of simple structures', *J. exp. Psychol.*, vol. 64, pp. 177–83.

OSGOOD, C. E., SUCI, G. J., and TANNENBAUM, P. H. (1957), *The measurement of meaning*, University of Illinois Press.

RIBBACK, A., and UNDERWOOD. B. J. (1950), 'An empirical explanation of the skewness of the bowed serial position curve', *J. exp. Psychol.*, vol. 40, pp. 329–35.

SAMPSON, E. D. (1963), 'Status congruence and cognitive consistency', *Sociometry*, vol. 26, pp. 146–62.

THORNDIKE, E. L., and LORGE, I. (1944), *The teacher's word book of 30,000 words*, Teachers College, Columbia University, Bureau of Publications.

VOLKMANN, J. (1951), 'Scales of judgement and their implications for social psychology', in Rohrer, J. H., and Sherif, M. (eds.), *Social psychology at the cross-roads*, Harper, pp. 273–94.

WOODWORTH, R. S., and SCHLOSBERG, H. (1954), *Experimental psychology*, Holt.

WUNDERLICH, R. A., YOUNISS, J., and DE SOTO, C. B. (1962), 'Schemas and kinship', *Psychol. Reports*, vol. 11, pp. 495–8.

10 P. C. Wason

The Effect of Self-Contradiction on Fallacious Reasoning

P. C. Wason, 'The effect of self-contradiction on fallacious reasoning', *Quart. J. exp. Psychol.*, vol. 16 (1964), pp. 30–4.

Introduction

In deductive reasoning a valid inference follows necessarily from its premises, i.e., it would be inconsistent to assert the premises and deny the inference. A fallacious inference is an invalid inference which has the appearance of validity. An individual who commits a fallacy is being deceived into accepting a conclusion which merely looks correct. For example, an individual presented with the statement, 'all A are B' might suppose that 'all B are A' follows from it. On the other hand, this mistake would not be made if a statement of the same form had been used to express a known fact, e.g., 'all monkeys are animals'. The abstract nature of the material about which inferences are made is one variable which affects the tendency to reason fallaciously (Wilkins, 1928); another is the emotive quality of the material (Lefford, 1946). The aim of the present investigation is to make the individual aware of his deception by forcing valid inferences to be inconsistent with previously made fallacious inferences in a serial task. This obliges the individual to contradict himself. The hypothesis is investigated that this self-contradiction reduces the tendency to make further fallacious inferences of the same type.

Method

The fallacies and the tasks

An attempt was made to induce two logically equivalent fallacies connected with conditional statements. In order to explain them the logic of conditionals will be briefly discussed. A statement in the form 'if p then q' is false only in the case in which the antecedent p is true and the consequent q is false. If this conditional statement is true, it follows that (i) if p is true, then q must be true, and (ii) if q is false, then p must be false. However, to deny the antecedent, i.e., to infer that if p is false, then q must be false, or to affirm the consequent, i.e., to infer that if q is true, then p must be true, is to be guilty of a fallacious inference.

Two tasks were used: an 'antecedent task', designed to induce the denial of the antecedent ('if not-p then not-q'), and a 'consequent task', designed to induce the affirmation of the consequent ('if q then p'). The following incomplete rules were used in the antecedent and consequent tasks respectively:

'Any employee aged 34 years, or more, will receive a salary of at least £— a year.'

'Any employee aged — years, or more, will receive a salary of at least £1,900 a year.'

In the antecedent task it would be valid to infer that the 'critical salary', i.e., the salary omitted in the rule, *could not be* more than that received by any employee aged at least 34, but fallacious to infer that it *must be* more than that received by any employee under 34. In the consequent task it would be valid to infer that the 'critical age', i.e., the age omitted in the rule, *must be* more than that of any employee receiving less than £1,900, but fallacious to infer that it *could not be* more than that of any employee receiving at least £1,900.

The incomplete rule for the antecedent, or the consequent task, was presented, followed by the ages and salaries of ten hypothetical employees, making a series of ten trials. These particulars allowed valid inferences on the odd numbered trials and fallacious inferences on the even numbered trials. At each trial the subjects were required either to make, or withhold, a deductive inference about the possible limits of the critical salary (age), and then state their current estimate of it. The estimates were intended to motivate the subjects and provide a check on the inferences.

Design

Sixty subjects (psychology undergraduates) were allocated at random before the experiment started to four groups: an experimental and a control group for each task. Inconsistency between fallacious and valid inferences was introduced in the experimental groups, but not in the control groups. In the antecedent task control group the salaries received by employees over 34 are all higher than the salaries received by employees under 34. It follows that successive valid and fallacious inferences about the limits of the critical salary are not forced to contradict each other. In the experimental group, however, the first four trials are the same as those in the control group, but thereafter the salaries given decrease successively. For example, on trial 4 an employee aged 24 receives £1,800, but on trial 5 an employee aged 37 receives £1,600. Hence the valid inference on trial 5, that the critical salary could not be more than £1,600, is inconsistent with the fallacious inference on trial 4 that the critical salary must be more than £1,800. But on trial 6 an employee aged 25 receives £1,500. The fallacious inference on this trial is consistent with the valid inference on trial 5. Thus the valid inferences on trials 5, 7 and 9 are forced to be inconsistent with the fallacious inferences which *precede* them, but are consistent with the fallacious inferences which *succeed* them. In the consequent task the particulars given in the control group are similarly arranged so that valid and fallacious inferences are consistent. In the experimental group inconsistency is again introduced on trial 5. For example, on trial 4 an employee receiving £2,300 is aged 35, but on trial 5 an employee receiving £1,500 is aged 37. The valid inference on trial 5, that the critical age must be more than 37, contradicts the fallacious inference on trial 4 that the critical age could not be more than 35. On the remaining trials the pattern of consistent and inconsistent inferences follows that in the antecedent task.

At every trial one type of question was asked in order to discriminate a valid inference, and another type to discriminate a fallacious inference. Hence one question was redundant at each trial. In the antecedent task the following types discriminated valid and fallacious inferences respectively: '*Could* x *be less than the critical salary?*' and '*Could* x *be more than the critical salary?*' (where x=the salary received by an employee on any given trial). In the consequent task the corresponding types of question were: '*Could* x *be over the critical age?*' and '*Could* x *be under the critical age?*' (where x = the age of an employee on any given trial). A negative answer to these modal questions indicates that an inference has been made. Such an answer rules out one of two possibilities, either (i) that a given salary (age) is less than the critical salary (age), or (ii) that it is more than the critical salary (age). An affirmative answer, on the other hand, is consistent with the truth of either possibility. Hence it is the correct answer when the information allows a fallacious inference: it constitutes a refusal to make one.

Procedure

Subjects were tested individually and instructed as follows:

This is a reasoning task which I want you to think about carefully.

In a certain organization the following rule held without exception: (here the rule for the appropriate task was given). *Your task is to try to find out the critical salary (age) in the rule.* I shall show you the ages and salaries of a number of employees in the organization, one at a time. After examining the particulars of each, you will answer two questions about the critical salary (age), and then write down your estimate of it. You will not be timed. Have you any questions?

The rule was displayed on a card in front of the subject, and then the particulars of the first trial, and the two questions, were presented on a slip of paper. If the subject failed to answer the relevant question correctly, i.e., failed to make a valid inference, his response was queried by the experimenter who waited until the correct answer was given. This procedure was carried out only on the first trial. After the subject had recorded his estimate, the particulars of the second trial were presented, those of the first remaining on the table in front of the subject. When the second trial had been completed, the particulars of the first were removed, and those of the third presented. This procedure continued throughout the remaining trials. Thus after the first trial the subjects were able to consult the particulars, the answers and the estimates of each immediately preceding trial. The subjects were allowed to make notes on rough paper provided, but were not allowed, of course, to correct their responses to any previous trial.

Results

Consistency between answers and estimates

The estimates of the critical salary and the critical age were consistent with the inferences (whether valid or fallacious) on 412 out of a possible 419 trials. This suggests that, regardless of whether the subjects were reasoning fallaciously, they were not random in their behaviour. On the remaining 181 trials inferences were withheld.

Initial susceptibility to fallacious inference

The criterion for initial susceptibility to making the fallacies was the occurrence of fallacious inferences on trials 2 and 4. (Twenty-seven out of the thirty subjects, classified as not susceptible, withheld fallacious inferences on both these trials.) In the antecedent task ten out of thirty subjects were susceptible, and in the consequent task twenty out of thirty subjects were susceptible. These frequencies differ significantly from the expected ones ($\chi^2 = 5 \cdot 4$, $p < 0 \cdot 025$, two tail test) and indicate that the affirmation of the consequent is a much more deceptive fallacy than the denial of the antecedent.

Effects of self-contradiction

Table I shows the number of subjects, initially susceptible to making fallacious inferences, who withhold subsequent fallacious inferences at different stages of the tasks, or make the maximum number of fallacious inferences, i.e., make no correction, in the experimental and control groups in each task. Once one of these subjects had withheld such an inference, they never succumbed to making one again. The differences between the distributions of the experimental and control groups within each task were tested by Whitfield's dichotomous tau (Whitfield, 1947). In the antecedent task the chance probability of the difference between the groups $=0.05$; in the consequent task the chance probability $=0.08$ (one tail tests). In spite of the significant difference between the tasks (ten subjects susceptible to making fallacious inferences in the antecedent task and twenty in the consequent task), it is clear that the effects of self-contradiction are similar in both. When the S values and variances of the tasks are combined, the chance probability of a difference $=0.03$.

Four subjects failed to make valid inferences on subsequent trials, one failing on three trials, and three failing on a single trial. Only one of these subjects was in an experimental group. Thus it is evident that, although self-contradiction occurrred when a valid inference was made, it did not cause *these* inferences to be subsequently withheld. Nine of the total subjects had to be corrected on the first trial, four in the antecedent task and five in the consequent task.

Table 1

Number of Subjects, Initially Susceptible to making Fallacious Inferences, who resist making Subsequent Fallacious Inferences at Different Stages of the Tasks, or make the Maximum Number of Fallacious Inferences, i.e., make no Correction

| | Antecedent task | | Consequent task | | Combined task | |
	Experimental group	Control group	Experimental group	Control group	Experimental group	Control group
N	4	6	10	10	14	16
6th trial	3	0	5	2	8	2
8th trial	0	1	1	0	1	1
10th trial	0	1	0	0	0	1
No correction	1	4	4	8	5	12

Discussion

In this exploratory experiment the attempt was made to induce fallacious inferences initially by using tasks which embodied a familiar situation: a positive correlation between age and salary. It is a plausible inference (other things being equal) that older employees *probably* earn more than younger ones. This inference, however, is inductive but the questions posed in the tasks could elicit only deductive inferences, i.e., inferences which are certain rather than probable. But it seems likely that the habitual tendency to reason inductively was responsible for the fallacious inferences to some extent. A similar interpretation of errors made in syllogistic reasoning has been proposed by Chapman and Chapman (1959).

In the experimental groups self-contradiction occurs when a valid inference is forced to be inconsistent with previously made fallacious inferences. The results show that these valid inferences are not withheld, but that subsequent fallacious inferences (which are consistent with preceding valid inferences) do tend to be withheld. This suggests that inconsistency allowed the subjects to gain insight into the fallaciousness of their reasoning, rather than weakened the response associated with making a fallacious inference. In addition, it is clear that the effects of inconsistency tend either to work when it is first introduced, or not at all. In the combined experimental groups eight of the fourteen subjects (57·2 per cent), initially susceptible to making fallacious inferences, withheld them at trial 6 (the first trial on which the effects of inconsistency could be felt), compared with two out of sixteen subjects (12·5 per cent) in the combined control groups. But on subsequent trials there is little difference between the groups. In the experimental groups one of the six remaining subjects (16·7 per cent) withheld fallacious inferences, compared with two out of fourteen (14·3 per cent) in the control groups.

It has been shown that self-contradiction can be used to extinguish fallacious inferences, and it presumably does so by creating a *reductio ad absurdum* to remind the individual that he has inferred a conclusion which does not necessarily follow. But it is worth noting that a fallacious inference is a special kind of error. It is not analogous to a conceptual mistake in mathematics, for it is not necessarily the result of using a rule wrongly. Rules of reasoning are not taught as part of general education, nor are deductions about past events coded into an explicit system for future reference. Hence, whether the present method of correcting error has any generality, and whether it has any advantages over didactic correction is a matter for future research.

References

CHAPMAN, L. J., and CHAPMAN, J. P. (1959), 'Atmosphere effect re-examined', *J. exp. Psychol.*, vol. 58, pp. 220–6.

LEFFORD, A. (1946), 'The influence of emotional subject matter on logical reasoning', *J. gen. Psychol.*, vol. 34, pp. 127–51.

WHITFIELD, J. W. (1947), 'Rank correlation between two variables, one of which is ranked, the other dichotomous, *Biometrika*, vol. 34, p. 292.

WILKINS, M. C. (1928), 'The effect of changed material on ability to do formal syllogistic reasoning,' *Arch. Psychol.*, vol. 102.

Part Three   INDUCTIVE REASONING

Inductive inferences range from 'guessing' whether it will be
fine today, to the estimation of future sales, and to the testing
of a scientific hypothesis. Psychologists have approached the
study of inductive behaviour in many ways. Sir Frederic
Bartlett distinguishes between thinking within two different
systems: 'closed' systems characterized by a finite number of
identifiable units which do not change with the progress of
thinking, e.g., problems using numbers; and 'open' systems
analogous to scientific research. The extract (11) we have chosen
deals with some experiments in the transitional area between
these two types of system. De Groot (12) examines some of the
factors underlying a conspicuously inductive skill – playing
chess. He stresses the role of experience upon the way in which
a chess master *perceives* a position, as opposed to the deductive
skills of calculation which might be supposed to be important
in chess. This theme is supported by the evidence of Rayner
(13) in his experimental study of the game of pegity. A striking
weakness in our ability to think inductively is demonstrated
by Wason (14) in a paper specially written for this volume.
People appear very reluctant to risk proving themselves wrong.
Finally, Gilson and Abelson (15) have studied the types of
generalization that people will accept on the basis of general
statements presented in the form of an argument.

11 F. C. Bartlett

Adventurous Thinking

Excerpt from F. C. Bartlett, *Thinking*, Allen & Unwin, 1958, chapter 6, pp. 99–111.

Transitional Experiments

There are many situations which possess some of the characteristics of closed systems, and also some of those that belong to scientific experiments. For example, suppose, starting from a particular place, we are given an objective indicated, in a general way only, as N., S., E. or W. of the starting-point. We have a sectional map which indicates a possible choice of directions along which we may move. When we reach the boundary of the first sectional plan, we are given another sectional map, and so on in stages, until we reach the end of the journey. In some respects, obviously, all of this procedure works within a closed system. The whole road scheme is complete before we begin the projected journey. No decisions as to direction that we may make at successive stages on the way to the final objective can have any possible effect on the disposition of the roads in the sectional maps not yet reached. But in some other respects our position is not unlike that of the experimenter. At every decision we make, with every consequent move up to the limit of a sectional plan, fresh information, or more evidence, is made available, and although descriptively this is just the same as it would have been if we had made different decisions, its significance relative to the objective is very closely dependent upon the moves, and the extent of the moves, that we have already made.

It is true that with sectional map-reading, additional information is made available and new decisions are called for at predetermined stages, whereas in the scientific experiment additional evidence is being developed, or seems to be being developed, all the time; and decisions are being shaped, or seem to be being shaped, continuously. At the same time, it is not unlikely that the ways in which additional clues are used, and the conditions which lead up to particular decisions, remain much the same in both cases. At any rate it is worth trying to find out whether this is so.

Any of the many other possible situations in which an objective is defined in general terms to begin with and there are several

133

possible lines of exploration, some of which yield information that may eventually pin-point the objective, might similarly be shown to have some characteristics in common with scientific experimentation.

H. C. A. Dale (1955, pp. 247–55), for example, has attempted to develop a technique which may have a direct bearing upon much of the procedure of the experimental scientist. He sets up what he calls a 'searching task' which must be carried out in stages. There are two main cases: (1) 'structured situations, in which all points encountered during the search yield information regarding the direction in which to proceed', and (2) 'unstructured situations in which this information is unavailable.'

I now propose, therefore, briefly to consider (a) map section reading; and (b) searching in a structured system as possible transitional experiments leading up to a more direct discussion of the principal characteristics of the thinking of the experimental scientist. Obviously other situations might have been selected, and I hope it will be equally obvious that each of these 'transitional experiments' raises psychological problems of much interest, and that they would repay more prolonged and careful study and analysis than I can give to them here.

Probably everybody will notice immediately that there is another important respect in which both these transitional cases differ radically from scientific operations which are designed chiefly to advance knowledge, rather than to answer some specific question. They both have definite stopping-points which are inherent in their design. When these terminal stages have been reached the operation is over, and there is nothing in them to open up new avenues of exploration. When the experimental scientist completes what he would call a 'fruitful' experiment this is not the case; his stopping-point is temporary only and leads beyond itself.

(a) Some points about sectional map-reading

I cannot claim to have made anything more than a very limited beginning of a study of the possible use of sectional maps as an experimental way of opening up some of the problems of scientific thinking, and even, perhaps, of suggesting likely answers to these problems. Enough has, I hope, been done to show that this general technique, and others which could be based upon it, are worth an extended exploration. The varieties of design, of serial presentation, and of overall structure that can be used, are very numerous, and here I shall attempt to take up and illustrate only a few of the many points which could well be raised.

The basic plan can be illustrated simply. The observer, or 'explorer' is given in succession a number of road section maps. Figure 1 shows a relatively straightforward instance.

Instructions given with the first section plan are:

You set out from the point marked S and your aim is to get to a spot somewhere to the N.W. Choose which road to start on, and when you have got as far as you can on this plan you will be given another sectional map, and so on until you get to the final map on which the place you want to reach will be marked O. At any stage you can, if you wish, go back to the starting-point or to some position short of the starting-point.

The observer ('explorer') may be given the information on the basis of which he chooses his route in a number of different ways. Each successive section can, for instance, be superimposed upon what goes before it, so that at every stage he has the complete map up to the finish of that stage. Or he may have to remember one, some, or all of the preceding stages.

Furthermore, the overall road system may appear to have no determinable principles of structure, and particular roadways may seem to wander about much as they appear to do to the uninstructed traveller in most rural districts in this country. Or there may be a graded structuration up to the most complete regularity of lay-out.

Again, there may be no dead-ends, as in the illustration given, and all roads out from S may eventually reach the objective, though along routes of varying length. Or there may be dead ends, so that there are bound to be return journeys unless an open route has been selected. An instance combining regularity of lay-out with dead-ends might be as illustrated in figure 2 (see p. 138).

It will be seen that, provided the whole lay-out is going on in this regular way, each 'stage' or section has two ways out, one of which gives a choice of two roads and the other of three; that always roadways marked 2, 3, and 4 are dead-ends, and that of the remaining two routes, road one will give a two-choice, and the other a three-choice situation; that at some section stage (here marked III) either the two-choice or the three-choice situation will make a change of direction towards the objective defined in general terms at the beginning of the experiment.

All that I propose to attempt to do at present is to indicate, without detailed analysis, some of the suggestions which emerge from these sectional map-reading experiments, in so far as they

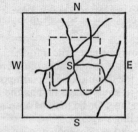

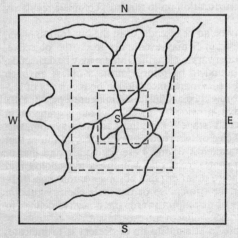

Figure 1

Figure 1—*continued*

4

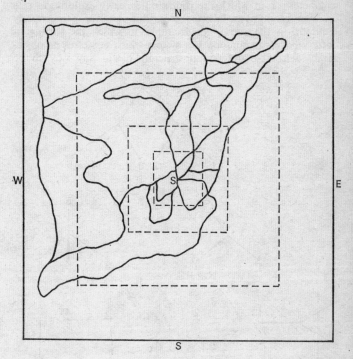

may help to provide an orientation to more direct studies of scientific thinking.

Firstly, there is the persistent question of how and when response to direction takes charge of thought activities. Obviously in these map-reading instances 'direction' is to be taken in a literal spatial sense. The map-reader moves, in imagination, along a given line of route and can estimate at once whether when he comes to the edge of his section he is likely to be nearer to or farther from his general objective. The road system designed can, of course, for this kind of 'direction', have whatever characters the experimenter selects. Initially no route may lead towards the objective (as in figure 2), or all routes may lead towards the objective, or one (as figure 1) route may lead towards the objective, or there may be any desired intermediate case. When all, or no, routes set out towards the general end given, and there is no other noticeable characteristic in which the routes differ, early exploration gets as near random as it ever does. But it never gets entirely random, in the sense, for example, in which the sorting of lottery tickets is random. If a system which possesses no objectively detectable differential structure has in any way to be

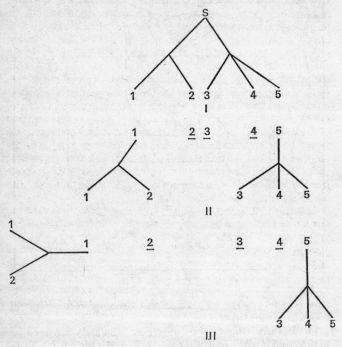

Figure 2   The objective is given as N. of S.

dealt with by a human being he cannot avoid treating it as if it had such a differential structure, so that as soon as ever he has anything to do with such a system it is true to say that not all of the things he might do are equally likely. Perhaps a simpler and more 'natural' way of putting this would be to say that in such instances an interest, or interests, which an observer has already formed may come into play. Then the same basic function which settles whether the observer will do anything or nothing about evidence, at the same time gives an unavoidable bias to what he can do.

In sectional map exploration, direction, in the sense just described, tends to be given priority at all stages of experimental search, but most decisively in the early stages. Thus, in figure 1, given it is very nearly certain that any normal map-reader will start out along the only route that runs nearly N.W., he will keep along this same route without deviation until the third sectional plan is reached. At this point the preferred route turns directly E., and it can be seen that two other of the starting routes have joined and seem to be going more nearly in the direction required. At this stage it appears that a small majority of explorers will prefer to continue along their chosen route while the others will retrace this path part or all of the way back and set out afresh. But the later in a sectional map series such a change of apparent direction occurred, the greater was the proportion of readers who nevertheless kept their route unchanged. None of the subjects of these map-reading experiments knew ahead how many sections would complete a series, also none knew at any stage until the last one how near he was to his objective. It is, however, the case that this kind of literal directional evidence was given absolute priority in the early stages of experimental search, and then with diminishing effect as the search went on.

The fact that once a route has been consistently followed for some time a fair number of people (probably most people) either prefer to continue along it, or are averse to moving away and starting afresh, even though the evidence that induced them to select that route is now apparently contradicted, may well be worth further study. It can be said at once, however, that, at least in this variety of prospective extrapolation, a lot of people see no overwhelming virtue in economy of route. Whether or not they may say that 'the best way is the shortest way', this is not a dominating principle in their action.

A related question is whether the number of possibilities that seem likely to be opened up by any particular move in a series of moves continues to be as important when thinking becomes freer and more adventurous as it seems to be in the fully closed system. The indication in the case of closed systems was that the strongly preferred move is one that reduces the number of probable next moves. It was in the hope of obtaining some experimental evidence about this that I used map sections in which, to begin with, either all routes, or no routes, were in the direction of the objective, but some routes consistently divided into more next possible roads than others. One very simple instance is given in figure 2; there are many other possible variations on the same theme.

In the case of figure 2, once the first step was taken any subject who was prepared to treat the road system as possessing a constant structure quickly realized that after the first step, neither direction gave him a true multiple choice. For at each succeeding stage roads 2, 3, and 4 were 'dead ends'. Obviously, however, it is easy enough to design sectional map systems in which multiple choice may be set against dual choice for as many stages and in whatever number may be desired. Under such conditions, so far as my own experiments have gone, no strong or consistent preference was shown for routes offering a smaller number, or a progressively diminishing number of next moves. When the map sections offered a succession of either/or alternatives, and also a succession of multiple choices, it was a little more likely that exploration would begin and continue along the latter, to return to the former only if at some stage one of the either/or routes took a decisive change of direction towards the general objective, and not always even then.

This may perhaps be a case somewhat specialized to operations like route finding on incomplete evidence. But if a generalization is legitimate from these map-section results it would seem that, when a thinker is working in an open, or relatively open, system (roads, for example, may proceed in *any* direction) he inclines to prefer the evidence which releases the greater rather than the smaller number of possibilities. I do not wish to suggest that in adopting this kind of procedure the thinker is following any clearly formulated or definitely articulated hypothesis about probabilities. It seems certain, indeed, that he must be working according to some kind of probability criterion which, however, may remain for him hardly defined at all. In any system having little known fixity of structure, on the whole, moves which release a larger number of possible next moves will be preferred to those which release a smaller number. The *working*, though not the formulated, rule seems to be that it is better to explore along the line of the greater number of possibilities, because it is more likely that the one sought will be found when there are a lot of chances than where there are only a few. It seems extremely likely that there must be some limit to this, and that when the number of possible next openings exceeds a certain range, the fact that with very many possibilities the small probability that any single one is the one wanted will override everything else. But I have not been able to determine this limit. Anyway there seems to be little warrant for the assumption that has often been made that the human brain shows an inherent preference for dual-choice systems, or for short cut, or clear-cut, situations in general. Already, in these transitional experiments, where thinking takes place within a sort of pseudo-open system, we can see that there is something attractive to the thinker about risk and adventure. He will often move, perhaps deliberately, and perhaps without much realization of what he is doing, along a line that opens up a large number of chances, though, so far as he can know, any one of these can have little likelihood of leading him where he wants to go. Maybe what this amounts to in a psychological sense is that a larger number of chances are being treated as a bunch, and that in the lump they outweigh the attraction of the smaller number of chances. Perhaps, also, we are now moving into a sphere in which thinking becomes more of a sport or a game than it can well be in the genuine closed system.

There is an obvious objection that all sectional maps which are actually used for any practical reason will contain many more concrete, representational details than those devised for these experiments. There will be river-courses, railway-lines, and often outstanding geographical and 'cultural' features. During the war of 1939–45, for example, when sectional area maps were much used by airmen, both 'natural' and 'man-made' features of a landscape were often specially marked. It is not difficult to show that such descriptive features, which make use of knowledge that the explorer already possesses, are given greater and greater importance as he gets his general route more and more opened up. How specialized knowledge enters more and more into the later natural development of thinking no matter what its field, will perhaps become clearer as we go on.

(b) Searching in a structured system

H. C. A. Dale has attempted by experiment to discover something about the principles that come into play when a person has to decide how to search for an assigned objective, and that objective is known to lie within some more or less defined system. He distinguishes between 'structured' and 'unstructured' systems; but this distinction is not of any great importance from our present point of view. For him a system is unstructured if it is such that search for the assigned objective can just as well begin at any stage in the system as at any other. If, under such conditions, the first attempt is successful it is so only fortuitously. If it is not successful nothing whatever has been learned about any preferred order or direction for subsequent search. There is indeed no possible objectively preferential order. But, as everybody knows, plenty of systems can be found in which particular search-points or check-points can be used to settle the most economical order and direction of subsequent search.

Dale says: 'An example of an unstructured situation is that of searching for a ball in a field. A ball lying at one point in a field has no effect whatever on the rest of the field, therefore no amount of effort expended in searching one corner will give any indication of whether it is best to look next in the middle, or in the opposite corner or anywhere else.'

This is obviously correct so long as the searcher is confined to search in a limited area by action, but if he can ask questions, provided only the ball, the field, or both do not change in some way that affects relative positions, then – in theory at any rate – there are always certain questions which, whatever the answer, will indicate the order and direction of those subsequent questions which will find the missing ball by the most economical route. In fact there is literally no 'unstructured' situation unless it is one in which changes are going on at random all the time.

However, the study of systems which present a number of possible check-points and some of them give more, some less, information about how to proceed in an economical manner, is one of great interest and importance. The case that Dale takes is that of the location of a fault in an electronic circuit. Throughout the whole of these discussions I have treated thinking as a process which generally, though not inevitably, proceeds through a succession of steps or stages, and that there is some connexion of necessity, or of preference, from step to step. I have all the time agreed that there is also the intuitive kind of thinking in which the steps are not articulated, and more consideration must yet be given to this kind.[1] But provisionally I have accepted the view that although in intuitive thinking the steps are not stated, they could be, without any change of issue. Dale's case, therefore, is particularly interesting in any study of experimental thinking, for 'electronic circuits consist basically of chains of "stages", and if a signal is fed into the input, checks will show it to be correct at all points up to the faulty stage and incorrect at all points beyond it.' Thus information is made available both about the direction and about the order in which to proceed.

The details of Dale's inquiry may be gathered from his paper. The general result is that, especially with naïve, although intelli-

1. See also Cartwright, 1955, pp. 9–12.

gent searchers, it is most likely that the method of search adopted will be an uneconomical one. Theoretically search-points ought to be chosen so as to get maximum possible information. 'This is best done if the searcher proceeds by asking general questions, "Is my objective in this half or that?" To begin a problem by asking "Is the objective in this stage?" is a very inefficient procedure.' However, in Dale's main series only one of his twenty-four subjects used the theoretically best method. Also those who began by using a method which demanded more work than was necessary did not readily change to the better way.

In 'unstructured' systems, in Dale's sense, there is no objectively best method of search. But with these also there was little sign that direct consideration of what might constitute short paths to solution had much to do with adopted methods. The subjects whom Dale considered to be the more intelligent, however, did tend to take check-points in a straightforward order of succession, and the effect of this could be to diminish the psychological load as much as possible by avoiding any difficult strain of remembering.

(c) Provisional conclusions

These transitional experiments have three main issues, all for the present to be treated as provisional only.

As the thinker takes up his search in the more open type of system, in the early stages directional features, belonging to the structure, or to an assigned structure, of the system in which he is working, but themselves of a general character, are predominantly effective.

As the search proceeds, these features may become less independently important, and in particular, empirical characteristics which the thinker has found in the course of his search tend to have a greater weight.

At no stage does the thinker necessarily show any strong bias towards either/or situations; towards short cuts and economical lines of search; towards numerically few risks.

The suggestion perhaps is that as thinking moves towards greater freedom one thing that happens is that the thinker is less and less concerned with the likelihood of items and more and more with that of packets, or groups of items. He is less detail-ridden, more 'schematic'-minded. If we should ask for the reasons why these lumping schematizing developments take place, our present answers can of course be no more than speculation. My guess is that there are two chief reasons – they are more efficient and they are a lot more fun.

References

CARTWRIGHT, M. L. (1955), *The mathematical mind*, James Boyce Memorial Lecture, Oxford U.P.

DALE, H. C. A. (1955), *Searching in a structured system*, A.P.U., Cambridge.

12 A. D. De Groot

Thought and Choice in Chess

Excerpts from A. D. De Groot, *Thought and choice in chess*, Mouton, 1965, sections 58 and 62.

Reproductive Factors in Productive Thinking: Knowledge and Experience

[. . .] The rapid insight of the chessmaster into the possibilities of a newly shown position, his immediate 'seeing' of structural and dynamic essentials, of possible combinatorial gimmicks, and so forth, are only understandable if we realize that as a result of his experience he quite literally 'sees' the position in a totally different (and much more adequate) way than a weaker player. The vast difference between the two in efficiency, particularly in the amount of time to find out what the core problem is ('what's cooking really') and to discover highly specific, adequate means of thought and board action, need not and must not be primarily ascribed to large differences in 'natural' power for abstraction. The difference is mainly due to differences in perception.

It is above all *the treasury of ready 'experience'* which puts the master that much ahead of the others. His extremely extensive, widely branched and highly organized system of knowledge and experience enables him, first, to recognize immediately a chess position as one belonging to an unwritten category with corresponding board means to be applied, and second, to 'see' immediately and in a highly adequate way its specific, individual features against the background of the category.

It is no accident that the word 'seeing', as used here, stands both for perception and abstraction. The two processes tend to fuse together; they are difficult to distinguish. But if a master and a weaker player are compared, often the former literally 'sees' possibilities that are deeply hidden for the latter, possibilities that the latter must first try to discover, calculate, think out, or deduce in order in his turn to be able to 'see' them. In other words, the difference in achievement between master and non-master rests primarily on the fact that the master, basing himself on an enormous experience, *can start his operational thinking at a much more advanced stage* and can consequently function much more specifically and efficiently in his problem-solving field. ·

145

It is not easy to appreciate fully the enormous effect of the expert's *reproductive completion of the perceived situation*, as his perceptual advantage might be called. In fact, the more 'experience' a person has collected in any field, the more difficult it becomes for him to understand the behavior of the have-nots. Thus every teacher knows the following frequent brand of overestimating his students: opining that from the given problem situation his students can 'immediately' derive (see) some property or means that he himself finds quite obvious – whereas in reality, in order to 'see' it, much perceptive and abstractive experience is required. The teacher has had this experience for so long that he is no longer aware of it. An experienced problem solver in any field is particularly apt to forget about his primary and fundamental problem transformations even *before* he starts his own consciously operational thinking. This is especially true when these problem transformations have shifted, over the long run, from the field of thought to the perceptual field – as they usually have in chess.

A simple example to illustrate the general idea can be borrowed from Köhler's experimental adventures with anthropoids. We humans are struck by the inability of these otherwise quite intelligent animals to take a ring off a nail – a possibility that we 'immediately see'. Due to our experience with nails and rings and their usage, we *see* the situation in a totally different way than the ape does. Similar examples can be given touching upon the relation between adults and children.

The relation between chessmaster and weaker player is – within a somewhat more limited universe – wholly comparable. The master's inability to identify with the weaker player and his difficulties is often striking. Generally it shows up in a lack of respect; anyone who does not belong to the elite is a 'patzer'. The virtuoso cannot possibly respect as a chessplayer a person who cannot even think out in half an hour what is completely obvious to him, since he himself immediately *reads* it from the perceptual situation.

Pure means abstraction is, in itself, never more than one step with a limited scope. Generally, it derives its power from the problem conception or situation perception from which it starts. As a result of the fact that it often occurs as an 'illumination' to the subject and/or as a striking find or discovery to the observer, the importance of the operation has often been overdrawn – just as with the composer's inspiration. We should keep in mind, however, that *all* 'masterly' achievements – fascinating discoveries included – in general as in chess, are based on a body of 'mastery' that is acquired by experience (and hard work), namely, mastery over an extensive, differentiated system of immediately actualizable dispositions for typical problem transformations; or in other words: mastery over a highly composite set (program) of general and specific perceptual and thought habits (routines).

The gist of the preceding discussion might be summarized by saying that a master *is* a master primarily by virtue of what he has been able to build up by experience; and this is: (*a*) a schooled and highly specific *way of perceiving*, and (*b*) a system of reproductively available methods, *in memory*.

In using the latter term we must take care, however, to distinguish between *knowledge* and *intuitive experience*. They can both be regarded as mutually interwoven subsystems of experiential linkings (in the domain of chess) that result from learning processes and are 'located' in memory, but they differ, by definition, in that knowledge ('knowing that') can be verbalized while intuitive experience cannot. Knowledge can be explicitly formulated by the subject and thus communicated, in words, to others; it is retrievable from memory by verbal cues. Intuitive experience, on the other hand, is an intuitive know-how – as distinct from 'knowing that' – that is only actualized by situations (on the chessboard or in the thought process) where it can actually be used. Here, too, adequate methods are immediately available from memory but, if used, the subject could not describe them, let alone write his own heuristic program. In principle, intuitive experiential linkings may at any time become knowledge ('knowing that', in addition to 'knowing how'), namely, at that moment when the subject becomes fully aware of them.

It will be clear now that the differentiated system of thought habits (routines) which forms the essence of chess mastership, consists partly of knowledge but largely of intuitive experience. The latter is possible and may be highly efficient in chess because the game has in fact nothing to do with verbalization; types of positions and corresponding playing methods – moves, manoeuvres – have a language of their own. In this respect the chess player's system of thought habits is rather comparable to a system of motor habits such as that of a billiard or tennis player. In fact, most *skills* depend largely on 'intuitive experience', i.e., on a system of methods that one cannot explicitly describe.

Specific Traits of Chess Thinking

In what aspects does chess thinking differ from non-chess thinking? Does the needed mentality for chess mastership extend to other fields? Can we define specific characteristics, possibly specific methods of thinking, that are peculiar to chess?

In attempting to answer these questions, we can initially resolve that *chess thinking is typically non-verbal*. The chess player is concerned with moves on the board, with movements and manoeuvres, with spatial relationships, and with the dynamics of captures, threats, and control – all of which can be objects of perception, imagination, and thought, without any dependence on verbal formulations and concepts. It is true that spoken and written language play an important part in learning to play chess and, of course in communication, but for the essence of the game language is of secondary importance. Illiterates and deaf-mutes can learn to play chess; strong 'natural players' who never studied any theory still exist. Chess players can communicate very well with each other without the benefit of a common tongue: the moves themselves – like the notes as they sound in music – much more adequately than any verbalism express the underlying ideas and mental processes. A game of chess may in itself be viewed as a dialogue, a sharp discussion in moves, not words. In fact, this dialogue can almost be subsumed under current definitions of 'language' except that the purpose is not 'mutual understanding' but mental competition in a specific field.

Thus chess thinking is non-verbal thinking and especially *thinking in terms of spatial relationships and possibilities for movement*. This is one reason for the particular *importance of intuitive experience* in the field of chess. One need never state why a particular action is undertaken or why a move is played, since the actions on the board are essentially self-explanatory. It is not necessary to formulate playing methods provided that one has them 'intuitively' available. The chess player's experience need not be explicit knowledge – although in the long run 'experience' generally tends to become knowledge, particularly when specific circumstances (such as writing a chess column, giving lessons, exchanging thoughts with colleagues) induce him to give an account of his own thought habits.

Other specific features of chess thinking follow from the necessity for the player to calculate mentally and in advance what may happen: 'if . . . and if then . . ., then. . . .' It is true that the master more conspicuously distinguishes himself by his extremely adequate selection of what to investigate than by his depth of calculation, but the fact remains that the choice of a good move rests largely on *foreseen possibilities* for action and on the evaluation of their *foreseen results*.

In principle, these calculations can always be considered instances of the general method of trying out. The extraordinary importance of this thought method is certainly a basic characteristic of chess thinking. For this reason we have repeatedly drawn the thought process as an *empirical thought investigation:* 'empirical' since it is by trying out and by (mental) experimentation that one seeks to approach the truth; again 'empirical' – as well as inductive – because there is no *a priori* or deductive way to establish with certainty how much can be attained and what can be proved. Here the contrast with solving a mathematics problem is striking.

Correspondingly, there is a *striking resemblance with processes of 'real' empirical research,* where processes of thinking and testing reality are interwoven. Especially, if the research goal is a practical one: if the decisions to be taken (moves to be made) depend on expected quantitative results, the parallel can be stretched a long way. First, the progressive deepening of the investigation: ideas recur more than once; solution proposals are tested with increasing thoroughness and are finally compared and weighed against each other. Just such a process is found in the development of scientific research: indeed, the 'subject' may shuttle back and forth between plans *A* and *B*. If, for instance, the goal is to improve the durability of some material, this may be achieved in more ways than one. First, the researcher is likely to do some small scale experimentation with one of the available methods (the provisional favorite). If this proves unsuccessful he will try out a second method – maybe a modification of the first – fitting into the same general framework. If he again fails to attain an immediate success the researcher may return to the first method which will be tried out more thoroughly this time. There is 'progressive deepening', indeed. Perhaps 'sample variations' and an explicit 'striving for elimination' of certain means may occur; finally, the researcher will probably try to prove scientifically that his 'favorite' method is the best one. Phases of specialized, detailed investigations can be discriminated from periods in which the investigator returns to a more general goal, or checks and recapitulates his partial results, or analyses the problem and weighs the pros and cons in a process of 'dialectical deepening'. In short: there occur pronounced 'transitional phases' with all the characteristics we know from chess thinking.

A further important point of resemblance is *the decisiveness of the quantitative moment.* The goal remains throughout to improve the durability of the material, but there is no *a priori,* objectively fixed limit to the amount or degree of improvement. The 'expectancy interval' the researcher has in his mind will change, and, particularly, get smaller (become more precise and realistic) during the empirical investigation.

Apart from research other *processes of rational choice* parallel the chess player's process provided that the decision is based on rational estimates or experimental determination of various quantitative consequences of a number of given alternatives. This obtains, for example, for certain decision processes in modern management.

Furthermore, *the function of a plan* in chess is no less than the planning procedures in industrial and commercial management or in economics in general – where the final goal is at least as quantitative as in chess. A plan is a framework for guiding future actions which will come about in the form of separate decisions or steps (moves); it is based on the features of the present situation, one into which a better insight can be obtained through the 'investigation of possibilities' (research, market analysis, etc.). Typically, the planned strategy is never certain to be right: it is formed on the basis of an insufficient set of data, permitting it to be changed in mid-stream.

Here we hit upon another important characteristic of chess thinking: decisions are based on *necessarily incomplete evidence*. Nearly every argumentation is incomplete: it does not generally provide certainties, but at best a high likelihood that the choice is a good one – or the best possible. There is room for 'intuitive completion'; in fact, there is a strong need for this method to enable the subject to build up the subjective certainty he requires for actual decisions.

By pulling together some of these characteristics of chess thinking, to wit, the *empirical attitude* of the player, his *relative* examination of possibilities, the uncertainties resulting from the *incompleteness of the evidence*, and finally the decisiveness of *quantitative* results, another one can be inferred: the *relativistic attitude* it requires. The incessant alternation between elaborating ideas and evaluating them leads to 'disappointments' so often that the player should not and, in fact, is conditioned not to 'believe' easily in any particular principle, plan, or method. Everything is tried out, tested, and checked – and often rejected; *a priori* nothing is accepted as true or taken for granted. In the chessmaster's empirical, specifically inductive way of thinking there are no primary principles from which deductions can be made; nor are there any empirical rules without exceptions. Often a plan or board goal must be given up right after the opponent moves: if shifting to another plan is more 'advantageous'. A dogmatist is just as unfit for playing chess as he is for leading a dynamic enterprise. The chessmaster is of necessity a relativist or even, so to speak, an opportunist in his thinking.

One more characteristic of chess thinking that should be mentioned is the *complexity of the hierarchical system of problems and subproblems* that the player must keep track of during his thought process. He must not, of course, get entangled in his own branches, nor may he disarray the subproblems and partial results, for instance. Indeed, it would seem that this requires a high degree of 'discipline' in thinking as well as a capacity for retaining complex structures of data. In this respect, however, chess is not unique.

13 E. H. Rayner

A Study of Evaluative Problem Solving

Excerpts from E. H. Rayner, 'A study of evaluative problem solving.
Part I. Observations on adults', *Quart. J. exp. Psychol.*, vol. 10 (1958),
pp. 155–65.

Problems often present several possible solutions, some of which
are better than others. The task imposed by such problems lies in
anticipating the possible alternatives and in choosing the best.
Such situations are evaluative and frequently met with in everyday life; for example, in deciding upon a means of reaching a
destination or in deciding the batting order. Board games also
present the individual with similar evaluative problems and may
provide material simple enough for experimental investigation.

This paper describes some observations carried out upon the
game of pegity. In this game two individuals play opposite one
another at a board with 24×24 holes in it, one has a pile of red
pegs and the other a pile of yellow pegs. Placing their pegs alternately each player tries to get five of his own pegs in an unbroken
straight line. Once a peg has been placed it must not be moved so
that as the game proceeds the number of pegs on the board increases. It is a game in which the rules are simple enough to be
understood by a four year old, and yet is interesting enough for
adults to play for long periods. The subjects are free to do as they
like within the limits of good recording. After the first instructions
the experimenter is a passive observer.

It seemed that the most fruitful exploratory study of problem
solving in this game would be to examine the developments in
thinking with age and also as an individual learnt the game. Individuals between the age of four and adulthood were observed,
each playing a fairly long series of games. This paper will deal
with some observations carried out on young adults. A later
paper, Rayner (1958), describes observations carried out on
children.

(a) Design of the experiment with adults

Six individuals were asked to play a league type series of games.
In this, each individual played a set of 5 games with every other
individual. Thus every subject played 5 sets, each with a different
opponent, and, as each set was of 5 games, he played 25 games in

all. The whole league series was of 75 games divided into 5 rounds. There was an interval of about a week between each round.

The pairing of individuals for each round, the starter of each game, and the player's peg colour were all decided randomly.

The subjects were second year students in psychology at University College, London.

The two players sat on opposite sides of a table on which was placed the pegity board. [. . .]

The experimenter sat beside the pegity board and recorded the position and time of every move. Each move was recorded on a replica of the pegity board.

At the start of the first session for each pair of players the rules of the game were given. These were understood without difficulty. They were warned not to talk. The experimenter then told them who was to start the first game and with what colour. The game continued without interruption until one player had got five of his own coloured pegs in an unbroken line, when he was proclaimed the winner.

The next game was started by the experimenter allocating the starter and colour of peg. This continued for the 5 games of the set. In subsequent sessions the experimenter merely ascertained whether the subjects remembered the rules before starting the first game off by allocating who was to start and his colour of peg. [. . .]

(b) Description of the pegity problem as it faces the player

The player must try to place a pattern of pegs on the board which can be made into five in a line no matter what the opponent does to stop him, and must therefore, at the same time, scan his opponent's pegs for dangerous lines which must be 'stopped' by the player placing one of his own pegs on a dangerous line to prevent it being expanded. Thus the pegity player, to be successful, must think of both attack and defence before each move.

More specifically, the player must realize that four pegs in an unbroken line with holes at both ends is unbeatable, for at whichever end the opponent places his next peg there is still a hole at the other end to allow the player to make five. A line of three pegs with holes at both ends is dangerous; that is, it must be stopped on the very next move if it is not to be made into an unbeatable four. Constructing lines of pegs with clear holes at both ends is thus of central importance in the game; in future we shall refer to such lines as 'open-ended'. The making of such single lines of pegs will be referred to as single line strategies. But, just as an open-ended four is unbeatable so is two open-ended threes crossed in a single peg. With this 'crossed-threes' pattern, whichever of the two lines of three the opponent chooses to stop there is still the other that can be made into an unbeatable four on the player's next move. The main point of making this 'crossed-threes' is that the pattern of pegs just prior to the placing of the critical peg that crosses the two threes doesn't look dangerous, yet it must be stopped to prevent defeat. We shall call it a 'potentially crossed-threes'. It will be noticed that a combination of two lines of threes in any direction crossing in any peg of either line will form an unbeatable crossed threes. The making of such sequences of moves will be referred to as a 'crossed-line' strategy.

Another aspect of these strategies is the anticipation of moves ahead required of the player to carry out successfully or defend against a given strategy. The single line strategy of making fours from open-ended threes is unbeatable three moves from the end of the game; e.g., the fourth peg in a line is placed, then the opponent places his peg in an attempt to stop it, lastly the line of five is completed by the player. The crossed threes strategy, on the other hand, is unbeatable five moves from the end, that is when the lines are crossed in a single peg. It also involves the placing of pegs on two intersecting lines.

Beyond these there are other strategies involving more lines, which are unbeatable even more moves from the end and which look even less dangerous. For example, a combination of an open-ended three with a potentially crossed three involves three lines and is unbeatable seven moves from the end. It is possible in this way to make an ordering of strategies in a table, in terms of the number of lines involved and the number of moves before the end of the game at which the strategy is unbeatable. Figure 1 below gives a sample of strategies ordered in this way.

(c) Psychological functions that may be investigated by observation of the game

First, we have just suggested that successful play depends on developing strategies which are unbeatable more moves ahead than the opponent can comprehend as dangerous. A scale of strategies, in terms of the number of lines involved and the number of moves ahead that each strategy was unbeatable, has been proposed. It could be thought of as a sort of measure of the anticipatory thought achieved in playing the pegity game. By means of this scale the development of thought by the player can be examined, both on a long time base by observing the change in performance with age through childhood, and also over a short time base by observing the changes with learning the game over a series of sessions.

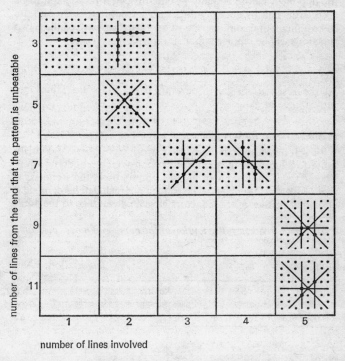

Figure 1   An example of a two dimensional scale of strategies

Next, it is possible to consider the conditions under which the subject tends to bias his thought. For example, the individual must scan the pegs on the board before he makes each move. The difficulty of perceiving dangerous lines embedded in a constellation of pegs on the board has already been mentioned. An aspect of this which has been investigated and will be reported upon later is the difference in the difficulty of discriminating lines that are

155

orthogonal as opposed to diagonal in the individual player's plane of vision.

Lastly, again considering the subject's possible tendency to bias in thought, it has been mentioned that the player must anticipate his own possible offensive moves and the possible moves of the opponent before actually placing his peg if he is going to be successful. This balance of attack and defence in thought appears to be difficult and some aspects of an inbalance between these two functions will be reported upon. [. . .]

Results

All the observations given below are based on the first, third and fifth rounds of games.

1. Simple quantitative summaries

1a. – It has been mentioned that two factors possibly contributing to success in the games were controlled by randomization. The first was the colour of peg the players used, the second was that of the starting player. The results, not included here, made it clear that neither of these factors gave an advantage to the adult player.

1b. – *The frequency distribution of the number of moves per game*

Table 1

Moves per game	Rounds		
	I	III	V
30–34	4	–	2
25–29	5	2	1
20–24	4	5	5
15–19	–	4	3
10–14	2	4	4
	26·0	20·9	20·1
Mean number of moves per game		22·2	

This suggests that the number of moves per game decreased as players gained experience.

1c. – Mean times per move (in seconds)

Table 2

Rounds			
I	III	V	Overall
17·3	21·0	20·4	19·2

Here no significant tendency occurred as the players gained experience.

2. Examples of investigations into the development of anticipatory thought in problem solving

2a. – In considering the possible strategy sequences described in figure 1 it will be realized that in a free game situation the placing of pegs could be fortuitous, one can never be sure that a strategy sequence of moves was in fact intentional. However, there are several criteria by which it is possible to estimate whether an individual had reached the level of intentionally thinking out a strategy of a given complexity before he made it. These can be enumerated:

(*a*) If a subject failed to complete a certain strategy when there was nothing to prevent him doing so, then it was most unlikely that he had anticipated the possible moves of the strategy correctly.

(*b*) If the subject failed to defend against a certain strategy then it was most unlikely that he had anticipated the strategy.

(*c*) If a subject successfully stopped a pattern of pegs that was dangerous by a certain strategy then he may have anticipated it correctly.

(*d*) If a sequence of moves was consistent with a certain strategy then the subject may have anticipated the strategy before carrying it out.

Introspective reports were excluded because the subjects were reluctant to give them repeatedly for the many sessions they had to attend.

In the games it seems that many players go no further than making open-ended threes. They try to make an open-ended three which is so embedded in the scattered constellation of pegs on the board that their opponent does not spot it until it is too late, they go on to make an unbeatable four and then a five. However, some players do seem to develop the crossed lines strategy. We shall be concerned here only with strategies where two lines are crossed, no player made more complex sequences of moves. In order to discriminate the making of such crossed line strategies the following sequences of moves may be grouped under four headings and enumerated:

(*a*) *Subject failed crossed line attack*
This is the case where the individual built up a potentially crossed lines, was in the position to cross them and go on to win for certain, but failed to do so.

(*b*) *Subject failed crossed line defence*
Here the opponent made a potentially crossed threes (or stopped fours) and the subject failed to stop it.

(*c*) *Subject stopped a potentially crossed lines pattern*
The subject was faced with an opponent's potentially crossed lines pattern; he stopped one or both of the lines.

(*d*) *Subject completed a crossed lines sequence*
In this case the subject built up a potentially crossed threes (or stopped fours). On the next move possible, without endangering himself, he made a crossed threes. On the move after that he made a four and then a five. All these without irrelevant moves. Moves that fell into these categories are enumerated in Table 3.

Table 3
Frequencies of Moves Recorded Indicating Crossed Line Strategies

| | *Rounds* | | | |
	I	*III*	*V*	*Total*
Fails attack	22	7	5	34
Fails defence	15	10	12	37
Crossed line defence	17	6	7	30
Crossed line full sequence	3	8	6	17
Total number of moves	365	314	302	981

Here there is a clear indication on all criteria, except that of crossed line defence, that the players carried out more crossed line strategies for the third and fifth rounds of games as opposed to their first round. Thus, as one would expect, strategy thinking develops with practice.

2b. Development of forethought with practice. – An increase in crossed line strategies as the individuals gained experience is perhaps the fruit of longer forethought developed with practice. An indication of longer forethought can be obtained from the times of the last moves in each game. These are shown in figure 2.

It will be noted that for the first round of games the time per move remained at about that for the mean of the whole game right up until the next to last move, then the ending move speeded up.

At the third round of games the time per move increased above the mean for the whole game three moves from the end and then suddenly speeded up for the last three moves. This seems to suggest that the third move from the end was pondered over but that for the last three moves the outcome was certain as far as the players were concerned and the moves were carried out quickly. In fact it often seemed that the players carried out these last moves as a mere ritual to please the experimenter, who often had to ask them to complete them. They foresaw the finish and

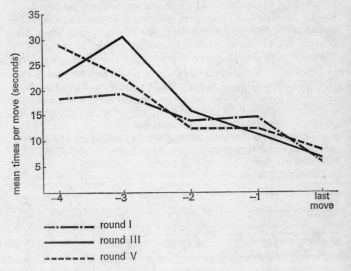

Figure 2   Mean times per move for the last five moves in each game

considered it a waste of time to place the ending pegs. In the fifth round of games the speeding up took place even earlier than in the third round. As one would expect, forethought seems to have developed with practice.

3. Examples of problem solving functioning being biased by the nature of the stimulus

3a. – Orthogonal and diagonal lines. – It seems clear that a necessary pre-requisite of efficient thinking about the pegity problem is the scanning of the stimulus pattern. This scanning must take the form of perceptual grouping, first into own and opponent's pegs, then grouping into lines of pegs which can be in any direction in the visual field but noted as having so many holes and gaps.

From the casual comments of subjects it was suspected that lines of pegs in the orthogonal direction would be more easily discriminated than in the diagonal. We set out to test this in the following manner. The player must respond to dangerous lines of open-ended threes, fours or fours stopped at one end, by stopping them. If the player failed to stop such a dangerous line then he clearly had failed to discriminate it as dangerous. This discrimination of the danger in a line first required the perception of the line itself then of its dangers. At present we are interested only in the perception of the line itself, the necessary additional discrimination of danger a confounding factor. However, if a comparison of the adequacy of scanning orthogonal as opposed to diagonal lines is required, as in this case, then the additional factor of recognition of danger can be considered to be the same for lines in either direction, so that it was possible to use the stopping of dangerous lines as a test of difference in discrimination of orthogonal as opposed to diagonal lines.

A two by two table was constructed enumerating the numbers of orthogonal or diagonal dangerous open-ended threes, fours, and fours already stopped at one end, that were stopped or not stopped, in Rounds I, III and V.

Table 4

	O	D	Total
S	88	79	167
$\overline{S}$	23	66	89
Total	111	145	256

O – orthogonal. D – diagonal. S – stopped. $\overline{S}$ – not stopped.

$\chi^2 = 17 \cdot 1$ df $= 1$
$P(\chi^2 \geqslant 17 \cdot 1) < 0 \cdot 001$

It must be noted that the χ^2 test is not strictly valid as the cell entries are not completely independent. However, it is clear that diagonal lines were missed more often than orthogonal lines. This may be due to the difference of direction in the visual plane or to the greater distance apart of the pegs on the diagonal lines.

3b. – *An indication that the subject tended to conform to his oppo-*

nent's timing of moves. – With the adult subjects there were very marked individual differences in the times taken in making their moves.

It was noticed that those subjects who normally took a long time over each move, often speeded up when faced by a quicker moving opponent. On the other hand, the normally quick moving subjects tended to slow down when faced by a slow opponent. This would be a sort of temporal 'Sherif effect'. To analyse such a tendency it is necessary to obtain firstly a measure of the difference between the timing made by the opponent facing the subject and the subject's own overall average timing of moves. Then to be compared with this, there must be a measure of the change the subject made in timing his own moves when faced by this particular opponent. [. . .]

The co-variation between these measures (product moment correlation$=0.76$) suggests that the adults altered the speed of their moves towards that of their opponents. It must be added that, when the subjects were told of this conformity to their opponent's timing after the experiment, they were very surprised. It could be said, then, that this was an example of the subject varying his thinking about the problem in a way that was dependent upon the actions of the other player and which was unconscious.

4. Observations of bias towards attack or defence

A perfect player would anticipate equally both his own possible moves and those of his opponent. But subjects reported difficulty in doing this. Several individuals reported that they failed to 'see' a critical stimulus pattern (dangerous or potentially offensive) because they 'were thinking too hard about attacking'. It may be said that they were in a way 'blind' because they were thinking about attacking.

Quantification of this effect was gained from the subjects' performances by classifying all moves in the following four ways:

(*a*) Attacking responses. Placing a peg to make three or more in a line. It will be assumed that before making such a move the player was thinking predominantly about attacking, that is, of his own possible moves to win.

(*b*) Non-attacking responses. Placing a peg that does not fall into the above category (e.g., making less than three in a line or stopping the opponent).

(*c*) Inappropriate responses. When faced by either a potentially winning or a dangerous stimulus pattern the player failed to respond appropriately by going on to win or stop the dangerous stimulus respectively.

(d) Other responses. All moves that were not inappropriate.

From these a 2×2 table could be made as follows:

	Attacking responses	Non-attacking responses
Inappropriate responses	Inappropriate attacking responses	Inappropriate non-attacking responses
Other responses	Other attacking responses	Other non-attacking responses

The results of such a cross classification are shown in Table 5.

Table 5

	Round I		Round III		Round V		Overall	
	Attack	Non-Attack	Attack	Non-Attack	Attack	Non-Attack	Attack	Non-Attack
Inappropriate	53	54	7	15	9	18	69	87
Other	94	222	82	155	89	143	265	520
χ^2	14·1		0·02		0·26		6·2	
Significance level	0·001		Insignificant		Insignificant		0·025	

There is evidence here that in the first round of games the subjects tended to miss critical stimulus patterns more often when they were attacking than when they were making any other sort of move. However, they showed a striking decrease in this 'blindness' when attacking after the first round of games.

Speculative Conclusions

Anticipatory thinking

All possible moves of a pegity game can be represented by a 'tree of possibilities' as suggested by Von Neumann and Morgenstern (1947). For pegity there would be 576 (24×24) branches at the first level each representing a possible first move. At the second level there would be 575 branches for each branch at the first level, and so on. The full tree for a pegity game would be enormous, but a perfect mechanical or 'logical' player would, before moving, have to anticipate all possible sequences of the game in a way that is isomorphic with the tree of possibilities. This would be very laborious and it is clear that no human plods through such a routine. But it seems that if an individual consistently carries out a certain strategy, such as a crossed threes strategy, then he must in all likelihood have anticipated the moves ahead in a way that is isomorphic with the part of the tree of possibilities representing that strategy. Such anticipatory thought need not be conscious.

The tree of possibilities suggests two further points concerning the nature of anticipatory thinking. Strategy thinking requires the representation of long sequences of events in which the individual must remember the first part when he comes to the end. This requires a short-term memory of something imagined, not perceived; a type of memory not easily investigated. Beyond this, strategy thinking requires the simultaneous comparison of several anticipated sequences to decide the best. This has been referred to as evaluation. It requires an immediate memory span of several imagined sequences at one time, a load which clearly taxes the human mind. However, although it seems that the individual must have anticipated the possible moves of a strategy at some time before he intentionally carried it out, there would be no necessity for him to do this on every succeeding occasion. Instead, he seems to be able to use a labour saving device. When the individual perceives a pattern of pegs from which the possible moves have been anticipated in the past, instead of anticipating again, he can refer to his memory as to what these possibilities were and what the outcome was. In this way, for instance, the percept of a pattern of pegs that in the past had been anticipated as leading to an opponent's five in a line could immediately be recognized as dangerous. By this means the player can build up a repertoire of memories of groups of pegs that had been anticipated as dangerous or potentially winning. This is a type of symbol formation.

In this process of the formation of symbols for possible sequences it will be clear that it is not only after actual experience of a set of moves that the perception of a group of pegs can come to be a symbol for the moves. The only pre-requisite is that the player should have anticipated the moves.

Of course, a use of symbols is open to error, for example, a perceived group of pegs may have been recognized as dangerous, when in fact they were not. This was the case when the subjects made inappropriate defensive moves.

Spatial generalization is another labour-saving device. For example, if an individual anticipated a group of pegs lying in one direction as leading to five in a line, he could recognize that all groups of pegs, bearing the same relation to themselves as this, were dangerous no matter what the orientation. In this way the repertoire of groups of pegs symbolizing known outcomes could be greatly extended without the actual experience of playing with these patterns or even of anticipating their outcome individually.

Thus the good player would be one who not only scanned the groups of pegs on the board accurately, and anticipated possible moves ahead without error, but also one who had a large repertoire of symbols of groups of pegs with known outcome. It is a concept formation. In this connexion it will be noticed that although actual anticipation from a pattern of pegs need not have been carried out, the internal thought, if correct, must still conform in part to the tree of possibilities.

The results show that human beings found it difficult to comprehend spontaneously even the simplest strategy in the course of their game. This seems strange when relatively simple machines could be conceived of to play the game. But in order to anticipate moves ahead, the human must carry out operations which conform to the structure of the tree of possibilities. In a game-playing machine this structure would be built into it by an artisan. But the human being is not like this. Not being specially designed to play pegity, he must achieve the structuring himself by learning. It is because of this structuring by learning that an understanding of thinking may be gained by observing the development of solving the problem, both as the individual gets older and as he gains specific experience in this game.

References

RAYNER, E. H. (1958), 'A study of evaluative problem solving. Part II. Developmental observations', *Quart. J. exp. Psychol.*, vol. 10, pp. 193–206.
VON NEUMANN, J., and MORGENSTERN, O. (1947), *Theory of games and economic behavior*, Princeton.

14 P. C. Wason

'On the Failure to Eliminate Hypotheses . . .'
– a Second Look

This paper has been specially written for this edition. (Eds.)

It is easy to obtain confirmations or verifications for nearly every
theory – if we look for confirmations.

POPPER

In my paper, 'On the failure to eliminate hypotheses in a conceptual task' (Wason, 1960), I discussed an experiment about the
extent to which people acquire confirming and disconfirming
evidence for their beliefs about a rule.

The subjects were told that the series, 2 4 6, conformed to a
simple rule which they had to discover by generating successive
series of their own. After each series they were told only whether
their numbers conformed to the rule which was 'numbers in
increasing order of magnitude'.

The paper provoked some criticism, e.g., 'the subjects' task is
misleading' (Wetherick, 1962); 'we question whether the model is
an appropriate one' (L. H. Shaffer, personal communication). Two
points especially aroused suspicion and anxiety: 1. The rule was
deemed grossly unfair in the sense that few subjects would consider order of magnitude to be a rule. 2. The generation of a large
number of positive instances of a hypothesis does not increase
the probability of its correctness, i.e., confirming evidence alone
is completely useless. It seems that the rationale of the experiment
was not made clear. This second look attempts both to clarify
its aims and to discuss some subsequent research.

Unlike most concept attainment tasks the point was not to see
whether the subjects discovered the rule. The point was to see how
they behaved when their hypotheses had been corroborated by
confirming evidence. This aim necessitates a task in which a
number of plausible hypotheses, other than the correct rule, will
spontaneously occur to the subjects. These hypotheses should be
more specific than the correct rule, but any series of numbers which
satisfy them should also satisfy the correct rule, i.e., these hypotheses should entail the rule. Hence the very general 'unfair' rule
was selected in order to facilitate more specific hypotheses such as,

'an equal interval between three ascending numbers' (arithmetic progression).

What can the subjects do with their hypotheses? Suppose a subject had entertained the hypothesis, 'intervals of two between ascending numbers', on the strength of these confirming instances: 8 10 12, 15 17 19, 20 22 24. He could announce his hypothesis to the experimenter as being the rule, or he could generate a series such as 3 6 9 in order to test his hypothesis. If he is told that such a series conforms to the rule, as this one does, then he has eliminated 'intervals of two' decisively. Thus the subject can either offer his hypotheses to the experimenter for judgement and wait for him to say, 'that isn't the rule', or 'that is the rule', or he can acquire this knowledge by himself by the internalized process of elimination which De Groot (1965), in a different context, calls 'negative proof'. This consists essentially in an attempt to refute one's own hypotheses rather than simply trying to confirm them. It is clearly the sort of procedure which occurs in a scientist's thinking and experimenting. In real life inferences can only be assessed in relation to the evidence for them – there is no authority to pronounce them right or wrong.

The task was intended to simulate the understanding of an event for which several superficial explanations are possible. Since the real explanation would be merely a concealed component in the superficial ones it will most frequently defy detection until the more obvious characteristics have been varied. The analogy is not to creative thinking but to the search for simplicity, in the sense of minimal assumptions.

Although the task is artificial it does possess two novel features. The correct rule cannot be proved but any incorrect hypothesis can be disproved. Moreover, an infinite number of series exemplifying any hypothesis can be generated. The subject cannot run out of numbers which confirm his hypotheses. Secondly, the subject is not shown stimuli from which he can select instances as possible evidence. He has to generate both his own hypotheses and his own evidence.

The details of the experiment and the quantitative treatment of the results may be found in the original paper. Only an outline will be given here. The subjects, twenty-nine undergraduates, were told that the rule was concerned with a relation between three numbers, and it was stressed that they were to announce their hypotheses about it only when they were highly confident that they were correct. At each trial the subjects wrote down both their series and their reasons for choosing it on a record sheet.

The experimenter said each time either, 'those numbers conform to the rule', or 'those numbers do not conform to the rule', according to whether they were in an increasing order of magnitude. If the correct rule was announced, the experiment was concluded. If an incorrect rule was announced, the subjects were told it was wrong and asked to carry on with the task. The session continued until the correct rule was announced, or the time exceeded forty-five minutes, or the subject gave up.

Twenty-two out of the twenty-nine subjects announced at least one incorrect rule, nine of these announced a second incorrect rule, and two of these nine announced a third incorrect rule. Six subjects announced the correct rule without any incorrect ones, and the results showed that these subjects varied their hypotheses much more frequently than those who announced one incorrect rule. Six representative protocols are given below, the first three from subjects who announced the correct rule without any incorrect ones, and the last three from those who made one or more incorrect announcements. The words which follow each series are the hypotheses, and the announcement of rules is printed in italics.

Examples of the Protocols

No. 1. Female, aged 25

12 24 36: unit figures are even and increase in twos; 8 10 12: even numbers increasing in twos; 2 6 10: even numbers increasing in fours; 6 4 2: even numbers decreasing in twos; 2 6 8: even numbers ascending; 8 54 98: even numbers ascending; 1 17 23: ascending numbers; 1 18 23: ascending numbers; 1 2 3: ascending numbers.
The rule is ascending numbers (9 minutes).

No. 2. Female, aged 21

3 6 9: three goes into the second figure twice and into the third figure three times; 2 4 8: perhaps the figures have to have an L.C.D.; 2 4 10: same reason; 2 5 10: the second number does not have to be divided by the first one; 10 6 4: the highest number must go last; 4 6 10: the first number must be the lowest; 2 3 5: it is only the order that counts; 4 5 6: same reason; 1 7 13: same reason.
The rule is that the figures must be in numerical order (16 minutes).

No. 3. Male, aged 25

8 10 12: continuous series of even numbers; 14 16 18: continuous series of even numbers; 20 22 24: continuous series of even numbers; 3 5 7: continuous series of odd numbers; 1 2 3: continuous series but with smaller intervals; 3 2 1: reverse; 2 4 8: doubling series; 2 2 4: two numbers the same; 6 4 2: reverse of original numbers; 1 9 112: simple ascending numbers.
The rule is any ascending series of different numbers (10 minutes).

No. 4. Female, aged 19

8 10 12: two added each time; 14 16 18: even numbers in order of magnitude; 20 22 24: same reason; 1 3 5: two added to preceding number.
The rule is that by starting with any number two is added each time to form the next number.

2 6 10: middle number is the arithmetic mean of the other two; 1 50 99: same reason.
The rule is that the middle number is the arithmetic mean of the other two.

3 10 17: same number, seven, added each time; 0 3 6: three added each time.
The rule is that the difference between two numbers next to each other is the same.

12 8 4: the same number is subtracted each time to form the next number.
The rule is adding a number, always the same one to form the next number.

1 4 9: any three numbers in order of magnitude.
The rule is any three numbers in order of magnitude (17 minutes).

No. 5. Female, aged 19

1 3 5: add two to each number to give the following one; 16 18 20: to test the theory that it is simply a progression of two. These are chosen so that they are more complex and not merely simple numbers; 99 101 103: to test the progression of two theory, using odd numbers.
As these numbers can hardly have any other connexion, unless it is very remote, the rule is a progression of adding two, in other words either all even or all odd numbers.

1 5 9: the average of the two numbers on the outside is the number between them.
The rule is that the central figure is the mean of the two external ones.

6 10 14; the difference between the first two numbers, added to the second number gives the third; 7 11 15: to test this theory; 2 25 48: to test this theory.
The rule is that the difference between the first two figures added to the second figure gives the third.

7 9 11, 11 12 13, 12 9 8, 77 75 71.
Subject gives up (45 minutes).

No. 6. Male, aged 23

8 10 12: step interval of two; 7 9 11: with numbers not divisible by two; 1 3 5: to see if rule may apply to numbers starting at two and upwards; 3 5 1: the numbers do not necessarily have to be in ascending or descending order; 5 3 1: could be in descending order.
The rule is that the three numbers must be in ascending order separated by intervals of two.

11 13 15: must have one number below ten in the series; 1 6 11: ascending series with regular step interval.

The rule is that the three numbers must be in an ascending series and separated by regular step intervals.
The rule is that the first number can be arbitrarily chosen; the second number must be greater than the first and can be arbitrarily chosen; the third number is larger than the second by the same amount as the second is larger than the first.
1 3 13: any three numbers in ascending order.
The rule is that the three numbers need have no relationship with each other, except that the second is larger than the first, and the third larger than the second (38 minutes).

It will be noted that in the first three protocols specific hypotheses are first of all considered, i.e., 'numbers increasing in intervals of two', 'successive multiples', and 'a continuous series of even numbers'. But in each case these hypotheses are eliminated by the second, third or fourth series. On the other hand, in the last three protocols examples of fixated behaviour can be found. In No. 4 virtually the same rule of arithmetic progression is announced three times in different terms. Similarly, in No. 5 the same rule is announced twice. In No. 6 a particularly interesting phenomenon occurs which was exhibited by two other subjects. The same rule is merely reformulated after it had been pronounced wrong, but before generating any further series. It would seem that in such cases there was an almost obsessional regard for verbal precision.

The most frequent incorrect rules were 'numbers increasing in intervals of two', 'increasing multiples of the first number', 'consecutive even numbers' and 'arithmetic progression'. A few rules were announced only once or twice throughout the task, e.g., 'arithmetic or geometric progression', 'the second number is the first number plus one and the third is the first number plus four'. (It is of interest to note that the latter rule is contradicted by the initial series, 2 4 6.)

After the announcement of an incorrect rule it would be expected, on a rational basis, that a high proportion of the immediately succeeding series would be inconsistent with the rule just announced, i.e., subjects would relinquish their hypotheses. In fact, over the entire experiment, sixteen such series were consistent and fifteen inconsistent with the rule announced. This experiment strongly suggested that the subjects were either unwilling, or unable to eliminate their hypotheses in this task.

In order to get more insight into the subjects' behaviour I conducted two further experiments. The first one, carried out in 1960, tried to determine whether subjects were merely unwilling to eliminate their hypotheses. One group of subjects was given ten shillings and told they could keep it if they announced the correct rule, but would forfeit half-a-crown for every incorrect rule announced. A control group did the same task without the money. The financial incentive only had the effect of significantly increasing the number of series generated before making an announcement. It appeared to have no effect on the tendency to announce incorrect rules as such. One subject remarked sourly, 'Dr Wason, the average subject is more concerned with pleasing the experimenter than with making money.' The failure to eliminate does not seem to be due to lack of motivation.

In the second experiment, which was carried out at Harvard in 1963, with the assistance of Martin Katzman, an improved technique was used. The twenty-two subjects (students) were told that they could announce only one rule during the task. If an incorrect rule was announced, they were not told it was wrong, but were asked, 'if you were wrong, how could you find out?' This question was asked in sixteen cases, i.e., to 73 per cent of the sample. Nine subjects replied that they would continue to generate series consistent with their hypotheses and wait for one to be negative; two replied that they would try out other hypotheses; two that they would generate series inconsistent with their hypotheses (the rational answer); three replied that no other rules were possible. 'I can't be wrong since my rule is correct for those numbers.' 'Rules are relative. If you were the subject and I were the experimenter then I should be right.' One subject did not make any announcement. Unfortunately he developed psychotic symptoms in the middle of the experiment and had to be removed by ambulance. Nothing similar has occurred with any other subject before or since. The present task seems to demand a level of functioning which most people readily tolerate, but it may impose severe strain on a few predisposed individuals: numbers and number-systems, for instance, sometimes have a peculiar fascination for people suffering from schizophrenia.

These subsidiary experiments suggest that in an abstract task most people are unable to use the procedure of negative proof – it would appear to be a totally alien concept. In 1961 Tirril Gatty did an experiment concerned mainly with correlations between behaviour in the task and the personality variables of 'rigidity', 'flexibility', 'ascendancy' and 'submissiveness'. None of the correlations approached significance. However, in an ingenious pilot study the subjects (students) were given an 'eliminative set', i.e., an instruction to discover the possible rules which *could* hold for the series, 2 4 6, other than the particular rule which the experimenter had in mind. The subjects were told to announce these 'not-rules' only when they were highly confident that they had discovered them. They were also told that if, in performing their main task, they happened to become completely confident about the correct rule, they were to announce that as well. Thus the subjects were alerted to the possibility of different rules, and invited directly to eliminate hypotheses.

These instructions had little effect. Six out of the eleven subjects announced at least one incorrect hypothesis as being *the correct rule*. These incorrect hypotheses were of the same type as those in my original experiment. The 'not-rules' were also similar but a few were more idiosyncratic, e.g., 'each number has the same number of digits', 'all the numbers must be different'. It is of interest to note that this latter rule is even more general than the correct one. Three subjects reformulated their 'not-rules', two doing so twice. Five subjects, in spite of the instructions, generated series to confirm a hypothesis first of all, and only then attempted to eliminate. Only two of the eleven subjects appreciated that one series was sufficient to prove conclusively that a hypothesis was incorrect. It would seem that the positive set is so strong in this task that specific instructions to eliminate do not break it.

What does apparently diminish this set, to some extent, is the initial presentation of a negative rather than a positive series, i.e., a series which does not conform to the rule. In 1962 Barbara Thompson retained the same rule, numbers in increasing order of magnitude, but gave her subjects the negative series, 7 5 3, with instructions to discover what relation must exist between three numbers in order for them not to conform to the rule. Similarly, Wetherick (1962) presented the negative series, 4 2 6, and instructed his subjects to discover the rule. In neither of these experiments were the results significant, but in both there was a trend suggesting that it is helpful to start with a negative series. The results, of course, are hardly surprising because a series which is not in increasing order of magnitude would be very likely to alert the subject to the possibility of order being relevant. Numbers, by convention, generally go up rather than down. The rule, instead of being an implicit component in a more specific hypothesis, becomes a factor of obvious importance.

All these experiments have been concerned with a relation between three numbers. In 1962 Jonathan Penrose attempted to generalize the problem in a pilot study by using as his task the inverted form of the game of 'Twenty Questions'. In the ordinary game a person asks questions of increasing specificity in order to discover a particular object. In the inverted game a person thinks of a logical class which another person has to discover by finding out whether objects fall under it. Penrose selected the class of 'living things' (analogous to numbers in increasing order of magnitude), and gave as the initial instance 'a Siamese cat' (analogous to the series 2 4 6). The subjects (students) were instructed to keep a written record of both their instances and their hypotheses. They were told to announce the class only when they were highly confident they had discovered it.

Only three out of the ten subjects announced the correct class without announcing any incorrect ones. 47·1 per cent of their instances confirmed their hypotheses and 52·9 per cent disconfirmed them. On the other hand, 86·5 per cent of the instances generated by the remaining subjects confirmed their hypotheses and only 13·5 per cent disconfirmed them. All the instances generated by the successful subjects, which resulted in the refutation of an hypothesis, led to consistent changes of hypotheses. But among the unsuccessful subjects there were eleven cases in which hypotheses were retained although logically excluded by one or more instances. A few cases of extreme fixedness of behaviour were observed. For example, one subject only changed his hypothesis from 'pets' to 'animals' over a period of twelve trials. These results suggest that the phenomena observed in the previous experiments are not specific to numbers.

In spite of the small samples used in these experiments – some were no more than pilot studies – there would appear to be compelling evidence to indicate that even intelligent individuals adhere to their own hypotheses with remarkable tenacity when they can produce confirming evidence for them. What makes people so narrow minded and so cognitively prejudiced? Why did they find these trivial games so difficult?

One answer is that these tasks are simply *Einstellung* problems similar to Luchin's (1942) jar problems. The subjects appeared to display rigid or fixated patterns of behaviour because they failed to overcome the set created by their confirming evidence. In my original experiment, however, a hypothesis such as arithmetic progression might have been announced out of desperation – simply because the subject could not imagine any more general rule. Indeed, Wetherick has argued that hypotheses are not directly eliminated at all, but are only changed when another more general rule comes to mind (Wetherick, 1962; Wason, 1962). This argument is perhaps plausible when an individual progresses from relatively specific hypotheses, e.g., 'increasing intervals of two', to more general ones, e.g., 'arithmetic progression'. But it loses much of its force when the progression is in the opposite direction – when simple hypotheses are eliminated and more complex and vulnerable hypotheses are conceived. These cases are rare but they are of the greatest interest. A beautiful example was observed by Gatty. One of her subjects generated eight series and at the same time eliminated these hypotheses, 'increasing intervals of two' and 'the second number is the first number times two, and the third is the second number plus two'. He then announced this hypothesis as the rule: 'the first and second numbers are random but the third is the second plus two.' On being told it was wrong he next acquired further evidence (six series) and announced this hypothesis as the rule: 'the first and second numbers are random, but the first is smaller than the second, and the third is the second plus two.' On being told that it was also wrong he proceeded as follows:

261 263 101, 3 17 17, 51 53 56, 671 671 3, 671 673 900, 42 43 45, 41 43 42, 41 43 67, 67 43 45. *The rule is that either the first number equals the second minus two, and the third is random but greater than the second, or the third number equals the second plus two, and the first is random but less than the second.* (Subject gives up: 50 minutes).

It seems highly probable that this subject could have conceived other hypotheses, as complex and as arbitrary as those which he announced, had he not been bemused by the confirming evidence for his own hypotheses. It was just this evidence which provided a sufficient warrant to make his particular hypotheses seem correct. There is no suggestion in his protocol that he was in any way bereft of ideas, or lacking in originality.

If one knows the correct rule in advance, then of course the subjects' behaviour may seem quixotic and absurd. It is only by doing the task or by watching someone else perform it, that one can really appreciate the helpless predicament into which the subjects so easily fall. At the end of the session in my original experiment the majority of the subjects, who had announced incorrect rules, were surprised and amused by what they recognized to be their own stupidity, but they claimed the experience, far from being humiliating, was both instructive and even cathartic. On the other hand, those subjects who announced the correct rule without announcing any incorrect ones, adopted an air of bland condescension and could not see any point in the experiment.

In the real world, as opposed to the psychological laboratory, the fixated, obsessional behaviour of some of the subjects would be analogous to that of a person who is thinking within a closed system – a system which defies refutation, e.g., existentialism and the majority of religions. These experiments demonstrate, on a miniature scale, how dogmatic thinking and the refusal to entertain the possibility of alternatives can easily result in error. Maybe it was the realization of this which seemed to have a profound effect on some subjects. But whether these tasks are any more than lessons in reasoning, and whether they can be generalized to other domains is uncertain.

References

DEGROOT, A. D. (1965), *Thought and choice in chess*, Mouton.

GATTY, T. (1961), 'Further investigations into the failure to eliminate hypotheses, with special reference to personality and set', Unpublished paper.

LUCHINS, A. S. (1942), 'Mechanization in problem-solving', *Psychol. Monogr.*, vol. 54.

PENROSE, J. (1962), *An investigation into some aspects of problem solving behaviour*, Unpublished Ph.D. thesis, University of London.

THOMPSON, B. (1962), 'The effect of positive and negative instruction on a simple "find the rule" task', Unpublished paper.

WASON, P. C. (1960), 'On the failure to eliminate hypotheses in a conceptual task', *Quart. J. exp. Psychol.*, vol. 12, pp. 129–40.

WASON, P. C. (1962), 'Reply to Wetherick', *Quart. J. exp. Psychol.*, vol. 14, p. 250.

WETHERICK, N. E. (1962), 'Eliminative and enumerative behaviour in a conceptual task', *Quart J. exp. Psychol.*, vol. 14, pp. 246–9.

15   C. Gilson and R. P. Abelson

The Subjective Use of Inductive Evidence

C. Gilson and R. P. Abelson, 'The subjective use of inductive evidence',
J. Pers. soc. Psychol., vol. 2 (1965), pp. 301–10.

An important area of inquiry into the psychology of thinking
has been much neglected of late, namely, the study of subjective
logic. Research in this area some fifteen or twenty years ago
reached the limited conclusion that distortions in syllogistic
reasoning commonly occur because of emotional and other
factors (Lefford, 1946; Thistlethwaite, 1950). Notwithstanding
the current interest in 'naive psychology' (Heider, 1958), in
'psychologic' (Abelson and Rosenberg, 1958; Osgood, 1960;
Piaget, 1957, p. 25), and in personal calculi distinct from normative
or objective logic (Colby and Gilbert, 1964; Shneidman and Farberow, 1959), there has been a paucity of good experimental
research aimed at the study of subjective logic in its own right.
The few novel studies that have been done seem not to have
aroused a great deal of interest (De Soto and Kuethe, 1959; De
Soto, London and Handel, 1965; McGuire, 1960).

Our approach to this area flows indirectly from an interest in
cognitive resistance to persuasive communications. Modes of
resistance to persuasion are referred to in the psychological
literature with various terms: 'defensive avoidance' (Hovland,
Janis and Kelley, 1953, pp. 88–89; Janis and Terwilliger, 1962),
'denial' (Abelson, 1959), 'misunderstanding' (Kendall and Wolf,
1949), 'incredulity' (Osgood and Tannenbaum, 1955), etc.
Additional terms have been invoked to characterize the lack of
critical resistance to communications, for example, 'rationalization' and 'wishful thinking' (McGuire, 1960). These types of
processes are assumed to be motivated by affects such as anxiety,
or by 'desires', or by unstable tension states, such as 'cognitive
imbalance'. All of these dynamics have in common the supposition
that resistance or overacceptance is triggered by the *evaluative*
implications of the communication. For example, the 'incredulity
response' is postulated by Osgood and Tannenbaum (1955) to
occur whenever a highly positively evaluated object and a highly
negatively evaluated object are associated via a positive assertion,
for example, 'Queen Elizabeth praises hatchet-murderers'.

It is theoretically insufficient, however, to place total reliance on evaluative or motivational processes in accounting for the acceptance or rejection of communicated assertions. Clearly there is also a 'reality component' involved. Unpleasant realities (e.g., 'Civil rights progress risks social disorder') are not always rejected out of hand, nor are pleasing absurdities (e.g., 'Sophia Loren is the Tennis Champion of Japan') necessarily found credible. To complete the theoretical picture, it is necessary to interrelate motivational and reality components (Abelson, 1963; Rosenberg and Abelson, 1960). Since so little is known about the reality component, it seems wise as a first step to study those mechanisms by which individuals evaluate the credibility or 'subjective truth value' of assertions in cases in which the motivational component is minimal.

The purpose of the present study was to begin an attack on the broad problem area sketched above. It was postulated that one way people assess the credibility of a general statement is by induction from examples or instances of that statement. For example, to the assertion, 'Senators take bribes', one might say yes, Senator X does take bribes, or X-type Senators do take bribes, or one might say yes, Senators take excessive campaign contributions (positive instances). But what if one also knew that Senator Y, or Y-type Senators do not take bribes, or that Senators do not take free yachts (negative instances)? The process of establishing 'inductive credibility' is similar to the process of inductive inference as referred to by logicians and mathematicians (Carnap, 1960; Watanabe, 1960), and to the processes involved in concept formation (Bruner, Goodnow and Austin, 1956; Hunt, 1962). However, we are interested in 'psychologic' rather than logic. Moreover, the literature on concept formation turns out to be surprisingly irrelevant to our present purposes. Studies of concept learning generally involve the *recruitment of a hypothesis* to account for the *given evidence*, whereas we are concerned here with the *recruitment of evidence* to test *a given statement*. That is, we are concerned with performance rather than learning, with the psychology of testing broad generalities rather than generating precise hypotheses. Other differences from traditional concept-formation studies will become clearer below.

A 'sentence' as considered here, consists simply of a subject, verb, and object. A 'positive instance of a sentence' is defined as a new sentence formed by leaving the verb unchanged and substituting instances of the subject and object for the original subject and object, respectively. Denote the instances of the subject, A, by $A_1, A_2 \ldots A_j \ldots$ and the instances of the object, B, by B_1, B_2

... B_k .... Positive instances of the statement 'A verb B' are provided by all sentences of the form 'A_j verb B_k'. [. . .] Negative instances of the sentence 'A verb B' are defined by the form 'A do not verb B_k'.

The array of evidence provided by instances relevant to the original sentence can be displayed in an *evidence matrix*. Reserving Row j for sentences involving A_j, and Column k for sentences involving B_k, one may enter in cell (j, k) of the matrix a 'plus' to denote the positive instance A_j verb B_k, a 'minus' to denote the negative instance A_j do not verb B_k, and a 'zero' to denote the absence of either type of evidential instance. This matrix can in principle display any pattern of entries, and we may now define our general research task as the study of the inductive credibility of sentences as a function of the form of the evidence matrix and the semantic nature of the sentence components.

Certain forms of the evidence matrix will produce more or less obvious consequences. For example, if the matrix consists almost entirely of positive entries, with one or two empty cells, there will be a strong tendency for an individual to 'fill in' these empty cells with plusses and to accept the universality of the associated assertion. (There is good suggestive evidence for effects of this general type from a classic study by Wolfle, 1932.) However, if plusses and minuses are scattered throughout the matrix, it is not at all clear what the consequences will be.

Fortunately, a tentative, general hypothesis about the evidence matrix was available when we entered this research program. Part of a computer program by Carroll, Abelson and Reinfeld (reported in Abelson and Carroll, 1965) is a set of routines which assess the inductive credibility of assertions by looking at the 'evidence matrix' of their instances. This computer program was written with the intention of simulating the real psychological processes involved, and several assumptions about these processes were made on the basis of introspective intuition.

The crucial assumption on the use of instances was as follows: the general statement A verb B is considered credible if more than half of the instances A_j of A are found to be connected with at least one instance B_k of B in sentences of the form A_j verb B_k. Thus, if the program is concerned, for example, with determining in general whether lawyers play card games, it will proceed by 'thinking of' instances of lawyers (which may be such generic instances as administrative lawyers, patent lawyers, American lawyers, or the like, or may be the specific lawyers, Smith, Jones, etc.) and asking if at least one instance of 'play card games' (e.g., 'play bridge', 'play poker', etc.) can be found appropriate to each. If more than half of the encountered instances of 'lawyers' meet this test, the general assertion is considered acceptable. [. . .]

In order to probe the validity of the above assumption, a pilot study was run with ten different evidence matrices. This study also began an exploration of the effects of semantic variables on the credibility of assertions.

Pilot Study

Table 1 displays the ten different evidence matrices used in the pilot study. They are grouped in the table according to the relative number of positive entries and according to a categorization of the 'specificity' of the evidence. By an 'object-specific' matrix we mean one in which the positive instances are all specific to certain designated objects, and the negative instances are all specific to other objects, irrespective of the subject. An example of an object-

Table 1

Evidence Matrices Used in the Pilot Study

Fraction of positive instances	Evidence Form		
	Object-specific	Subject-specific	Mixed
3/9	1. $\begin{bmatrix} + & - & - \\ + & - & - \\ + & - & - \end{bmatrix}^a$	2. $\begin{bmatrix} + & + & + \\ - & - & - \\ - & - & - \end{bmatrix}^b$	3. $\begin{bmatrix} + & - & - \\ - & + & - \\ - & - & - \end{bmatrix}$
1/3	4. $[+ \ - \ -]$	5. $\begin{bmatrix} + \\ - \\ - \end{bmatrix}$	none
6/9	6. $\begin{bmatrix} + & + & - \\ + & + & - \\ + & + & - \end{bmatrix}$	7. $\begin{bmatrix} + & + & + \\ + & + & + \\ - & - & - \end{bmatrix}$	8. $\begin{bmatrix} + & + & - \\ + & - & + \\ - & + & + \end{bmatrix}$
2/3	9. $[+ \ + \ -]$	10. $\begin{bmatrix} + \\ + \\ - \end{bmatrix}$	none

[a, b] See discussion in text.

specific evidence matrix (of Type a in Table 1) for the assertion 'People have gadgets' is as follows:

Altogether there are three people – A, B, C.
Altogether there are three gadgets – X, Y, Z.

A has X	A doesn't have Y	A doesn't have Z.
B has X	B doesn't have Y	B doesn't have Z.
C has X	C doesn't have Y	C doesn't have Z.

In this example, the entire burden of positive evidence lies specifically with the object, 'X', and the entire burden of negative evidence with 'Y' and 'Z'. In order to say yes to the question, 'Do people have gadgets?' (given only the above evidence), an individual must generalize from Gadget X to the gadgets in general. That is, object-specific evidence matrices require generalization over objects in order to reach a conclusion.

Conversely, a 'subject-specific' evidence matrix is one in which the positive instances and negative instances are, respectively, specific to different subjects. An example of a subject-specific matrix (of Type b in Table 1) for the same assertion, 'People have gadgets', is as follows:

A has X	A has Y	A has Z.
B doesn't have X	B doesn't have Y	B doesn't have Z.
C doesn't have X	C doesn't have Y	C doesn't have Z.

In this case, in order to say yes to the question, 'Do people have gadgets?' an individual must generalize from Person A to the people in general.

In effect, the assumption made in the Carroll, Abelson, and Reinfeld computer program specifies that subject-specific evidence inhibits generalization, but that object-specific evidence does not. In other words, it is easier to generalize over objects than over subjects. In the case of the two examples above, the first example should be more likely to elicit the answer yes than the second when the question 'Do people have gadgets?' is posed. Tests of this prediction and its psychological interpretation are discussed below.

A third type of evidence matrix used in the pilot study is a type we have labeled 'mixed', in which the positive and negative instances are symmetrically distributed. Common sense would suggest that a mixed matrix would provide the strongest evidential support with a fixed number of positive instances.

In the pilot study, the preliminary investigation of semantic variables was begun by using ten different subject-object pairs and two different verbs. Following Heider's (1946) important distinction between 'sentiment relations' and 'unit relations', the verbs 'like' and 'have' were chosen for study.

Method

Twenty-item questionnaires were constructed. Each form of evidence matrix in Table 1 was used twice in each questionnaire, once with the verb 'like' and once with the verb 'have'. [. . .]

Each item was introduced by phraseology indicating that only

179

the presented evidence was to be used in answering the 'yes' or 'no' question following the item. The general introduction to the questionnaire stressed that none of the questions admitted of strictly logical answers, but rather that intuitive impressions were to be given.

Twenty subjects were recruited from a pool of Yale students (typically sophomores) subject to a requirement of participation in psychological experiments. Two subjects received each of ten counterbalanced forms.

Results

There were no apparent differences among the ten subject-object pairs in the tendency to elicit yes responses. The results are given in Table 2 for the ten evidence matrices and the two verb forms, aggregated over subject-object pairs. Each entry is the proportion of yes responses, based upon twenty responses, one per subject.

It is apparent from the table that when two-thirds of the evidential instances were positive, there was an almost universal tendency to agree with the general assertion. Confining our attention, then, to the upper portion of the table representing the cases in which but one-third of the evidential instances were positive, the following suggestive tendencies should be noted: (a) the 3/9 and 1/3 cases produced virtually identical results; (b) the object-specific case produced more positive generalization than the subject-specific case, but this difference was large only for the verb have, not for the verb like, the latter having produced generally low agreement rates; (c) the mixed case produced generally high agreement rates.

Discussion

The tendency for object-specific evidence to be more powerful than subject-specific evidence supports the asymmetrical assumption of the computer program. The apparently strong difference between have and like came initially as a surprise. Verbs have been found by others, however, to make a considerable difference in various ratings of sentence properties (Gollob, 1964; Szalay, 1962) and in generalizing from one symbolic sentence to another (De Soto and Kuethe, 1959).

The main study was designed to explore verb properties further, to be more systematic in the examination of subject and object properties and to retain control over the very interesting variable, subject-specific versus object-specific evidence.

Main Study

Eight verb forms were chosen for use in the main study: three representing 'unit relations' (produce, buy, have), three representing what might broadly be considered 'sentiment relations' (get angry with, understand, like), and two with apparently ambiguous standing on Heider's dichotomy (steal, avoid). These latter two are ambiguous in that 'steal' may imply both positive sentiment and a condition of ownership, and 'avoid' has connotations

Table 2

Proportion of Subjects Giving 'Yes' Response as a Function of Evidence Matrix and Verb

$(N = 20)$

Fraction of positive instances and verb	Evidence form		
	Object-specific	Subject-specific	Mixed
3/9			
Like	0·35	0·25	0·70
Have	0·75	0·30	0.80
1/3			
Like	0·40	0·20	—
Have	0·80	0·30	—
6/9			
Like	1·00	0·95	1·00
Have	1·00	0·95	1·00
2/3			
Like	1·00	1·00	—
Have	0·95	0·90	—

NOTE. – For the pattern of positive and negative instances representing each matrix form, see Table 1.

both of negative sentiment and negative unit relation. (The other six verbs are not really completely unambiguous either, and a discussion of verb variables will prove warranted following the presentation of results.) [. . .]

In Table 3 are presented the sets of subjects, verbs, and objects used in the study. These terms were picked in part so as to make potentially reasonable any possible combination of subject, verb, and object (e.g., 'Families like foods', 'Artists buy animals', etc.). For purposes of greater generality, the nonsense words 'Gleeps' and 'Fung' were included along with the variety of more commonplace terms.

As far as the evidence forms were concerned, only two forms, rather than ten, were included, as described below.

Method

A 128-item questionnaire was constructed, consisting of 64 core contents presented so as to embody each of two forms of evidence: object specific, with one (randomly placed) positive instance out of three, and subject specific, likewise with one positive instance out of three. (See the row of Table 1 labeled 1/3.) Examples of

Table 3

Subjects, Verbs and Objects Used in Main Study

Subjects (*and instances*)	Verbs	Objects (*and instances*)
Gleeps (1 legged, 3 legged, 5 legged)	Produce	Fung (green, yellow, red)
Families (urban, suburban, rural)	Buy	Magazines (sports, news, fashion)
Tribes (Southern, Northern, Central)	Have	Animals (big, small, medium-sized
People (poor, rich, middle-class)	Get angry with	Gadgets (X, Y, Z)
Men (old, young, middle-aged)	Understand	Daughters (red-headed, blonde, brunette)
Artists (unknown, fairly well-known, very well-known)	Like	Paintings (modern, classical, impressionistic)
Candidates (A party, B party, C party)	Steal	Ideas (economic, military, social)
Women (fat, thin, average)	Avoid	Foods (sweet, salty, spicy)

these two respective forms of items with the content 'Tribes have magazines' are:

1. Altogether there are three kinds of tribes – Southern, Northern, Central.
   Southern tribes have sports magazines.
   Northern tribes do not have sports magazines.
   Central tribes do not have sports magazines.
   Do tribes have sports magazines?
2. Altogether there are three kinds of magazines – sports, news, fashions.
   Southern tribes do not have sports magazines.
   Southern tribes do not have news magazines.
   Southern tribes have fashion magazines.
   Do Southern tribes have magazines?

Table 4

Proportion of 'Yes' Responses as a Function of Semantic Elements and Evidence Form

Subject	SS[a]	OS[b]	Verb	SS	OS	Object	SS	OS
Gleeps	0·62	0·71	Produce	0·72	0·83	Fung	0·59	0·67
Families	0·59	0·69	Buy	0·73	0·81	Magazines	0·57	0·66
Tribes	0·62	0·71	Have	0·72	0·88	Animals	0·62	0·71
Candidates	0·55	0·69	Steal	0·70	0·84	Ideas	0·62	0·74
People	0·62	0·69	Get angry with	0·62	0·70	Gadgets	0·63	0·69
Men	0·65	0·73	Understand	0·44	0·44	Daughters	0·61	0·69
Artists	0·59	0·71	Like	0·47	0·63	Paintings	0·64	0·75
Women	0·67	0·71	Avoid	0·51	0·50	Foods	0·64	0·72

Note. – N = 34 subjects × 8 items = 272.
[a]SS = subject-specific evidence form.
[b]OS = object-specific evidence form.

The 64 core contents were selected as a balanced subset of the total set of $8 \times 8 \times 8 = 512$ possible combinations of subject, verb, and object. A Latin square design was used such that each of the eight verbs was used in combination with eight different subject-object pairs, balanced over subjects and objects.

Twelve filler items were also included in the questionnaire. Since all of the main items presented exactly one positive instance out of three, it was thought possible that subjects might tend to respond 'yes' as they began to suspect that no items would ever appear with a more favorable proportion of positive instances.

Table 5

Analysis of Variance of Transformed Item Proportions

Source	df	MS	F
Verb (V)	7	1·5703	58·16***
Subject (S)	7	0·0390	1·44
Object (O)	7	0·0579	2·14*
Evidence form (E)	1	1·4049	52·03***
E × V	7	0·0951	3·52**
E × S	7	0·0206	<1
E × O	7	0·0073	<1
Residual	84	0·0270	—
(Estimated base-line variance)		(0·0184)	

$* \ p \leqslant 0.05$
$** \ p \leqslant 0.01$
$*** \ p < 0.001$

In order to identify the potential presence of any such context effects, twelve filler items (with otherwise unused core contents) containing two positive instances out of three were inserted at the beginning of half of the questionnaires. In the other half of the questionnaires twelve parallel filler items each with one positive instance out of three were inserted at the beginning.

The subjects were 34 Yale undergraduates recruited from the same subject pool as was used for the pilot study.

The instructions were the same as for the pilot study, emphasizing that no test of formal logic was involved, and that each item should be answered only on the basis of the particular evidence presented.

Results

There were no significant or even suggestive differences attributable to the type of filler items, and therefore all thirty-four questionnaires were combined into a single analysis of the main items. Table 4 displays the proportion of 'yes' responses by subject, verb, object, and evidence form. (Data for each semantic element were aggregated over the eight items embracing combinations of the other two elements.)

Cursory inspection of the table suggests that the object-specific evidence rather consistently produced more yes responses than subject-specific evidence; and further, that the verb made a considerable difference, whereas neither the subject nor the object seemed to matter.

The design of the questionnaire permitted a systematic analysis of variance. [. . .]

Table 5 summarizes the analysis of variance on the (arc-sine) transformed proportions for the 128 questionnaire items. [. . .] Clearly the factors of *verb* and *evidence form* are significant. Relative to these effects, all others are of much smaller magnitude. The interaction of verb and evidence form is statistically significant, though small. The object factor is of borderline significance, and the subject factor seems not to be significant unless one wishes to argue that the error term is artifactually large enough to mask its effect. The remaining two tests yield rather clearly nonsignificant outcomes. [. . .]

Discussion

This study confirmed, once again, as did yet a third study by Abelson,[1] that the tendency to form inductive generalizations is an asymmetric function of the evidence form. Subjects in all three studies generalized more freely over objects than over subjects. In the pilot study, this tendency might perhaps have been attributable to the fact that the subject instances were singular, while the object instances were plural. Thus, there was perhaps a felt contradiction in generalizing, for example, from Mary (singular) to girls (plural), a contradiction not present in the generalization over objects. However, this 'bug' in the pilot study was eliminated in the main study, and the asymmetry

1. In this small-scale study, an eight-item questionnaire was administered orally to a colloquium audience of thirty-nine persons. The verbs 'have' and 'like' were used in subject-specific and object-specific forms with one positive instance out of three. Two different sentence contents were used. There were 36·5 per cent more yes answers to generalizations involving have than like, and 13·5 per cent more yes answers to object-specific than subject-specific forms. There was no interaction between these two effects.

between subjects and objects remained (though it was not quite as strong an effect as it had been in the pilot study).

What explanation is there for the apparently stronger tendency to generalize over objects rather than over subjects? One line of explanation is syntactic: the subject of a sentence comes first, and is perhaps thereby made more salient than the object. The attachment of two negative instances out of three to the salient sentence subject might then have a more inhibiting effect on the generalization than would the attachment of two negative instances out of three to the less salient object. This explanation offhand does not seem very compelling, but at least it is not inconsistent with a second, more 'psychological' explanation, and in any case, it can be tested in further studies by using reversed sentences such as, 'Animals are bought by tribes.'

The second line of explanation proceeds from the assumption that differences among types of people are psychologically more important than differences between types of objects. It has been argued that one forms an impression of a person as an individual entity, as a unit distinct from all other units (Asch, 1946). In our main study, the sentences involved person types (e.g., 'fat women', 'rural families', etc.) rather than individual persons, but one might argue that person types are perceived in unitary fashion also, as in the process of stereotyping. Therefore, subjects are unwilling to generalize from a particular subject type to people in general. That one type of person steals does not mean that most people do. On the other hand, objects may be seen as much more readily interchangeable. That one type of object is stolen may well indicate that other types of objects are stolen.

The reader may note a flirtation with tautology in the above explanation: there is less of a tendency to generalize over subjects than over objects because there is more of a tendency to distinguish among subjects than among objects. Certainly if we are to begin to avoid circularity of this sort, we must specify in structural and/or functional terms some cognitive differences between concepts representing 'things which act' and those representing 'things acted upon'.

The computer program which served as the inspiration for our series of experimental studies does in fact recognize differences between these two types of concepts. They are stored in memory in somewhat different fashion, and there is a process difference as well. While it is not appropriate here to go into this process difference in detail, we may briefly indicate the nature of the difference by noting that memory search operations are hierarchically governed by concepts representing 'actors', rather than those representing 'actees'. We believe that one substantial asset of a computer simulation approach to cognitive processes is that it forces the operational specification of otherwise vague or tautological notions.

Regardless of the evidential form of the questionnaire items, why do the verbs act differently? From Table 4 one sees that the verbs 'have', 'produce', 'buy', and 'steal' generate more 'yes' responses than the other four verbs. An intuitive explanation might be that one does not have to have all the types of Xs to have 'X'; no one has all the Xs; thus, not to have a particular X does not imply a very negative relationship between the subject and X. Similar considerations apply to the verbs 'produce', 'buy', and 'steal', all possessing the character of unit relations. This explanation is reminiscent of Cartwright and Harary's (1956) argument that it is difficult to establish negative unit relationships.

With respect to the other four verbs, 'like', 'understand', 'avoid', and 'get angry with', the situation is different. It is possible for someone to like all types of X, or avoid most types of X. Since one may like or understand many things, an instance of not liking or understanding X carries greater negative force than not having X. Thus, generalizations are not made so readily with verbs such as like when over half the instances are negative.

Another possible clue to the differences between verbs may lie in the aforementioned tendency to view individuals as units. Asch (1946) has shown that some descriptive words are much more important in the formation of impressions than others. De Soto and Kuethe (1959) have also found that certain verbs heavily determine the overall impression of the person. No doubt, the verb steal is such a verb. Thus, if it is attributed once to a person, one is left with an overall impression of the person as a thief. In other words, one positive instance with a verb of this nature applied to a person (or type of persons) may be sufficiently powerful to override a majority of negative instances.

To summarize our two major lines of explanation of the verb results (no doubt there are others), it seems that subjects will generalize more often if either the negative form of the verbs does not imply a very negative relationship between subject and object, or if the verb is such as to lead to a holistic impression of the subject class. It is not clear which explanation should take precedence, and indeed, the two overlap considerably with respect to the present limited selection of verbs. One also wonders how to designate our two groups of four verbs. It seems awkward to follow Heider and refer to 'unit verbs' and 'sentiment verbs'. The former term lacks suggestiveness, and the latter does not seem broad enough. One possible terminology which preserves much the same meaning is to denote the verbs have, buy, produce, and steal as *manifest* verbs, and like, understand, avoid, and get angry with as *subjective* verbs. At any rate, distinctions between verb classes are very important in studies of subjective logic using verbal materials, and the matter is much worth pursuing in further studies.

From the first, it has been obvious that more effects the judgement of credibility of an assertion than the evidence matrix of its instances. Another aspect of the computer program (Abelson and Carroll, 1965) which assesses the credibility of an assertion consists in the examination of concepts of which the given statement is an instance. This involves going up the 'tree' of evidence instead of down. It will be necessary in later studies to see whether verbs and evidence form play a part here, too.

References

ABELSON, R. P. (1959), 'Modes of resolution of belief dilemmas', *Conflict Resolution*, vol. 3, pp. 343–52.

ABELSON, R. P. (1963), 'Computer simulation of "hot" cognition', in Tomkins, S., and Messick, S. (eds.), *Computer simulation of personality*, Wiley, pp. 277–98.

ABELSON, R. P., and CARROLL, J. D. (1965), 'Computer simulation of individual belief systems', *American Behavioral Scientist*, vol. 9, pp. 24–30.

ABELSON, R. P., and ROSENBERG, M. (1958), 'Symbolic psychologic: a model of attitudinal cognition', *Behav. Sci.*, vol. 3, pp. 1–13.

ASCH, S. E. (1946), 'Forming impressions of personality', *J. abnorm. soc. Psychol.*, vol. 41, pp. 258–90.

BRUNER, J. S., GOODNOW, J. J., and AUSTIN, G. A. (1956), *A study of thinking*, Wiley.

CARNAP, R. (1960), 'The aim of inductive logic', in *Proceedings of the international congress for logic and methodology of science*, Stanford U.P., pp. 1–38.

CARTWRIGHT, D., and HARARY, F. (1956), 'Structural balance: a generalization of Heider's theory', *Psychol. Rev.*, vol. 63, pp. 277–93.

COLBY, K. M., and GILBERT, J. P. (1964), 'Programming a computer model of neurosis', *J. math. Psychol.*, vol. 1, pp. 405–17.

DE SOTO, C. B., and KUETHE, J. L. (1959), 'Subjective probabilities of interpersonal relationships', *J. abnorm. soc. Psychol.*, vol. 59, pp. 290–4.

DE SOTO, C. B., LONDON, M., and HANDEL, S. (1965), 'Social reasoning and spatial paralogic', *J. pers. soc. Psychol.*, vol. 2, pp. 513–21.

GOLLOB, H. (1964), *A combined additive and multiplicative model of word combination in sentences*, Unpublished doctoral dissertation, Yale University.

HEIDER, F. (1946), 'Attitudes and cognitive organization', *J. Psychol.*, vol. 21, pp. 107–12.

HEIDER, F. (1958), *The psychology of interpersonal relations*, Wiley.

HOVLAND, C. I., JANIS, I. J., and KELLEY, H. H. (1953), *Communication and persuasion*, Yale U.P.

HUNT, E. B. (1962), *Concept learning: an information processing problem*, Wiley.

JANIS, I. L., and TERWILLIGER, R. F. (1962), 'An experimental study of psychological resistances to fear arousing communications', *J. abnorm. soc. Psychol.*, vol. 65, pp. 403–10.

KENDALL, P. L., and WOLF, K. (1949), *The analysis of deviant cases in communications research*, Harper.

LEFFORD, A. (1946), 'The influence of emotional subject matter on logical reasoning', *J. gen. Psychol.*, vol. 34, pp. 127–51.

MCGUIRE, W. J. (1960), 'A syllogistic analysis of cognitive relationships', in Rosenberg, M. J., *et al.*, *Attitude organization and change*, Yale U.P., pp. 65–111.

OSGOOD, C. E. (1960), 'Cognitive dynamics in the conduct of human affairs', *Public Opinion Quart.*, vol. 24, pp. 341–65.

OSGOOD, C. E., and TANNENBAUM, P. H. (1955), 'The principle of congruity in the prediction of attitude change', *Psychol. Rev.*, vol. 62, pp. 42–55.

PIAGET, J. (1957), *Logic and psychology*, Basic Books.

ROSENBERG, M. J., and ABELSON, R. P. (1960), 'An analysis of cognitive balancing', in Rosenberg, M. J., *et al.*, *Attitude organization and change*, Yale U.P., pp. 112–63.

SHNEIDMAN, E. S., and FARBEROW, N. L. (1959), 'Suicide and death', in Feidel, H. (ed.), *The meaning of death*, McGraw-Hill, pp. 284–301.

SZALAY, L. (1962), 'Untersuchungen zur semantischen Struktur der Zeitwörter', *Zeitschrift für experimentale und angewandte Psychologie*, vol. 9, pp. 140–63.

THISTLETHWAITE, D. (1950), 'Attitude and structure as factors in the distortion of reasoning', *J. abnorm. soc. Psychol.*, vol. 45, pp. 442–58.

WATANABE, S. (1960), 'Information-theoretical aspects of inductive and deductive inference', *IBM Journal of Research and Development*, vol. 4, pp. 208–31.

WOLFLE, D. L. (1932), 'The relation between linguistic structure and associative inference in artificial linguistic material', *Language Monographs*, vol. 11, p. 55.

THINKING AND REASONING

Part Four MATCHING PROBLEMS AND CONCEPTUAL THINKING

Bruner *et al.* (1956) were not the first psychologists to compare performance in a conceptual task with some ideal 'strategy'. A pioneering study was performed by Whitfield (16). The subject's task was to discover the required arrangement of eight objects into a number of designated areas. Whitfield was able to demonstrate a discrepancy between the difficulty of a task and a measure of its theoretical difficulty. This research has attracted the attention of psychologists in the Soviet Union, and has been repeated by them. Donaldson (17), using a similar matching problem technique, has investigated the phenomenon demonstrated by Bruner *et al.* (1956) that people are either unwilling or unable to assimilate negative information, i.e., information about what is *not* an instance of a concept. Campbell (18) has investigated Bruner's claim that people are reluctant to adopt indirect methods in conceptual tasks. The study of concept attainment has proceeded rapidly in the U.S.A. under the influence of Bruner. Haygood and Bourne (19) present some interesting evidence about learning a large number of different logical concepts. They show a difference between the learning of rules when one knows the relevant attributes in a concept, and learning the relevance of attributes when one knows the rule governing the concept. Nearly all previous studies of conceptual thinking have confounded these two variables. A highly original approach to the study of conceptual thinking is associated with the work of George Miller and Noam Chomsky, and the research on the 'Grammarama Project' at Harvard. Some of the preliminary experiments are described by Shipstone (20) in a study of people's ability to discover a sequential pattern in strings of nonsense syllables which are generated by a simple set of rules.

References

BRUNER, J. S., GOODNOW, J. J., and AUSTIN, G. A. (1956), *A study of thinking*, Wiley.

16   J. W. Whitfield

An Experiment in Problem Solving

Excerpt from J. W. Whitfield, 'An experiment in problem solving', *Quart. J. exper. Psychol.*, vol. 3 (1951), pp. 184–97.

Introduction

The need for description of a task

This experiment was performed as an attempt to describe in both quantitative and qualitative terms the behaviour of individuals faced with a 'trial-and-error' problem-solving task. It has long seemed to the writer that there is an inadequacy of description of tasks, and of stages in solution, in both problem-solving experiments and in learning experiments. Tasks are frequently described in terms of psychological theory or inferences from behaviour. As examples, the descriptive adjectives may be 'trial-and-error' or else 'insight'. If, instead, we consider tasks as modified by knowledge of results in stages during the solution, we may find a more satisfactory mode of description, referring to the problems themselves, and not to theory nor even necessarily to behaviour. It may thereby become possible to establish an independent base line from which behaviour may be measured or described. Considering briefly the two types of problem mentioned above – 'trial-and-error' and 'insight'; it would appear that the 'trial-and-error' problem is one in which there is a reasonably high probability of achieving some degree of success fairly early in the attempt at solution, and that both the correct and the incorrect elements of the partial success, if known and acted upon, constrain behaviour closer and closer to the completely correct solution. An attempt at solving an 'insight' problem, on the other hand, is almost certain to be either completely right or completely wrong, and in the latter case, except for the narrow information that this specific attempt is wrong, very little information is gained. The problem remains approximately of the same difficulty until complete solution is obtained.

The term 'difficulty' having been introduced, it would be as well to consider its meaning in this context. Its usual reference in psychology is derived from behaviour, measured by the mean time or mean number of trials required for solution or for fulfilling an accepted criterion – or alternatively, in terms of what proportion

T – T.R. – G

of a standard population under standard conditions obtain a solution. But it would seem possible, theoretically at any rate, to consider a more objective form of difficulty, associated purely with the problem and not dependent on the behaviour. To take an example, if we present a multiple-choice intelligence test question the difficulty of the question is dependent partially on the number of possible 'answers' presented. This is merely stating that the task lies mainly in the choice; the judgement of the fitting-ness of the question to each of the possible given answers. Other things being equal, the 'difficulty' is a function of number of answers given. This is, of course, only partially true, in the sense that behavioural 'difficulty' can be modified without changing the number of answers – i.e., if all except one of the given answers are obviously absurd then the task is simplified. But this is an entirely different notion of 'difficulty'. These two types of difficulty may perhaps be named 'stimulus difficulty', referring to the possible descriptions or measurements inherent in the form of the task, and 'phenomenal difficulty' referring to the perceptual and cognitive aspects of the content or the mental processes required for solution. The analogy with terms in the psychology of perception is deliberate. As in the study of perception, 'stimulus' is intended to be described in objective or physical terms, and 'phenomenal' in terms of the behaviour of the observer.

As mentioned earlier, the case of problem solving adds the further complication that difficulty is going to be affected by partial success and knowledge of results. At first sight it would seem not easy to allocate this change of difficulty to either stimulus or phenomenal difficulty, in that knowledge of results requires appreciation by the observer to be effective. However, if it is considered as information now made available, to be added to the basic information given in the problem, it can clearly be treated as a change of stimulus difficulty.

Thus for the study of problem solving it is desirable that the problems chosen should be such that a measure of stimulus difficulty can be made, and that changes in stimulus difficulty in the process of solution can also be measured. The phenomenal difficulty should be measurable from the behaviour of individuals. Further, the problems chosen ought to be such that qualitative observations, which may hint at the modes of solution attempted or the mental processes involved should be capable of record.

Design of suitable experimental problems
Simple derivatives of matching tasks were devised as problems

conforming to the suggested requirements. Let us consider the simple task in which four objects are to be matched against four spaces – or four other objects. For a first trial, there are 4! or 24 ways of arranging the objects. Thus the initial stimulus difficulty can be considered as a function of 24. Of these 24 arrangements, one is completely correct. In this case the stimulus difficulty ceases to exist, the problem is solved. Six of the possible first-trial arrangements give two correct matchings and two incorrect. We have now a great deal of information. For example, we may know that A goes on α, B goes on β, C does not go on δ, and D does not go on γ. Altogether this information adds up to the statement that the solution must lie in interchanging the two incorrect objects. Thus, instead of the initial 24 possible arrangements, there is now only one possible arrangement. The stimulus difficulty has been reduced to some function of one. The phenomenal difficulty need not of necessity be similarly reduced – the objects may so closely resemble each other that it is almost impossible to remember which object was where. Eight of the possible first-trial arrangements have one correct matching and three incorrect. One of these is

	1st trial		2nd trial choice of			
α	A		A		A	A
β	C	leading to	(B or D)	$\rightarrow$ either	B or D	
γ	D	$\rightarrow$	{B or C}		C	B
δ	B		(C or D)		D	C

– two possible arrangements, one correct, the other giving sufficient additional information for the correct arrangement to be the only possibility for the third trial.

And still further, nine of the possible first-trial arrangements are without any correct matches. But they still give information.

	1st trial		2nd trial choice of
α	B		A, C or D
β	C	leading to	A, B or D
γ	D	$\rightarrow$	A, B or C
δ	A		B, C or D

which has nine possibilities. Tabulating the possibilities (continuing the correct solutions throughout) we have:

(For the first trial the number of possible arrangements is 24.)

Trial 1		Trial 2		Trial 3		
Frequency	No. of possible arrangements for Trial 2	Frequency	No. of possible arrangements for Trial 3	Frequency	No. of possible arrangements for Trial 4	
1	0	12	0	23	0	All
6	1	10	1	1	1	correct
8	2	2	2			at
9	9					Trial 4

Thus we can see how the stimulus difficulty is changing, and the variation in change with the degree of success achieved.

The number of possible arrangements is not a very convenient measure to use directly. [. . .] For the first trial, the number of possible arrangements is $n!$, where n is the number of objects to be ordered. This number is reduced trial by trial. It seems reasonable to reverse the factorial process; if x arrangements are now possible, for this to be measured as y, where $y! = x$. In the majority of cases x is not a true factorial, but the use of Γ function tables overcomes this. Thus 'y' is the number, which if it could have a factorial, would have x as its factorial. This value y can be referred to as the 'Equivalent Series', i.e., the problem is now at the same value of stimulus difficulty as would be presented for the first trial of a series of y objects. Thus after a first matching trial of four objects, none of which is correctly placed, $x = 9$, and the Equivalent Series is 3·31.

In one sense this is absurd, as 3·31 objects cannot be matched, but the transformation serves two useful functions. It restores the measure to a scale linearly related to the number of objects presented in the simple case (magnitude therefore can be simply appreciated). It also reduces skewedness so that simple statistical procedures are applicable [. . .]

The matching problems

The case of simple matching will be referred to as the 8(1) condition of problem. Here there are 8! possible arrangements (40,320) on the first trial.

A second matching problem using the same material was devised. Instead of matching eight objects to eight spaces, and being told after each trial which objects were correctly matched and which were not, eight objects were to be 'placed', two in each of four cells. The information given for each cell was whether there were 0, 1, or 2 objects correctly placed. If one was correctly placed and the other was not, the correct one was not specified, the information being that one was correct and one incorrect. The initial stimulus difficulty is less than in the 8(1) condition, as order within each cell is irrelevant. There are 2,520 initial possible arrangements, one sixteenth of 8!, the Equivalent Series being 6·65 (again referring to the equivalent as a simple matching problem). But the information gained from a trial may be conditional.

Consider the first trial:

Correct	1st Trial	Possible arrangements for 2nd trial
AB	AE −1 correct	either A with B, C, D or F; or E with B, C, D or F.
CD	CF − 1 correct	either C with A, B, D or E; or F with A, B, D or E.
EF	BD −0 correct	Two from A, C, E and F.
GH	GH −2 correct	G and H.

There are eight possible arrangements, but the A, E and the C, F alternatives may have to be remembered for subsequent trials. [. . .]
This problem is referred to as the 4(2) condition.

The third variation of the problem is on *a priori* grounds simpler still. The eight objects are to be allocated, 4 to each of 2 spaces. There are only 70 ways in which this can be done. One of these is completely right, one is completely wrong, giving the information that a straight interchange of the objects is all that is necessary. As in the 4(2) condition, information is given as to the number correct in each cell – it is bound in this case to be the same for both cells. This is the 2(4) condition. [. . .]

Experimental material, instructions, and design

The eight objects employed were:

(1) Block of wood	W
(2) An empty safety match box	M
(3) A piece of brass plate	P
(4) A piece of brass tube – like a napkin ring	R
(5) A meccano 1 inch gear wheel	G
(6) A wood screw	S
(7) A bolt with hexagonal head	Bo
(8) A small metal bracket	Bk

197

For the 8(1) condition a sheet of cardboard was divided into 8 spaces from left to right. For the 4(2) condition another sheet was marked out into quadrants, and for the 2(4) condition a sheet was divided into 2 cells, Left and Right. For an experimental session the subject sat at a table with one of the cardboard sheets on it, and the eight objects placed in a heap randomly beside it. In the 8(1) condition the instructions were:

Here are eight objects, and on the sheet of cardboard in front of you there are eight spaces. Each object has been allocated to a space at random, and your task is to find out which object goes where for them all. The procedure is this; after a trial (and a trial means all eight objects placed one in each space) I will place a card with the word 'Correct' against each object which is in its correct cell. I will put nothing against an incorrectly placed object. You will then have half a minute to look at the display without manipulating it. At the end of that time I will take the cards away, shuffle the objects and return them to base and you will have another try. Except for the half minute for looking at the display there is no time limit.

Similar instructions were given in the 4(2) and the 2(4) conditions, except that they were told that 0, 1 or 2, or 0, 1, 2, 3 or 4 cards would be placed in appropriate cells, but that in the conditional cases they would be told not which objects were correct, but only the total correct in the cell.

Three random 'correct' allocations were used and rotated between the conditions. The effects of order of trial (at least 48 hours interval between sessions was maintained) were minimized by a factorial design:

Subject	8(1)	4(2)	2(4)
1	1st	2nd	3rd
2	1st	3rd	2nd
3	2nd	1st	3rd
4	2nd	3rd	1st
5	3rd	1st	2nd
6	3rd	2nd	1st

Similarly for subjects 7–12 and 13–18.
For subjects 1–6 the correct orders were:

8(1)	Bk	R	M	P	G	Bo	W	S
4(2)		G	W		P	Bk		
		S	R		M	Bo		
2(4)	M	P	G	S	W	R	Bo	Bk

for subjects 7–12:

8(1)	G	W	P	Bk	S	R	M	Bo
4(2)			M	P	G	S		
			W	R	Bo	Bk		
2(4)	Bk	R	M	P	G	Bo	W	S

and for subjects 13–18:

8(1)	M	P	G	S	W	R	Bo	Bk
4(2)			Bk	R	M	P		
			G	Bo	W	S		
2(4)	G	W	P	Bk		S	R	M	Bo

The eighteen subjects were students, research workers and staff from the Psychological Laboratories at Cambridge and University College, London.

Thus the experiment is balanced for straightforward comparison between the three conditions. Record was made of where each object was placed in each trial. The number of possible arrangements left at the end of each trial was computed and transformed into the Equivalent Series.

Results

The mean equivalent series, trial by trial, is shown for the three conditions in Table 1. It will be seen that, compared with expectation, human performance in the 8(1) condition is reasonably good. But it is considerably poorer in the 4(2) and the 2(4) condition. Phenomenal difficulty in the latter two conditions would seem to outweigh stimulus difficulty to some extent. Nine subjects in the 8(1) condition behaved with perfect consistency – i.e., they never repeated an error nor forgot a correct match. Three subjects did so in the 4(2) condition and only 2 in the 2(4) condition. Similarly, as a crude indication of failure to take account of all information, we may consider those instances where complete information had been obtained (i.e., if full account was taken of all information, the next trial would be completely correct) but where the subject failed to respond and produced a wrong arrangement.

Table 1

Performance of Subjects compared with Theoretical Performance:
Equivalent series after trials

Trials				Theoretical*	Observed
8(1) Condition:					
1	..	..	..	6·487	6·491
2	..	..	..	4·656	4·701
3	..	..	..	2·508	2·726
4	..	..	..	0·810	1·183
5	..	..	..	0·128	0·462
6	..	..	..	0·006	0·111
7	..	..	..	0·000025	0·056
8	..	..	..	0·000	0·000
4(2) Condition:					
1	..	..	..	4·863	4·785
2	..	..	..	2·623	3·244
3	..	..	..	0·818	1·525
4	..	..	..	0·079	0·667
5	..	..	..	0·0001	0·333
6	..	..	..	0·000	0·222
7	..	..	..	—	0·167
8	..	..	..	—	0·056
9	..	..	..	—	0·056
10	..	..	..	—	0·056
11	..	..	..	—	0·056
12	..	..	..	—	0·000
2(4) Condition:					
1	..	..	..	3·908	3·993
2	..	..	..	3·095	3·143
3	..	..	..	2·156	2·421
4	..	..	..	1·200	1·401
5	..	..	..	0·355	1·179
6	..	..	..	0·110	0·778
7	..	..	..	0·016	0·722
8	..	..	..	0·000	0·722
9	..	..	..	—	0·667
10	..	..	..	—	0·556
11	..	..	..	—	0·389
12	..	..	..	—	0·333
13	..	..	..	—	0·278
14	..	..	..	—	0·278
15	..	..	..	—	0·222
16			—		0·111

* In all conditions these values represent the calibration of the problems
in terms of the average expected stimulus difficulty, trial by trial, throughout

In the 8(1) condition 6 Ss made 1 unnecessary trial
„ „ „ „ 1 S „ 2 „ trials
„ „ 4(2) „ 4 Ss made 1 unnecessary trial
„ „ „ „ 2 „ „ 3 „ trials
„ „ „ „ 1 S „ 4 „ „
„ „ „ „ 1 „ „ 7 „ „

„ „ 2(4) „ 3 Ss „ 1 „ trial
„ „ „ „ 1 S „ 5 „ trials
„ „ „ „ 4 Ss „ 6 „ „
„ „ „ „ 2 „ „ 7 „ „
„ „ „ „ 2 „ „ 11 „ „

In the 2(4) condition two of the subjects failed to find a solution in 16 trials, at which point the experimental sessions were suspended.

The observations can be alternatively described in terms of the number of trials required for solution, compared in all cases with the number of trials expected on a hypothesis of perfect memory, but otherwise random behaviour.

Table 2

Observed and Expected Number of Trials for Solution

	8(1) Condition		4(2) Condition		2(4) Condition	
	E	O	E	O	E	O
1st	0·000	0	0·007	0	0·257	0
2nd	0·110	0	0·429	0	1·029	0
3rd	1·916	1	5·700	1	2·057	1
4th	6·975	5	10·454	6	4·038	4
5th	6·975	6	1·408	5	5·611	2
6th	1·916	4	0·002	2	3·572	2
7th	0·110	1	—	1	1·131	
8th	0·000	1	—	2	0·285	
8+	—		—	1	—	9

An additional behavioural measure can be made in terms of survival of information. If we take the first trial, this has given some information, and any subsequent trial can be tested against it to see whether it is consistent, or infringes the information

the performances. They represent the average of all possible performances by a machine which had perfect memory, but which otherwise acted purely at random.

201

gained in trial 1. If the later trial is consistent, we have no real way of deciding whether this was deliberate or not, whether the subject had remembered and was using the information gained earlier, or whether the consistency had occurred by chance or was derived from information gained in intervening trials. If, however, the trial is not consistent, then we can assume either that the subject has forgotten the information, or for some reason is deliberately refraining from using it. Thus we can take, trial by trial, a measure of the survival of information. On the parallel with other survival distributions, we can assume this to be quasi-logarithmic in form, and take either the logarithmic decrement, or the half period as the measure of survival.

Table 3

Survival Time of Information

8(1) Condition		4(2) Condition		2(4) Condition	
Trial	($\frac{1}{2}$ period in trials)	Trial	$\frac{1}{2}$ period	Trial	$\frac{1}{2}$ period
1	6·81	1	2·41	1	1·71
2	4·96	2	1·65	2	1·33
2+	5·02	3	1·62	3	1·00
		3+	2·95	4–8	1·37
				8+	2·23
All	5·55		2·16		1·55

This agrees with the other quantitative data in indicating the relative phenomenal difficulty of the tasks. The differences between the trials may just be a normal memory effect, as shown in Ebbinghaus' work on serial learning. It may alternatively be a function of approach to the problem by some individuals who deliberately referred back to their first trial after subsequent trials, testing the observations gained against it and paying less attention to intervening trials. The improvement in consistency with later trials may be due to the fact that the problems were nearer solution, and most of the information was now systematized.

Behaviour in the first trial

The first trial differs from the succeeding trials in that the subject has no information to go on at all. He has been told that the correct matchings have been assigned by chance, and might therefore be expected to respond in an equally random manner. He does not in general do so.

In the 8(1) condition, the arrangement

1	2	3	4	5	6	7	8					
W	M	P	.	.	.	.	.	was given by 7 subjects				
W	P	M	.	.	.	.	.	,,	,,	,,	2	,,
.	.	.	.	.	P	M	W	,,	,,	,,	3	,,

Thus 12 out of 18 subjects adopt some rudimentary form of a size or size and shape classification for their first trial.

Similarly in the 4(2) condition, in the first trial:

W and M in same cell	12 subjects
R and G in same cell	9 ,,
P and Bk in same cell	8 ,,
S and Bo in same cell	8 ,,

5 subjects had all 4 pairs
6 ,, ,, 2 of the pairs
4 ,, ,, 1 pair
and 3 ,, ,, 0 pairs.

And further, in the 2(4) condition, 6 subjects divided the objects into W M P Bk on one side and R S G Bo on the other (a shape classification – square *versus* round). A further 5 had W M P on one side with some object other than Bk.

It will be seen how important it was to interchange the random 'correct' layouts between the three conditions, as there obviously exist commonly preferred orders, and one of the random arrangements might be nearer to these than the others.

Discussion and Qualitative Observations

The first conclusion to be drawn from the observations is that phenomenal difficulty (measured from the behaviour) and stimulus difficulty (measured in the manner described) are not in agreement. It is suggested that this difference lies primarily in the nature of the information gained by the subject, varying as it does from the unequivocal 'correct-incorrect' information in the 8(1) condition, through the simple conditional form – the 'either this is right or that is right' – sometimes found in the 4(2) condition, to the more complex conditional form of one or two or three out of four are correct, found in the 2(4) case. Furthermore it is suggested that these differences force the subjects to adopt different methods of solution for the three tasks. A feature common to all three tasks is the attempt on the part of the subjects to impose methods of or aids to solution on to the task. The first of these has already been mentioned; the laying down of the material on the first trial in some sort of meaningful order. The advantages of this procedure are obvious: instead of having to remember the position of eight objects, all that is necessary is to remember the basis of the classification. It is the introduction of a generalization, not as a method of solution, but as a means of organizing, and consequently of simplifying the data. The majority of subjects adopted some form of classification, easily identifiable from the records, in all three tasks. In the 8(1) condition, many subjects adopted additionally a systematic approach to the solution, the best such system being 'scanning'. This is best illustrated by example.

Correct order	M	P	G	S	W	R	Bo	Bk	
1st trial ..	*W*	*M*	*P*	*R*	*G*	*S*	*Bk*	*Bo*	(size classification)
2nd trial ..	*Bo*	*W*	*M*	*P*	*R*	*G*	*S*	Bk	(moved one to right)
3rd trial ..	*S*	*Bo*	*W*	*M*	*P*	*R*	*G*	Bk	(continued)
4th trial ..	*G*	*S*	*Bo*	*W*	*M*	R	*P*	Bk	,,
5th trial ..	*P*	*G*	*S*	*Bo*	W	R	*M*	Bk	,,
6th trial ..	M	P	G	S	W	R	Bo	Bk	,,

Nine subjects used this method from the beginning, two others took it up after early trials. Some other systems adopted for part or all of the time were reversal of trial 1 order or interchange of adjacent pairs. In no case did there seem to be a complete absence of system of some form or other.

The combination of an initial classificatory layout, and systematic change between trials reduces the phenomenal complexity of the problem enormously, the only problem remaining is memory of the items correct – the others are taken care of. It is perhaps worth noting that two individuals, faced with a sudden large increase in the number correct on one trial, broke down on the system. One subject failed to remember an item which had been in its correct position for two trials, and the other failed to move one of the incorrect objects to its next scanning position. These may represent the effect of change from a set to avoid repeating errors to a set to retain the correct responses, but more evidence would have to be forthcoming for any definite conclusion.

The two other tasks, however, do not lend themselves to such systematic solution. In the 4(2) condition, several individuals attempted a systematic approach, even though it ignored some of the information.

As an example:

Correct	M	P	G	S	W	R	Bo	Bk
Trial 1	*Bo*	*Bk*	*P*	S	*G*	*M*	*R*	*W*
,, 2	*Bo*	*W*	*Bk*	S	*G*	*P*	*R*	*M*
,, 3	*Bo*	M	*W*	S	*G*	*Bk*	*R*	*P*
,, 4	P	M	*Bo*	S	*G*	*W*	*R*	Bk
,, 5	P	M	*R*	S	*Bo*	*W*	*G*	Bk
,, 6	P	M	G	S	R	W	Bo	Bk

In this case the information from the first trial (i.e., that except for either P or S, none of the objects was in its correct position) was not wholly employed. Instead, Bo, S, G and R were left in position and the others were scanned.

This may have an advantage, in cases where several cells have no correct entry, in making any information gained unconditional – as appears in the example given, at trial 3, where M is certainly placed. But if there are cells initially containing one correct object, certainty is not achieved. In the example, trial 2 gives one correct entry in cell 2, as had been the case with trial 1. Although on a probability basis it is likely that this is S, it is not certain, as the same information would have been given were P and Bk the correct objects for that cell. A system like this, or some of the other less definite forms observable in the records implies a surrender of information, reducing the chance of early success in an endeavour to reduce the memory load of the task. Records of eight subjects indicate similar non-acceptance of information in keeping with some form of system.

Loss of information is even more marked in the third 2(4) condition, though it is less easy to relate this to any systematic approach. Rather than producing a system, and acting on it, individuals seem to make a hypothesis as to which objects are correct, and to test this hypothesis, and modify it trial by trial. This involves reference back to earlier trials. In a few cases trials appear to be referred to the first trial only. An example:

			Trial consistent with trials
Trial 1	..	..	
,, 2	..	..	1
,, 3	..	..	1, 2
,, 4	..	..	1, 2, 3
,, 5	..	..	1, 2
,, 6	..	..	1, 2 (repetition trial 5)
,, 7	..	..	1, 2, 3
,, 8	..	..	1, 2, 7 (rep. of trials 5 and 6)

Trial 9	..	..	1, 3, 7
,, 10	..	..	1, 3, 7 (rep. trial 9)
,, 11	..	..	1, 2, 4, 5, 6, 8, 9, 10
,, 12	..	..	1, 2, 3, 7 (rep. of trial 4)
,, 13	..	..	1, 2, 4, 9, 10, 11, 12
,, 14	..	..	1, 2, 3, 5, 6, 8, 9, 10, 13
,, 15	..	..	1, 3, 4, 5, 6, 8, 11, 12, 13, 14
,, 16	..		Consistent with all

Every trial is consistent with the first trial. The second trial also has some effect. But every move was just another attempt at solving the problem as left at the end of trial 1. This can be seen from the repetitions of trials – particularly the two instances of immediate repetition. It is worth noting that, had the information been accepted, the problem would have been solved on the fifth trial. It is also worth noting that there are only 16 possible arrangements consistent with trial 1, and it is somewhat surprising, given this consistency with the first trial, that the solution was not reached earlier as a matter of chance.

Another method of attempted solution lay in referring trials back to their immediate predecessors, neglecting information obtained earlier. As an example:

Trial consistent with trials

Trial 1	..	..	
,, 2	..	..	1
,, 3	..	..	1, 2
,, 4	..	..	2
,, 5	..	..	1, 2
,, 6	..	..	2, 4, 5
,, 7	..	..	2, 5, 6
,, 8	..	..	1, 2, 4, 7
,, 9	..	..	6, 8
,, 10	..	..	2, 9 (repetition trial 4)
,, 11	..	..	2, 4, 5, 9, 10
,, 12	..	..	1, 3, 4, 5, 6, 9, 10, 11
,, 13	..	..	all

In this case, except for trials 4 and 5, all the trials are consistent with the trial immediately preceding, and several are consistent with the two immediately preceding trials, but on the whole information gained earlier than that is ignored. This procedure stands in contra-distinction to the example given immediately above, and yet there is one important feature in common. These individuals (like almost all of the subjects) either could not or would not act upon all the information. The difference lies in their selection of information.

In a few instances there were examples of assumptions made which were erroneous. Some of these cases bear striking resemblance to fixated behaviour more usually mentioned in connexion with experimental studies of conflict. As an example:

Correct order	..	..	Bk	R	M	P		G	Bo	W	S
Trial 1	..	..	*G*	R	*W*	P		*Bk*	Bo	*M*	S
„ 2	..	..	*Bo*	*S*	*W*	P		G	*R*	*Bk*	*M*
„ 3	..	..	*G*	R	*S*	P		*Bk*	Bo	W	*M*

At this stage the subject decided that G and R should be placed in the left hand cell. For the next eleven trials these two objects were taken up first and placed confidently on the left, the subject then studying the remaining six objects. After the fourteenth trial this broke down, and G was correctly transferred to the right hand cell. Repeatedly during the eleven trials information was presented which indicated that both G and R could not be on the left, but it was ignored.

If an analogy with another type of problem is possible, these three examples are like three different attempts at a jigsaw puzzle. The first is like taking one piece and trying the other pieces against it; the second like taking one piece and trying another against it, taking a third piece and trying it against the second, and so on; whereas the third example is rather like deciding that 'this brown piece must be part of the horse's head'.

Another interesting feature of the observations on this condition is that behaviour, with respect to the information of correct or incorrect does not correspond to the actual value of the information given. As the objects are to be placed in either of two cells, it follows that the information that an object is incorrectly placed is equal in value to the information that it is correctly placed – merely requiring the subject to reverse its position. Information that none of the objects are in their appropriate cells is complete information. Three subjects reached this position. Two failed to act upon the information, although a subsequent report from one subject implied that this was a memory failure rather than a failure to appreciate the value of the information. The third subject responded correctly, after a long pause, and with the observation 'Would I be naïve if I thought that if I reversed them they would all be right?'

Similarly, information that one object in each cell was correctly placed is equal in value to information that three objects are correctly placed in each cell. Both leave only sixteen possible arrangements, whereas the condition of two right in each cell leaves 36 arrangements. Behaviour was not consistent with this, however, for if we take survival times of information from trials with these 'success' scores we have:

1 correct each cell $\frac{1}{2}$ period of survival of information 0·72 trials
2 ,,   ,, ,, ,, ,, ,, ,, ,, ,,   1·09 ,,
3 ,,   ,, ,, ,, ,, ,, ,, ,, ,,   4·84 ,,

The phenomenal difficulty of the task after a one correct trial is thus much greater than after a three correct trial even though the stimulus difficulty is the same. This may mean that the value of 'correct' is increased over 'incorrect' by the emotional implications of the terms. Or it could merely be a carry over from more normal problem situations (as in the two other experimental conditions) where this equality of value in terms of stimulus difficulty does not hold. Or as a third possibility it could be that the subjects' set was towards the placing of four correct objects into a cell, rather than the placing of each object into one of the two cells, and that the complementary nature of the two cells, being one stage removed in the formulation of the problem, did not affect their behaviour.

The nature of trial and error problem solving

The nature of the trial-and-error problem has already been discussed, with its emphasis on the progressive reduction of number of possible modes of behaviour during the course of solution. Ideally, the aim of the solver – human, animal or mechanical – is to make this reduction as efficiently as possible. The experimental results indicate that the human subject, under some conditions, does not show mechanical efficiency. Some speculation is possible as to the nature of this distinction and its relation to efficiency in the psychological sense of use of the subject's own perceptual, memory and cognitive abilities. The number of objects used in these experiments was partly chosen because of its divisibility into the three experimental conditions, and also partly as it is about the normal maximum for immediate memory span for position. Twelve objects would have suited the experimental design, even more so than eight, but even trial-to-trial consistency would have been problematic, in the face of the immediate memory task involved. Even with eight objects it is doubtful whether the normal individual's ability to remember would, by itself, have enabled him to solve any of the problems. Thus memory aids, or a judgement of the important information to be remembered are a necessity. The most customary memory aid, notes on paper, was denied. The initial classification of objects, observed in all experimental conditions, and the systems such as scanning, in the first condition, are very good substitutes. The simple matching problem is so greatly reduced in phenomenal difficulty by them that it almost ceases to be a problem, and is certainly the easiest of the three. The memory load is reduced to immediate memory of correct and incorrect and direction of scanning for each trial only, without any necessity to carry information over longer periods by sheer memory. The two generalizations, of order and of movement together take up all the information and reduce it in its psychologically quantitative size to an amount easily coped with by the individual. The same essential feature is observed in the other conditions, only in these cases the reduction has to be made by the selection of information – after the initial memory aid of classification of objects. This selection takes place in different ways, mainly by selecting some of the objects and ignoring the others, or by selecting some of the trials and ignoring others, or by selecting some inferences from trials and ignoring others. In real life problem-solving situations, in addition to these methods of selection (which may be persistent behavioural characteristics of the individuals) there are usually preformed evaluations of the value of different pieces of information, evaluations carried over from previous experience or training, etc. This only differs in the experimental situation in that the experiment has an initial trial, which can be considered as effectively absent in the real life situation.

It could be paralleled experimentally, by the use of material in which there were inherent clues as to the correct position; by instructing the subjects that there was some sense in the arrangement not just a random allocation. Some earlier experiments showed that inherent clues produced a greater chance of early success, but if this were not attained they interfered with any later solution. These experiments were performed using the simple matching problem only (like the 8(1) condition); it would be of interest to see whether, in the more conditional cases the inherent clues took greater priority of attention.

It is tempting to speculate on the relation of intelligence to these describable aspects of problem solving. For a functional definition, intelligence is bound to be concerned with ability to solve problems but the working definitions on which most measurements of intelligence are based restrict it either to an appreciation of the formal structure of problems, or the ability to comprehend and manipulate all the information for a series of simple problems.

The choice of generalization, or the process of selection and rejection of information are very rarely demonstrated in intelligence tests, and yet it may be that these are far more important in the normal use of intelligence; the production of a tentative 'solution' to problems, the formal structure of which escapes comprehension.

The experiment described does not throw any light on this. Its design, balanced with respect to the three conditions, makes it difficult to compare subjects. In addition, the variation in chance success in the first trial, assumed to be balanced as far as conditions are concerned by using eighteen subjects and rotating the experimentally 'correct' orders between the conditions, is bound to lower any correlation of subject's performance between the three conditions. An experiment specifically aimed at this end is perfectly feasible. It would presumably require more subjects, and some standard system of constructing the 'correct' order from the subject's first trial devised. It ought then to be seen whether there was any correlation in performance, and perhaps more important, any persistence in the qualitative methods of solution adopted. The observations would have to be validated against an external criterion of degree of success in coping with real life problems, if anything of the nature of intelligence is to be associated with the performance.

Positive and Negative Information in Matching Problems

M. Donaldson, 'Positive and negative information in matching problems', *Brit. J. Psychol.*, vol. 50 (1959), pp. 235–62.

Introduction

In the study of problem solving it is possible, in certain circumstances, to calculate the formal value of a piece of information and compare this with the psychological value of the information for a given subject. It is also possible to equate, for formal value, information given positively and negatively, and then compare, for psychological value, these two different modes of communication. Much of the work on this topic has been done within the framework of the concept attainment problem.

Studies of the utilization of negative instances in concept learning have been made by Smoke (1933), Hovland and Weiss (1953) and Bruner *et al.* (1956). Smoke found no significant difference between the time required for learning from positive instances and that required for learning from a combination of positive and negative instances; but, as Hovland and Weiss point out, Smoke does not say what information was provided by his negative instances and so no measure of formal as opposed to psychological information value can be obtained from his data. This defect is remedied in the other two studies, both of which provide evidence that positive information is more efficiently utilized in concept attainment than is negative information.

Hovland and Weiss express the view that a major remaining research task is that of determining the factors responsible for this finding and suggest that perceptual factors must play some part since: 'Positive instances have the required characteristics directly perceptible. Negative instances, on the other hand, do not have the correct combination of characters in direct view.' This suggestion emphasizes an important feature of the concept attainment problem, namely, that the characters are normally presented to the subject in all possible combinations and the information consists in telling the subject whether each combination, as it appears in visible association before him, is a positive or a negative instance of the concept. But there is a situation which, from the point of

211

view of logical structure, resembles the concept attainment one, and yet differs from it in this respect: that the characters are originally presented in complete dissociation from one another (if indeed they are presented non-verbally at all) and the information consists in instructions to the subject to link them or keep them apart in various ways. This occurs in any matching problem. Evidence of unequal difficulty in the handling of positive and negative information in matching problems will then be relevant to the Hovland and Weiss hypothesis concerning the role of perceptual association; and evidence is provided by a matching problem experiment of Whitfield's (1951) that negative and positive information which is formally of the same value is not always recognized as equally useful even by subjects of superior intelligence – this, too, in a simple binary situation. It therefore appears that an explanation other than that of directly given perceptual association must be looked for.

Bruner *et al.*, in their discussion of the use of negative information in concept attainment, make no mention of perceptual links but emphasize, rather, that negative information must usually be transformed into positive information. They speak of the 'inability or unwillingness' of their subjects to use negative information and suggest that information resulting from 'in-the-head' transformation may be distrusted, perhaps because of awareness of the risk of error.

It appeared that some further evidence bearing on these issues might be obtained by a study of matching rather than of concept attainment and, specifically, by having the subjects construct, rather than solve, a matching problem. The construction of a problem calls for an explicit consideration of structural characteristics to a degree not generally necessary in the solution of the problem. It thus provides admirable opportunity for subjects to display their awareness of formal equivalence. (It may also provide them with an opportunity to develop their awareness by obliging them to render explicit that knowledge of structure which often appears to remain implicit in ordinary problem solving. Bartlett and Piaget have both, in recent years, emphasized the importance of awareness of structural characteristics, but the word 'awareness' is ambiguous and Piaget stresses the fact that the subject, in one sense, generally does not know what he is doing. The construction of a problem as opposed to the solving of it may prove to be an excellent way of helping him discover what he is doing and may thus have educational significance, as some teachers realize. It may also be a valuable means of tackling what Bruner *et al.* (1956)

describe as 'the great technical problem' in the study of thinking: namely, the externalizing of linked sequences of behaviour for purposes of observing them.) Further, it is possible to impose conditions which make certain ways of proceeding preferable to others, within the context of the task. In the present instance, the advantage of this is that the task can be set in such a way as to place high value on the use of negative information and so give the subject good cause to prefer it to its positive counterpart if he understands the formal equivalence of the two. Suppose n objects $(a, b, \ldots, n)$ to be matched one to one with n other objects $(a', b', \ldots, n')$. Then information necessary for this matching may be given in one of the following ways. (The possibility of using disjunctive information is omitted from consideration.) (i) $n-1$ positive statements, associating a with a', b with b' and so on (information concerning the final association, n to n', being, of course, redundant, since n and n' will be the only objects remaining). (ii) $n-2$ positive statements, associating a with a', etc., and 1 negative statement, dissociating $n-1$ from n' or $(n-1)'$ from n. (iii) $n-3$ positive statements and 3 [2+1] negative statements, which latter may be given in a variety of ways so long as two of them combine to rule out one pairing and the third rules out another. Thus the three negatives dissociating $n-1$ from n', $n-2$ from n' and $n-2$ from $(n-1)'$ would be adequate for this purpose; but the three negatives dissociating $n-1$ from n', $n-2$ from $(n-1)'$ and n from $(n-2)'$ would not. (The three negatives which are adequate will be described as being in strong combination; the three which are not will be said to be in weak combination.) (iv) $n-4$ positive statements and 6 [3+2+1] negative statements in strong combination. And so on, until the following extreme is reached. (v) $n-n$ positive statements (i.e., none) and

$$[(n-1)+(n-2)+ \ldots 1]$$

negative statements in strong combination.

This being so, if each positive piece of information is valued at n points and each negative piece at 1 point, then the total 'score' for an all-negative construction (see (v) above) will be lower than that for any construction containing positives, and subjects can be told of this scoring system and instructed to achieve the lowest possible score.

It can be demonstrated that, with negatives valued at 1 point, n points is the least whole number weighting for positives which makes the all-negative construction the most 'economical'. For, as we have seen, the all-negative model contains

$$[(n-1)+(n-2)+(n-3)+\ldots 1]$$

negatives. Now for each positive that is introduced, the first term of the negatives is omitted: that is, the introduction of 1 positive makes it possible to dispense with $n-1$ negatives; the introduction of a second positive makes it possible to dispense with a further $n-2$ negatives; and so on. If, then, an all-negative construction is to be the most economical, the weighting of the positives must be greater than the greatest number of negatives which a positive can ever replace, namely $n-1$. That is to say, the weighting of the positives must be n.

In the problem used in this inquiry, $n=5$. Each positive was therefore valued at 5 points and the possible ways of providing information were 5 in number, containing 4, 3, 2, 1 and 0 positives respectively. These different possible constructions will be referred to as the $(4, \bar{0})$, $(3, \bar{1})$, $(2, \bar{3})$, $(1, \bar{6})$ and $(0, \overline{10})$ models.

Procedure

In the first inquiry, nineteen subjects, aged 14 years to 14 years 6 months, took part. All of them had I.Q.s within the range 112–18 on each of two Moray House group intelligence tests which had been administered two and three years previously. They had all been taking part in a more extensive investigation which had involved the solution of a matching problem similar to that which they were now to construct. In this earlier problem, information was provided on the $(1, \bar{6})$ model. It must, therefore, be recognized that a set towards this model may have resulted and no reliance can be placed on the evidence of the frequency of its occurrence in this inquiry. However, the subjects' previous work with a matching problem was considered advantageous in so far as it reduced the likelihood of confusions arising merely from a failure to understand what was required. The job of explaining to the subjects what they were to attempt in the problem-construction task was certainly made much easier by this circumstance. The actual wording of the instructions was as follows. (They were read aloud to the child and then the typed sheet was given him to consult.)

Problem A

Do you remember the question about the five boys and the five schools? This time I want you to make up a problem like that instead of solving it. I'll tell you what the answer is to be and you are to tell me what

214

information would have to be given to the children who are to solve the problem. We'll call the boys by their initials. Let's say their names are Arthur, Bob, Charles, Dick and Edward. And we'll just call the schools 1, 2, 3, 4 and 5.

Now here is the answer:

$$\begin{array}{ccccc} A & B & C & D & E \\ 4 & 2 & 1 & 3 & 5 \end{array}$$

That is, Arthur goes to school number 4, and so on.

Now you can give information in two ways. Either you can say something like 'Arthur goes to school 4' (which we can write as $A = 4$, for short), or you can say something like 'Arthur does not go to school 2' which we can write as $A \neq 2$, for short). Pieces of information like $A = 4$ we'll call *positive*. Pieces of information like $A \neq 2$ we'll call *negative*. Every positive piece of information that you give will cost 5 points; every negative piece will cost 1 point. You have to try to give enough information for some one who does not know the answer to be able to find it out, and you have to try to do it in such a way as to make the lowest possible score.

When the subjects had made their attempts at construction, they were given a second task which was as follows.

Problem B

$$\begin{array}{cc} A & B \end{array}$$

| × × × × | × × × × |

Here are two boxes labelled A and B. The crosses in the boxes stand for the numbers 1–8. You are to find out which numbers are in A and which are in B, but you do not have to worry about the way in which the numbers are arranged inside the boxes – that is, if you discover that 3 is in A you do not have to go on to ask whether it is the second cross or the third one or so on.

You will ask me for the pieces of information you think you will need. You may ask me either for a piece of *positive* information or for a piece of *negative* information; and you may tell me whether you want it to be about box A or about box B. If you ask me for a piece of positive information about box A I shall give it to you in the form:

'One of the ×'s in A is 5' – or whatever it may be.

If you ask for negative information about A I shall tell you:

'None of the ×'s in A is 7' – or whatever it may be.

Now each positive piece of information will cost you 2 points, each negative piece 1 point. You are to try to find the answer making the lowest possible score.

This second problem was suggested by Whitfield's paper (1951) and was introduced as a further check on awareness of the equivalence of positives and negatives. The order of presentation of problems A and B was not varied because it was considered that the number of subjects was too small for any valuable estimate of the effects of differing order to be obtained and that with a group of this size there was more to gain by keeping the conditions of administration constant for all subjects.

Subjects were tested individually and a record was made of all in their comments and explanations. They were encouraged to make full use of pencil and paper in working out and checking their constructions, and they were allowed to continue with each problem until they declared themselves satisfied that they had made the lowest possible score. They spent, on the average, 32 minutes on the first problem and 8 minutes on the second one.

In the second inquiry the subjects were ninety women students in their third year at a Scottish teachers' training college. They were tested as a group with problem A, worded in more general terms and without reference to earlier experience of matching problems, which these subjects had not been given. The time allowed was 25 minutes. Problem B was not administered. It could not be given as a group test without radical alteration.

Results

(a) First inquiry – problem A

Fourteen subjects were able finally to provide information on the $(0, \overline{10})$ model. No one, however, achieved this at the first attempt. The average number of attempts for all the subjects was 3·4 with a range of from 2 to 8.

Table 1

First Construction Attempts

Col. 1		Col. 2		Col. 3		Col. 4		Col. 5		Col. 6 Total
Model	f	Model	f	Model	f	Model	f	Model	f	f
4, $\overline{0}$	—	—	—	—	—	—	—	—	—	—
3, $\overline{1}$	1	3, $\overline{2}$	1	—	—	—	—	—	—	2
2, $\overline{3}$	2	2, $\overline{4}$	1	2, $\overline{5}$	2	—	—	—	—	5
1, $\overline{6}$	4	1, $\overline{7}$	1	1, $\overline{8}$	1	1, $\overline{9}$	2	1, $\overline{10}$	1	9
0, $\overline{10}$	—	0, $\overline{11}$	1	0, $\overline{16}$	1	0, $\overline{18}$	1	—	—	3

Table 1 shows the construction made by each subject on his first attempt. Models in column 1 are the formally correct variants described in the introduction, though, of course, only $(0, \overline{10})$ is 'correct' in terms of the special conditions imposed. In all the other columns, the models contain redundant information. The models are arranged by rows according to the number of positives in decreasing order from top to bottom of the table, and by columns according to the number of negatives in increasing order from left to right of the table. Thus, the top left corner contains models with most positives and the bottom right corner contains models with most negatives. The cross-totals of frequencies (col. 6) indicate how often 4, 3, 2, 1 and 0 positives respectively were used. Three subjects (models $(1, \overline{7})$, $(2, \overline{4})$ and $(2, \overline{5})$ in columns 2 and 3 of Table 1) began by trying to use only negatives but could not keep this up and introduced positives in the course of their first attempt. No one tried to start by giving four pieces of positive information. All must, therefore, presumably have appreciated in some manner that the use of negatives was advantageous.

The four who began with model $(1, \overline{6})$ proved to be the best subjects. All proceeded to model $(0, \overline{10})$ at the second attempt and made no errors at all, unless their initial inclusion of one positive be termed 'error'. It has already been pointed out that, since the subjects had all had practice in solving a problem constructed on model $(1, \overline{6})$, a set towards it might be anticipated. This would not, however, seem to explain why the four who began in this way all moved very rapidly on to successful completion of the task. What is probable is that some at least of the nine subjects who began by using one positive (see Table 1, fourth row) were influenced by the problem they had solved previously but that only these four were capable of avoiding redundancy from the start. Perfect recollection of the $(1, \overline{6})$ model in the absence of good understanding would seem highly improbable, especially as the names used were changed.

Analysis of the construction attempts showed that there were three main errors.

(i) *Positive/negative redundancy.* – This amounts to failure to realize that a positive statement linking two characters makes any negative statement involving either character superfluous. Thus, if $C=1$, it follows without further statement that $C \neq 2$, that $D \neq 1$, etc. Six children made the error of providing such superfluous negatives.

(ii) *Negative/negative redundancy.* – Logically this is barely distinguishable from positive/negative redundancy, since it is only when negatives combine to equal a positive statement that further negatives can be called redundant. Thus, logically, if positive/negative redundancy is understood and avoided one

217

would expect the same to be true of negative/negative redundancy. But this was not found to be the case. Thirteen subjects made errors of negative/negative redundancy, as compared with six in the positive/negative category (four of these being however in both categories), and there was evidence that psychologically the two were not equivalent. Here is an example of negative/negative redundancy associated with explicit awareness of the need to avoid positive/negative redundancy. Words spoken by the experimenter are in brackets.

S. 7. *A* doesn't go to 2. . . . *A* doesn't go to 3. . . . *B*. . . . I am trying to work out whether it would be best to say that *B* goes to 2 or that he doesn't go to any one. (How could you do that?) – Pause – Could I score out '*A* doesn't go to 2' and put '*B* goes to 2'? (Yes. Why did you score that out?) Well, as it is only one boy that goes to a school and you're saying that *B* goes to 2, to say that *A* doesn't go to 2 would be a waste of a point.

Thus this subject shows clearly that he understands positive/negative redundancy. But a little later he goes on:

Well, I see one way to do it but I don't know that it's the lowest of them. You could say *A* doesn't go to 2, 1, 3 or 5, but you would have twenty points. (Why?) Well, as there is one point for every negative you do you would have four points for every letter and there are five letters.

The subject gives the twenty negatives accordingly, but then says he knows this is not the lowest possible score and proposes to reduce it as follows:

Well, you could try saying *A* goes to 4 and you could take away the 4 from *B*, *C*, *D* and *E*.

That is, he proposes to reintroduce a positive so as to be able to reduce the negatives. He shows no awareness that his first four negatives are exactly equivalent to a positive in respect of making such a reduction possible. It is true that, at his last attempt (he needs six in all), he says he 'has a theory that brings it down to 10' and is then able to explain that 'if you have four negatives for the first one you only need three and then two and then one'.

There was no example of awareness of the risk of negative/negative redundancy associated with lack of awareness of the positive/negative variety. The two cases of positive/negative redundancy in the protocols of children who did not make negative/negative redundancy errors arose when difficulty in bringing negatives into strong combination (see (iii) below) had led subjects to the introduction of a positive towards the end of a construction attempt. This positive then rendered earlier negatives redundant and the fact was not noticed by the subjects.

(*iii*) *Use of negatives in weak combination.* – Some of the children showed themselves unable to decide effectively which negative statements would be of most value. For instance:

S. 9. *A* does not go to 2, 1 or 3 and that leaves 4 or 5. And *C* does not go to 4. And *B* does not go to 5. That has told all the ones they don't go to. . . .

or again:

S. 5. Bob does not go to 1 or 3. Arthur does not go to 2 or 5. Charles does not go. . . . Bob must go to 2, 4 or 5. Arthur must go to 1, 3, or 4. Charles not to 4 or 5. It's not really telling you anything! So Arthur not to 5 and Charles not go to . . .1, 4 or 2. So Dick to either 5 or 3. And Bob . . . I'm getting myself tied up now. (Are you trying to do it all with negatives?) Yes.

This subject is finally able to produce a solution with one positive and ten negatives, that is, with four superfluous negatives.

Errors of this kind were made by seven children.

Six children made a direct statement at one point or another to the effect that, in their opinion, at least one piece of positive information would have to be given; and there seemed to be a very general expectation that 'to do it all with negatives' would be costly because so many would be required.

Here is an example.

S. 11. I think you would have to say one of the schools one of the boys goes to . . . because if you gave it in negatives I think it would add up to more than five points. (What makes you think that?) Well, you have to give at least four negatives to make one positive, and if you have the positive I think it makes. . . . If you are giving a reason and you have a positive you don't always have to say the three letters because the three letters or the four letters do not go.

This is certainly not very coherent but the 'at least' is revealing: it should, of course, be 'at most'. It looks, again, as if the subject realizes that a positive can make certain other information superfluous ('you don't always have to say the three letters') but does not recognize that a combination of negatives can do so equally effectively. She seems to be trying to explain that the value of one positive in terms of the knowledge it gives is greater than the value of four negatives. Thus the four negatives 'make' the positive in one sense but do not fully equal it in function.

(b) First inquiry – problem B

Thirteen subjects finally made the lowest possible score by asking for four negative pieces of information relating to the same box. Among the six who failed to do so were four of the five subjects who failed with problem A.

The number of attempts necessary was much less than for problem A. Ten subjects took only one attempt, though among these were four who failed. (It will be recalled that the experiment stopped when the subject said he was sure he had the lowest possible score.) Eight subjects took two attempts and one took three attempts.

In each attempt, it was possible for the subject either to ask for information about one box only or about both boxes; and to ask for negative information or for a mixture of positive and negative information. (Theoretically he could of course also have asked only for positive information but this did not occur.) From Table 2, which shows the numbers in these categories on the first attempt,

Table 2

	One box	Two boxes
Negative only	6	8
Positive and negative	0	5

it will be seen that fourteen of the nineteen subjects have been able to recognize at once, in this situation, the possibility of dispensing with positive information. Only six, however, began by confining their attention to one box alone. The most common tendency was to ask for information about *A* and about *B* in fairly strict alternation.

A number of children tried to look for a principle of distribution: for instance, that all the odd numbers were in *A* and all the even ones in *B*. When this became evident, the subject was at once told that there was no rule to be discovered.

(c) Second inquiry – problem A

Of the ninety subjects who took part in the second inquiry: (i) fifty-six provided information adequate for solution and free of redundancy, and of these forty-nine did so using the $(0, \overline{10})$ model, while four used the $(1, \overline{6})$, two the $(2,\overline{3})$ and one the $(3, \overline{1})$ model; (ii) twenty gave more information than necessary; (iii) seven gave less than necessary but considered they had given enough; and (iv) seven papers were unfinished.

Among the twenty-seven finished papers where information was either redundant or inadequate – (ii) and (iii) above – there were twenty-three instances of negative/negative redundancy, three of positive/negative redundancy and one of negatives in weak combination. (Notice that the fact of giving less information than is necessary for solution in no way rules out the possibility of giving redundant information: in what information *is* provided there may be duplication.)

Scrutiny of the fifty-six papers in (i) above showed that, in many cases, earlier attempts had been written down. Some of these had obviously been abandoned mid-way and sometimes two or three attempts had been scored out in such a way that it was hard to tell where one ended and the other began. Thus, no exact count of errors in these earlier attempts could be made; but it seemed that, on the whole, the proportion of positive/negative to negative/negative redundancy obtained by analysis of the twenty-seven papers in groups (ii) and (iii) above was maintained.

Discussion and Conclusion

The finding that logically equivalent positive and negative information is not always psychologically equivalent is confirmed in this inquiry. It is confirmed with particular force by virtue of the fact that the problem situations were not neutral with respect to positives and negatives. Rather the conditions of the tasks were such as to give the negatives privileged status and encourage the subjects to work with them. Evidence of 'inability or unwillingness' to do so is, then, in these circumstances, all the more strong.

There is some unambiguous evidence of inability, as opposed to unwillingness. This is to be found in the fact that three subjects began by trying to produce an all-negative construction for problem A, found themselves in difficulties and introduced positives to simplify their task. It is certainly true that the use of negatives calls for an appreciation of the structure of a matching problem in a way that the use of positives does not. Lack of this appreciation shows itself in the failure to bring negatives successfully into strong combination and, when this happens, resort to positives is only to be expected. But this sort of difficulty with the structure of the problem cannot account for all the evidence of lack of equivalence between positive and negative information. In particular, it cannot explain the evidence that positive/negative and negative/negative redundancy are psychologically distinct – evidence obtained both from the individual studies (see S.7 and S. 11) and from the group inquiry which showed that, with older subjects, one of these errors

221

had largely disappeared while the other continued to be extremely prevalent and, indeed, to be the only common source of trouble remaining, since the difficulty of understanding how to bring negatives into strong combination had also diminished to vanishing point.

How, then, are we to interpret the fact that it is possible to understand quite well the way in which negatives can 'add up' to 'equal' a positive, yet not see that to provide negative information which duplicates this derived positive is to introduce redundancy as surely as if one provides negative information which duplicates a directly stated positive?

The suggestion made by Bruner *et al.* (1956) that the need for 'in-the-head' transformation explains the peculiar difficulty of negatives will not serve for this purpose. In the matching problem construction task, repeated transformation in both directions was called for. What we have to explain is the fact that one particular sequence of transformations – from negative to positive and back again – is especially difficult, a 'block' of some kind occurring commonly after the first transformation has been made. Nothing of the kind was ever observed to occur when the opposite sequence – from positive to negative and back to positive – was in question. No subject showed any sign of regarding negative information that had been derived from positive information as in any way different in status or usefulness from directly given negative information. The possibilities for transforming positives into negatives were not always fully exploited – witness the occurrence of positive/negative redundancy – but once this transformation had been carried out there was no suggestion that the derived negatives could not be further utilized.

There appear to be two possible explanations of failure to use the derived positive. One is that negative information is in some way distrusted. However, the distrust would not, in this case, seem to stem from awareness of the risk of error in the course of transformation, as Bruner *et al.* suggested it might do, but rather from a less rational feeling that negative information is not such good currency as positive information and that complicated and far-reaching transactions cannot safely be made with it. There is, indeed, occasional evidence in the protocols that negative information is distrusted even when no transformation is involved. For instance, S. 2 comments '*E* doesn't go to 4 and *A* does, so *E* can't be 4'. Here a directly given negative is reinforced by a positive before it is accepted as quite conclusive.

Another possibility, however, which must not be overlooked in considering the limited transformability of negatives is that this particular manifestation of lack of equivalence is to be explained by reference to the attitude of the subjects to positive information. It may be due, in part, to a feeling of finality attaching to positive statements and deriving from the knowledge that positive matchings are the ultimate end of the endeavour. What may be lacking is the ability to see them as ends in themselves and yet at the same time as means to further ends within the framework of the problem.

The results of problem B are, on the whole, easier to interpret than those of problem A. As Table 2 shows, most of the subjects were able to recognize at once the formal equivalence of positive and negative information in this simpler situation. But it should, of course, be noted that they had all just previously tried to solve problem A. That even after this experience five subjects still included positives – and one of them went so far as to state explicitly that at least one positive was absolutely necessary for the solution of B—is quite impressive evidence of unwillingness to rely on negatives alone. In this case, it does seem appropriate to talk of unwillingness rather than inability, because no subject in problem B relied entirely on positives and, in this problem, to understand how one piece of negative information can be used to assign a number positively to the other box might be said to be evidence of 'ability' to assign all numbers in this way. The insistence on retaining one positive appears, then, as a security measure rather than a failure of understanding.

The greatest source of difficulty in problem B lay in understanding the importance of asking for information about one box only. This, of course, can be regarded as yet another instance of difficulty with negatives – or at least with indirect information – since it depends on failure to realize that to know the complete contents of one box is to know where the remaining numbers are not located, which, in this binary situation, is to know where they are located – that is, to know the complete contents of both boxes.

It should be noticed that the tendency for subjects to ask about boxes *A* and *B* in systematic rotation was less likely to lead to rapid success than a more haphazard procedure whereby there was a chance that all spaces in one or other box would be allotted before seven pieces of information had been obtained. When this happened, the subject generally realized that he had all the information he needed, and this realization, coming when more than one of the eight spaces remained unfilled, seemed to facilitate the understanding that only four pieces of information were necessary.

The tendency to look for a rule or principle was probably an obstacle in the way of this crucial understanding, for the subject who had a hypothesis presumably based his decisions about which box to choose on irrelevant considerations relating to the testing of the hypothesis. 'Looking for a rule' in this situation perhaps exemplifies a general tendency observed by Bruner *et al.*: the tendency for subjects to feel that they must, on pain of failure, try to anticipate trends, rather than wait for what the data reveal.

References

BRUNER, J. S., GOODNOW, J. J., and AUSTIN, G. A. (1956), *A study of thinking*, Wiley.

HOVLAND, C. I., and WEISS, W. (1953), 'Transmission of information concerning concepts through positive and negative instances', *J. exp. Psychol.*, vol. 45, pp. 175–82.

SMOKE, K. L. (1933), 'Negative instances in concept learning', *J. exp. Psychol.*, vol. 16, pp. 583–8.

WHITFIELD, J. W. (1951), 'An experiment in problem solving', *Quart. J. exp. Psychol.*, vol. 3, pp. 184–97.

18 A. C. Campbell

On the Solving of Code Items Demanding the Use of Indirect Procedures

A. C. Campbell, 'On the solving of code items demanding the use of indirect procedures', *Brit. J. Psychol.*, vol. 56 (1965), pp. 45–51.

Subjects in categorization (concept attainment) experiments markedly prefer direct to indirect tests of the hypotheses they propose (Bruner, Goodnow and Austin, 1956). An hypothesis is proved indirectly through elimination of all rival possibilities. Consider a subject who, faced with two mutually exclusive alternatives X and Y, assumes that alternative X leads to the desired goal. The direct test of this hypothesis is to try X. The indirect test of the hypothesis is to try Y and, according as Y does or does not lead to the goal, to draw an inference as to the tenability of the original hypothesis about X. The preference of subjects for direct tests is found to persist even in circumstances where, unlike the instance just cited, indirect procedures would be more appropriate, economical and efficient. Bruner *et al.* suggest that avoidance of indirect procedures may stem from an appreciation that errors are liable to be made during the 'in the head' transformations of data that indirect procedures entail. They further suggest that avoidance of indirect procedures may well be general to a variety of cognitive activities, and not confined just to categorization. Whether subjects are unable competently to cope with indirect procedures, or merely unwilling to attempt their use when direct – although extremely laborious and inefficient – alternative procedures are available is left an open question.

Relevant to these issues is a study by Donaldson (1959). Subjects were asked to construct a set of statements which, taken together, would give sufficient information for five objects (A, B, C, D, E) to be matched one to one with five other objects (a, b, c, d, e). A positive statement such as 'A goes with a' ($A=a$, for short) scored 5 points. A negative statement such as 'A does not go with b' ($A \neq b$) scored only 1 point. Subjects had to try to make as low a score as possible, which means that negative statements had 'privileged status'. The most economical solution consisted of $[(n-1)+(n-2)+(n-3)+\ldots+1]$ negative statements which, for $n=5$, works out at 10 negatives. For example:

(1) $A \neq b$ (5) $B \neq c$ (8) $C \neq d$ (10) $D \neq e$
(2) $A \neq c$ (6) $B \neq d$ (9) $C \neq e$
(3) $A \neq d$ (7) $B \neq e$
(4) $A \neq e$

An optimal solution implies the derivation of positive statements from given sets of negative ones. Thus statements (1)–(4) lead to the derived positive statement $A = a$. From this derived positive statement can be further derived the negative statement $B \neq a$. This, in conjunction with statements (5)–(7), leads to a second derived positive statement $B = b$, etc. This sort of transformation sequence occasioned much difficulty for school children and college students alike. Some sort of 'block' typically occurred after the derivation of the first positive statement ($A = a$). Donaldson suggests that perhaps so strong a feeling of finality attaches to positive statements that subjects fail to see them as means to further ends within the framework of the problem. Positive matchings are after all the ultimate end of the endeavour. A second possibility is that negative information is, in a somewhat irrational way, distrusted as a foundation for transactions that are at all far-reaching.

With solutions of less than optimum economy, containing one or more positive statements, there is scope for transformations in the direction opposite to that considered above, i.e., from a given set of positive statements may be derived negative statements which, in turn, lead to further positives. Take the solution:

(1) $A = a$ (2) $B = b$ (3) $C \neq d$ (4) $C \neq e$ (5) $D \neq e$

From the positive statements (1) and (2) may be derived the negative statements $C \neq a$ and $C \neq b$. These, in conjunction with statements (3) and (4), enable the derivation of the positive statement $C = c$. This sort of transformation sequence occasioned no undue difficulty. The suggestion of Bruner *et al.* that avoidance of indirect procedures stems from awareness of the risk of error in the course of transforming data is accordingly rejected. There is risk of error in all transformations, yet subjects displayed ineptitude only with transformations involving the development of positive statements derived, at an earlier stage, from given sets of negative statements. Only three subjects attempted an all-negative solution straight off. All three encountered difficulty and introduced positives despite their high 'cost'. Donaldson takes this as unambiguous evidence of inability (as opposed to unwillingness) to take full advantage of the transformation possibilities of negative information and hence competently to handle indirect procedures. But fourteen of the nineteen school children and forty-nine of the ninety college students did win through to an all-negative solution in the end, which renders an unqualified 'inability' interpretation untenable. Rather would it seem that subjects are unable competently to handle indirect procedures straight off, but many develop the ability to do so with a little practice.

Experiments with Compound Code Items

The experiments reported here follow from those of Bruner *et al.* and Donaldson. They seek to determine (*a*) whether difficulty with and avoidance of indirect procedures extend to the solving of compound code items. If so, (*b*) what is the locus of the difficulty? And (*c*) is it inability to cope therewith, or unwillingness to make the attempt, that leads to the avoidance?

Test Materials

The code items consist of five 5-letter words listed across the page, with coded versions listed vertically, in a different order, underneath. The code is arbitrary (i.e., not based on any rule of alphabetical sequence) and solution is dependent on structural rather than semantic features of the words. The coded words are incomplete, but contain sufficient letters for the attainment of a unique and unequivocal solution. For example:

(1) FOLKS	(2) TABLE	(3) DRIFT	(4) LIBEL	(5) STEAK
–	–	– C	–	( )
–	–	–	–	( )
Q	–	–	–	( )
C	– Q	– U		( )
U	–	–	–	( )

Item (*i*)

C occurs in first and fourth positions, and could stand for F (the first coded word representing DRIFT and the fourth FOLKS) or for L (the first coded word representing TABLE and the fourth LIBEL). Q occupies first and third positions, and can only stand for L. Hence the third coded word is LIBEL and the fourth FOLKS (and the first therefore DRIFT). Since $C - Q - U$ is FOLKS, U stands for S. The fifth coded word has a U in first position and so must represent a word beginning with S. Of the two words as yet unidentified only STEAK meets this requirement. The fifth coded word is therefore STEAK and the coded word for which no letters are given must, by default, be TABLE.

Ten items similar to Item (i) constitute Test A. Ten further items having the same sets of words but with a slightly different choice and distribution of coded letters constitute Test B. Item (i) for example becomes:

(1) FOLKS	(2) TABLE	(3) DRIFT	(4) LIBEL	(5) STEAK
–	–	–	C	– ( )
–	–	X	–	– ( )
Q	–	–	J	– ( )
C	–	Q	–	– ( )
–	–	–	–	– ( )

Item (ii)

A single X and a single J replace the pair of U's from Item (i).

FOLKS, LIBEL and DRIFT are identified exactly as before, but STEAK and TABLE can no longer be identified by matching up pairs of coded letters against pairs of letters occurring in the same ordinal positions in the uncoded words since no appropriate letter-pairs are given. Turning to the single letters, since $Q--J-$ is LIBEL therefore J stands for E. What X stands for is not known. If the coded counterparts of STEAK and TABLE are to be identified by other than arbitrary allocation this can, in terms of the letters given, only be accomplished indirectly. X, as well as being a positive instance of a class of letters unknown, is also a negative instance of the class of E's. From the positive statement 'J stands for E' ($J=E$) can be derived the negative statement 'X does not stand for E' ($X \neq E$). The latter may alternatively be expressed in positive form as 'X stands for *not-E*' ($X = \bar{E}$). The fact that the second coded word has an X in third position can now be interpreted to mean that it represents a word that does not have an E in third position. This eliminates STEAK. Hence the second coded word is TABLE and the fifth STEAK, rather than vice versa. This final stage of the solution sequence is indirect in the sense in which Bruner *et al.* use the word: it involves elimination of all (here only one) alternative possibilities by showing them *not* to be the case. In addition, the elimination is achieved via transformations of data akin to those discussed by Donaldson.

The first five items of Test B are similar to Item (ii) above. Each of the remaining five items has only *one* letter-pair among the coded letters. In illustration, Item (ii) could be restructured as follows:

(1) FOLKS	(2) TABLE	(3) DRIFT	(4) LIBEL	(5) STEAK
–	–	–	C	J	( )
–	–	X	–	–	( )
Q	–	–	–	–	( )
C	–	–	Z	–	( )
U	–	M	–	–	( )

Item (iii)

Solution of Item (iii) is far less direct than for Items (i) and (ii). There is a greater demand for elimination of alternative possibilities, and this entails much manipulation and transformation of data. That no item in Test B is soluble without some use of indirect procedures is in contrast with the tasks used by Bruner *et al.* and Donaldson. In their tasks direct procedures could always be used, albeit at high cost or the expenditure of excessive effort. Success via the use of direct procedures only is precluded for Test B items; the only alternative to the use of indirect procedures is arbitrary allocation.

Procedure and results

Experiment 1. – Seventy-nine first-year psychology students at the University of Edinburgh were assigned at random to two groups. One group ($N=39$) did Test A; the other group ($N=40$) Test B. A 20 min. time limit was imposed. Both tests were prefaced by two sample items, neither of which demands any indirect procedure. (If sample items involving indirect procedures had been given straight off, and Test B not found unduly difficult, it would remain a matter of speculation whether such difficulty might have been found had sample items involving indirect procedures not been given, i.e., had subjects not been acquainted with the appropriate solution procedures and instructed in their use.) Results appear in Table 1. The difference between groups is significant at beyond the 1 per cent level for number of whole items correct. (All P values cited come from Mann-Whitney U-tests.) The other differences, although they fail to reach the 5 per cent level of significance, are all in the direction indicating inferior performance on Test B as regards both speed (number of words attempted) and accuracy (error ratios). That Test B, whose items call for the utilization of indirect procedures, is found more difficult than Test A (in which no such demand is made) indicates that many subjects are not able *spontaneously* to apply indirect procedures to the solving of compound code items. Experiment 2 seeks to determine whether this is due to some difficulty inherent in the indirect procedures themselves, or merely because the subjects lacked acquaintance with and knowledge of the appropriate procedures.

Table 1

Means, Ranges and Error Ratios for Tests A and B in Experiment 1

	Test A ($N = 39$)		Test B $N = 40$)	
	Mean	Range	Mean	Range
Single words correct (maximum 50)	18·3	0–50	12·9	0–32
Whole items correct (maximum 10)	3·4	0–10	1·9	0–6
Words attempted	19·6	0–50	15·9	0–35
Error ratio (percentage of words incorrect)	52/764=6·8%		120/636=18·9%	

Table 2

Means, Ranges and Error Ratios for Tests A and B in Experiment 2

	Test A ($N = 19$)		Test B ($N=20$)	
	Mean	Range	Mean	Range
Single words correct (maximum 50)	19·6	0–50	12·8	0–30
Whole items correct (maximum 10)	3·8	0–8	2·1	0–6
Words attempted	21·6	10–42	16·4	5–32
Error ratio	39/411 = 9·5%		73/328 = 22·3%	

Experiment 2. – Thirty-nine first-year students were assigned at random to two groups: nineteen did Test A; twenty Test B. Test B was this time prefaced by an additional sample item whose solution is partially indirect. The solution of this item was gone through *in detail*, and every effort was made to ensure that the data transformations involved were fully understood by the subjects doing Test B. Conditions were otherwise exactly as for Experiment 1. Results appear in Table 2. Performance on Test B is again inferior to that on Test A, P values being significant beyond the 5 per cent level both for number of words and number of whole items correct. The difference in difficulty between Tests A and B is just as pronounced as in Experiment 1, if not more so. Certainly it has not been reduced by the provision of instruction in the use of indirect procedures. (Compare the finding of Bruner *et al.*

that despite detailed explanation of the nature of disjunctive concepts subjects persist in making choices and using information in ways specifically unsuited for disjunction.) It could be objected that a single sample item involving indirect procedures is scarcely sufficient to acquaint a subject therewith but, even allowing this objection, there would still seem to be difficulty associated with or inherent in the indirect procedures themselves.

Discussion

Experiments 1 and 2 have shown that lack of facility in the use of indirect procedures does extend to the solving of compound code items. And since on Test B one must either use indirect procedures or fail (apart from chance successes), the high failure rate is strongly suggestive of inability on the part of the subjects who failed. The possibility does, however, remain that failure was preferred to the labour that indirect procedures entail. As Bartlett points out (1958, p. 84), subjects sometimes convey the impression that they cannot do anything with a problem when all that this really means is that they are not sufficiently interested to go to the trouble of working out what to do with it.

That the difficulty of the Test B items *is due* to their involving indirect procedures can be seen by comparing the error patterns for the two tests. Errors on Test A are few in number, and so distributed that no one word in any item is wrongly identified more frequently than is any other. Errors are due mainly to 'carelessness'. Subjects rush through the items and do not bother to check their solutions. Errors on Test B are far more prevalent, and no longer mainly due to carelessness. They are concentrated on words whose identification entails the use of indirect procedures, and it would seem that subjects are brought to a halt by these words and resort is had to guessing. On the first five items of Test B, where only the final pair of words cannot be identified by direct matching of coded with uncoded letter-pairs, there is a 50 per cent chance of guessing incorrectly. This contributes to the error scores. But there is also a 50 per cent chance of guessing correctly, which means that the number of subjects failing to work eliminatively and resorting to guessing is almost certainly greater than the error scores alone suggest. On the five remaining items of Test B the number of words not able to be decoded by direct matching procedures has increased from two to three. Since there are six possible matchings of three coded with three uncoded words, the probability of chance success is now only 1 in 6. Unfortunately the error patterns for these items could not be studied because few subjects had time to attempt them in the 20 minutes allowed.

Turning now to the nature of the psychological difficulty associated with indirect procedures, an important contributory factor is a lack of appreciation that any instance is, simultaneously, a member of more than one class. All A's for example are, at the same time, $\bar{B}$'s and $\bar{C}$'s and . . . $\bar{Z}$'s. Difficulty in viewing the same thing as simultaneously of two different classes has been demonstrated repeatedly by Piaget, e.g., the difficulties experienced by young children in grasping number as being both cardinal and ordinal, or in regarding daffodils as belonging simultaneously to the subordinate class 'daffodils' and the supraordinate class 'flowers'. It is not only children who experience this sort of difficulty, judging by the failure of so many first-year university students to appreciate that a letter of the alphabet – A for instance – belongs not only to the class of A's but also to the various supraordinate 'equivalence' classes $\bar{B}$'s, $\bar{C}$'s, . . . , $\bar{Z}$'s that are the complementaries of the classes of the letters of the alphabet other than A itself. Why does there exist this lack of competence in dealing with classes such as the class of $\bar{X}$'s? Heidbreder (1945, 1948) argues that people prefer to work with cues that are directly perceptually apprehensible. The various $\bar{X}$'s tend not to bear any particular perceptual similarity one to the other, and this may lead to a reluctance to work with them. But the problem is less a matter of reluctance than one of failure even to conceive of such a class as that of $\bar{X}$'s a class which, when united with the X's, exhausts the contents of the supraordinate class 'letters of the alphabet'. Linguistic factors may have something to do with this. Classes such as $\bar{X}$'s are purely verbal, the only feature the various class members have in common being that they can all be labelled '$\bar{X}$'. In at least one experiment (Bruner and Olver, 1963) linguistic convention has been found to be used but infrequently as a basis of classification.

A second major factor contributing to the difficulty of Test B items is their demand for transformations involving a change of logical subject. Take Item (ii) above. The transition from $J=E$ to $X \neq E$ involves the derivation, from a statement about J, of a statement about something other than J. The opposite transition from $E=J$ to $E \neq X$ is probably easier. Both are statements about E. But this transition, while equivalent to the former from the point of view of formal logic, is not the one that subjects doing the code items actually attempt. Donaldson (1956) tentatively suggested that transformations of data are the more difficult if they involve a change of logical subject. The present results substantiate this. Donaldson's further suggestion (1959) that a feeling of finality may attach to positive statements is also relevant here. Such a feeling would contribute to failure with the seemingly simple transition from $J = E$ to $X \neq E$, the positive $J = E$ being regarded purely as an end in itself rather than as also a means to a further end within the framework of the problem.

Conclusions

The experiments with compound code items reported in this paper provide further support for the suggestion of Bruner *et al.* (1956) that lack of facility with indirect procedures may extend to a variety of cognitive activities other than categorization. Many subjects seem truly unable – rather than merely unwilling – to employ the indirect procedures appropriate to the solving of the Test B items. It is suggested that the difficulty experienced with these items stems from the need to work with equivalence classes that are negatively defined and purely verbal, and/or the demand for data transformations involving a change of logical subject.

References

BARTLETT, F. C. (1958), *Thinking. An experimental and social study*, Unwin.

BRUNER, J. S., GOODNOW, J. J., and AUSTIN, G. A. (1956), *A study of thinking*, Wiley.

BRUNER, J. S., and OLVER, R. R. (1963), 'Development of equivalence transformations in children', *Monogr. Soc. Res. Child Developm.*, vol. 28, pp. 125–41.

DONALDSON, M. C. (1956), *The relevance to the theory of intelligence of the study of errors in thinking*, Ph.D. thesis, Edinburgh University Library.

DONALDSON, M. C. (1959), 'Positive and negative information in matching problems', *Brit. J. Psychol.*, vol. 50, pp. 253–62.

HEIDBREDER, E. H. (1945), 'Towards a dynamic psychology of cognition', *Psychol. Rev.*, vol. 52, pp. 1–22.

HEIDBREDER, E. H. (1948), 'The attainment of concepts: VI. Exploratory experiments on conceptualization at perceptual levels', *J. Psychol.*, vol. 26, pp. 193–216.

19 R. C. Haygood and L. E. Bourne, Jr

Attribute- and Rule-learning Aspects of Conceptual Behaviour

Excerpts from R. C. Haygood and L. E. Bourne, Jr, 'Attribute- and rule-learning aspects of conceptual behavior', *Psychol. Rev.*, vol. 72 (1965), pp. 175–95.

Problems used in experimental studies of conceptual behavior have two major features, either or both of which may be initially unknown to the subject. First, there are the stimulus characteristics which make up the specific concept-to-be-learned. Second, there is the type of concept, represented by a rule which combines or otherwise elaborates the relevant attributes to define the concept. For example, a bidimensional principle for classification might specify that 'all red square figures are examples of the concept'. In such a concept color and form are the relevant dimensions, while red and square are the relevant attributes or values of the dimensions; the conceptual rule is conjunction or joint presence of attributes.

Attribute identification

In most concept-learning studies, particularly the concept identification experiments (e.g., Archer, Bourne and Brown, 1955; Bourne, 1957), interest has centered primarily on the discovery or identification of relevant attributes. Typically the general form of solution is described and illustrated for the subject with preliminary instructions and practice problems and, as such, constitutes a 'given condition'. Indeed, the majority of these experiments have employed simple and familiar unidimensional or conjunctive concepts or solutions. Once the unknown relevant attribute(s) is (are) discovered, through an inductive process based on the subject's observations of a series of examples and non-examples of the concept, the problem is to all intents and purposes solved.

Correspondingly, concept-identification studies have explored variables which appear to be important to the identification of relevant attributes, such as number of relevant and irrelevant stimulus dimensions (Walker and Bourne, 1961), amount of intra- and interdimensional variability (Battig and Bourne, 1961), and redundancy between dimensions (Bourne and Haygood, 1959; Haygood and Bourne, 1964). Theoretical interpretations of concept identification have been based largely upon processes involving stimulus features of a single problem, such as the conditioning and adaptation of relevant and irrelevant cues (Bourne and Restle, 1959) and the sampling and testing of hypotheses about these features (Restle, 1962; Trabasso and Bower, 1964).

Conceptual rules

Aside from incidental comparisons of the difficulty of unidimensional and conjunctive concept identification (Bourne and Haygood, 1959; Walker and Bourne, 1961), there has been no concern in this series of studies with type of concept or conceptual rule as a variable. The tacit assumption has been that identifying relevant attributes will be affected in much the same way by important variables regardless of the rule. Indeed, preliminary evidence, showing that the effects of number of relevant and irrelevant dimensions are the same for concepts based on conjunctive and biconditional rules, has been reported (Kepros and Bourne, 1963). There is, however, some recent evidence (e.g., Conant and Trabasso, 1964; Hunt and Kreuter, 1962; Neisser and Weene, 1962; Shepard, Hovland and Jenkins, 1961) to indicate that, under certain circumstances, types of concepts differ considerably in their difficulty. For this reason, it seems important to consider in detail the role that conceptual rules may play in concept learning. Although there are many rules for combining stimulus attributes and generating concepts, this paper will be limited to a system of constructing nominal, or discrete, concepts with, at most, two relevant attributes.

Consider first a closed stimulus population (Hovland, 1952) generated by x independent dimensions of y values each. When both x and y are two or more, it is possible to select two values from separate dimensions to be focal attributes. This selection maps the entire stimulus population on to the four categories or contingencies defined by the presence and absence of the focal attributes. For example, if redness (R) and squareness (S) are chosen as focal attributes, the four contingencies so defined are RS, $R\bar{S}$, $\bar{R}S$, and $\overline{RS}$.[1]

When these two focal attributes are further selected to be relevant attributes in defining a concept, the four contingencies are

1. The bar over a symbol stands for 'not', hence the categories read 'red, square'; 'red, not square'; etc. In logical terminology the symbols T (true) and F (false) are used, representing the presence and absence, respectively, of the attribute specified. Thus in general terms, the contingencies are TT, TF, FT, and FF.

mapped on to a two-response system: positive and negative instances of the concept. This second mapping creates 16 binary partitions of the stimulus population, two of which are trivial because they place the entire population in either the positive or negative response category. The remaining fourteen nontrivial partitions are defined by the unique distribution of the four attribute contingencies (RS, $R\bar{S}$, $\bar{R}S$, and $\overline{RS}$) into either the positive or negative category. The partitions are shown in Table 1. Capital letters are assigned arbitrarily to the fourteen mappings of the stimuli on to the response system, with '$+$' indicating those patterns which are positive instances and '$-$' indicating those which are negative.

The number of stimulus patterns which are instances of each contingency is, obviously, a function of both interdimensional (x) and intradimensional (y) variability. Manipulation of interdimensional variability does not affect the proportions of patterns within each contingency, whereas a change in intradimensional variability clearly does. The pattern sets resulting in the cases of two-value and three-value dimensions are presented in Table 1.

Neisser and Weene (1962) have shown that there are only ten different rules within this set of fourteen mappings. This results from the fact that the following pairs are precisely the same except for a change of relevant attributes: B and C, E and G, H and I, and L and N. The ten remaining mappings fall into five complementary pairs having the property that any instance which is positive under one member of the pair is a negative instance under the other. Table 2 describes these complementary pairs both symbolically and verbally.

Levels of rules

A symbolic description, using the operations of negation, conjunction, and disjunction as primitives, suggests that the ten mappings may be further broken down into levels based on the complexity (or length) of the descriptive expression. The unidimensional (Level I) represents the simplest, followed by those six expressions which involve single conjunctions or disjunctions of both relevant attributes (Level II). Finally, the most complex expressions entail both conjunctive and disjunctive operations (Level III). Neisser and Weene pointed out that the successive levels form a hierarchical structure, with the elements of Level II expressions being the Level I statements and the elements of Level III being Level II statements. Further they offer the hypothesis that the order of structural complexity within the system will

Table 1
Fourteen Mappings of a Stimulus Population with Two Focal Attributes on to a Binary Response System

| Dimensions and levels | | Pattern sets | | | Partitions | | | | | | | | | | | | | |
Color R	Form S	Contingencies	Two level	Three level	A	B	C	D	E	F	G	H	I	J	K	L	M	N
T	T	RS	RS	RS	+	+	+	+	+	+	+	+	−	−	+	−	−	−
T	F	R$\bar{S}$	RT	RT, RC	+	+	−	+	+	−	−	−	+	+	−	+	−	−
F	T	$\bar{R}$S	GS	GS, BS	+	−	+	+	−	−	+	+	−	+	−	−	+	−
F	F	$\bar{R}\bar{S}$	GT	GT, GC, BT, BC	−	+	+	+	+	+	−	+	+	−	−	−	−	+

Note. – The following abbreviations are used: S – square, T – triangle, C – circle, R – red, G – green, and B – blue.

Table 2
Conceptual Rules Describing Partitions of a Population with Two Focal Attributes

| | | Basic rule | | | | Complementary rule | |
	Partition	Name	Symbolic description	Verbal description	Partition	Name	Symbolic description[a]	Verbal description
Level I	E	Affirmation	R	All red patterns are examples of the concept	H	Negation	R̄	All patterns which are *not* red are examples of the concept
Level II	K	Conjunction	R∩S	All red *and* square patterns are examples	D	Alternative denial	R|S [R̄∪S̄]	All patterns which are *either not* red *or not* square are examples
	A	Inclusive disjunction	R∪S	All patterns which are red *or* square *or both* are examples	N	Joint denial	R↓S [R̄∩S̄]	All patterns which are *neither* red *nor* square are examples

Level	Code	Name	Symbolic	Verbal description
	C	Conditional	$R \to S$ [$R \cup S$]	If a pattern is red *then* it must be square to be an example
	L	Exclusion[b]	$R \cap \bar{S}$	All patterns which are red *and not* square are examples
Level III	F	Biconditional	$R \leftrightarrow S$ [$(R \cap S) \cup (\bar{R} \cap \bar{S})$]	Red patterns are examples *if and only if* they are square
	J	Exclusive disjunction	$R \bar{\cup} S$ [$(R \cap \bar{S}) \cup (\bar{R} \cap S)$]	All patterns which are red *or* square *but not both* are examples

a Symbolic descriptions using only the three basic operators, ∩, ∪, and negation, are given in brackets.
b There is no special symbol for exclusion in general use.

be reflected in an order of difficulty when actual concept problems are given to human subjects for solution. [. . .]

Neisser and Weene report a study of the relative difficulty of attaining concepts at the three levels implied by their system, and the results clearly support the hypothesis that concepts of hierarchically higher levels are more difficult to attain than those of lower levels. In addition, although there is a general improvement in performance across two successive concept problems of the same type, the difference in difficulty is still evident on the second problem. Exploring fewer different concept types, Hunt and Kreuter (1962) found similar results.

Rule learning

The analysis above immediately raises the question of why, from a psychological point of view, higher level concepts are more difficult to attain. Hunt offers an interpretation based on the fact that any deterministic rule can be expressed as a tree of decisions. The tree specific to any rule is learned by the subject, assumedly through the utilization of a general strategy applicable to all conceptual problems. Theoretically, the subject begins by trying to solve the problem as a conjunction of attributes, but, in doing so, may uncover (when a nonconjunctive solution holds) subproblems which require special treatment. The general strategy may be realized in a computer program which yields results close to the order of concept difficulty observed in real data (Hunt and Kreuter, 1962). Neisser and Weene, on the other hand, lean toward an interpretation based on the hierarchical organization of concepts, which pictures the subject as working up from simple to more complex groupings of stimuli. To identify correctly an instance of a Level III concept, the subject must have Level II concepts available as components. Similarly, to utilize Level II concepts, the subject must be familiar with Level I components. Thus to attain a complex concept, the subject must use and therefore have attained concepts at a lower level. This interpretation implies that the subjects do not learn Level III concepts as such, but rather construct or induce them from their component parts.

There are at least two other relevant considerations. [. . .] Level I concepts have one relevant dimension, whereas Level II and III concepts have two; number of relevant dimensions (or bits of relevant information) has been shown to be a powerful determiner of task difficulty (e.g., Bulgarella and Archer, 1962). The greater difficulty of Level III as compared to Level II concepts may result from differences in the mapping of the four stimulus contingencies as shown in Table 1 (i.e., TT, TF, FT, and FF) on to the two response categories. All Level II concepts involve a 3:1 split of the contingencies, whereas Level III concepts are based on a 2:2 split. In a sense there is more uncertainty in the stimulus-category systems of Level III concepts (Garner, 1962). This uncertainty is reflected in the lack of homogeneity or commonality among individual stimulus patterns in either the positive or negative category of Level III concepts. Indeed, each category within Level III concept types consists of two subsets whose members have, by definition, no relevant attributes in common. Thus the highly efficient strategies based on discovery of common attributes (Bruner, Goodnow and Austin, 1956) are eliminated, and must be replaced by different, and perhaps more difficult and less efficient, strategies based on multiple contingencies. This interpretation suggests that differences in difficulty among concept levels (and perhaps within levels as well) result from differences in stimulus uncertainty – in effect, from differing information requirements to solve the problems.

It is also possible that the observed ordering between rules is little more than a reflection of differing familiarity with the rules and their appropriate strategies. With equal familiarity, concept forms at Levels II and III may be equally difficult to attain. Suggestive of this is Wells' (1963) demonstration that the evident preference of naive subjects for conjunctive as opposed to disjunctive concepts in problems which could be solved by either rule (Hunt and Hovland, 1960) can be modified by preliminary training and familiarization with disjunctive concepts. Extensive training on several mappings of Table 1 may produce equal facility with each type of concept, thus modifying the hierarchy described by Neisser and Weene (1962).

Two aspects of conceptual behavior

With the exception of that of Conant and Trabasso (1964), each of these studies of comparative rule difficulty has required the subject both (a) to identify the relevant attributes, and (b) to learn the assignment of values on relevant dimensions to response categories as prescribed by the rule. That is, for the subject each problem had two unknowns. This confounding of attribute identification with rule learning creates certain difficulties in the interpretation of results. For example, it has not been established that the rules differ in difficulty in the absence of the necessity to identify relevant attributes. Clearly, the strategies appropriate for identifying relevant attributes differ among rules, and it may be that those which are useful in a conjunctive problem are easier to learn or employ than those associated with a biconditional. This possibility is supported by the finding of Conant and Trabasso that naive subjects learn to use a positive-focus strategy in a conjunctive problem earlier than they learn to use a negative focus in a disjunctive problem. However, it is possible that attribute identification under different conceptual rules might not differ if adequate instructions and training on the relevant rule were given.

This suggests that there is a distinction between two independent kinds of behavior: (a) rule learning, in which the subject attains or discovers the principle for partitioning the stimuli in a particular problem and acquires the rule in general form so that he can use it in any problem; and (b) attribute identification, in which the subject attains or discovers the relevant attributes. One major purpose of this paper is to provide some experimental evidence on the validity of this analysis, to demonstrate the separability of the two forms of behavior, and to indicate the unique features of each.

Experiment 1

In the first experiment, each subject was presented with a series of five concept problems, based on the same rule but with a different pair of relevant attributes. Each subject served in one of three main conditions which are labeled rule learning (RL), attribute identification (AI), and complete learning (CL). In the RL condition, the subject was given the names of the two relevant attributes at the start of each problem. His task was to learn the proper assignment of a set of stimulus patterns to the response classes according to some unknown but preselected rule combining these attributes. In the AI case, one rule was explained and illustrated for the subject at the outset, leaving him the task of identifying the attributes relevant to the concept in each problem. This case represents in essence the experimental procedure used in earlier studies of concept identification. In the CL case, the subject was told neither the rule nor the attributes at the outset, but had to attack each problem given only a description of the stimulus population and the size of the concept (two relevant attributes).

One specific purpose for separating out RL was to determine whether the rules are intrinsically different in difficulty when the subject is not required to identify relevant attributes. If so, then it can be expected that, at least on the initial problems, different rules will yield different numbers of errors and trials to solution.

In contrast, the AI condition (which provides thorough preliminary instruction on the rules) was designed to assess the relative difficulty of identifying relevant attributes under different rules. Whereas expectations regarding RL are not clear, there is some evidence in the literature to support the expectation that AI problems will differ in difficulty even though rule instruction is given. Bruner, Goodnow, and Austin (1956) have demonstrated the utility of a powerful holist strategy for identifying the relevant attributes of a conjunction. This strategy allows the subject to form and test a composite hypothesis which embodies on any trial all tenable solutions. Thus, with this strategy there is no need for the subject to consider independently all possible pairs of relevant attributes. Such a strategy is, in general, not appropriate to the disjunction or to any of the other rules to be studied in this experiment. The strategies which are available for these other rules provide no convenient way of forming a composite hypothesis which simultaneously represents all possible solutions.

The CL condition was included for two reasons. First, it provides continuity with the experiments of Neisser and Weene (1962), and of Hunt and Kreuter (1962). Second, CL provides a base line for comparison to AI and RL to determine the effectiveness of instructions that, in one case, provide the relevant attributes and, in the other, the relevant rule. If knowledge of either feature is important to concept learning, performance on even the first problem should show significant differences between CL and the other two conditions.

To determine the effects of practice, a series of five problems having the same solution form was given in all conditions. Assuming the effectiveness of instructions, improvement across successive problems could be attributed to the following factors. In RL, to an increasing familiarity with the way a rule assigns stimulus patterns to the response categories; in AI, to the development and utilization of strategies appropriate to the identification of relevant attributes under a given rule; and, in CL, to both factors.

Method[2]

Subjects and design. – Sixty students from introductory psychology classes participated individually as subjects and were assigned in order of appearance to one of twelve treatment combinations.

The experimental design was a 4×3 repeated-measures factorial, incorporating concept problems generated by four different rules and three instructional conditions. The rules used – conjunction,

2. This section has been abridged. (Eds.)

inclusive disjunction, joint denial, and conditional – were selected arbitrarily to include (a) only Level II types (Neisser and Weene, 1962) and (b) one pair of complements. The three instructional conditions were AI: the rule and all stimulus dimensions were described and illustrated, but the relevant attributes were unknown to the subject; RL: all the stimulus dimensions and the relevant attributes, stated in TT form, e.g., red square, were given, but the rule was not explained; and CL: all dimensions, but neither the rule nor the relevant attributes were described. Each subject solved five successive problems utilizing the same rule within the same instructional condition. A different pair of relevant attributes was used in each problem, and five different sequences of pairs were used to avoid confounding with ordinal position.

Materials and apparatus. – The stimulus patterns were geometric designs, prepared on 4×6 inch cards and varying along four three-value dimensions. Dimensions and their values were: number (one, two, and three figures), size (large, medium, and small), form (square, triangle, and hexagon), and color (red, yellow, and blue).

Task and procedure. – The subject was required to sort, or classify a series of visually presented stimulus patterns into two categories. The correct classification for any stimulus was determined both by the pair of attributes relevant in the particular problem and by the conceptual rule which specified the relationship between these attributes. In each problem two dimensions were irrelevant to solution.

Emphasis was placed on finding the two attributes which characterized the class of positive instances; despite this emphasis on the positive category, the subjects were warned that both the presence and absence of particular attributes might be important. Instructions given to all groups were identical except for those portions restricted by the nature of the experimental conditions.

To each successive stimulus card, the subject was required to respond 'yes' or 'no' thus indicating whether it was an example of the concept or not. Following the subject's response, the experimenter provided feed-back by saying 'right' or 'wrong' and by placing the stimulus card face up on the desk in an area marked YES or NO as appropriate. All problems were self-paced in that the subject was allowed as much time as desired to respond, and instructions stressed accuracy rather than speed.

The criterion of problem solution was 16 consecutive correct responses.

Results and discussion

The mean numbers of errors and trials to solution observed for all five problems in each of the twelve main conditions of the experiment are reported in Table 3. Overall analysis of variance on errors demonstrated four statistically reliable effects. First, for all concept types CL, wherein both the rule and the relevant attributes were unknown, was more difficult than AI, which in turn yielded a greater number of errors than RL ($p < 0.01$). Second, there was steady improvement in performance over problems ($p < 0.01$) and no evidence of interaction between problems and instructional conditions. Third, rules differed generally in difficulty ($p < 0.01$) and according to the order observed by Hunt and Kreuter (1962). Finally, the interaction of rules and successive problems was reliable ($p < 0.01$) reflecting the fact that the difficulty of joint denial, disjunction, and conditional concepts changed markedly in comparison to conjunctive concepts. Identical results held for the analysis of trials to solution.

Further inspection and analyses of the data in Table 3 revealed that, in RL conditions, essentially perfect performance was reached by all subjects on the fourth problem on all rules except the conditional. Initial expectation of and familiarity with the conjunctive rule was clearly evidenced by the fact that only one subject made any errors on these RL problems, and he made these only on two of the five problems. Fractional mean errors on later disjunction and joint denial problems resulted, in both cases, from a single subject making one or two errors per problem. Complete mastery of these three rules is demonstrated by the immediate solution of each problem by the subjects upon being provided with the relevant attributes.

The overall greater difficulty of the conditional rule appeared to result from two sources. First, the size and nonhomogeneity of the class of positive instances: inspection of Table 1 shows that the conditional rule classifies a greater number of instances as positive than any other and moreover uniquely requires both TT and FF (e.g., red square and not red, not square) to be grouped together. One implication of this is that focusing on the negative category (Hunt, 1962), which was not encouraged by the instructions of this experiment, would facilitate the learning of conditional concepts. Second, the asymmetry of the rule: whereas the partition generated by any of the other three rules is invariant with commutation of attributes, e.g., red and/or square is identical to square and/or red, only one of the two possible attribute orderings

245

Table 3

Mean Number of Errors (E) and Trials (T) to Solution in Experiment 1

Rule	Instructional condition	Problem									
		1		2		3		4		5	
		E	T	E	T	E	T	E	T	E	T
Conjunction	AI	4·0	13·4	3·4	12·0	1·6	11·6	3·4	15·5	2·2	7·4
	RL	0·2	0·2	0·4	0·4	0	0	0	0	0	0
	CL	3·6	14·0	3·0	6·4	3·2	11·8	4·0	16·2	2·0	7·6
Disjunction	AI	12·1	32·8	7·6	32·0	4·0	18·0	4·2	9·8	4·2	16·0
	RL	8·0	33·3	0·6	4·2	0·2	1·0	0·4	0·4	0·2	2·6
	CL	37·0	120·8	17·0	52·4	22·2	75·6	11·0	38·8	13·0	49·2
Joint denial	AI	9·2	32·6	11·4	35·6	6·4	21·5	8·6	27·0	3·4	16·6
	RL	8·6	28·6	3·4	11·8	1·6	4·6	0	0	0·4	4·0
	CL	17·0	67·0	12·0	49·4	16·2	62·6	18·6	67·0	17·2	65·6
Conditional	AI	26·8	49·4	12·2	47·8	12·6	54·0	13·8	54·5	9·0	34·0
	RL	16·4	57·5	10·4	45·8	6·8	23·5	7·6	23·0	6·4	30·5
	CL	38·4	116·3	11·4	27·8	11·2	30·6	20·6	60·6	11·0	37·6

is correct for a conditional problem. The effect is to place special emphasis on the difference between T F and F T instances. Because the order of attributes was not stressed in the instructions, the subject was posed the additional task of making this basic distinction. Additional evidence on the difficulty of this task is provided by Experiment II.

Once the subject has learned the rule, it is obviously possible to categorize patterns without error in any R L condition. In contrast, A I requires, on logical grounds, the presentation of a certain minimal number of instances since the subject must discover which dimensions and values are relevant. Even the most efficient search strategy will be accompanied by a number of errors commensurate with the number of trials necessary to eliminate all but the correct pairing of attributes.

While it is impossible to determine exactly what strategies, if any, were used by the subjects, inspection of the error data suggests that the subjects were not responding in accord with randomly selected binary hypotheses prior to solution, for such a strategy would give an error total equal to about half the number of trials. Instead, the actual mean errors approaches the minimum commensurate with the *theoretical minimum trials* for all rules except conditional. In other words, it would appear that error performance in conjunction, inclusive disjunction, and joint denial was about as efficient at the end of five problems as it can be. The small ratio of errors to trials suggests that many subjects solve the problem in parts, for example, by initially discovering one but not both of the relevant attributes (Trabasso and Bower, 1964).

The overall difficulty of the conditional rule is reflected in performance within the A I condition. Numbers of trials and errors are greater over all five problems than for any other rule. The failure of the subjects to obtain conditional rule mastery in five consecutive R L problems suggests that part of the difficulty within the A I condition results from a lack of understanding of the rule itself.

Except for conjunctive concepts, C L yields more errors and requires more trials than A I, even for the fifth problem. This result demonstrates the effectiveness of prior instructions about the rule, and provides further evidence that both R L and A I are involved in the solution of conceptual problems. The improvement in C L performance is consistent with the findings of Neisser and Weene (1962). It is indicative of the possibility that, with further training, the subjects will become as facile with problems of a non-conjunctive nature as they are with conjunctive problems at the outset – within the constraints of the amount of information required for problem solution. However, failure of the CL groups, in general, to attain the same level of performance as AI groups after several problems indicates that rule learning proceeds more slowly when the subject must, in the same problem, identify relevant stimulus attributes. Clearly, then, CL is more than the simple sum of AI and RL.

At least after the first problem, performance on the disjunctive and joint denial concepts is virtually identical, as would be suggested by the fact that they are complementaries. The difference between these concepts on the first problem, which is not statistically significant, may be attributable to the initial effect of instructions emphasizing the class of positive instances, but the evidence is far from compelling.

Experiment II

The RL condition of Experiment I provided training for the subject in the assignment of stimulus patterns (or attribute contingencies) to response categories by a single rule. If the subject can be trained to perform adequately on two or more rules, it becomes feasible to present to him a conceptual task which may be labeled, for sake of consistency, rule identification (RI). In RI the subject is given the relevant attributes and is required to identify which of the known rules determines problem solution. The task, obviously, is designed as an analogue of AI problems, wherein the subject must identify which of several known attributes determines solution under a given rule. From Table 1 it is clear that the assignment of one or more of the four contingencies of relevant attributes will differentiate any two rules, and that presentation of all four contingencies will determine uniquely which rule is correct. Thus the subject's performance may be compared to an efficient algorithm, which solves such RI problems in four trials if each trial provides an example of a different contingency of the relevant attributes. In general, a certain minimal number of instances, positive or negative, is required to eliminate all but the correct solution for any RI problem, just as in AI. Assuming prior familiarization and equalization of rules through RL, however, no difference in rule difficulty would be expected.

The purpose of Experiment II is to investigate RI performance after prior RL training on four different rules selected to represent both Levels II and III from the Neisser and Weene (1962) hierarchy and a high degree of diversity in the way they assign stimulus patterns to categories.

Method[3]

Subjects and design. – Twenty-four students from introductory psychology classes served as subjects.

The experiment consisted of two parts, an RL and an RI phase. In the RL phase, the subjects were presented with a series of concept problems based on three different rules, viz., disjunctive, conditional, and biconditional. The six possible sequences of rules were used, each for an equal number of subjects. Successive problems utilized different pairs of relevant attributes, which were named for the subject before each. The purpose of this phase was to train the subjects in the use of these three conceptual rules, plus a fourth, the conjunction, which was explained in detail and illustrated during initial instructions.

For the RI phase, a balanced incomplete-blocks design, with four rules, two pairs of relevant attributes, and two successive problems, was used. The two problems were based on two of the four rules on which the subject was trained during the RL phase. The two pairs of relevant attributes, which were named for the subject at the outset of each problem, were counterbalanced with problem order and with relevant rule.

Materials and apparatus. – The stimulus patterns were the same as those used in Experiment I.

Task and procedure. – The task and instructions were essentially those used in the RL condition of Experiment I, with the exceptions that (*a*) equal emphasis was placed on observing instances of both the positive and negative categories and (*b*) an elaborate explanation of each rule was given after performance on its associated problem. The subject was told that there would be three training problems, each employing a different rule, and that subsequently there would be two problems in which the solution could be any one of the four rules.

Results and discussion

Mean numbers of errors and trials to solution of all problems are given in Table 4. Analyses of variance on the two dependent response measures showed identical outcomes; therefore, only significance tests based on errors are reported. During the RL phase, sources of variance identified with rules, ordinal position of problems and their interaction were statistically significant ($p < 0.01$). The initial order of difficulty among rules is precisely the same as that observed by Neisser and Weene (1962) and by

3. This section has been abridged. (Eds.)

Hunt and Kreuter (1962); these differences, however, are atten-uated on the latter two R L problems. Because, in this phase, only one working problem of each type was given to each subject, ordinal position and interaction effects are attributable to a general transfer among rules, particularly from other rules to the biconditional, rather than (as in Experiment I) a specific process of learning how to solve problems characterized by a single rule.

Number of trials to present at least one stimulus pattern repre-sentative of each type of attribute contingency sets one logical limit on the minimum information necessary to categorize all patterns correctly. These values, computed directly from the stim-ulus sequences used, are presented in Table 4. A comparison of trials to solution with this base line indicates that, with the possible exception of later disjunctive problems, the subjects do not solve problems with maximal efficiency during the R L phase. This is hardly unexpected in view of the training routine employed and the relative unfamiliarity of these rules at the outset.

There are significant differences in difficulty among conceptual rules in the R I phase ($p < 0.01$) with biconditional and conditional problems producing a greater number of errors than the conjunc-tive and disjunctive. The reliability of these differences is enhanced by the limited variability in performance on conjunctive and dis-junctive problems, wherein solutions were attained in a minimal number of trials in 75 per cent and 83 per cent of cases, respec-tively. Identification of the conditional and biconditional rules was accomplished in a minimal number of trials by only 33 per cent and 25 per cent of the subjects, respectively. [. . .]

General Discussion

The preliminary analysis outlined in this paper discloses two aspects of conceptual problems as they are commonly posed for subjects in the laboratory, viz., the learning of rules and attributes. Research to date has been concerned largely either with (a) the processes by which subjects, given the correct rule, discover or identify relevant attributes of a concept, or (b) performance in situations wherein both the relevant attributes and the rule are unknowns. The present experiments considered the third case, attributes given and rule unknown, for purposes of logical and empirical comparison with the first two. Primarily, this study provided a comparison of performance characteristics in R L and A I problems; its aim was to determine the advantages to be gained, if any, from a separation of attribute and rule aspects in studies of

Table 4

Mean Number of Trials (TS) and Errors (E) to Solution and Number of Trials Necessary to Present at Least One Representation of Each Attribute Combination (TP) in All Problems, Experiment II

						Problem									
	Rule learning									Rule identification					
	1			2			3			4			5		
Rule	E	TS	TP	E	TS	TP	E	TS	TP	E	TS	TP	E	TS	TP
Conjunction	—	—	—	—	—	—	—	—	—	1·8	8·0	8	3·2	5·8	5
Disjunction	6·3	19·5	7	2·3	6·9	7	2·8	8·4	5	1·5	4·2	5	2·3	7·2	5
Conditional	8·8	24·4	9	10·5	27·0	5	6·3	15·5	9	3·5	8·8	7	6·8	16·3	6
Biconditional	29·1	65·5	7	4·4	16·0	7	8·6	27·4	5	8·5	30·2	9	6·2	27·8	5

Note. – There were no conjunctive problems given during the R L phase.

conceptual behavior. Secondarily, interest centered on the question of differences in difficulty among rules, and the possibility that these differences may be attenuated through training.

Rule Learning

In Experiment I the observed improvement across a series of RL problems demonstrates that through training the subject does acquire knowledge about how a rule assigns stimulus patterns to response categories. At least for the rules which are initially least difficult, conjunction, inclusive disjunction, and joint denial, it has been shown that RL proceeds regularly to a level of mastery such that, given the relevant attributes, the subjects categorize stimulus patterns essentially without error.

Training on a single rule bears obvious similarity to the regimen of learning-set studies (Harlow, 1949). Solving each of a series of individual problems yields continuous improvement, producing optimal performance on a given type of task. In the present situation, where some rules are familiar and relatively easy at the outset, while others – because of lack of training or interfering expectations – are relatively difficult, this procedure operates to reduce or eliminate initial differences in difficulty. It may also be noted that the process called RL is not unlike concept formation, as that phrase is used by Piaget (1929; see also Flavell, 1963). When one of Piaget's children learns the concept of conservation of quantity, he has acquired, in effect, a general rule or way of responding in a variety of problematic situations. For example, the attainment of conservation is implied when a child indicates that (a) emptying a container of beads into another of different shape and capacity does not affect the quantity of beads, or (b) different spatial arrangements of poker chips on a table do not entail a change in number of chips. In the last analysis, it is not the specific attributes, inextricably tied to the rule, which the subject acquires as the concept, but rather the rule itself.

Processes in rule learning and identification

Rule learning may be construed as the process by which the subject acquires information on the assignment of all combinations of values on relevant stimulus dimensions to response categories. In the stimulus population used in the present experiments, this means a mapping of nine different patterns (combinations of three values on each of two relevant dimensions) on to a two-response system. Evidence from Experiment II, however, argues that RL introduces an additional, simplifying factor or heuristic into the categorization process. Simplification results from collapsing the 3×3, in general $m \times n$, matrix (representing combinations of values on relevant dimensions) to a 2×2 matrix, each cell of which contains a set of patterns, called here contingencies, characterized by the presence or absence of the two relevant attributes. To say, then, that the subject has learned a rule is to say that he understands how it uniquely assigns contingencies to response categories.

It is conceivable that a subject who achieves, with practice, the capacity to react to all instances of each contingency as members of the same class might derive an algorithm for learning a new rule or for attaining solution to any RI problem: *observe the assignment of one example of each of the four contingencies, then classify all future instances according to this scheme.* This plan reduces a potentially unlimited population of instances to four, then merely maps these four on to a twofold response system. While it is probably true that this algorithmic process is not carried out formally by the subjects, it is not unreasonable to assume that many subjects perform a similar routine on a more intuitive level.

General RL, for at least some subjects, may be conceived, then, as a two-stage process involving: (*a*) reductive coding of a stimulus population to the matrix of attribute contingencies and (*b*) acquisition of the assignment of contingencies to response categories which is unique to each of a variety of rules. Neither the data nor this analysis indicate that Step *a* is mastered before the subjects learn anything about a rule. Both imply only that sophisticated and efficient performance in problems which require the learning of a new rule or the identification of a familiar one will include an intervening step which reduces the effective complexity of the stimulus population. Evidence from Experiment II, however, makes it clear that some subjects used the collapsing or coding heuristic prior to complete learning of the more difficult conditional and biconditional solutions. The similarity of the coding principle to the formal truth table is obvious. If the foregoing interpretation is correct, the results imply the utilization, as a mediator, of some informal version of this device, which of course is well known to have considerable power in logic.

Rule difficulty

If the subject learns a rule as a specific and unique mapping of contingencies, and uses differences in the assignment of contingencies as a means of identifying the rule, the implication is that all rules which in some way entail the combination of two (or any

253

fixed number) relevant attributes are equally complex or difficult. It is well established that rules for combining two relevant attributes are not equally difficult at the outset even when the attributes are known and probably take different amounts of practice to learn. However, there is evidence in the present experiments that such differences may be reduced through RL and probably eliminated. Initial differences may be attributable to differing amounts of pre-experimental experience with the various rules used here, and to peculiar, unfamiliar, or 'unexpected' assignments of contingencies to response categories, such as the assignment of both TT and FF instances, which have no common relevant attributes, to the same response class. It is possible, moreover, that variation in the uncertainty of pattern-to-response or contingency-to-response assignments, e.g., Level III versus Level II rules (Neisser and Weene, 1962), may account for differences in initial difficulty. All of these sources of differential rule difficulty in RL apparently may be rendered ineffectual through training, leaving the subject with a repertoire of habits or strategies for solving RI problems with equal facility regardless of the rule. This repertoire may, in fact, be analogous to the knowledge of stimulus attributes which, it is assumed, the subject brings with him to most experimental situations.

Rule and attribute identification

Rule-identification tasks are analogous to those requiring identification of relevant attributes. In both, one aspect of the problem is unknown, either the rule (RI) or the relevant attributes (AI). In both, given a complete understanding of the possible values of the unknown and a systematic plan or strategy for isolating the correct value(s), the subject may solve the problem in a computable minimal number of stimulus instances which depends almost exclusively on the number of possible values of the unknown.

The dichotomy implied by the terms RL and RI is debatable. The problem is that acquisition is in this case essentially a process of gradual change in performance with practice. It takes some arbitrary criterion to distinguish the attainment of habits from their utilization. One cannot appeal to superior performance during any so-called identification problem as evidence of a difference between learning and utilization of conceptual rules. Such superiority, which indeed exists, can be construed as reflecting in the identification phase merely a continuation of the improvement shown in the RL problems. The differentiation between RL and RI rests not on performance but in the nature of the experimental task. As the subject learns new rules, in fact, as soon as he has learned two, it is possible to present him with a problem requiring the identification of which of the known rules is correct. If the subject has not completely mastered either or both rules, some RL may occur. The degree to which the subject actually has mastered the set of rules is the degree to which any problem involves true RI.

It is difficult to specify the degree to which improvement in performance over a series of AI or RI problems results from increasing familiarity with the rule(s), or from the development and utilization of strategies appropriate to the identification of unknowns. Rules differ in familiarity to the unsophisticated subject (Wells, 1963), and it is virtually impossible to equate them on this factor through preliminary instructions, no matter how detailed. Thus, 'true' AI or RI conditions would necessitate thorough understanding of the relevant rule(s), such as might be provided by the RL conditions of the present experiments, prior to the presentation of identification problems. The effects of such prior training should be explored more thoroughly in subsequent experiments.

Theoretical comment

[...] The model of efficient performance in RL and RI tasks presented here presumes that the subject achieves an encoding of known *stimulus attributes* into an effective truth table; the unique distribution of the attribute contingencies of the truth table into categories then identifies the relevant rule. Most theoretical interpretations of conceptual behavior (e.g., Bourne and Restle, 1959; Restle, 1962) have been concerned primarily with a different case (AI) wherein it can be assumed that the subject knows the *rule* and must identify the relevant attributes only. Analytic separation of attribute- and rule-learning aspects of conceptual behavior does not preclude the development of a theory capable of describing performance when both rule and attributes are unknown (CL). Yet, available evidence is clearly too fragmentary to sustain any set of strong theoretical assertions.

It may be noted that the RL model implies a hypothesis-testing strategy which yields a simple test among alternative possible solutions. Each new contingency reduces the number of possibilities until only the correct one remains. Restle (1962) and others have conceived of AI as proceeding along similar lines. That is, the subject selects, tests, and rejects stimulus attributes (as hypotheses) until the correct one or combination is discovered. In view of the considerable success of these models in providing detailed, quantitative accounts of performance in simple concept-identification tasks, it is reasonable to suggest an extension to more complicated CL problems.

If both the rule and the relevant attributes are unknown, the subject may (a) randomly select a pair of attributes on a provisional basis for encoding in a truth table, (b) test for systematic assignment of the attribute contingencies to response categories, and (c) reject the pair and select a new one if tests for consistent assignments fail. This extension implies a formal model with two independent processes, corresponding to discovery of the two unknowns. The processes obviously overlap, however, in the sense that the subject must test for systematic contingency assignments to response categories subsequent to the selection of any attribute pair.

It is clear that any such theory has little or no validity as an account of the behavior of naive subjects in CL tasks. Present data show that the subjects begin to encode relevant attributes only after an appreciable amount of practice on experimental problems, and even then only when the relevant attributes are given at the outset. Thus, the accuracy of this description is very likely limited to those cases wherein the subject has attained *mastery* of several rules. Observations of the naive subject in the present experiment are closer to expectations based on Hunt's (1962) interpretation. Most subjects presume the problem to be conjunctive at the outset, with the obvious and predictable result that CL and AI conjunctive problems do not differ in difficulty. When the conjunctive strategy is insufficient, the subject discovers a set of partial solutions which, taken together, permit him to attain criterion. Thus, Hunt's model may provide an adequate description of the subject's performance on initial CL problems. While solution to such problems may be attained through the acquisition of a decision tree, as Hunt suggests, present data indicate that certain generic decisions in the tree – corresponding to the relevant rule – are transferable across problems, for evidence of learning to learn (or solve) is provided by both experiments. Since both inter- and intrarule transfer were observed, it seems likely that generic decisions somehow contribute to the formation of an intuitive truth table. The nature of this acquisition process is, however, obscure.

Suggestions and conclusions

The analyses and results presented here immediately suggest certain problem areas requiring further study. First, and perhaps most obvious, is the exploration of parameters affecting RL and RI. Many of the variables which exert a pronounced effect in AI, such as number of irrelevant dimensions, may be expected to have little or no effect in RL. On the other hand, possibilities which are irrelevant to AI, such as the number of known rules, may have direct and measurable effects in RI.

Second, there is a need for more rigorous study of AI under rules other than the conjunction. Consideration of previous results and the present analysis suggests that a large part of the differences across rules in previous experiments may be attributed to differential prior training and familiarization. Further study in which subjects are thoroughly trained on the relevant rule, so that it constitutes a true 'given' in the problem, should clarify the question of inherent rule difficulty in AI. It may be anticipated that somewhat different strategies will be utilized when different rules are in effect, since it is apparent that those appropriate to conjunctive problems are not efficient for other rules (Bruner *et al.*, 1956). Whether important determiners of conjunctive concept identification will have a different effect when other rules are used, however, is not clear. The results of Kepros and Bourne (1963) with biconditional problems suggest no difference in at least one case, that of increasing the number of irrelevant dimensions. But additional experiments to determine, for example, whether increasing the amount of intradimensional variability has a similar effect on AI with a variety of rules are needed.

Third, although previous work has shown that the proportion of positive instances has a significant effect on solving conjunctive problems (Hovland and Weiss, 1953), it is not safe to generalize this result to all concept types and problems, for it may be no more than an artifact of the appropriateness of a positive focus for conjunctive strategies (Hunt, 1962). Rules which are more easily solved with a negative focus may well show a significant superiority for negative instances. Apart from the question of strategies, the present analysis suggests that the proportion of the four stimulus contingencies may be an even more powerful determiner of solution in certain problems than the raw proportion of positive and negative instances.

Fourth, the present experiments dealt only with rules based on the sentential calculus, i.e., rules reducible directly to expressions involving only negation, conjunction, and inclusive disjunction. Other classes of rules, expressing such relationships as equality, order, inclusion, and so forth, remain to be explored. It is of interest to observe how the subject determines the relevant relationship between given or known attributes, and to compare such performance with that on the logical rules used in the present study. [. . .]

References

ARCHER, E. J., BOURNE, L. E., Jr, and BROWN, F. G. (1955), 'Concept identification as a function of irrelevant information and instructions', *J. exp. Psychol.*, vol. 49, pp. 153–64.

BATTIG, W. F., and BOURNE, L. E., Jr (1961), 'Concept identification as a function of intra- and interdimensional variation', *J. exp. Psychol.*, vol. 61, pp. 329–33.

BOURNE, L. E., Jr (1957), 'Effect of delay of information feedback and task complexity on the identification of concepts', *J. exp. Psychol.*, vol. 54, pp. 201–7.

BOURNE, L. E., Jr, and HAYGOOD, R. C. (1959), 'The role of stimulus redundancy in concept identification', *J. exp. Psychol.*, vol. 58, pp. 232–8.

BOURNE, L. E., Jr, and RESTLE, F. (1959), 'Mathematical theory of concept identification', *Psychol. Rev.*, vol. 66, pp. 278–96.

BRUNER, J. S., GOODNOW, J. J., and AUSTIN, G. A. (1956), *A study of thinking*, Wiley.

BULGARELLA, R. G., and ARCHER, E. J. (1962), 'Concept identification of auditory stimuli as a function of amount of relevant and irrelevant information', *J. exp. Psychol.*, vol. 63, pp. 254–7.

CONANT, M. B., and TRABASSO, T. (1964), 'Conjunctive and disjunctive concept formation under equal-information conditions', *J. exp. Psychol.*, vol. 67, pp. 250–5.

FLAVELL, J. H. (1963), *The developmental psychology of Jean Piaget*, Van Nostrand.

GARNER, W. R. (1962), *Uncertainty and structure as psychological concepts*, Wiley.

HARLOW, H. F. (1949), 'The formation of learning sets', *Psychol. Rev.*, vol. 56, pp. 51–6.

HAYGOOD, R. C., and BOURNE, L. E., Jr (1964), 'Forms of relevant stimulus redundancy in concept identification', *J. exp. Psychol.*, vol. 67, pp. 392–7.

HOVLAND, C. I. (1952), 'A "communication analysis" of concept learning", *Psychol. Rev.*, vol. 59, pp. 461–72.

HOVLAND, C. I., and WEISS, W. (1953), 'Transmission of information concerning concepts through positive and negative instances', *J. exp. Psychol.*, vol. 45, pp. 175–82.

HUNT, E. B. (1962), *Concept learning: an information processing problem*, Wiley.

HUNT, E. B., and HOVLAND, C. I. (1960), 'Order of consideration of different types of concepts', *J. exp. Psychol.*, vol. 59, pp. 220–5.

HUNT, E. B., and KREUTER, J. M. (1962), *The development of decision trees in concept learning: III. Learning the connectives*, Western Management Sciences Institute, Los Angeles.

KEPROS, P. G., and BOURNE, L. E., Jr (1963), 'The identification of biconditional concepts', *Amer. Psychologist*, vol. 17, p. 424. (Abstract.)

NEISSER, U., and WEENE, P. (1962), 'Hierarchies in concept attainment', *J. exp. Psychol.*, vol. 64, pp. 640–5.

PIAGET, J. (1929), *The child's conception of the world*, Harcourt, Brace.

RESTLE, F. (1962), 'The selection of strategies in cue learning', *Psychol. Rev.*, vol. 69, pp. 329–43.

SHEPARD, R. N., HOVLAND, C. I., and JENKINS, H. N. (1961), 'Learning and memorization of classifications', *Psychol. Monogr.*, vol. 75, whole no. 517.

TRABASSO, T., and BOWER, G. (1964), 'Concept learning in the four-category concept problem', *J. math. Psychol.*, vol. 1, pp. 143–69.

WALKER, C. M., and BOURNE, L. E., Jr (1961), 'Concept identification as a function of amounts of relevant and irrelevant information', *Amer. J. Psychol.*, vol. 74, pp. 410–17.

WELLS, H. (1963), 'Effects of transfer and problem structure in disjunctive concept formation', *J. exp. Psychol.*, vol. 65, pp. 63–9.

20 E. I. Shipstone

Some Variables Affecting Pattern Conception

Excerpts from E. I. Shipstone, 'Some variables affecting pattern conception', *Psychol. Monogr.*, vol. 74 (1960), whole no. 504.

This approach to the study of concept formation is based on the assumption that there is an implicit conception of structure (patterning behavior) in adult human beings and that this can be classified into hierarchically organized categories. In order to give a more definite conception of what this means, we begin with an annotated protocol recorded for a single subject. The procedure described in this sample protocol is slightly different from that used in the main experiments described below; it was chosen, however, in order to unravel for the reader in some detail the process of strategy construction in concept formation. This technique is replaced by a simpler and more concise one in the experiments to be described later.

An Illustrative Study (Experiment I)

The subject sits at a table; across from him is the experimenter. The subject has just finished reading the following instructions:

During the last war an army base was receiving important code information, one message at a time. This information had to be sorted for filing as it was received. Now suppose you were the officer on duty with this important job of receiving and filing this information. You will now be presented with the same information, single message on single card, two cards at first, then one card at a time. You are to study the card and then decide how you are to file it. You can put the cards into as many piles or boxes as you wish and you are free to move around a card from one box to another any time you wish. You will not be limited in time since the decisions you make are very important, but work rapidly. Read these instructions again until you understand them thoroughly and read them again in between if you should forget them.

Any questions?

Now, one further point. As you work with these cards, think aloud as if you were talking to yourself. Talk freely about what you are doing throughout your performance.

Any questions?

'Here,' says the experimenter, 'are the first two cards.' The subject is handed two cards, 5 in. × 8 in., in which are typewritten: ZIR PAG ZIR ZIR PAG NEN; and ZIR PAG NEN PAG NEN PAG NEN PAG NEN PAG NEN PAG NEN PAG ZIR NEN. Only three nonsense words, NEN, PAG, ZIR, arranged in various different orders, are typed on any of the cards; it is convenient to abbreviate them, N, P, and Z. The subject looks at the two cards, laughs selfconsciously, and places them separately on the table in front of him.

He says, 'It seems as though the main difference in the way things repeat is first according to the symbols that appear and then in the order in which they appear.'

There is a silent pause. The experimenter says, 'Now you will have to tell me when you are ready for the next card.'

'Next card, please.'

The next card contains the message ZPZN. The subject places it on the table by itself. All three cards are separately placed, so that the experimenter asks, 'Why did you place that card there?'

'Oh, well,' the subject says, 'there seems to be a difference in the lengths of the messages. And I don't have enough information to really decide on categories. I am just setting them aside until I gather a little more information.'

The experimenter, who has seen some people base their entire classification on the length of the messages, makes a special note that the first basis of classification mentioned by the subject is length. Will he stay with this aspect, or will he look further?

The next card is ZPZZZZZZZZZZZZPN. The subject says, 'Now this card is more similar in length to one of the other ones I received, and it contains a large number of ZIRs as the other one, so I will put these two together, possibly in the same category.' He places together ZPZZZZZZZZZZZZPN and ZPZZPN; since he does not combine ZPZZZZZZZZZZZZPN and ZPNPNPNPNPN-PNPZN, he seems to have rejected length as a basis of classification. For the moment, apparently, his attention is caught by another aspect, the repeating unit ZIR.

The next card is ZPNPZN. The subject reads it silently. There is a long pause. 'Whatever you are thinking,' says the experimenter, 'please say it aloud. I know that is not easy.'

'Well,' says the subject, 'I just noticed that all of the five cards start with the same syllable and the syllables appear to be ordered. Similarly, the second syllables in all the cards are the same. A difference arises in the third syllable, so there is a possibility of arranging these cards according to the syllables. Alphabetically, in other words. But for the time being I will put this card in with the one which has similar length, that is, with the same number of syllables, like six or so.' He proceeds to file them by length, as follows: ZPNPZN and ZPZZPN are put together, ZPNPNPNPNPNPNPZN and ZPZZZZZZZZZZZ-ZZZPN are put together, and ZPZN is left by itself. Although he is beginning to pay attention to the way the messages begin, and to consider the possibility of an alphabetical ordering, he rejects it in favor of a classification on the basis of length. He has destroyed his first tentative grouping on the basis of a repeating unit and has returned to the earlier hypothesis.

The next card is ZPPN. 'Again,' says the subject, 'all the cards start with the same two syllables. But I am going to set this card aside for a separate category for no other reason than that I want to gather more cards before I make a classification.' There is a pause. 'Am I to assume that this is coded information? I mean, information like language information?'

The experimenter replies, 'I am sorry I cannot answer that question for you. These are messages you are receiving and you are trying to file them.'

'Messages are coming in and I am trying to organize them. Hmm . . . temporarily, I am going to rearrange the cards and put them in alphabetical order according to the syllables, starting from the beginning.' The subject seems to hope that something not presently obvious will appear as he tries different spatial arrangements of the cards. As he works at alphabetizing them, he says, 'I've just noticed something that had not occurred to me before, that there are only four symbols.' In fact, of course, there are only three. 'Somehow,' he continues, 'in the beginning I assumed there were going to be more. So, now I am arranging them first of all according to syllables, that is, the syllable order and the first three syllables, and then according to the lengths of the messages.' Since the first two syllables are identical on all the cards that he has seen, any attempt to alphabetize must take into consideration at least the first three syllables of the message.

The experimenter notes that the subject is beginning to combine his rules in an effort to find some new basis for classification. Like most subjects, this one began with relatively simple rules – counting and alphabetizing – ready-made operations he has learned in other contexts; he transfers them bodily to the present task. For some reason, however, the results do not satisfy him and he is now beginning to search for something else. As he collects more cards, he wants to come to terms with them in a way that respects their peculiarities and particularities, not by some ready-made rule that might fit almost anything.

As shown in the chart below, the next card is ZPNPNPNPNPZN. The subject studies this card in silence for almost 60 seconds, looking back and forth between it and other cards spread out on the table before him. Then he makes a new observation, 'I notice now that when I look at these cards in categories that there are units within each card that seem to repeat between cards. Like, for instance, I have two cards here both of which start with ZIR PAG NEN and end in ZIR NEN, and in between they have the unit PAG NEN, but in slightly different numbers. I mean, one card will have more of these units than another card. It seems like relationships are starting to emerge.'

The more complex rule that the subject has just discovered is one that the experimenter has watched many subjects come to; the experimenter calls such formulations 'Initial-Middle-Final Rule'. Although the rule is here applied to only two cards to form a single category, it contains the germ of the filing system that this subject will use for all the remaining cards. Note that it is a rule designed to fit the present situation and to use the particular information provided by this set of messages; it is not a rule that would apply equally well to all imaginable sets of messages.

The order in which the messages were presented to the subject was:

1. Z P Z Z P N
2. Z P N P N P N P N P N P Z N
3. Z P Z N
4. Z P Z Z Z Z Z Z Z Z Z Z Z P N
5. Z P N P Z N
6. Z P P N
7. Z P N P N P N P N P Z N
8. Z P Z Z Z Z Z P N
9. Z P Z Z Z Z Z Z Z Z Z Z Z P N
10. Z P P P P N Z N N N N N P
11. Z P P P N Z P
12. Z P N Z N P
13. Z P N P N P N P Z N
14. Z P P N Z P
15. Z P Z Z Z Z Z Z Z Z N P
16. Z N Z N N N N P
17. Z P N P N P N P N P N P N P N P Z N
18. Z P Z Z Z P N
19. Z P Z Z Z Z Z P N
20. Z P N P N P N P N P N P N P Z N
21. Z P P P P P P P P P P N Z N N N P
22. Z P Z Z Z Z Z Z P N
23. Z P Z Z Z Z Z Z Z Z P N
24. Z P N Z N N P
25. Z P N P N P N P N P Z N
26. Z P Z N
27. Z P N P N P N P N P N P N P N P Z N
28. Z N Z P
29. Z N Z N P
30. Z P P P P P N Z P

263

[. . .] After the subject has received 30 cards and has arranged them as follows (though not necessarily in this order within classes):

A. ZPPN
    ZPZZPN
    ZPZZZPN
    ZPZZZZPN
    ZPZZZZZPN
    ZPZZZZZZPN
    ZPZZZZZZZZPN
    ZPZZZZZZZZZPN
    ZPZZZZZZZZZZZPN
    ZPZZZZZZZZZZZZPN

B. ZPZN
    ZPNPZN
    ZPNPNPNPZN
    ZPNPNPNPNPZN
    ZPNPNPNPNPNPZN
    ZPNPNPNPNPNPNPZN
    ZPNPNPNPNPNPNPNPZN
    ZPNPNPNPNPNPNPNPNPZN

C. ZPNZNP
    ZPNZNNP
    ZPPPPNZNNNNNP
    ZPPPPPPPPPPNZNNNP

D. ZPPNZP
    ZPPPNZP
    ZPPPPPZP

E. ZNZNP
    ZNZNNNNP

Two cards, ZNZP and ZPZN, remain unclassified.

'Okay,' the subject says. 'Well, I'll start out with my biggest and main categories because the relationships are clear, so I'll make sure that they follow all the way through. Now, they all have the same beginning and end syllables. There is no question about that. And, similarly, the second and next-to-last symbol in all – the beginning and end units are similar in all cards. In my first category the intermediate symbols are always ZIRs and they occur in varying numbers. Let's see, one, two, three, skip some; I can order these according to the number of ZIRs in between. I don't suppose it matters as long as I am classifying rather than trying to interpret the information. I can't seem to decide between these: they seem to be homogeneous.'

He shifts to Set B. 'I'll take the next one. Again, we have two syllables that are the same – I mean, they are the same from card to card, beginnings and ends. And we have in between them, rather than one syllable repeating, a pair of syllables repeating . . . and always ending in the same one. So I order these according to the number of insertions.'

He shifts to the Set C. 'Now I am going to look at one of the more complicated categories. Here it seems there's a beginning unit that consists of two syllables on each of the two cards and the end unit which consists of only one syllable' [short pause]. 'In addition, there is a middle unit that consists of NEN ZIR, or whatever it is. And in between there are varying numbers of syllables between the beginning units and the middle unit. In this category there are varying numbers of syllables PAG, so I am going to arrange them in this order. This will be my primary ordering process. And, should there be duplication in the number of PAGs, then I would check the number of symbols on the other side of the middle part, and order them according to their number' [pause]. 'I see that this does occur . . . so, they are ordered first with respect to the symbols between the beginning and the middle, and then with respect to the symbols between the middle and the end. Should there be any ambiguity in the first order . . . it appears like a very nice. . . .' He combines his next three categories into one on the basis of the rule just stated; the result is a third category:

C. ZNZNP
    ZNZNNNNP
    ZPNZNP
    ZPNZNNP
    ZPPNZP
    ZPPPNZP
    ZPPPPNZNNNNNP
    ZPPPPPNZP
    ZPPPPPPPPPPNZNNNP

'Now,' he continues, 'I have the cards in three main categories, and I'll see if they will hold up. Again, they begin with, and end with, the same unit; and the same pattern of middle syllables repeats.'

He shifts to the remaining odd cards, ZNZP and ZPZN. 'Now let's see if my last category. . . . I'm not sure what to do with that – make sure if it doesn't fit into one of the old ones . . . it doesn't as such . . .' [long pause]. 'I'm glancing over all the categories now to make sure that this last category doesn't fit into a subset of those' [pauses while looking]. 'I think. . . .' He picks up ZPZN. 'I now notice that one of these cards does fit in to the, ah, my earlier category. . . . It's curious, I didn't notice it before, but it seems to be identical with the first one in one of my categories. Well, I'll place it there.'

There is a long pause, while he considers the remaining odd card,

ZNZP. 'It seems a shame to have a one-card category. I'll look over once more to see if we can find a place to put it . . . this odd card.'

After a little more search, he gives up. 'I will leave it as it is,' he says, 'I am happy with my classification.' [. . .]

The Problem

After watching a dozen or more subjects perform in a similar manner, one is impressed with several things. The first is the similarity between this laboratory episode and ordinary behavior shown in dealing with our daily environment. All day long stimuli impinge upon an organism in a haphazard array; unless he can rapidly sort and file information in the right compartments his life will quickly revert to chaos. [. . .]

A second impression one gathers is that men have learned to behave in this orderly manner without any specific instructions and without any knowledge of results provided by a teacher or an experimenter. Man seems to respect structure in the world where-ever he finds it, regardless of consequences. [. . .]

Since the notion of structure, or pattern, as proposed by the Gestalt psychologists, seems essential for the description of our subject's behavior, it becomes the starting point of our inquiry. The notion of 'pattern', however, as we use it here, is something of a special case of the Gestalt notion. We are interested in what Miller and Chomsky (1958) have called 'pattern conception'. For the purpose of the present experiments we define pattern as the invariance of a sequence of symbols in the context of lawful change, and we simplify its meaning by defining pattern in terms of internalized rules, or relations, a subject employs to organize novel information. Rules usually imply a notion of abstraction and generalization; they go beyond the information given. [. . .] By the use of rules the subject searches for pattern in order to recode the sensory input into manipulable, meaningful units. Perhaps a limitation on the information capacity of the human channel makes such behavior (recoding) necessary. In any case, it was our wish to find out something about these rules or patterns by which the subject handles information. [. . .]

Materials

Miller and Chomsky (1958) have pointed up some of the difficul-ties of method and material in laboratory studies of concept for-mation. In the earlier concept formation studies the subject was constrained by the nature of the task to find the rules as the experimenter defined them. Furthermore, the use of geometrical patterns differing in size, shape, and color effected a certain stereo-typy in material and usually limited them to a finite number of possible alternatives from which the positive instances were to be selected. Miller and Chomsky proposed the use of a new kind of material in the study of pattern conception, viewing it as a different kind of task: instead of spatial patterns, they proposed to study sequential patterns. By using finite state systems for materials one could study pattern conception in a situation 'modelled after the task of a grammarian'.

A finite state language is an artificial language consisting of the set of strings (sentences) that can be generated by a set of simple rules (see Chomsky and Miller, 1958). This set of rules is a kind of algebra, or grammar, for identifying the grammatical sentences in a particular language. [. . .] Figure 1 is a graphical representa-tion of the finite state generator used in the introductory illustra-tive study. The numbered circles represent the states of the system and the arrows represent the rules of transition permitted from one state to the next. From S_2, for example, the grammar permits us to move to S_5, then back again to S_2, thus: $S_2 \rightleftarrows S_5$. This loop can be traversed any number of times. The nonsense words asso-ciated with the arrows represent the finite set of symbols that comprise the given vocabulary of the language. This particular finite state system has a vocabulary of three words – NEN, PAG, and ZIR, abbreviated as N, P, and Z for convenience. One of these words is generated each time we move from one state to the next. For example, in S_3 the rules say either move to S_4 by generating the word PAG, or make a loop by returning to the same state itself by generating ZIR any number of times. A well-formed string is generated by starting in S_0 and following any route in the diagram and ending in the first visit to $S_{0'}$. The well-formed strings selected by the generator in figure 1 are: ZPZN, ZPPN, ZNZP, ZPZPN, ZPNZP, ZNZMP, ZPNPZN, ZPNZNP, etc. Of these well-formed strings the first three we consider as basic strings. The important feature defining a basic string is that no state is visited more than once. When loops are inserted, states are revisited; basic strings with their loops are termed *formulas*. Basic strings are significant because, as Chomsky and Miller have shown, they provide the pattern for all the longer sentences in the language; in grammatical terms, they are the linguistic 'frames' into which the elements must fit. Any number of different sentences can be generated by following the rules and using the loops any number of times; if we indicate loops by parentheses, however, all the sentences in the system shown in

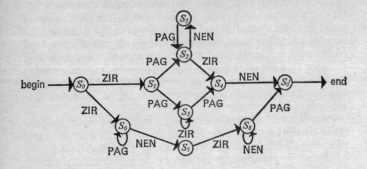

rules of transition

(O,Z,1)	(1,P,3)	(3,Z,3)	(5,P,2)	(7,Z,8)
(O,Z,6)	(2,N,5)	(3,P,4)	(6,P,6)	(8,N,8)
(1,P,2)	(2,Z,4)	(4,N,O′)	(6,N,7)	(8,P,O′)

basic strings	canonical notation		
ZPPN	ZP	(Z)	PN
ZPZN	ZP	(NP)	ZN
ZNZP	Z(P)	NZ	(N)P

*Figure 1   A graphical representation of the finite state generator of
sentences used in the illustrative study. (An admissible string is any
sequence of words generated by starting in state O and ending on the first
visit to O′. All admissible strings can be expressed by means of the
canonical notation given below the figure. Loops have been omitted in the
basic strings. The rules of transition given beneath the diagram comprise
an equivalent description of the generators. Each rule defines the state in
which it is applicable, the symbol it generates, and the next state in which
the rule leaves the system.)*

figure 1 can be represented by a canonical notation of the general
formulas:

$$ZP(Z)PN$$
$$ZP(NP)ZN$$
$$Z(P)NZ(N)P$$

[. . .]

General Procedure

At the beginning of an experimental session a finite set of sentences from a particular language is presented to a subject in a rectangular array of cards on a table surface. The cards have been
previously arranged by tables of random numbers and are all

exposed simultaneously before the subject. (This procedure of presenting all the cards to the subject at once is different from the procedure followed in the illustrative study.) Each 3 in. × 5 in. card contains one string of words only; the string is typed in capital letters on a single line. The subject sits facing the cards; he reads the typed instructions, then repeats them to the experimenter in his own words.

Neutral instructions:

Here is an array of cards to be sorted into groups, into as many or as few groups, as you wish to make and for whatever reason you wish to make them. When you are satisfied with your groups inform the experimenter.

If a subject has any questions regarding the time limit he is informed that there is none. When a subject begins to study the cards the experimenter starts a timer manually; the experimenter stops the timer as soon as the subject is through with his sorting. After the subject has made his groups he is asked to generate two sample strings to match each of his groups and the experimenter records the results of the subject's sortings along with any comments that the subject is willing to make about the way he performed the task. [. . .]

An Exploratory Study (Experiment II)

This experiment was a pilot study (*a*) to explore the kinds of strategies subjects use in grouping a given set of strings generated by finite state grammars (if, indeed, they used any strategy at all), and (*b*) to define some quantitative methods to measure the amount of 'pattern' in each system of categories developed by a subject. [. . .]

A strategy may be successful or less successful. It is considered successful if it corresponds completely with the basic strings of the experimenter's grammar. It is less successful if it deviates from the experimenter's rules. The degree of correspondence between the experimenter's rules and a subject's rules determines the degree of the subject's success. No strategy used by a subject is labeled as completely unsuccessful.

Procedure

In this exploratory study nine different finite state systems were set up in a 3 × 3 design; three different generators (grammar) of three, four, or five basic strings (see diagrams in Figures 2a, 2b, and 2c) were combined in all possible ways with three sizes of vocabulary, either of three, six, or nine words. Nonsense words were used in all the languages in order to minimize possible associations with the stimulus sequences. As a control, a tenth language consisted of sequences of random strings which were generated with the help of tables of random numbers. A vocabulary of three words was used for this set.

The languages were constructed with the following principles in mind: (a) Grammar III (five basic strings) is a hybrid composition from Grammars I and II. (b) The grammars are constructed to facilitate the experimenter in detecting objectively the strategy used by a subject. This principle places a constraint of congruence of certain parts – initial and/or final – in the structure of the basic strings. (c) The placement of symbols on transitional arrows is determined partly by the reason given previously, partly by haphazard assignment. (d) The number of instances (samples) in all ensembles in this study is 16. [. . .]

Sixty subjects were run individually, six subjects per condition. Subjects were distributed one per condition in the order in which they came. [. . .]

Qualitative analysis of strategies

Out of the billions of possible partitions of the 16 instances only about 20 strategies, not always markedly different from each other, were found to be used by subjects. The five most common strategies were labeled as follows:

Length: subject puts together instances having the same number of words.

Alphabet: subject alphabetizes the whole set of instances, treating it as a single category.

Initial: subject sorts by similarity found in the beginnings of sentences. This similarity could range anywhere from one to four words.

Initial-Final: subject sorts by the identicalness both of the beginnings and the endings of sentences.

Formula: this strategy approximates to the experimenter's rules for the finite state generator.

Miscellaneous: this category is a cover-all group for isolated cases of sorting such as sorting by a single striking word, or by the repetitive elements, or by rhythm, etc. [. . .]

Results

The distribution of subjects in the Random group is compared in Figure 3 with two groups (I,3 and III,9) with respect to the kinds

a grammar I

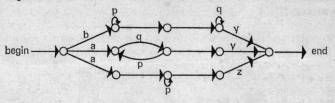

b grammar II

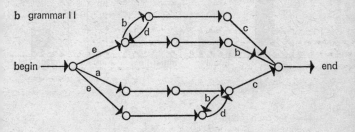

c grammar III

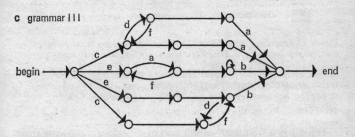

Figure 2   Finite state generators for sentences used in the Exploratory Study (Experiment II). (The small letters on arrows indicate similarities and differences in the initial, final, and loop positions of symbols in the sentences generated.)

of strategies used in each. The bars for the Random group and the (III,9) group are longer at the opposite ends. Condition (I,3) has more affinity with the Random group than is apparent from the figure; three of its subjects who were classified under the Miscellaneous condition in the type of strategy used actually used

271

some kind of differentiated counting technique that was slightly more complex than the plain counting involved in the Length strategy. [. . .]

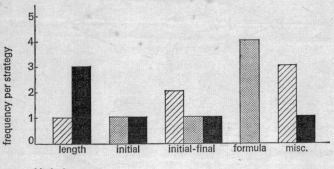

N = 6 for each group
▨ (I,3) group
▧ (III,9) group
■ random group

Figure 3   Frequency comparison of strategies by subjects in the Random and two grammar groups. (The Random group worked with 16 strings that had been haphazardly generated. The (I, 3) group worked with 16 well-formed strings that had been generated with three formulas and a vocabulary of three words. The (III, 9) group worked with 16 well-formed strings that had been generated with five formulas and a vocabulary of nine different words.)

Table 1 is a frequency tabulation of all subjects showing their distribution by the kinds of strategy they employed and the experimental conditions under which they had worked. There are just about five or six types of strategy that cover all subjects under the various conditions tested. The better or more successful strategies are used under some conditions more than in others. For example, none of the 18 subjects used the Length or the Alphabet strategies when the number of alternative words used was nine. Ten of these subjects used some form of the Formula strategy. When the sentences were formed with a vocabulary of only three words, on the other hand, 5 of the 18 subjects used the simpler

Table 1
Frequency Distribution of Subjects in the Respective Language Groups by the Type of Strategy They Used

T – T.R. – L

Grammar	Kind of strategy						N
	Length	Alphabet	Initial	Init.-Final	Formula	Misc.	
Random	3		1	1		1	6
(I,3)	1			2		3	
(II,3)	1	1	1				
(III,3)	1	1	1	3	4		
Total	(3)	(2)	(1)	(5)	(4)	(3)	18
(I,6)	2		1	1	1	1	
(II,6)	2		2		2		
(III,6)			2	2	1	1	
Total	(4)	—	(5)	(3)	(4)	(2)	18
(I,9)			3	2	4		
(II,9)			1	1	2		
(III,9)			1	1	4		
Total	—	—	(4)	(4)	(10)		18
Sum Total	10	2	11	13	18	6	60

Note. – Figures in parentheses are sums of frequencies immediately preceding those totals.

strategies and only 4 discovered the Formula strategy; all of those 4 subjects came from the same condition group. [. . .]

Discussion

Pattern conception. – What we had observed as a dramatic instance of orderly responses demonstrated in the introductory study, was confirmed by the responses of more than fifty subjects in this exploratory experiment. It is not a fortuitous matter that no subject, not even one from the Random group, handed the cards back to the experimenter in some haphazard arrangement or declared the task insoluble. On the contrary, in each case the subject used some kind of a system by which he had looked for relations among the instances to create his categories. Even with the Random group some subjects worked very hard and long trying to find some sort of scheme to organize their information. By and large, the subject could verbalize the type of relations that he had discovered in terms of a rule or rules though he was not always able to do this with precision.

Hierarchy in rules. – The thing that amazed us most was that nearly all subjects could be classified so easily within the same general types of five or six strategies – strategies which were, by and large, the same ones we noted earlier in the responses of our single subject described above in the illustrative study. In other words, a hierarchy in rules that was indicated in the individual's responses seems to characterize the group responses as well. This is a two-sided observation: it points first, to the fact that responses under all conditions of card sorting described above are classifiable within five or six easily detectable strategies; and second, that these strategies themselves can be ordered in complexity.

We can classify these strategies into two types: the ready-made type and the invented type. Ready-made rules are independent of the nature of the information to be processed. The rule of counting, for instance, to make groups of equal length, already exists in a subject's repertory and can be easily transferred to almost any kind of material. The ready-made rule applies whether the materials be heads of cattle, pictures in an art gallery, or the coded messages about the enemy's moves. This rule of counting is an instance of a simple quantitative strategy that is highly useful in dealing with certain kinds of information, but not so appropriate for certain other kinds. The counting rule may take on slightly different shades, as counting the number of different words, or counting the number of repetitions of any word, etc., but essentially it is the same rule that is applied.

Alphabetizing is here classified as a ready-made strategy because this rule, too, already exists in the everyday repertory of a college student. Since it is always possible to alphabetize a given series of words of any language, it requires little ingenuity on the part of a subject to apply this rule.

It is important to note that a subject loses information by applying the simple strategies of counting and alphabetizing to these not-so-simple sequences. We have, therefore, evaluated such strategies as being less successful. A strategy is rated as less successful in proportion to the amount it deviates from the finite state grammar which governs the given strings. In the simpler strategies a subject seems to work more with the perceptual characteristics of the information than with the structural ones.

Subjects in the Random group, which is the control group for all the nine experimental groups, seem to resort to the simple strategies, particularly the one of counting, more than the subjects in the grammar groups seem to do, except the subjects of the (I,3) group. The responses of this group have close kinship with the responses of the Random group. When a subject in any group either finds the task too difficult for him or when he does not wish to exert himself, functionally, he is treating the grammar strings as if they were random strings. Hence the strategies that subjects would be found to be using in these instances would be close kins to counting or to alphabetizing strategies. It seems highly probable that subjects in the (I,3) group were treating the grammar strings as random strings.

The observed fact that a subject in the Random group follows a counting strategy does not necessarily imply that the subject has worked with one strategy only. Subjects' protocols bear evidence to the contrary. Several subjects described complex strategies that they had tried to apply to the strings, but which they had discarded because they always seemed to find too large a number of single cases. Notice that a subject is uneasy about having too many one-case categories, and this is virtually what he would find in the random set where each instance is unique. After having searched for abstract relations, a subject is forced by the stimulus properties of the set to settle for something less. This sample of behavior is apropos to the basic argument in this thesis.

Strategies labeled Invented are different from the ones just described. We classify the Initial-Final strategy and the Formula strategy under this label because it is the nature of the materials which suggests these strategies to the observer. A high degree of discovery, however, is also involved in these strategies, but since a subject is unaware of the embeddedness of any formulas within the materials, we prefer to call them the Invented rules rather than the Discovered rules. This label, however, applies most appropriately to the Formula strategy. In this strategy the subject has to go beyond the obvious information. The subject has to tease out an invariant sequence of words in each of the instances, as also he must find the recursive units. The search for invariance and variance yields formulas which are the basic framework for the grammar strings. This type of response calls for a certain degree of abstraction in order to discover the true pattern implicit in the strings.

Invented strategies correlate more closely with the information given. Since the instructions a subject receives are neutral, his only source of information is the set of strings he has before him. The amount of information he is able to extract from them is a critical factor in the way he will process the information. His efficiency in extracting the maximum amount of useful information depends largely upon two, sometimes interdependent, conditions of motivation and stimulus complexity. [. . .]

Subjects who do not get seriously involved in the task may or may not end with the Invented strategies. One subject in the Random group worked with her 16 cards for 41 minutes. She tried to make groups by initial similarities, by ratio relations, by sequence relations, and by a method of substitution. But when none of these strategies worked by her criterion of success, she resorted, according to her own version, to 'the simplest strategy of counting'. The task of seeing relations among the random strings is perhaps psychologically more complex than the task of seeing relations where relations do in fact exist.

The results from all nine grammar group conditions of finite state systems where relations do in fact exist, do not distribute under the Invented strategies only. Some do and some do not. In Table 1 we notice that the stimulus condition, where nine alternative words were used to develop the strings of sequences, as compared to three in the Random group, and three and six in the other two conditions, more than 50 per cent of the subjects evolved the Formula strategy as compared to the 0 per cent of the Random group and 22 per cent in each of the other two. Of these, the 20 per cent of subjects in the vocabulary three group, all come from a single condition (II,3), meaning that none of the subjects from Condition (I,3) or (III,3) or (0,3) arrived at the Formula strategy.

Are these differences, indicated in the percentages of subjects who evolve the Invented strategies and those who do not, functionally related to the complexity of the experimental variables under which subjects work? If so, what constitutes experimental complexity? That is the question we turn to in the next section.

Experimental Variables

In the exploratory study of the previous section evidence for a search for pattern was found. Sometimes this search was creative, sometimes transitive, but what was not clear from the data was why this difference existed in the quality of performance. Informal evidence suggested that instruction was one variable that needed to be controlled more precisely and the data indicated that some stimulus features of the input were contributing to the outcome. Accordingly, some experiments were carried out to assess the effect of the following four variables:

1. Instructions. Four different instructions were tested to select one that would maximally involve the subject in the task, but with minimal guidance from the nature of the instructions.

2. Number of instances. The number of different instances per basic formula was varied from two instances to three to four, to test the effect of the amount of evidence on the quality of strategy.

3. Number of different alternatives (Vocabulary). Three or nine different words comprised the vocabulary for developing the different language systems.

4. Structural similarity (Grammar). The effect of the formal structure of the languages, three rules as against five rules with variation in similarity between the rules, was also investigated. [. . .]

The instructions, to the extent to which they were varied, did not produce a strong effect on the quality of the performance. Other variables (complexity of grammar, number of different alternatives, number of instances) seem to be more important because they can make the problem so hard that they mask out the effects of instructions. When conditions are optimal for instructions to have an effect, the main effect that changed instructions produced was to slow subjects down to make them stop, look, and think more carefully. [. . .]

The results show that the variety of symbols (number of different alternatives) with which the messages are constructed is far more critical in controlling pattern conception than is the length or the structure of the messages. Two sets of messages, identical in length, in rules of formation, and in the instruction given subjects, but differing in the number of symbols, elicit qualitatively different responses. A large variety of symbols tends to elicit the invented strategies whereas the small variety generally leads to ready-made rules. This result indicates that the subject is able to recode the given information more effectively when there is a variety in the symbols from which it is composed.

A parallel advantage is observed by increasing the amount of evidence provided to a subject for a given rule. The number of instances per rule was varied from two to three to four instances, while other factors of vocabulary, grammar, and instructions were held constant. The strategies that subjects used under each of these conditions were evaluated in terms of two statistical techniques developed specifically for the purpose of strategy analysis. As the amount of evidence increased, the strategies improved. A larger quantity of evidence facilitates recoding of the sequences in terms of variant and invariant symbols.

Earlier experiments on perception have indicated that redundancy may be of several kinds, and that the influence of redundancy upon responses varies with its quality. Although we have not applied an information measure of redundancy to our materials (the finite state systems that we used are too simple to require such statistical treatment) we have worked with a related conception of structural similarity (rules of formation) in linguistic sequences. Languages varying in number and complexity of rules of formation, but similar in length and size of vocabulary, do not yield markedly different results. The fewer rules embedded in a language do not necessarily make that language simpler. Data indicate that structural redundancy is less critical in pattern conception than is the variety in symbols or the amount of evidence. More experiments with better controls on redundancy are needed to determine the effect of this variable on pattern conception.

Two specific difficulties were found to characterize the responses of many subjects in almost all of the experimental groups. These difficulties we shall label as: the zero concept difficulty and the double loop concept difficulty. [. . .]

The zero concept: it was not infrequent to find a subject puzzled about the basic string of a formula. For example, if one of the formulas in a grammar was: a (c) b b a, its basic string, a (c)^0 b b a, was often held as a separate card for a considerable period of time and was even placed in a separate category by some subjects. When a subject had decoded a grammatical rule as the experimenter had structured it, he could easily see the arithmetical progression in the development of a loop move from 1 to n, even though quite deliberately some exponents in the progression had been left out.

But it seemed difficult for a subject to see that the exponent of the loop could also be zero. Viewed historically, the zero concept was not easily come by either. Perhaps it is difficult for one to think of starting a series with nothing. Normal counting frequently begins with 1 and moves up to n. It is, therefore, quite possible that this way of counting interferes with the necessity to begin the series with the zero notation in our formulas.

The double-loop concept: the zero concept seemed even more difficult for subjects to handle in the double-loop formulas. This was so because the double-loop in itself was a hard concept for the subject. We have described the double-loop as a formula consisting of two variables, instead of just one, within an invariant sequence of symbols. It has been schematized thus: a (c) b c (b) a.

Some subjects broke up the double loop subset into three further sub-subsets as follows: a $(c)^{1-n}$ b c a, a b c $(b)^{1-n}$ a, and a $(c)^{1-n}$ b c $(b)^{1-n}$ a. The basic string was either held as a separate category, or it was placed with one of the first two sub-subsets. In watching subjects at work, it was fairly obvious to the experimenter that subjects were having considerable difficulty with the double-loop subset. They insisted upon applying the simple rule of one loop varying from 0 or 1 to n to this complex formula, and were confused with the similarity within the three sub-subsets. This can be very clearly seen in the thinking-aloud responses of our subject in the Illustrative Study. One could explain this difficulty on the basis of two characteristics of pattern response. The first, that the subject formulates his method early in the game and more or less stays with it; and the second, that the subject seeks to apply one pattern consistently throughout to all parts of the system.

Reiss (1958) pointed out that a subject constructs his 'model' fairly early, and then begins to stabilize around it as he tests it with successive negative or positive instances. From the thinking-aloud responses of our subjects and on the basis of data from other studies on the evolution of strategies not reported here, Reiss seems to be right. Those subjects who initiated a Counting strategy in the beginning showed a strong counting bias, and those who used the Initial strategy stuck pretty closely to the left-to-right rule of comparing sequences. Exceptions did occur in the Random group, or when the method of presentation of instances was varied. In the Random set, one could find the subject trying all sorts of strategies, and finally settling on a perceptual one, when nothing else seemed to work. But in the sets where the subject had once perceived the structural order in a subset fairly early, or even later, he did not give it up. This does not mean, of course, that there is no further refinement of the strategy with an increase in the amount of evidence. It simply means that more instances only help to sharpen or modify the 'model' already constructed.

This kind of fixation in strategy ties in with the point we are making about consistency in sorting. By and large, most subjects work with one method of classification for all the subsets they make. They do not seem to want to shift gears in their strategy from subset to subset. This characteristic way of responding is independent of the input, and it seems to give us some information about the human channel itself. It is, therefore, important to note that not only does a subject organize the input sequences into categories, but that he does this on the basis of a consistent principle. [. . .]

Pattern conception, apparently, is not a simple function of any one experimental variable. This point was most clearly evident from the time measures, which did not correlate consistently with any one experimental condition. It was reasonably clear, however, that the longer time measures correlated positively with the better strategies. Presumably, the central processes of recoding and thinking take time, which causes the delay in response. There was little evidence for an increase in time with the increasing length of the set.

Finally, all studies led us to conclude that, irrespective of the type of finite state system used – its structure, vocabulary, length, or anything else – the average number of categories that subjects make is five or six. Although we were not looking for this point, this result is in keeping with the findings from some studies on 'channel capacity', Miller (1956), and it indicates that thinking like memory is centrally affected by the channel capacity of the organism.

References

CHOMSKY, N., and MILLER, G. A. (1958), 'Finite state languages', *Inform. Control*, vol. 1, pp. 91–112.

MILLER, G. A. (1956), 'The magical number seven, plus or minus two: some limits on our capacity for processing information', *Psychol. Rev.*, vol. 63, pp. 81–97.

MILLER, G. A., and CHOMSKY, N. (1958), 'Pattern conception', Paper delivered at conference on pattern detection at University of Michigan.

REISS, D. (1958), *Subjective models of a simple finite-state grammar: a study of their attainment and characteristics*, Unpublished honors thesis, Harvard University.

Part Five INFORMATION PROCESSING MODELS AND COMPUTER SIMULATION

As we noted in the Introduction, it is difficult to compare human performance with a computer simulation of it. Hence it is not surprising that more theoretical than empirical investigations have been carried out in this area. The value of such theoretical research, however, is that it suggests the operation of analogous mechanisms which control human thinking. For example, Gilson and Abelson (15) report an empirical study inspired by a computer program. Craik (21), in a chapter of his book *The nature of explanation*, written before the development of electronic computers, points the way towards simulation in his speculations about the analogies between mind and mechanism. Miller, Galanter and Pribram (22), in a chapter from their book *Plans and the structure of behavior*, survey the influential work of Newell, Shaw and Simon on simulation of human problem solving, and the ideas of the mathematician, G. Polya, on the heuristics of problem solving. Just as a computer is controlled by its program, Miller *et al.* postulate that human beings organize their behaviour by means of 'plans', and their chapter is concerned with how we develop plans to cope with new situations. The notion of a plan is based on the *test-operate-test-exit* or TOTE concept which represents the simplest type of feedback loop: test for a discrepancy between what is and what should be, if none then exit; if there is discrepancy, operate to reduce it; test again, and so on. Neisser (23) distinguishes two types of human thinking – rational, controlled and routine as opposed to irrational, uncontrolled and creative. He postulates two underlying patterns for their organization: a single sequential process for rational thinking, and multiple parallel processes interacting with each other for creative thinking. The same dichotomy is realized in a program described by Reitman *et al*. (24) which simulates the solution of simple analogy problems by human beings. Finally, Hunter (25), in a paper hitherto unavailable in English, describes the plans utilized by a human calculator – the eminent mathematician, A. C. Aitken – in the course of performing prodigious mental calculations.

21 K. J. W. Craik

Hypothesis on the Nature of Thought

Excerpt from K. J. W. Craik, *The nature of explanation*, Cambridge University Press, 1943, chapter 5.

One of the most fundamental properties of thought is its power of predicting events. This gives it immense adaptive and constructive significance as noted by Dewey and other pragmatists. It enables us, for instance, to design bridges with a sufficient factor of safety instead of building them haphazard and waiting to see whether they collapse, and to predict consequences of recondite physical or chemical processes whose value may often be more theoretical than practical. In all these cases the process of thought, reduced to its simplest terms, is as follows: a man observes some external event or process and arrives at some 'conclusion' or 'prediction' expressed in words or numbers that 'mean' or refer to or describe some external event or process which comes to pass if the man's reasoning was correct. During the process of reasoning, he may also have availed himself of words or numbers. Here there are three essential processes:

1. 'Translation' of external process into words, numbers or other symbols,

2. Arrival at other symbols by a process of 'reasoning', deduction, inference, etc., and

3. 'Retranslation' of these symbols into external processes (as in building a bridge to a design) or at least recognition of the correspondence between these symbols and external events (as in realizing that a prediction is fulfilled).

One other point is clear; this process of reasoning has produced a final result similar to that which might have been reached by causing the actual physical processes to occur (e.g., building the bridge haphazard and measuring its strength or compounding certain chemicals and seeing what happened); but it is also clear that this is not what has happened; the man's mind does not contain a material bridge or the required chemicals. Surely, however, this process of prediction is not unique to minds, though no doubt it is hard to imitate the flexibility and versatility of mental prediction. A calculating machine, an anti-aircraft 'predictor', and Kelvin's tidal predictor all show the same ability. In all these latter cases, the physical process which it is desired to predict is *imitated* by some mechanical device or model which is cheaper, or quicker, or more convenient in operation. Here we have a very close parallel to our three stages of reasoning – the 'translation' of the external processes into their representatives (positions of gears, etc.) in the model; the arrival at other positions of gears, etc., by mechanical processes in the instrument; and finally, the retranslation of these into physical processes of the original type.

By a model we thus mean any physical or chemical system which has a similar relation-structure to that of the process it imitates. By 'relation-structure' I do not mean some obscure non-physical entity which attends the model, but the fact that it is a physical working model which works in the same way as the process it parallels, in the aspects under consideration at any moment. Thus, the model need not resemble the real object pictorially; Kelvin's tide-predictor, which consists of a number of pulleys on levers, does not resemble a tide in appearance, but it works in the same way in certain essential respects – it combines oscillations of various frequencies so as to produce an oscillation which closely resembles in amplitude at each moment the variation in tide level at any place. Again, since the physical object is 'translated' into a working model which gives a prediction which is retranslated into terms of the original object, we cannot say that the model invariably either precedes or succeeds the external object it models. The only logical distinction is on the ground of cheapness, speed, and convenience. The *Queen Mary* is designed with the aid of a model in a tank because of the greater cheapness and convenience of the latter; we do not design toy boats by trying out the different plans on boats the size of Atlantic liners. In the same way, in the particular case of our own nervous systems, the reason why I regard them as modelling the real process is that they permit trial of alternatives, in, e.g., bridge design, to proceed on a cheaper and smaller scale than if each bridge in turn were built and tried by sending a train over it, to see whether it was sufficiently strong.

Many mechanistic views of life and behaviour have been advanced, for instance those of Hartley and Cabanis. But on the one hand there has been a tendency to *assert* a mechanistic theory rather than to regard it as a hypothesis which should, if followed out, indicate exactly how and where it breaks down; and on the other hand, there has been little attempt to formulate a definite plan of a mechanism which would fulfil the requirements. Hull has, however, made some models which show response to an altered stimulus, or conditioning. I have not committed myself to a definite picture of the mechanisms of synaptic resistance, facilitation, etc.; but I have tried, in the succeeding pages, to indicate what I suspect to be the fundamental feature of neural machinery – its power to parallel or model external events – and have emphasized the fundamental role of this process of paralleling in calculating machines. Thus, it is perhaps better to start with a definite idea as to the kind of tasks mechanism can accomplish in calculation, and the tasks it would have to accomplish in order to play a part in thought, rather than to draw analogies between the nervous system and some specific mechanism such as a telephone exchange and leave the matter there. A telephone exchange may resemble the nervous system in just the sense I think important; but the essential point is the principle underlying the similarity.

Now it may be that a mind does not function only in this way; but as this is *one* way that 'works', in fact the only way with which we are familiar in the physical sciences, and as there is abundant evidence of the great mechanical possibilities of the nervous system, it does not seem overbold to consider whether the brain does not work in this way – that it imitates or models external processes. The three processes of translation, inference, and re-translation then become the translation of external events into some kind of neural patterns by stimulation of the sense-organs, the interaction and stimulation of other neural patterns as in 'association', and the excitation by these of effectors or motor organs.

Without inquiring into the relation between such neural patterns and the unitary symbols of thought – words, numbers, etc. – we can study to some extent the scope and limits of this modelling or imitative process, by studying the scope and limits of the two great classes of symbols – words and numbers.

Any kind of working model of a process is, in a sense, an analogy. Being different it is bound somewhere to break down by showing properties not found in the process it imitates or by not possessing properties possessed by the process it imitates. Perhaps the extraordinary pervasiveness of number, and the multiplicity of operations which can be performed on number without leading to inconsistency, is not a proof of the 'real existence' of numbers as such but a proof of the extreme flexibility of the neural model or calculating machine. This flexibility renders a far greater number of operations possible for it than for any other single process or model. [. . .]

We have now to inquire how the neural mechanism, in producing numerical measurement and calculation, has managed to function in a way so much more universal and flexible than any other. Our question, to emphasize it once again, is not to ask what kind of thing a number is, but to think what kind of mechanism could represent so many physically possible or impossible, and yet self-consistent, processes as number does.

The key may possibly lie in the following fact: in causal chains and physical or chemical combinations, the possibility of a given combination tends to be limited by other factors than the mere self-consistency of the combination. If you try to determine whether the series of integers can be extended to infinity by piling bricks on top of one another, you find that after a time the bricks fall down, or you cannot reach to pile any more up, or you run short of bricks or die; all these are extraneous difficulties. More subtle are the difficulties of adding nine oranges to nine apples, or of trying to produce a physical four-dimensional object. In all these cases we have not been satisfied with simply finding whether a given combination can exist along with other combinations; we have chosen a combination of combinations (i.e., a *number* of *objects*) which of course limits the number of possible self-consistent combinations, just as in a game of rolling balls into grooves under a glass lid the number of times all are simultaneously in their grooves decreases as the number of balls is increased. In a mechanism such as a telephone exchange or a nervous system, where one is not trying to produce new objects but merely combinations of active or excited elements, the possible combinations are at a maximum, limited only by remoteness of excited elements (*vide* failure of association) or decrease of excitation with time (*vide* forgetting). Even these difficulties can be to some extent overcome by further use of written and spoken symbols to act as a kind of reinforcing or relay system.

This greatly extended power is not unique to a mind; it could be illustrated by calculating machines. A machine working on a graphical principle might try to represent squaring and cubing by pointers moving along the x, y and z axes; it would inevitably come to a standstill or repeat itself when the volume of the cube equalled its own volume. On the other hand, a machine working on the principle of picking up gear-teeth by a repeated-multiplication process could go on raising any number to any power however large if it had sufficient dials on it.

It is likely then that the nervous system is in a fortunate position, as far as modelling physical processes is concerned, in that it has only to produce combinations of excited arcs, not physical objects; its 'answer' need only be a combination of consistent patterns of excitation – not a new object that is physically and chemically stable.

We have now to inquire what meaning causality, implication, consistency and so forth can have when applied to such a mechanism. Again, our question is not 'What kind of thing is implication or causality?' but 'What structure and processes are required in a mechanical system to enable it to imitate correctly and to predict external processes or create new things?'

In examining this question, we can divide the process of thinking or reasoning into the same steps as before – representation by symbols, calculation, and retranslation into events.

The diversity of calculating machines, languages and words for numbers shows that a relation can be represented in several symbolic ways. *Unique determination* is the main principle; a symbol, a setting of a machine, or a neural pattern is liable to be misleading if it represents two distinct types of physical things or events.

Causality in the external world would be represented by some (causal) process of interaction between excited elements in our own brains. As a result of such interactive or associative processes we might have, for example, $A=B$, $B=C$, $A \neq C$, where A, B and C are neural patterns claiming to represent external things or processes. These patterns clearly cannot all remain simultaneously excited; inconsistency means a clash in the interaction of patterns.

My hypothesis then is that thought models, or parallels, reality – that its essential feature is not 'the mind', 'the self', 'sense-data', nor propositions but symbolism, and that this symbolism is largely of the same kind as that which is familiar to us in mechanical devices which aid thought and calculation.

I hope no one will be deterred by the idea that such a theory regards thought as an inactive halo round mechanical brain processes; for though my hypothesis assumes that thought processes and consciousness are dependent on mechanical processes, it tries to discover what function consciousness does perform, by seeing where a purely mechanical process fails to meet the facts. If it is true, it would be a hylozoistic rather than a materialistic scheme; it would attribute consciousness and conscious organization to matter when it is physically organized in certain ways. However, these are remote speculations; the important point is to propound the theory and to consider ways of testing it.

We shall not consider purely speculative consequences of it, but only inferences which have some possibility of being experimentally verified, though we cannot claim that they provide critical tests of it. There remains the vitalist possibility – that life and mind, something different and aloof from physical matter, enters, and that we are misguided in our attempts to explain any aspects of conscious processes in terms of their material basis. But if so, the failure ought to show itself somewhere, if we proceed with due caution in the proposal and testing of hypotheses.

It is generally agreed that thought employs symbols such as written or spoken words or tokens; but it is not generally considered whether the whole of thought may not consist of a process of symbolism, nor is the nature of symbolism and its presence or absence in the inorganic world discussed. Further, it has been usual to restrict the word 'symbol' to words or tokens, which still leaves the processes of the relating of words to form sentences and the processes of inference and implication mysterious and unique. Let us consider whether these processes are not paralleled by familiar mechanisms.

First, we have seen that the possibility of verbal or other symbolism is the fundamental assumption of all philosophy communicated by anyone to anyone else. Without falling into the trap of attempting a precise definition, we may suggest a theory as to the general nature of symbolism, namely, that it is the ability of processes to parallel or imitate each other, or the fact that they can do so since there are recurrent patterns in reality. The concepts of abilities and patterns and formal identity in material diversity are all hard ones; but the point is that symbolism does occur, and that we wish to explore its possibilities. There are three main steps: first, is there any evidence of such symbolism in inorganic nature? secondly, do we ourselves employ such symbolism in thought? and thirdly, is there any evidence that our thought processes themselves involve such symbolism, occurring within our brains and nervous systems?

There are plenty of instances in nature of processes which parallel each other – the emptying of pools and the discharge of a cat's fur which has become electrified, the transmission of sound and electromagnetic and ocean waves, and so forth. As mentioned above, human thought has a definite function; it provides a convenient small-scale model of a process so that we can, for instance, design a bridge in our minds and know that it will bear a train passing over it instead of having to conduct a number of full-scale experiments; and the thinking of animals represents, on a more restricted scale, the ability to represent, say, danger before it comes, and leads to avoidance instead of repeated bitter experience. In inorganic nature, because of its simpler organization, we should expect this function to be less fully exemplified. Indeed, there are very few examples at all. Perhaps the nearest approach is the fine trickle of water which first finds its way from a mountain spring down to the sea and smoothes a little channel for the greater volume of water which follows after it. But the *material* of symbolism – the parallel mechanisms – seem to be there; it is only the sensitive 'receptors' on matter, and means of intercommunication or nervous system, which are lacking.

Again, there is no doubt that we do use external and mechanical symbolization to assist our own thinking. Provided with a piece of paper we can perform long and complicated calculations which would be impossible in our heads; and the Busch differential analyser will solve problems which could not be tackled by any other method.

Finally, there is some, though scanty, evidence from anatomy and electrophysiology that our nervous systems do contain conducting sensory and motor paths and synapses in which there occur states of excitation and volleys of impulses which parallel the stimuli which occasioned them; so that, as far as experimental evidence goes, this symbolization is found to occur in the central nervous system. But what produces and occasions it, on such a mechanistic theory? In any mechanical system, the events which occur are those which result in the greatest possible equalization of energy – roughly speaking, the reactions take the path of least resistance. If parts of an organization are inter-connected by a system of communication such as the nervous system, the reactions can be directed along the 'lines of least resistance' by the expenditure of a very little energy in the appropriate 'lines of least resistance' in the nervous system. The situation is enormously complicated by natural selection, which causes the survival of certain organisms – those, for instance, in whom the passage of the 'monitoring' nerve impulse results in such activity of the whole organism as will tend to preserve it. In general, it is much more illuminating to regard the growth of symbolizing power from this aspect of survival-value, rather than from the purely physical side of accordance with thermodynamics; but it does not seem that there is any inconsistency between the two.

Thus there are instances of symbolization in nature; we use such instances as an aid to thinking; there is evidence of similar mechanisms at work in our own sensory and central nervous systems; and the function of such symbolization is plain. If the organism carries a 'small-scale model' of external reality and of its own possible actions within its head, it is able to try out various alternatives, conclude which is the best of them, react to future situations before they arise, utilize the knowledge of past events in dealing with the present and future, and in every way to react in a much fuller, safer, and more competent manner to the emergencies which face it. Most of the greatest advances of modern technology have been instruments which extended the scope of our sense-organs, our brains or our limbs. Such are telescopes and microscopes, wireless, calculating machines, typewriters, motorcars, ships and aeroplanes. Is it not possible, therefore, that our brains themselves utilize comparable mechanisms to achieve the same ends and that these mechanisms can parallel phenomena in the external world as a calculating machine can parallel the development of strains in a bridge?

The Formation of Plans

Excerpt from G. A. Miller, E. Galanter and K. H. Pribram, *Plans and the structure of behavior*, Holt, 1960, chapter 13.

Where do Plans[1] come from? Probably the major source of new Plans is old Plans. We change them around a little bit each time we use them, but they are basically the same old Plans with minor variations. Sometimes we may borrow a new Plan from someone else. But we do not often create a completely new Plan.

Consider the origins of the Plans we have discussed: instincts are inherited Plans and so are not created by the individual who executes them. Habits and skills are most frequently acquired by imitation or verbal instruction from another person, although they may develop inadvertently as we attempt to cope with the pattern of events around us. Shared Plans are normally communicated to us as participants, but even when we help to originate a new shared Plan we usually try to form it along lines already familiar. Plans for remembering attempt to exploit familiar situations and previously established associations. When we speak we usually try to say something that is not completely predictable, but the novelty of what we say is always subject to well-established grammatical Plans that we are not at liberty to revise. Even in thinking and problem solving we are continually executing Plans tediously mastered at school.

This attitude toward the question of where we get our Plans resembles the attitude of Boston matrons toward their hats: 'My dear, we don't *get* our hats, we *have* them.' The analogy could be improved, however, if they had a few hats and only the pattern for many others. When we say that most Plans are remembered, not created, we do not mean that the Plan is stored in memory ready for execution down to the very last muscle twitch. Often it is a metaplan that is stored – a metaplan from which a large number of different Plans can be generated as they are needed.

When do we store Plans directly and when do we store Plans for generating Plans? For example, the Plan for reciting the alphabet is probably stored – memorized – directly, like any other motor skill. And so is the Plan for counting, at least through the first few hundred integers. But as the numbers begin to get large it is likely

1. See the introduction to this section, p. 281.

that we work in terms of a metaplan, a set of rules for generating $N+1$ from N, rather than with a direct Plan for uttering the successive integers. There are interesting questions here concerning the mental economies involved – how frequently must a Plan be used before it is worth our while to memorize it directly rather than to remember a Plan for reconstructing it?

A kind of low-level creativity is displayed by any system complex enough to have metaplans. For example, in using an electronic computer to make calculations involving logarithms, a decision must be made whether to store a table of logarithms in the computer's memory or to give the computer a formula for calculating logarithms as they are needed. If the table is used, the logarithm will be rapidly found if it is in the table, but the computer will be unable to handle any numbers whose logarithms it has not been given explicitly. If the formula is used the process will be slower, but the computer will be able to 'create' the logarithms of numbers it has not seen before. Therein lies a great advantage of formulas, sets of rules, metaplans: they are easily stored, and when there is time to use them they can be projected into an infinite variety of unforeseen situations. The advantages of having Plans to generate Plans is so great that no intelligent automaton, living or dead, could get along without them. They not only permit the electronic computer to seem creative in a trivial way with logarithms, they permit men to be creative in significant ways in a wide variety of situations.

Consider some well-defined problem, such as finding a proof of a mathematical expression, and note the levels of metaplanning that are involved. The expression is itself a Plan that can be used to carry out some particular arithmetic operations – it has its own hierarchical organization and can be analysed in much the same way a sentence can be parsed. The proof is a sequence of those mathematical expressions and will characteristically have its own hierarchical structure. Thus, the proof is also a Plan. And it is a metaplan because the objects it operates on are themselves Plans. But the system cannot stop there. There is a third level of planning that we discover as soon as we think of the procedures that the mathematician used in order to generate the proof. If the proof is a path leading from the expressions that were given to the expression that was to be proved, then the mathematician had to explore a great variety of possible paths in order to find this one. Searches are generally conducted according to some kind of Plan, usually a heuristic Plan. So we must have a heuristic Plan for generating a proof Plan for transforming a mathematical

Plan for performing certain computations. Does it stop there? Is it necessary to add the students of heuristic – mathematicians, computer engineers, psychologists, teachers, etc. – who may someday be able to specify hierarchical organizations for generating heuristics? Is it possible for all Plans to have metaplans that write 'em, and so on *ad infinitum*? Or is heuristic the end of the line? It seems that heuristic Plans are as far as one can go in this regression, for the methods used to discover new heuristic Plans would themselves be heuristic Plans. A plausible account of heuristic Plans, therefore, will provide the general outlines within which a theory of thinking about well-defined problems can eventually be constructed.

In his popular text, *How to solve it*, Polya distinguishes four phases in the heuristic process:

First, we must understand the problem. We have to see clearly what the data are, what conditions are imposed, and what the unknown thing is that we are searching for.

Second, we must devise a plan that will guide the solution and connect the data to the unknown.

Third, we must carry out our plan of the solution, checking each step as we go.

Fourth, we should look back at the completed solution, reviewing, checking, discussing, perhaps even improving it.

Obviously, the second of these is most critical. The first is essentially the construction of a clear Image of the situation in order to establish a test for the solution of the problem; it is indispensable, of course, but in the discussion of well-defined problems we assume that it has already been accomplished. The third is the execution of a Plan, and although it may be costly or require much skill, we assume that it can be performed in a straightforward manner. The fourth phase is important for the student who wants to develop his ability to solve problems, for it facilitates storing the method for future use. However, it is in the second phase, the actual formation of a Plan, that something creative must happen. As Polya describes it:

We have a plan when we know, or at least know in outline, which calculations, computations, or constructions we have to perform in order to obtain the unknown. The way from understanding the problem to conceiving a plan may be long and tortuous. In fact, the main achievement in the solution of a problem is to conceive the idea of a plan. This idea may emerge gradually. Or, after apparently unsuccessful trials and a period of hesitation, it may occur suddenly, in a flash, as a 'bright idea' (1945, p. 8).

Polya presents the heuristic devices that mathematicians use in the form of questions, a kind of dialogue between a teacher and a student. The first question to ask is whether you know of a related problem. Usually there are many related problems and the problem is to choose the right one. A suggestion that points towards an essential common point is: look at the unknown and try to think of a familiar problem that has the same or a similar unknown. If this does not suggest a plan, can you restate the problem? If you cannot solve the proposed problem, perhaps you can solve some related problem. Can you decompose it into several simpler problems? Perhaps you can work backwards – from what antecedent could the desired result be derived? Each of these heuristic devices is discussed by Polya in terms of specific examples.

Consider this puzzle: how can you bring up from the river exactly six quarts of water when you have only two containers, a four-quart pail and a nine-quart pail? The answer is not immediately apparent. What related problem can we solve? We could get eight quarts by twice filling the small pail and emptying it into the large pail. Or we could get five quarts by filling the larger nine-quart pail and then pouring off as much as we can into the smaller four-quart pail. But the desired amount is six quarts. We are not making much progress working forwards from the given conditions to the desired result. Perhaps we could work backwards. What is the situation we are trying to reach? Imagine six quarts of water in the large pail. From what antecedent condition could this be derived? If the large container were filled and we could pour out three quarts, we would have the desired result. From what antecedent condition could this be derived? If the small pail already held one quart, we would have the condition we need. From what antecedent could this be derived? We could measure one quart by filling the nine-quart pail, discarding four quarts twice with the small pail, and then pouring the remaining one quart into the small pail. And so, by working backwards, we reach something that we know how to do. If we now reverse the whole process, we have our plan for measuring out the six quarts. This heuristic principle – said to have been described first by Plato – is to concentrate on the unknown and to try to see what could have led to it; it works not only in solving water-measuring problems but in a great variety of other problems as well. (The principle is perhaps most apparent when we note how easy it is to run a multiple-T maze from the goal box to the start, and how difficult it is to find the right path in the opposite direction.)

Working backwards is one of many heuristic methods known to all good problem-solvers.

A critic of the present argument would have the right at this point to register a number of protests. His complaints might run something like this: (1) Metaplans that generate metaplans that generate still more Plans are far too complicated. A good scientist can draw an elephant with three parameters, and with four he can tie a knot in its tail. There must be hundreds of parameters floating around in this kind of theory and nobody will ever be able to untangle them. (2) These rough, heuristic rules of thumb, these probes and questions, these maxims and proverbs can be used only by people with enough intelligence to understand them and see how to apply them. They cannot be seriously proposed as unambiguous components of a scientific theory. (3) Even if we took this approach seriously, there is no way to put it to the test of experimentation. The evidence for it is not even simple introspection – the argument is based on what must lie behind introspection. It violates all the rules of the behavioristic tradition and threatens to set psychology back at least N years (where N measures the intensity of the critic's emotional response).

These are good criticisms and they must be met. The answer to the first one is clear enough: if the description is valid, then the fact that it is very complicated cannot be helped. No benign and parsimonious deity has issued us an insurance policy against complexity. However, there is no need to become discouraged on that account, for within the past decade or so electronic engineers have begun to develop computing machines that are big enough and fast enough to serve as models for testing complicated theories. Describe the theory carefully, translate the description into a computer program, run the program on a computer, and see if it reacts the same way organisms do. Now that we know how to write such programs – especially since the work of Newell, Shaw, and Simon[2] – we can begin to test ideas that would probably have seemed impossibly complicated to an earlier generation of psychologists. Computer engineers have only just begun to explore the possibilities of self-programming automata – we can look forward to many new discoveries as they learn more and more about what Norbert Wiener calls 'the problems of organized complexity'.

The possibility of using electronic computers gives us an answer

2. The earliest description of the use of list structures to develop flexible information-processing languages in order to simulate cognitive processes with heuristic programs seems to be in the paper by Newell and Simon (1956).

to the second criticism, as well. If the heuristic devices that thinkers say they are using can be translated into programs that reproduce the results obtained by the person, then we have every reason to believe that the heuristic device was a true description of his procedure in solving the problem. If the heuristic method is ambiguous, the program simply will not work. With this test available, therefore, heuristic rules of thumb can indeed be proposed as elements of a serious theory of thinking.

The proposal that a theory of thinking and problem solving should include all the heuristic rules men have discovered does not originate with the present authors, of course. It has a long and distinguished history, for it appears implicitly in almost every subjective description of the problem-solving process. Without a good supply of heuristic methods no artist could create, no scientist could discover, no technician could invent. In most cases, however, the discussions of heuristic schemes have been little more than catalogues of useful tricks.[3] Only recently have workers begun to explore the possibility that the catalogue might be converted into a coherent theory.

Marvin Minsky, (1956, p. III–23), noting the extent to which language guides our problem-solving efforts, has suggested that one way to develop a theory of heuristic would be to design or evolve a language through which the machine can be given heuristic suggestions which it can try to realize in a variety of reasonable ways. We would then be able to communicate with the machine in much the same way Polya communicates with his students. Of course, the machine would have to provide an intelligent description of what it was trying to do, for otherwise it would be difficult to know what suggestions to make. But the machine would slowly accumulate its own private catalogue of heuristic tricks, just as the student does. Then we could take the machine apart and see how it worked – an analysis to which few students are willing to submit. In Minsky's view, which is broadly the same as the present authors', verbal information provides an organism with 'a set of instructions for constructing, in its head, out of parts available there, a machine to perform a response of the desired kind' (p. III–18). As he points out, a machine that uses language as we do would have to contain a fairly powerful, general-purpose machine that, under the direction of linguistic signals, could construct a variety of special-purpose machines. If such a machine was told to try to construct

3. For example, in Moles (1957) there is a list of twenty-one different heuristic methods that Moles has been able to distinguish and exemplify in the historical development of science and technology.

a Plan by working backwards, for example, it would presumably know how to do so. Children acquire their store of heuristic methods by listening to verbal suggestions and then trying to execute them, and perhaps that is also the best way to let the machines evolve. If we want to develop a self-programming automaton, maybe we should let it learn the way we do.

Yet the fact that students of heuristic talk about such schemes does not mean that they are able to carry them out. Our critic should not be put off by appeals to authority or by evidence that computers are both impressive and fashionable. Talk about self-programming machines could create an impression that all of psychology's problems have been locked tightly in a box labeled 'Plan Generator', never to be opened again. In order to meet the criticism head-on, therefore, we should, even before considering the third complaint, give some more concrete description of how heuristic Plans can be realized in actual machines.

Let us consider chess and the way a computer might use heuristic Plans in order to play that game. One's first thought, perhaps, is to compute all possible continuations from a given position, then choose one that led to a checkmate of the opposing king. Unfortunately, even the fastest electronic computers we have would be unable to execute that exhaustive Plan in a reasonable period of time. It is necessary, therefore, to use heuristic Plans. But what heuristic Plans do we have for playing chess? These can be found in any chess manual for beginners; they include such maxims as, 'Try to control the four center squares', or 'Always make sure your King is safe before you attack', or 'Do not attack the opposing position until your own position is developed', etc. How can these heuristic principles be used to control what the machine will do?

Newell, Shaw, and Simon (1958) have analysed the traditional chess heuristics into six independent 'goals': (1) King safety, (2) material balance, (3) center control, (4) development, (5) King-side attack, and (6) promotion of Pawns.[4] This ordering of the goals is significant, because the machine always tries to achieve them in that same order. That is to say, first the machine will look to see if its King is safe. If not, it will try to defend it; if so, it will go on to the next goal. The next thing the machine will do is to check up on the possible exchanges, to make sure that its pieces are adequately protected. If not, the machine will protect them;

4. This article contains, in addition to the description of their own work, an account of the history of the problem beginning with Shannon's paper in 1949.

if so, the machine will turn next to center control. Can it move its Pawns into the center? If so, it is done; if not, the machine turns to development, then to attacking the King; and finally, if none of those goals leads to a good move, the machine will consider the Pawn structure.

Associated with each of the goals is a set of rules for generating moves that are relevant to that goal. For example, when the machine applies the center-control heuristic, it will first propose moving Pawn to Queen 4, then Pawn to King 4, then will propose moves that may prevent the opponent from making these two key moves, then propose moves that prepare for making these moves (e.g., adding defenders to the Queen 4 or the King 4 squares, or removing some block to moving the Queen's Pawn or the King's Pawn).

When the move generator has proposed something to do, the machine does not automatically accept it, of course. The proposal must be evaluated to see if it really achieves the desired results. The evaluation cannot be limited to a single goal, however, for a move that would look very good to the center-control Plan might utterly destroy the King's position, or lose a piece, etc. The proposed move must be analysed in terms of all six goals. The value of a move is a vector. The value of a move for center control is obtained by counting the number of blocks there are to making the two key Pawn moves. The component representing material balance will assign the conventional numerical values to the pieces, examine certain continuations until no further exchanges are possible, and note the change in material. (The evaluation of moves with respect to material balance is exceedingly complex and involves numerous other heuristic principles.) And so the evaluation proceeds through the different goals.

Now, when the machine has found a move that all the different heuristic goals approve, the move may still not be made. There may be an even better move possible. Thus, the machine has the problem of making a choice among the moves after they have been evaluated. There are several different ways it could proceed, but there is one thing it cannot do: it cannot wait until all the possible proposals have been made and evaluated in order to select the one with highest value. There are far too many proposals possible. Newell, Shaw, and Simon suggest that the simplest choice procedure is to set an acceptance level arbitrarily (a mechanical 'level of aspiration') and simply to take the first acceptable move. In order to avoid the possibility that no conceivable move would meet the criterion, a stop-order can also be imposed; save the best move discovered up to this point and, if the time-limit expires before an acceptable move has been found, make the best one that was found.

A critic who still doubts that heuristic rules can be incorporated into completely deterministic programs suitable for guiding the behavior of an automaton will have to pursue his doubts into the original articles themselves. We should, however, pause long enough to try to express the Newell, Shaw, and Simon program in the language used in the present book – not because it adds anything to their description, but simply to make clear that their work does indeed illustrate, and lend credibility to, the less explicit notions about information-processing that we have applied to psychological questions in these pages.

There are several ways that TOTE hierarchies could be organized to play chess, all of them using the heuristics that Newell, Shaw, and Simon have programmed, but the one that seems simplest and nearest to the spirit of their work has two major subplans, one for generating the moves, the other for evaluating them. The prototest could be the question, 'Who plays next?' If the machine is to play, the operational phase, 'Make a move', is executed. This operation has two tests, 'What move?' and, when that has been answered, 'Is that the best move?' The operational phase of the move generator has six tests, all of the intuitive form, 'If you do not have a move, why not try to X?' where X is one of the six goals. If no move has been selected, then the operational phase of X will be executed. In the case of center control, for example, it will consist of a string of tests of the form, 'Have you tried P-Q4?' 'Have you tried P-K4?' 'Have you tried to prevent him from moving P-Q4?' and so on. Each of these can be further elaborated. Eventually a legal move is selected and then control is transferred to the evaluation routine. This also has six parts, one for each of the goals; and each question, 'How does it affect the safety of the King?' or 'How does it affect the balance of material?' etc., has associated with it operational phases which are more or less elaborate according to how difficult the question is to answer. We could, if it seemed desirable, permit any of the six individual evaluation routines to reject a proposed move if it tested out too badly with respect to that particular goal – that decision would make it difficult for the machine to offer sacrifices, however, so it is probably wiser to postpone any rejections until the result of all six evaluation routines are collected and compared with similar evaluations of other moves. Amateur chess-players are not always that wise, however, and will frequently reject a move because of some glaring disadvantage – only to discover its compensating advantages later when they study the games of a master. It is not our present purpose to offer alternatives to the Newell, Shaw, and Simon program, however, but merely to illustrate that their heuristic programs do not confute or conflict with the idea of Plans presented here.

There are many other heuristic devices that we might discuss. One of the most interesting is the use of a 'diagramming heuristic' in a geometry program written by H. L. Gelernter and N. Rochester[5] (1958). They used the heuristic programming techniques developed by Newell, Shaw, and Simon in order to make a computer tackle geometry problems in the same fashion as a high-school student. Geometric proofs are typically rather long and it is almost impossible to discover them by any exhaustive procedure of trying all possible sequences of transformations. In this situation the human geometer will draw a figure that contains the essential conditions of the problem and then study the figure until he develops some Plan for the proof. He may check with other figures in order to make sure he is not trapped by some accidental property of the one figure he has used. Or he may, following standard heuristic methods, try to restate the problem or analyse it into steps that create new problems, then construct figures to help him prove those ancillary problems. The ways in which he exploits this Image of the problem are quite interesting and complex, and it is a challenging task to try to convert them into explicit rules that can be programmed for a machine. The rules would be such things as, 'If the figure has an axis of symmetry and it is not drawn, then draw it.' Or, most important, 'If two line segments or angles are to be proved equal, determine by measuring on the diagram whether they are corresponding parts of apparently congruent triangles.' When the machine discovers by measurement that certain things are equal or proportional, it can set these up as hypotheses and inquire whether, if they are true, they will contribute to the construction of a proof.

It is certainly true, as our critic pointed out, that these systems become extremely complicated. There is, however, a kind of backhanded comfort to be found in that fact. Most scientific advances have reduced man's dignity, moved him out of the center of the universe, given him apes for cousins, subjected his brain to the fickle endocrines and his mind to the unconscious forces of lust –

5. The idea seems to have originated at the Dartmouth Summer Research Project on Artificial Intelligence in 1956, particularly in discussion among John McCarthy, Marvin L. Minsky, and Nathaniel Rochester.

the reduction of his cognitive processes to machine operations would seem to be the final crushing blow. At least we can take comfort in the fact that we are too complicated to reduce to simple machines. Thus far the human brain seems to be the most amazing computing machine ever devised – nothing else we know even approaches it. The more carefully we analyse the information-processing that must go on in order to solve even the simplest problems, the more respect we gain for this beautiful piece of biological equipment.

Before we try to meet our critic's final objection, however, let us consider two more heuristic methods. These two are quite general methods described by Newell, Shaw, and Simon (1960) and tested for their effectiveness in enabling a computer to solve problems in logic, chess, and trigonometry. They refer to them as 'means-ends analysis' and the 'planning method'. The former attempts to analyse a problem into a sequence of subproblems, and the latter attempts to find a plan by ignoring some of the complicating factors in the situation. Undoubtedly there are many other heuristics that we use to solve problems, but these two are certainly ubiquitous, important, and powerful.

The means-ends analysis runs something like this: first, see if you know any way to transform the given into the desired solution. If no way is known, then try to reduce the difference between them; find some transformation that reduces the difference, and then apply it. Then try the first step again – see if you know any way to transform the new version of the given into the desired solution. If not, search again for a way to reduce the difference, etc. Each time the difference is reduced, the problem gets a little easier to solve. Intuitively, the heuristic works something like this: 'I want to get from A to B, but I do not know how. What is the difference between what I have and what I want to get? The difference is D. How can I reduce D? Operator T will reduce D, but I do not see how to apply it. Transform A so that operator T will apply to it. Now apply operator T and get a new object A'. The new problem is to get from A' to B, but I do not know how. What is the difference?' And so the means-ends analysis continues.[6] The argument attempts to make progress by substituting

6. What Newell, Shaw, and Simon call 'means-ends analysis' is similar to the theory of productive thinking described by K. Duncker. From his analysis of the situation and of the goal, the person locates a source of difficulty that he then attempts to remove. See Duncker (1945). The important advance over Duncker's work, of course, is to be completely explicit in terms of a computer program.

for the achievement of any goal the achievement of a set of easier goals. Its success will depend upon how shrewdly the measure of difference is defined and the transformations are selected.

No doubt it is obvious that any method we can discover for breaking up a big problem into smaller problems will tremendously simplify the solution. This approach is valuable when the solution can be characterized by several simultaneous attributes. That is to say, if a situation differs from the goal with respect to *both* attribute *A* and atttibute *B*, we can try to factor the problem into two parts. Instead of looking for a Plan to remove both differences simultaneously, we can search first for a set of Plans that will take care of attribute *A*, then search through that smaller set of Plans for one that will also handle attribute *B*. When we proceed in this way we are free to decide in which order to search for each aspect, in which order to eliminate the differences. In the language of children's games, we get progressively 'warmer' as we solve each successive component of the problem.

A second very general system of heuristic used by Newell, Shaw, and Simon consists in omitting certain details of the problem. This usually simplifies the task and the simplified problem may be solved by some familiar plan. The plan used to solve the simple problem is then used as the strategy for solving the original, complicated problem. In solving a problem in the propositional calculus, for example, the machine can decide to ignore differences among the logical connectives and the order of symbols and to look only at what the symbols are and how they are grouped. The logical operators that add, delete, or regroup symbols are then applied to the abstracted propositions, regardless of their connectives. The steps required to get the right symbols correctly grouped then serve as a possible strategy for a complete proof. The critical feature, of course, is whether or not the neglect of the details changed the problem so much that the solution of the simple problem was irrelevant.

Most heuristic methods involve some way to use the information already acquired. If correct solutions are literally scattered at random through the set of possible solutions, then previous search through one part of the solutions can be of no aid to the subsequent search through the remainder. However, in most situations where men have been successful in solving problems, the successful solutions lie in a neighborhood of successful solutions. *Hamlet*, for example, is still an excellent play even when an actor accidentally changes a few of Shakespeare's lines, thus changing it into another, but very similar, play. The general concept of biological evolution is a good one, even though the sequence of development of different species may in some instances require revision in the light of future evidence. When we get into situations where the modification of any slight detail of a correct solution changes it into an incorrect solution – as in opening a combination lock, for example – we are usually unsuccessful. When the best solution is in a neighborhood of good solutions, however, it is possible to explore the neighborhood of any relatively successful solution to see if a better one turns up near by.

If some of the possible solutions are, in this loose sense, clustered together in a space defined by the attributes, or dimensions, of the problem, it may be possible to simplify the problem by ignoring one or two of the attributes entirely. If the simplified problem can be solved, the steps in its solution can suggest a Plan for solving the original problem. With luck, the steps that led to a successful region in the smaller space may still lead to a successful region in the larger space. This is the sort of heuristic we use, for example, when we try to find ways to settle disputes between nations by thinking how we might settle similar disputes between individuals. Another example is the use of the diagram heuristic by Gelernter and Rochester – the steps involved in solving the problem posed by a particular diagram may provide a Plan suitable for proving the general theorem.

Means-ends analysis and the planning method are two of the most powerful heuristic methods used by Newell, Shaw, and Simon in their development of a general problem-solving program, one general enough to deal with a wide range of well-defined problems in essentially the same way. Once they have succeeded, their computer programs will indeed have risen above the level of heuristic 'catalogues', such as those offered by Polya and others, to the status of a heuristic 'theory' of thinking.

After studying this pioneering work by Newell, Shaw, and Simon it is quite difficult to recapture one's innocent respect for parsimony in psychological theories. Certainly, we can no longer think that anyone who postulates complicated information-processing by an organism is appealing to mysterious, vitalistic, ambiguous, or unscientific principles. Complicated information-processing according to heuristic principles is not only conceivable – it has actually been accomplished, demonstrated on existing computers. Henceforth, it is not necessary to suspect metaphysical booby traps in every psychological process more complicated than a conditioned reflex. The work of Newell, Shaw, and Simon shows in detail how the processes of solving problems can be compounded out of more elementary processes that can be executed by machines. And it shows that those elementary processes, properly organized, can in fact solve complex problems; no ghostly assistance from an undefined source, human or divine, is needed.

But, while all of this work is clear progress in dealing with the problems of organized complexity, we still have hanging over our heads the third complaint by our patient critic. He may by now have finally granted that heuristic methods can be incorporated into machines, but he must still feel that the behavioral evidence can never be collected for really testing these ideas. It is a serious complaint. If people must be this complicated, and if things this complicated cannot be studied experimentally, then scientific psychology must be impossible. It is a complaint that, if true, would certainly be important to prove.

But is it true? Certainly, if one interprets 'scientific' to mean that all of a subject's verbal reports must be ignored, then it will be impossible to study thinking at the level of complexity required for programming computers or for understanding the neurology and physiology of the brain. But are such Spartan strictures necessary? They would protect us from long, violent disputes about 'imageless thoughts', perhaps, because they would make it impossible to say anything at all about thoughts, but that is a high price to pay for consonance.

The most valuable approach seems to be the 'thinking aloud' method used by Binet, Duncker, Claparède (1934), and many others. Unlike the usual introspective or retrospective methods that require a subject to analyse his experience into meaningless mental contents – sensations, images, feelings – thinking aloud requires merely that the person talk while he is working, that he should comment on what he is doing, what he is looking for, what his intentions are, what objects or relations catch his attention, etc. As Claparède pointed out, the method has many shortcomings – the task of talking may inhibit the thought processes, or slow them down, it may make the process sound more coherent and orderly than it would otherwise be, the referents for some of the utterances are not clear, the subject may fall silent at just the critical moment when the experimenter would most like to know what he is doing. But when the method is used intelligently and conscientiously, it can provide a tremendous amount of information about the detailed process of thought. The problem is not so much to collect the data as it is to know what to do with them.

The subject will say, in effect, 'I want to do *A*, but before I can do *A* I have to prepare for it by doing *B*.' He then proceeds to do *B*, which may lead on to unforeseen consequences that prevent his ever returning to do *A*. Nevertheless, the consideration of *A* was an essential step in the thought processes leading to *B*. If we are to develop an adequate heuristic description, one that will solve the problem in the same manner as the subject, it must consider *A*, then do *B*. But if we had not recorded the things the subject said he was considering, along with the things he actually did, the task would be hopeless. It is actually easier to simulate the person's spoken thoughts than to simulate only the decisions that appear in his behavior. Since thinking aloud permits more of the person's thought processes to project through the plane of perception, it helps to limit the variety of conceivable descriptions to a handful that are reasonably accurate.

Newell, Shaw, and Simon have found that the subject's description of what he is doing is exactly the kind of data they need to formulate a theory that will predict his behavior. They ask a subject to derive one logical expression from another by the application of a given set of transformation rules. The subject talks about the task as he does it. He may look at the two expressions he is given and say that the one he has to start with has too many propositions to the left of the main connective, so he will have to get rid of some (an application of the 'planning method'). He looks at the list of transformations until he finds one that gets rid of things to the left of the main connective, so he would like to apply that. But then he realizes that he cannot, because the proposition he wants to transform has 'and' in it, whereas the rule he wants to apply works only for 'or'. So, he says, the job is to get that connective changed in order to apply the transformation that will shorten the left side. He looks for a transformation that turns 'and' expressions into 'or' expressions and elects to try it as his first step. Now, it is possible to find a fairly simple set of heuristic methods to describe what this subject is doing (e.g., his method is to make the propositions more important than the connectives in guiding the choice of transformations), and to predict that he would mention the left-shortening transformation before he adopted the connective-changing transformation. But if the only datum that the experimenter records is the bald fact that the subject's first choice of a transformation was the connective-changing transformation, it is impossible to see how the subject's strategy can be inferred.

It is tempting to say that a successful theory 'predicts the subject's verbal behavior'. In fact, no one is yet much interested in the verbal behavior as behavior, but only in the meaning of what is said. The subject may say, 'Use number 8 next', or, 'Let's try that one again', or any of a variety of equivalent verbal behaviors, yet these differences are ignored when testing the adequacy of the theory. Obviously, therefore, the interest lies in the subject's Plan, not in his specific actions.

When the psychologist says that his subject in these experiments was following such-and-such a Plan, or was using a particular metaplan for generating Plans to solve the problem, it is clear that this is a hypothetical statement. The Plan, or the metaplan, represents the psychologist's theory about that chunk of observed behavior. Obviously, we can never know whether or not we have *the* theory for any domain of inquiry. There is always a variety of alternative Plans that could have led the subject to exhibit the same behavior; the best we can hope to do is to select the simplest one compatible with all the facts. But, because this kind of ambiguity is such a pervasive feature of behavioral analysis, it is important to reduce it as far as possible. In this endeavor, the subject's verbal report has one great recommendation in its favor, because language, for all its notorious shortcomings, is still the least ambiguous of all the channels open from one human being to another.

References

CLAPARÈDE, E. (1934), 'La genèse de l'hypothèse', *Archives de Psychologie*, vol. 24, pp. 1–154.

DUNCKER, K. (1945), 'On problem-solving', *Psychol. Monogr.*, whole no. 270.

GELERNTER, H. L., and ROCHESTER, N. (1958), 'Intelligent behavior in problem-solving machines', *IBM Journal of Research and Development*, vol. 2, pp. 336–45.

MINSKY, M. L. (1956), *Heuristic aspects of the artificial intelligence problem*, Group Report 34–55, Lincoln Laboratory, Massachusetts Institute of Technology.

MOLES, A. A. (1957), *La création scientifique*, René Kister.

NEWELL, A., SHAW, J. C., and SIMON, H. A. (1958), 'Chess-playing problems and the problem of complexity', *IBM Journal of Research and Development*, vol. 2, pp. 320–35.

NEWELL, A., SHAW, J. C., and SIMON, H. A. (1960), 'Report on a general problem-solving program', *Proceedings of the international conference on information processing*, UNESCO, Paris.

NEWELL, A., and SIMON, H. A. (1956), 'The logic theory machine: a complex information processing system', *IRE Transactions on Information Theory*, vol. IT-2, no. 3, pp. 61–79.

POLYA, G. (1945), *How to solve it*, Princeton U.P.

23 U. Neisser

The Multiplicity of Thought

Excerpt from U. Neisser, 'The multiplicity of thought', *Brit. J. Psychol.*, vol. 54 (1963), pp. 1–14.

Historical Survey

The psychology of thinking seems to breed dichotomies. Nearly everyone who has touched the subject has divided mental processes into two (or more) kinds: productive and blind, creative and constrained, intuitive and rational, autistic and realistic, and so on. These distinctions seem to overlap; they share a common core of meaning which is difficult to describe precisely. In this paper I shall propose yet another dichotomy, but one which can be rather sharply defined: the distinction between *multiple* and *sequential* processes. I hope to show that many of the phenomena which underlie the other classifications can be clarified by it. First, however, we must take a closer look at these formulations themselves.

Productive and blind thinking. – These terms are taken from Wertheimer's classical discussion (1959). Essentially the same distinction was made by Köhler (1927) emphasizing the terms 'insight' and 'trial-and-error', as well as by other Gestalt psychologists. Recently it has been stressed again in Bruner's (1960) discussion of the aims and problems of education, in a chapter entitled 'The importance of structure'. Insightful thinking is responsive to the real structure of the problem. The situation is viewed as a whole, simultaneously, rather than one isolated part at a time. The productive thought process (or the effective teacher) focuses on the central features – and on the gaps – that appear in this direct inspection. [. . .]

Creativity and constraint. – There is widespread interest in 'the creative process' in the identification of creative talent, and the like. Creativity here means much more than structurally sound thinking in Wertheimer's sense. Indeed, it is often opposed to 'problem solving'. It is not limited to abstract thought, but is usually meant to include the original activities of musicians, painters and poets, as well as of scientists. The defining psychological characteristic of creative activity is not the quality of the product (even bad work can be creative) nor its uniqueness in history, but a certain freedom from constraint in the process itself. Learning by rote, copying, simple induction or deduction, the stereotyped application of artistic formulas – none of these is creative; they lack the spontaneity and unpredictability that the term implies. Problem solving, no matter how elegant, always involves mostly a response to environmental demands, while creativity erupts more or less unconstrainedly from within the person himself.

It is generally agreed that the creative process is not a conscious one. Artists and scientists unite in reporting that their ideas (images expressions, etc.,) simply 'appear', more or less clearly, later to be elaborated consciously. '(Creative) production by a process of purely conscious calculation never seems to occur' (Ghiselin, 1952, p. 15). Many have argued, however, that a conscious period of preparation is necessary to initiate the 'incubation' process that occurs out of consciousness. Maslow (1957) has argued that creativity is intimately bound up with the Freudian 'primary process', and Kubie (1958) has stressed its relation to the pre-conscious.

Intuition and reason. – This distinction has probably always been with us. Some judgements and decisions seem to be 'rational', 'logical' in that the person who makes them can explain the basis of his judgement, to himself or to another person. Others – hunches, guesses, feelings – are of obscure origin. Intuition is quick, and often compelling; reason is plodding and pale. Some persons are said to be more intuitive than others; women perhaps more than men. Intuition plays a prominent part in interpersonal relations, in our judgements of other people and our behaviour towards them. Neither the therapist whose interpretations are appropriate, nor the actor gifted with a keen sense of timing seems to base his actions on rational deliberation. Hunches and intuitions play a role in many other situations as well; one may feel inexplicably certain that a particular line of attack will yield the solution to a problem, that there will be a change in the weather or a fluctuation in the stock market. Mental processes of this kind seem to be common wherever there are situations too complex for ready logical analysis.

Bruner discusses the difference between intuitive and 'analytic' thinking in detail: 'Analytic thinking characteristically proceeds a step at a time. Steps are explicit and usually can be adequately reported by the thinker to another individual. Such thinking proceeds with relatively full awareness of the information and operations involved. It may involve careful and deductive reasoning, often using mathematics or logic and an explicit plan of attack. Or it may involve a step-by-step process of induction and experiment. . . . Intuitive thinking characteristically does not advance in careful, well-planned steps. Indeed, it tends to involve manoeuvres based seemingly on an implicit perception of the total problem. The thinker arrives at an answer, which may be right or wrong, with little if any awareness of the process by which he reached it' (1960, pp. 57–8).

Intuition shares certain properties with the creative process. Tauber and Green (1959) consider them essentially identical, and group them together with dreams and subliminal perception as 'prelogical' experience, opposed to the 'logical' processes of reason. This point of view comes close to the positions of Freud and Kubie.

Autistic and realistic thinking. – This distinction was made by Bleuler (1912). Autistic thinking is dominated by affects; realistic thinking is sensibly and coherently goal-directed. 'It (autism) mirrors the fulfilment of wishes and strivings, thinks away obstacles, conceives of impossibilities as possible, and of goals as attained' (p. 404). Bleuler found it characteristic of the thought of schizophrenic patients and of dreams, noting also that it sometimes occurred in 'states of great distraction' and in mythology. McKellar (1957) has expanded these parallels. He regards imaging, creative activity, and other relatively 'uninhibited' mental states as essentially involving autistic thought.

In normal persons, autistic thinking occurs primarily in situations where the constraints of reality are loosened, as in sleep or in daydreams. Thus, there is no need for the thought process to restrict itself to the possible, to realistic representations, to ordinary sequences of time and place, and so on. It is relatively free to follow where impulse leads. This interpretation requires us to assume that ordinary people have powerful 'unrealistic' impulses, with certain characteristic modes of expression. Thus, it merges with the Freudian conception of the primary process, on which several of the dichotomies we have discussed are essentially based.

Primary and secondary process. – In *The interpretation of dreams* (1900) Freud found it necessary to assume that two fundamentally distinct modes of mental functioning were available to every person. The 'primary' process is revealed by the 'absurdity' and 'incorrectness' of dream experiences. Any train of thought which has suffered repression, and has been drawn in to the unconscious, will be governed by the primary process. Its characteristics include (1) condensation: the emotional loadings of various ideas pass freely from one to the other (along varied associative pathways), and the intensity of many may ultimately be concentrated in a single conceptual unit; (2) compromise: the formation and emotional stressing of new ideas intermediate among existing ones; (3) the use of very loose connexions (puns, clang associations, etc.), as associative channels; (4) toleration of contradictions: any thoughts whatever may coexist or combine. The function of the primary thought process is to find discharge for emotions. It takes place in the unconscious; that is, among ideas which have been permanently repressed and cannot become conscious. For this reason, the emotions involved are always infantile urges. In Rapaport's (1951, p. 693) terms, the primary process is 'drive-organized'.

The mental activities of the new-born infant are assumed to be almost entirely governed by the primary process. Gradually, a 'secondary process' develops in which this sort of activity is inhibited in favour of reality oriented thinking. The delays and detours which are encountered in the search for emotional discharge result in the growth of rational and conceptual thinking. The secondary process is 'conceptually organized' (Rapaport, 1951, p. 696). Conscious and preconscious ideas are governed by the secondary process. Freud assumed that primary-process thought never became conscious without substantial secondary censorship, like that of the dream. This differentiates the concept of primary process from that of autistic thinking; the latter term can describe conscious as well as unconscious processes.

Many psychologists and others have speculated that the primary process is the source of creativity. It seems to have the unpredictability and freedom from constraint which the creative process requires. This view is supported by the fact that the creative act is inaccessible to consciousness. A common modification of this theory (e.g., Rapaport, 1951, p. 719; Maslow, 1957) holds that creative and intuitive thinking result from suitable cooperation between primary and secondary processes. The former supplies spontaneity, vigour, and effortless invention; the latter elaborates and re-orders the products to adapt them for artistic, communicative, or other purposes.

Unconscious, preconscious, and conscious. – The primary process model has recently been challenged by Kubie in his provocative book on creativity and neurosis (1958). He rejects the simple dichotomy of the two processes because it assigns the same origins to creativity as to pathology: both are said to arise from the uncontrolled and uncontrollable unconscious. His own conviction is that creative activity is blocked by neurosis and released by psychotherapy. Nevertheless, he agrees that the source of creativity cannot lie in the systematic and communicable processes which Freud called 'secondary'. Thus, Kubie argues that a *tri*chotomy is needed to handle the facts: the communicable processes of consciousness, the quick and flexible thinking that results in creativity, and the deep unconscious restraints of anxiety and neurosis. The middle category he calls *preconscious*. This is a substantial extension of Freud's views. Freud thought of conscious and preconscious as similarly organized; the latter consisted simply of ideas that could become conscious (without censorship) but did not happen to be so at some given time.

Kubie shows, with many rich examples, that preconscious activity is fast, complex, and prolific. It has the functional properties that other theorists ascribe to the primary process, without being organized around either infantile drives or systematic conscious conceptions. However, it rarely operates independently of the other systems. 'Preconscious processes are assailed from both sides. From one side they are nagged and prodded into rigid distorted symbols by unconscious drives which are oriented away from reality and which consist of rigid compromise formations, lacking in fluid inventiveness. From the other side they are driven by literal conscious purpose, checked and corrected by conscious retrospective critique. The uniqueness of creativity, i.e., its capacity to find and put together something new, depends on the extent to which preconscious functions can operate freely between these two ubiquitous concurrent and oppressive prison wardens' (1958, p. 45).

Sequential and Multiple Processes in Computers

The common core of all these theoretical dichotomies seems to be the distinction between a relatively well-ordered, easily describable, and efficiently adapted thought process on one side, and a simultaneous and superficially confused profusion of activity on the other. Apparently there are two different modes of handling the external and internalized information with which the mind must deal. It cannot be a coincidence that two corresponding modes have appeared as alternate possibilities in the design of 'artificially intelligent' systems – that is, in programming computers to perform quasi-intellectual tasks. In that field, the two possibilities are often called 'sequential' and 'parallel' (Selfridge and Neisser, 1960).

'Intelligent' activity in computing machines

How is it possible for processes in machines to teach us anything about human thinking? Human mental activity is more complex than any existing computer program by many orders of magnitude. The 'intelligence' that has been achieved artificially is either extremely specialized or almost trivial. Moreover, the human mind may – indeed, probably does – have resources and methods that are unimaginable in machines such as those in existence today. Clearly, there is an empirical question here. Useful analogies may exist, or they may not. It is for the psychologist to decide whether a particular model or theory has value for him, regardless of its origin. However, he can make such a decision only after expending the effort necessary to become acquainted with the model in question. For this reason, we must consider some of the problems involved in programming computers to behave sensibly. [. . .]

What the machine does depends on the program of instructions that has been pre-stored in it. The information that has been put in may be modified, or new information may be written. These actions may be made *conditional* on the input, or on intermediate results. 'If the input has characteristic A, add 1 to the contents of register X; if it has characteristic B, copy the first ten cards of input into registers R for later use; if C, execute the series of instructions beginning at Y; if neither A, B, nor C proceed to the instructions at Z.' Eventually, the program may call for the *output* (on more cards, or tape, or typewriter) of some part of the internal information. What is put out will depend on what was put in and on the intermediate 'processing' that it has undergone. It is temptingly easy to give psychological names to different kinds of processing. Suppose the program takes one course of action if the input possesses a certain general property, and another if it does not: then this property has been 'abstracted'. Or suppose the program has some provision for modifying its own instruction sequence if certain intermediate results are obtained: it will handle further input differently and has 'learned'.

In fact, it is very difficult to write programs that will successfully 'abstract' interesting properties of the input. In computerman's language, this is called the problem of 'pattern recognition', and has received a good deal of attention (Minsky, 1961; Selfridge and Neisser, 1960). The difficulty arises partly because the precise informational basis of the properties we would like to abstract (of the patterns we would like to identify) is unknown, or variable, or both. Spoken words, or written letters, or pathological E.E.G. records, form classes of patterns that people can identify but for which the defining stimuli are hard to specify. We shall consider the recognition of letters in some detail, in order to illustrate the two modes of analysis referred to above. The input problem itself will be ignored; suppose that by some television-like process a photograph of any printed or written letter can be converted into an array of holes on punched cards and fed into a computer. What shall be done with this information to determine which of the twenty-six alphabetic characters it represents?

One possibility is to have a standard form of each letter stored away in advance, and compare the newcomer with each of these to determine the best match. For reasons discussed elsewhere (Selfridge and Neisser, 1960) this procedure is not advisable. It is better to base the decision on the presence of various subordinate features of the input: lines, curves, open spaces, and the like. If these can be identified, how shall information about them be used in deciding which letter the input represents? We shall consider two alternatives: sequential logic and parallel processing.

Sequential processes

Sequentially, one may proceed as follows: is there a vertical straight line? If so, the letter is B or D or E or ...; if not, the letter is A or C or V, etc. The question divides the universe of possibilities into two categories. The next question depends on the answer to the first. If there is a vertical line, one might ask if there is also a right angle. This divides E, F, T, etc., from N, M, U, etc. A series of such questions is called a 'logic' or a 'decision tree', and can easily be devised to make an unequivocal decision about every input. Many programs for letter recognition have been written on this basis. They work rather well, *provided the input is restricted to printed characters in particular founts*.

If the computer is given *hand-printed* characters to identify, such a program will score almost at random. The critical defining properties simply are no longer critical. A hand-printed E might have neither a vertical line nor a right angle, while an A might have both. Almost every conceivable kind of 'distortion' arises in hand-printing. These variations are not disturbing to the human reader; people can identify about 96 per cent of randomly selected hand-printed characters even without the aid of context (Neisser and Weene, 1960). Nevertheless, a sequential program is unable to cope with them. The reason is obvious: a process which goes consecutively from one decision to the next must go astray if even a single decision is wrong. Only where no uncertainty exists is such a program dependable. Error-correction procedures are possible, but they will become unmanageably complicated if the variability of the input is large. Such a program proceeds by rote, and like all rote procedures it is inadequate in the face of novelty.

Multiple processes

Evidently, we need a program that sees the letter 'as a whole'. How can this be accomplished? Essentially *by asking all the questions at once*, instead of letting each answer determine the next question. Suppose the program examines the input for many different properties simultaneously. Letters are ultimately identified by weighted averages of the results. Such features as vertical line and right angle are given weights which increase the probability that the program will decide T and decrease its chances of saying O. Even a great deal of variability need not lead the program astray, because letters are effectively defined by the totality of their features. Selfridge (1959) originally proposed that the identifying operations be called 'demons' and the entire program a 'pandemonium'. This term suggests more confusion than is actually involved. 'Parallel processing' is also misleading, since it suggests that the various operations are very similar and that they never meet; neither implication is desirable. I shall use the term 'multiple processing' for such systems.

A program which identifies hand-printed characters by multiple processing has been written and tested by Doyle (1960). It is very nearly as good at its job as people are, reaching an accuracy of about 90 per cent. It uses twenty-eight rather arbitrarily selected operations, most of which count gaps, or strokes, or concavities in various directions. Its accuracy is not much diminished if one or another of its operations is eliminated. The operations are not literally simultaneous; that would be impossible within the physical limitations of present computers. They are functionally simultaneous, in the sense that all of them are completed before any decision is made.

Multiple processing has several fundamental advantages over the sequential procedure. Not only is it effective in the face of ambiguous cues, but it displays a certain nonchalance about internal errors. In contrast, a single false step in a pre-arranged sequential program is fatal. Moreover, learning and adaptation are relatively easy to incorporate into a multiple process. A sequential program on the other hand is very difficult to improve. Suppose some sequence of operations has classified the input as A when it should have been R. Which operation went wrong? There is no obvious way to find out, and one cannot readily introduce experimental changes since any alteration of the sequence is likely to have major consequences. In a multiple process, on the other hand, small changes in the weights given to various features may produce improvement, and at least will not upset the system as a whole. Doyle's program went through a learning phase, to find the results of the twenty-eight operations applied to a sample of known letters; the operating phase then made use of combining weights based on these results. In other words, the programmer did not need to know the defining characteristics of hand-printed letters at all; he only provided an array of relevant operations for the computer's use.

It is important to stress that the various operations in a multiple program do not have to be independent of one another. They may be as redundant as desired, if computer space is available. On the other hand, they need not all be of one type, but can focus on very different kinds of features. Nor need these features be 'elementistic' in the sense protested by Gestalt psychology. It is easy to imagine an operation concerned with the degree of circularity of a pattern, or with the extent to which it is symmetric. This raises another point. How can the computer establish whether a pattern is circular? Only by a set of subordinate operations, which themselves may be organized either sequentially, or, again, in multiple. Thus, a multiple program naturally involves hierarchies of operations. A hierarchy may extend in the other direction also. For example, the identification of a letter may play the role of a single operation in a complex whose intent is the identification of printed *words*. The superordinate stage again could be programmed sequentially (each successive letter as it was identified might narrow the subset of possible words) or in multiple (all the letters might be examined and their results combined into a best guess at the word). Such hierarchies almost certainly play a major role in human cognitive processes.

Multiple processing is not always the best way to program a pattern recognition problem. It involves a great deal of wasted 'effort' (computer time or space) because every operation is applied to every input. In any situation where a correct and decisive sequence of operations can be established, sequential programming will be very much more efficient. Only where such a procedure is impossible or unknown can multiple processing be justified. Moreover, an organized sequence has a certain clarity which is absent in the 'pandemonium' of a multiple process. At any given moment in a sequence one can (in principle) say just what the machine is doing, and what it will do next. When a multiple process is operating (assuming true simultaneity of operations) no such statement is possible. Different parts of a multiple machine may appear to be engaged in quite unrelated and even useless activities. This is no mere appearance, for in any given instance many of the operations are indeed useless. Nevertheless, it is just this apparently incoherent and chaotic profusion of activity which enables the program to make quasi-intelligent identifications of patterns in its environment.

Implications for a Theory of Thinking

My thesis is that human thinking is a multiple activity. Awake or asleep, a number of more or less independent trains of thought usually coexist. Ordinarily, however, there is a 'main sequence' in progress, dealing with some particular material in step-by-step fashion. The main sequence corresponds to the ordinary course of consciousness. It may or may not be directly influenced by the other processes going on simultaneously. The concurrent operations are not conscious, because consciousness is intrinsically single: one is aware of *a* train of thought, but not of the details of several. The main sequence usually has control of motor activity. Cases where it does not (where behaviour does not correspond to consciousness) impress the observer as bizarre or pathological.

The characteristics of primary- and secondary-process thought

Before we examine the analogy in detail, a word about the role of motivation in thinking is appropriate. Why are some operations performed rather than others? Why do some processes become a part of the main sequence while others do not? The most consistent view is that all thinking is motivated; the course of processing depends on both the enduring and the cyclical needs of the thinker. Various needs have various consequences. One fundamental need is for the maintenance of an orderly and adaptive sequence in one's own behaviour. For social as well as physical and physiological reasons, our *actions* have to display a certain degree of self-consistency. This demand is probably responsible for the original development of a 'main sequence' within the multiplicity of thought. Certainly it accounts for the extent to which the main sequence is inviolable while we are awake, and

316

our consequent belief that men can think of only one thing at a time. (If the main sequence is *not* inviolable, if our actions are not governed by an orderly sequential process, the result must be either immobility or chaos, i.e., psychosis.)

The multiple operations can combine and influence one another in many ways. In the computer program for letter recognition discussed above, the processes which recognized various features were combined by a simple weighted sum. In human thinking, every sort of fusion, exclusion, disjunction, and so on may occur. The result of this facile interaction is the 'primary process' described by Freud, in which condensation, compromise, and disregard for logic are the rule. The 'secondary process' is the main sequence itself, proceeding sequentially through steps whose logic has been preprogrammed by realistic experience. Kubie's 'preconscious' consists of multiple processes, while the main sequential process is his 'conscious'. Indeed, both Freud and Kubie refer explicitly to simultaneous processing; e.g., 'It is really not easy to form an idea of the wealth of trains of unconscious thought striving for expression in our minds . . .' (Freud, 1900, p. 478).

Why is the primary process 'drive-organized'? What accounts for the 'autistic' (i.e., personally motivated) character of our multiple processes? Again, the answer is hardly original. All thinking is motivated, but personal motives show through more clearly in processes which do not have control of behaviour and thus are relatively unconstrained by realistic demands. 'Autistic thinking' in Bleuler's sense occurs when the main sequence is more or less detached from motor activity and is affected by logically irrelevant processes going on at the same time. Its 'irrational' characteristics stem from multiplicity, while its motivational and affective properties arise because the course of processing is governed by personal needs. Multiple processing is also the source of symbolism and over-determination in this kind of thought. One sequence of processes may be analysing the shape of something seen (or remembered) while others work with features that have emotional significance; all of them may recombine to turn the main sequence in a novel direction.

The existence of more than one process implies that the main sequence may be altered in 'unpredictable' ways at almost any moment. The change will usually be in a direction away from immediate adaptation to the external world and toward an emphasis on inner needs. Because such changes are often maladaptive they may produce anxiety, and restraints on the recombination of processes are usually developed during childhood. As a result of these restrictions on the flow of information, much of multiple activity in adulthood may have no effect, or its influence may be limited to certain stereotyped 'symbolic' expressions. These limitations are Kubie's 'unconscious'. People differ widely in the extent to which they are free to use the multiplicity of their own thoughts.

Limits on the complexity of multiple thinking

I propose that not only autism, but also intuitive, creative, and productive thinking depend on the use of multiple sequences of mental activity. This brings up an important question: what limitations are there on the nature and complexity of processes off the main sequence? If activities outside of consciousness had only the infantile logic of Freud's primary process it would be hard to see how they could be responsible for intelligent activity. In our approach to this problem, the analogy to a physically realizable computer may be helpful again. There are three different kinds of restrictions that limit the diversity and complexity of processes in a machine. It will be instructive to see what form they would assume in human thinking.

First, a computer may simply be constructed in such a way that certain operations can only be conducted one at a time. For example, most computers have a single 'central processing unit' in which all arithmetic operations must be carried out. This is the reason why the operations in Doyle's letter-recognition program were actually performed one by one, although they were 'functionally' simultaneous. However, one can imagine systems that are not so restricted (e.g., Holland, 1959). Some elementary mental activities are limited in just this way: seeing, for example, requires visually specialized regions of the nervous system. I am assuming that the parts of the brain underlying the processes of human thought are free of this limitation. (It is worth noting that, anatomically, the human cerebrum appears to be the sort of diffuse system in which multiple processes would be at home. In this respect it differs from the nervous system of lower animals. Our hypothesis thus leads us to the radical suggestion that the critical difference between the thinking of humans and of lower animals lies not in the existence of consciousness but in the capacity for complex processes outside it.)

A second limit on the achievements of computers arises simply because no one may know how to program the task in question. Either it cannot be performed with the operations available, or the way to perform it has not yet been discovered. Corresponding restrictions certainly apply to thought processes. Insoluble problems exist. However, this is true whether the activity of the mind is multiple or sequential, and thus is irrelevant to the present argument.

The final limitation on computer performance is a critical one. Any given machine has a finite capacity. There is only a certain amount of 'space' in which instructions and information can be stored. More complex programs take up more space. If two programs are executed simultaneously, each has less space available than if it were being carried out alone, and is thus more limited in what it can do. There is no way for human thinking to escape this principle. If several processes occur together, none can be as complex as the subtlest possible single processes. This must lead to problems in the allocation of mental resources: shall the main sequence use all the facilities, and prevent multiple processing altogether? Shall off-sequence processes occur only at a low level of complexity? Are a number of equally complex activities permissible? Can an off-sequence process be more complex than the main sequence itself? Of course, this 'problem' is not 'solved' by a planner. Some distribution of resources actually occurs, as the evolutionary result of interactions among ongoing processes and with the environment. We can safely predict that: (1) there will be individual differences in the depth which multiple processing attains; (2) the existing allocation of resources will usually not be the most efficient possible.

We are assuming that the main sequence (conscious activity) is in close touch with the environment because it must direct behaviour. Its activity is therefore crucial for adaptation, and we may reasonably suppose that it is accustomed to the lion's share of capacity. This conclusion is borne out rather directly by some of Broadbent's (1958) material, as well as by the 'primitive' character of autistic or prelogical thought. However, there is no reason to believe that this is necessarily or universally the case. At times when the activity of the main sequence is not demanding – for example, during sleep or the performance of routine activity – other sequences, out of consciousness, may attain high degrees of complexity. As we have seen, such states of disengagement do seem to play a critical role in creative thinking. Thus, considerations of capacity explain the role of the 'incubation' phase of thought.

It is not always easy to establish the relative 'complexity' of different mental processes. The information capacity which a computer requires to perform a particular task depends not only on the problem itself, but also on the mechanisms with which the machine is equipped and on the ingenuity of the program. One of the main lines of progress in the computer field is the development of 'programming languages' – and, to some extent, of computers specially designed for them – which make previously intricate operations comparatively simple. We do not know what simplifying mechanisms, both innate and acquired, are available for thinking. Plausible speculation is possible: for example, it seems likely that people are especially efficient at handling two- and three-dimensional properties of the visual input. In other words, the same amount of information may require less capacity coded in terms of spatial relationships than in terms of temporal sequence. (Unger, 1958, has designed a computer which would have this property to some extent.) This assumption would explain the predominance of visual imagery in dreams, and perhaps also our preference for visual models and metaphors for thinking, from 'insight' to 'point of view'.

Thus far, we have considered multiple processes which were relatively independent of one another and somewhat free of realistic constraints. To such processes we have ascribed 'autistic', 'prelogical', and 'creative' thinking, in its various guises. The 'productive' thinking which produces insightful solutions of problems does not seem to be quite the same kind. The primary process will not readily find the area of a parallelogram. Such problems require a grasp of the relationships among various parts or, perhaps, among various subproblems. There are lines that slant, angles, a central rectangle, a notion of what 'area' means, and so on. No part alone is enough, nor is just any concatenation of parts. But if the analyses of the parts go on simultaneously, along related sequences, there may come a moment when a higher-order operation (in the parallelogram case perhaps some part of the spatial systems hypothesized above) can combine them adaptively. In this situation, 'insight' seems to involve building a novel hierarchy of existing processes. There is ample evidence already that the 'components' of insightful behaviour must be established in advance (e.g., Birch, 1954). The present suggestion is that their *potential* existence is not enough: they must be *simultaneously* operative if a novel recombination is to emerge.

Empirical Evidence

All the foregoing is speculative. The fundamental assumption on which my argument rests is that people commonly or constantly think about several things at once. Is this really plausible? Can it be substantiated? In a sense, the most important evidence has already been presented: the theory stands or falls by its success in integrating the facts about human thinking. Nevertheless, a problem arises because the assumption of multiplicity contradicts the common belief of both laymen and psychologists. There is a widespread conviction that it is impossible, or at least unusual, to do even two things at once. This conviction is based marginally on objective evidence, but primarily on introspection. Everybody has had the experience of trying to think about two things at the same time, and ending with confusion about both. These experiences are valid, but what they show is only that we cannot be *conscious* of two complex processes together. They give no testimony about processes outside of consciousness. Our subjective certainty of the singleness of thought does not contradict the present theory. Indeed, it is incorporated in the concept of the main sequence.

A different kind of subjective experience confirms the possibility of simultaneity. In what is called a 'double take' we first hear a statement one way, then realize with a start that something quite different was said. Two analyses of the auditory input are represented here. The first initiates a conscious train of thought, which is interrupted by the results of the second. Thus, the second, significant, interpretation must have proceeded outside of consciousness until its importance was 'understood' and a consequent alteration of the main sequence occurred. Something like this must happen on a very large scale in cases of multiple personality. In such cases, one of the personalities often is aware of what another personality is doing or thinking, and can make use of its knowledge later.

Experimental findings

Within experimental psychology, there have been a number of studies indicating the difficulty of multiple response or multiple conscious activity (Woodworth and Schlosberg, 1954, pp. 87–90; Broadbent, 1958, Chapter 2). Subjects cannot follow two conversations at once, or make two responses at once, without decrement in performance. We cannot review these studies in detail. However, most of them would have required their subjects to have two 'main sequences'. The theory put forward here predicts that two things can be done at once only if (*a*) they do not both require response; (*b*) they do not both have a high level of complexity; (*c*) at least one of them is 'automatic' enough to be outside of consciousness. Ordinary experiments on overlapping activities do not meet these criteria.

To obtain more direct evidence, we have been conducting experiments on the visual scanning of printed lists. Preliminary results have been reported elsewhere (Neisser, 1963). Subjects scan a list of 'words' (actually consonant strings) until they find one that has some critical property. The search time, divided by the (variable) number of words *ahead* of the critical item, is a measure of the average time used by the subject to determine that each intervening item does *not* have the critical property. This measure is uncomplicated by reaction factors, since the subject makes no response to these non-critical items. In the present context, it is of interest to compare time-per-word if the critical property is a single letter (say Z) with time-per-word if the subject is looking for either of two letters (say Z *or* Q). All of our experiments agree that with practised subjects time-per-word is no longer in the latter case than in the former. Indeed, results of a recent experiment (unpublished) suggest that it takes no longer to scan for any of *ten* letters than for one alone. These results establish that multiple processing can occur, at least at the perceptual level. The theory proposed here also predicts that reactions to multiple cues will be slower in infra-human species than in man, but we have not carried out relevant experiments.

It is not as easy to generate novel predictions about thinking itself, because of the number of variables on which the successful problem-solving or imaginative thinking depend. It has been shown above that the tendency for ideas to arise during sleep or routine activity follows from considerations of capacity. One further prediction is worth mentioning. It has become common to have subjects 'think aloud' during experiments on problem solving (e.g., Newell, Simon and Shaw, 1958). If the views expressed in this paper are valid, such a procedure will substantially change the nature and course of the thought process, by limiting it to the main sequence. It may be possible to test this prediction experimentally.

References

BIRCH, H. G. (1954), 'The relation of previous experience to insightful problem solving', *J. comp. Psychol.*, vol. 38, pp. 367–83.
BLEULER, E. (1912), 'Autistic Thinking', in Rapaport, D. (ed.) (1951), *Organization and pathology of thought*, Columbia U.P., pp. 399–437.
BROADBENT, D. E. (1958), *Perception and communication*, Pergamon.
BRUNER, J. S. (1960), *The process of education*, Harvard U.P.

DOYLE, W. (1960), 'Recognition of sloppy hand-printed characters', *Proc. Western Joint Computer Conf.*, pp. 133–42.

FREUD, S. (1900), *The interpretation of dreams*, in Brill, A. A. (ed.), *The basic writings of Sigmund Freud*, Modern Library, pp. 181–552.

GHISELIN, B. (1952) (ed.), *The creative process*, California U.P.

HOLLAND, J. (1959), 'A universal computer capable of executing an arbitrary number of sub-programs simultaneously', *Proc. Eastern Joint Computer Conf.*, pp. 108–13.

KÖHLER, W. (1927), *The mentality of apes*, Harcourt, Brace, Penguin Books, 1957.

KUBIE, L. S. (1958), *Neurotic distortion of the creative process*, Lawrence, Kansas University.

MCKELLAR, P. (1957), *Imagination and thinking*, Cohen and West.

MASLOW, A. H. (1957), 'Two kinds of cognition and their integration', *Gen. Semantics Bull.*, vol. 20, pp. 17–22.

MINSKY, M. (1961), 'Steps toward artificial intelligence', *Proc. Inst. Radio Engrs.*, N.Y., vol. 49, pp. 8–30.

NEISSER, U. (1963), 'Decision-time without reaction-time: experiments in visual scanning', *Amer. J. Psychol.*, vol. 76, pp. 376–85.

NEISSER, U., and WEENE, P. (1960), 'A note on human recognition of hand-printed characters', *Information and Control*, vol. 3, pp. 191–6.

NEWELL, A., SIMON, H. A., and SHAW, J. C. (1958), 'Elements of a theory of human problem solving', *Psychol. Rev.*, vol. 65, pp. 151–66.

RAPAPORT, D. (1951), *Organization and pathology of thought*, Columbia U.P.

SELFRIDGE, O. G. (1959), 'Pandemonium: a paradigm for learning', in *Mechanization of thought processes* (National Physical Laboratory), H.M.S.O.

SELFRIDGE, O. G., and NEISSER, U. (1960), 'Pattern recognition by machine', *Sci. Amer.*, vol. 203, pp. 60–8.

TAUBER, E. S., and GREEN, M. R. (1959), *Prelogical experience*, Basic Books.

UNGER, S. H. (1958), 'A computer oriented toward spatial problems', *Proc. Inst. Radio Engrs.*, N.Y., vol. 46, pp. 1744–50.

WERTHEIMER, M. (1959), *Productive thinking*, Tavistock.

WOODWORTH, R. S., and SCHLOSBERG, H. (1954), *Experimental psychology*, Methuen.

24 W. R. Reitman, R. B. Grove and R. G. Shoup

Argus: An Information-processing Model of Thinking

Excerpt from W. R. Reitman, R. B. Grove and R. G. Shoup, 'Argus: an information-processing model of thinking', *Behav. Sci.*, vol. 9 (1964), pp. 270–81.

Argus is an information-processing system consisting of a central executive and a network of semantic elements. Many of these elements may be active simultaneously. The executive is related to the sequential processing organization used in the General Problem Solver (G.P.S.) (Newell, Shaw, and Simon, 1960). The semantic elements are derived from and functionally similar to the cell-assemblies conjectured by Hebb (1949).

The program described below is designed to explore problem solving in such a system. It is also a first step in the evolution of a more general conceptual tool. We anticipate that later versions of the program will be able to give an integrated account of cognitive structure and of such processes as understanding, cognitive learning, and a range of types of thinking extending from controlled, goal-oriented problem solving to daydreaming and free association (Reitman, 1964a).

Several other points may be noted, though they are only indirectly connected with the use of the program as a model and conceptual tool. For example, though Argus and G.P.S. hardly span the range of possible information-processing systems, taken together they do suggest the variety of fundamentally different systems of psychological assumptions that may be represented in list-processing languages and in computer models generally. Then, too, since Argus is partly modeled after G.P.S. and partly a reaction to the behavioral consequences of certain of its organizational concepts, what follows should indicate some of the ways in which one information-processing model may influence and affect the development of others. Finally, because Argus is intended less to simulate behavior than to explore the implications of a system of assumptions about cognitive organization and activity, it is relevant to current discussions concerning the range of uses to which such models may be put (Reitman, 1964b). [. . .]

Psychological Considerations: Distractability and Context Change

Probably the most significant work of the past decade on the processes underlying goal-directed thought is that of Newell, Shaw, and Simon (e.g., 1958, 1960; Newell and Simon, 1961), Gelernter (1960), and their associates. These investigators developed and applied information-processing models to research in this area, and they are mainly responsible for the recognition which these new conceptual and methodological tools have achieved (Feigenbaum and Feldman, 1963; E. Hunt, 1962; J. Hunt, 1961; Miller, Galanter and Pribram, 1960; Tomkins and Messick, 1963).

Given the need to justify and explain at the same time some particular theories and a complex and unfamiliar methodology, these earlier papers understandably focus for the most part upon the substantial similarities to be demonstrated by comparisons between human performance and the behaviors generated by the models. As a number of excellent recent discussions (e.g., Neisser, 1963; Newell, 1962b) make evident, however, the *differences* discovered through such comparisons may be equally significant keys to the underlying organization and structure of psychological activity. The program reported below arose in part in response to just such a pattern of informally observed differences – differences, incidentally, similar at many points to those noted and discussed by Neisser and Newell.

It is difficult to study the behavior of G.P.S. without being struck by its singlemindedness. So total a lack of distractability might perhaps occur in some perfect exemplar of the Pavlovian 'strong nervous system', but it is by the same token quite atypical of human thinking generally. Rarely are we capable of such utter tenacity.

Consider a few examples. Suppose the phone rings while you are writing a letter or working out a lecture. You answer, discuss some unrelated subject, and then return to your task. Only infrequently will interruptions and interpolated activity of this sort have any serious effect upon your work.

Many of us with 'weaker' nervous systems can be distracted by much less insistent stimuli – for example, by the occasional unexpected ideas that crop up in the course of our work. But even if a new thought arising in this way is carried forward for a bit, we generally encounter little difficulty in recovering the strands of our previous activity, particularly if we have taken down a note or two before following out the interrupting idea. Now and then, of course, we are *not* able to recover our previous context and at such times we may wonder unhappily whether we have not perhaps lost some great thoughts in the shuffle. But such outcomes are infrequent. As casual observation of any luncheon conversation will testify, the limited effect of such losses and confusions is amazing when we consider the range and frequency of the distractions orderly cognitive activity is subjected to.

Nor will anyone who has ever been really worried about some problem underestimate the difficulty involved in approximating the singlemindedness we see in G.P.S. It is no matter of closing one's door, unplugging the telephone, and concentrating on the day's agenda. Both normal and neurotic experiences attest to human inability to ignore anxiety stimuli or control their propagation. Over and over again, they return to interrupt. Quite apart from matters connected with a primary somatic signal such as pain, the recurrence of insoluble problems and their unwanted intrusions into remote cognitive contexts attest to fundamental differences between human information-processing and that which goes on in strictly sequential, centralized systems such as G.P.S.

Loss of Information

Finally, we would suggest that human ability to endure interruptions with a minimum of confusion is related to a more general insensitivity to loss of detail. Current computer programs typically presume perfect recall of a great deal of specific information. Errors or omissions at quite trivial levels can result in total derailment. With each subgoal it generates, for example, G.P.S. stores context information requiring some two hundred words of code. This is the information it needs if it is to operate meaningfully with that subgoal at any later time (Newell, 1962a, 1962b). Note that these subgoals have as their terms the abstract, sensorily empty expressions of symbolic logic. Empirical problems involving sense data no doubt would require a great deal more stored information. Like Tristram Shandy, such a system might soon spend much of its life recording the details of a single day. Humans, by contrast, seem generally less dependent upon a multitude of details, more able to regenerate what they need as the occasion arises. One might well argue that as a general rule, almost everything we experience tends to be forgotten. Only as an exception is an item of information long retained and ready at hand. [. . .]

We might account for our ability to handle telephone interruptions by analogy with mechanisms now utilized in many computer systems. Interruptions by worry or promising ideas are another matter, however. To explain them, we must assume a system sensitive to its understanding of, and interest in, the information it is processing, and capable of assessing the likely importance of incipient alternatives. If we are to account for its imperfect ability to put aside problems and ideas as it chooses, the system also must be assumed to include a *number* of parallel centers of activity, rather than just one as in G.P.S. Finally, we must specify how choices among alternatives might be determined by relative significance or urgency, or perhaps even by the relative sensitivity to disturbance of the information contexts serving to frame and define each of the alternatives. Available information-processing models enable us to pose and to think about such questions, but they are not a sufficient basis for dealing with them.

Alternatives to Strictly Sequential, Centralized Processing

In his Introduction to *The organization of behavior*, Hebb labels 'the failure . . . to handle thought adequately' as 'the essential weakness of modern psychological theory' (1949, p. xvi). Defining thought as 'some sort of process that is not fully controlled by environmental stimulation and yet co-operates closely with that stimulation' (p. xvi), Hebb then develops a schema intended to serve as 'a conceptual tool for dealing with expectancy, attention, and so on, and with a temporally organized intra-cerebral process' (p. xviii). The result, built around the cell-assembly concept, is very likely the most seminal systematic theory in psychology which appeared in the postwar era, and the idea of a system of active interacting elements is very suggestive when viewed against problems of the sort we have been discussing.

Substantial as its other merits may be, however, in no sense can Hebb's theory be considered a general theory of thought. In particular, Hebb never shows how his theory might account for goal-directed thinking, e.g., as one finds it reflected in protocols of problem-solving behavior. Nor have we been able to imagine any way in which a system consisting entirely of Hebian cell-assemblies might be made to do so. 'Thought', in fact, has only one index entry for the entire body of Hebb's book. 'Thinking' and 'problem solving' get none at all. Thus it is not surprising that though there have been computer models of information-processing based upon Hebb's theory, they have for the most part been concerned with the development of cell-assemblies from individual neurons (e.g., Rochester *et al.*, 1956) rather than with the processes of thought.

327

There is another difficulty involved in simulating thinking in a system of active parallel elements of the sort Hebb describes – the very vagueness of the concept of a parallel system itself. Just as the assertion that a system is nonlinear tells us nothing about the kinds of deviations from linearity it shows, so terming a system parallel implies nothing about the extent of parallel activity or the constraints to which it is subject. By presenting evidence bearing on things humans can *not* do, Broadbent (1958, 1962), Miller (1956), and others have suggested certain limitations that parallel models of human information-processing would apparently have to reflect. Within these limitations, however, many organizational principles remain which might serve as bases for explanation of those performances humans *are* capable of: with respect to selections from among these, psychological theory in general seems to have very little to say.

In his paper on the organization of G.P.S., Newell (1962b) points out that 'sequential processing ... encourages us to envision isolated processes devoted to specific functions, each passively waiting in line to operate when its turn comes. It permits us to think of the total program in terms of only one thing going on at a time'. Without a centralized, sequential arrangement, he suggests, information-processing might well be like an 'Alice-in-Wonderland croquet game, with porcupine balls unrolling themselves and wandering off, and flamingo mallets asking questions at inopportune times' (p. 398).

None the less, though the over-all organization of G.P.S. with its goal structures and associated context storage procedures clearly is an excellent basis for carrying on complex information-processing in an orderly fashion, discussions such as Hebb's and the informal examples of human experience considered above convince us that human cognitive activity must be organized at least in part in a fundamentally different framework. Though we cannot see how cell-assemblies and phase sequences *by themselves* can be made to provide an adequate general account of thought, perhaps a system linking a limited sequential control to an underlying structure of active elements fashioned after the Hebbian model might furnish the necessary basis.

Thus Argus is a first step toward a system that begins by positing active cognitive elements and gradual loss of information. It is being used to explore how an organism operating under these conditions might be enabled to get back to the right track close enough and often enough to achieve some semblance of progress in its work. In Newell's metaphor, in other words, Argus is an inquiry into the virtues of flamingoes given a modicum of order in Wonderland.

Program Structure and Operation

The program described below is written in IPL-V (Newell, 1964) and has been run on the Bendix G-20 at Carnegie Institute of Technology. As was noted above, Argus is written so as to make possible extended versions applicable to a broad range of cognitive functions. The versions now running, however, are limited to analogies problems of the form $A:B::C:(W, X, Y, \text{or } Z)$. To simplify the exposition, minor differences among the several versions of Argus are for the most part ignored here. All versions share the same basic organizational structure, and each is capable of finding solutions to the simple analogies problems used in testing the system. [. . .]

The main aspects of the system are the sequential *executive*, the *network* of active semantic elements, and the channels of *interaction* between them. There are also *experimenter* routines, but since these are concerned primarily with input and output, performance monitoring, and similar housekeeping tasks, they need not be described further. [. . .]

Executive

The activity of the executive is organized on four levels. From the top down, these are: subject, problem, strategy, and strategy step. We may think of an individual as someone who has available a variety of information-processing strategies along with some rules for their use in specific situations. An individual subject is therefore defined as a set of information-processing strategies and rules for their use. Given a subject, that is, a particular set of strategies and rules, the Argus experimenter generates a problem. All problems are analogy items at present, and each is read in as a list of seven words corresponding to the names of the three given semantic elements and the four answer alternatives. Using the strategies and associated rules specified, the executive now tries to solve the problem. Each strategy is a scheme built up of steps, the basic units of behavior available to the executive. Figure 1 depicts a simplified version of one such strategy. Though rudimentary and relatively ineffective as given here, the strategy illustrates the kinds of unitary behaviors assumed and the ways in which they may be organized in higher-order information-processing schemes. The implications of the various steps will be evident once we have discussed the structure of the semantic elements upon which they operate, and are ready to consider the executive cycle and the dynamics of the Argus system as a whole.

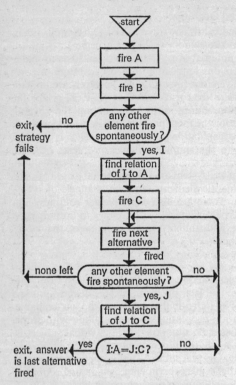

Figure 1   Rudimentary strategy (slightly simplified) for analogy problems of the form A:B::C: (W, X, Y, or Z). When an element is fired, activation and inhibition increments are added to related elements, altering their states.

Changes in the semantic network occur *within* steps. When a step commences the network is in some state *s*. By the end of the step, changes may have occurred in the status of individual semantic elements, and in the strengths of interrelations among the elements. Thus the network as a whole is in some new state *s'*. No further changes take place until the next step begins. The order in which changes within a step occur is only locally relevant. Such

330

changes become available to the executive *together*, and only after the step in which they occur has been completed. The step thus serves a double function. Like the method segment in G.P.S., it is the minimal unit of behavior. In an important sense, however, it is also the minimal unit of time; from the viewpoint of the executive, network changes occurring within the step may be thought of as taking place in parallel and at approximately the same time.

Cognitive Structure as a Network of Active Semantic Elements

[. . .] The basic units of the Argus cognitive structure are the semantic elements (see Reitman, 1965, chapters 3, 4 and 5). These correspond to Hebb's cell-assemblies in terms of the psychological functions they serve. Each semantic element is an IPL-V structure consisting of three description lists. The first two lists define the direct connexions or associations to other semantic elements in the cognitive structure. Since Argus at the present time has neither perceptual inputs nor behavioral outputs, the meaning of a semantic element is solely a function of the set of its direct and indirect interconnexions to the other elements of the cognitive structure.

Each relation to another semantic element is specified by an attribute-value pair on the first description list. For example, the relation of the semantic unit corresponding to the sensation of heat to the one representing its opposite, cold, would be given by the pair (OPPOSITE, COLD) on the first description list of the semantic element HEAT. The pairs on the second list specify the current strength of association for each such relation between the element and another semantic element in the cognitive structure.

The third description list gives the parameters defining the current state of the semantic unit. These parameters are named in terms reminiscent of Hebb's conceptual nervous system. This is an informal usage, however, primarily for mnemonic purposes, and carries no neurophysiological implications about corresponding elements in the human nervous system. That is, the Argus semantic elements are purely psychological or information-processing constructs. They correspond to units of meaning in human cognitive structures, and their existence is taken as given.

Five parameters are required to specify the current state. The first four give activation, inhibition, threshold, and size values for the semantic element. The fifth names the internal date when these values became current. Activation and inhibition values decay with time, and all of the first four parameters may vary with other changes occurring in the system. Thus the values recorded for these parameters, though correct as of the indicated internal date, will in general be wrong when the semantic element is called or acted upon subsequently. Any routine affecting or using a semantic element must therefore first call in sub-routines that compute appropriate current values for the first four parameters and update the fifth.

Activation, inhibition, and conflict. – It might seem simpler to replace activation and inhibition by a single parameter representing the net resultant. The modification certainly would be advantageous computationally. We maintain the distinction because we are working at an aggregate level, i.e., at the level of semantic elements, rather than with units corresponding to individual neurons. It is not obvious that we want to consider a semantic element which is high both in activation and inhibition to be psychologically equivalent to one having low values on these two parameters. On the contrary, semantic elements high both in activation and inhibition provide a very reasonable representation of one type of cognitive conflict, i.e., a conflict focused about a few specific elements of meaning in the system. [. . .]

Threshold, size, and propagation of activity. – The first two description lists of a semantic element specify the elements it is associated with and the strength of each of these associations. The set of all such pairs thus describes the structure of interconnexions within the cognitive structure as a whole. Following Hebb (1949, p. xix), we think of the semantic elements in Argus as generally open in the sense that usually changes in the state of an element might be expected to have some effects beyond its bounds. But there seems to be no good basis on which to specify the extent or significance of these constant low-level inter-element interactions. Worse yet, if they are extensive and frequent enough, there is no way in which a serial device can be expected to continue to simulate more than a small fraction of such interactions – the Tristram Shandy problem again. A second problem arises out of Hebb's conception of the firing of an element once activity within it rises above a certain level.

In Argus, both problems are handled by a single parameter, the threshold. Thus this concept in Argus is as much a programming convenience as it is a theoretical construct. Threshold marks the point of maximum activity within an element. Below threshold, activity within an element does not propagate. Once activity reaches threshold level, the element is said to fire.

The maximum impact any particular element may have on others is specified by its size. Size is thus an ancillary parameter, reflecting the assumption that some elements are 'larger' or otherwise more important than others in determining the direction of activity within the cognitive structure.

We have stated that propagation takes place within a step. The current step terminates only when no further elements are active enough to fire. Interminable firing loops are prevented by conventions, e.g., by permitting elements to fire only once within a step, or by reducing the activation level of a just-fired element to some arbitrary proportion of its threshold value. The latter procedure to some extent resembles the refractory period behavior of individual neurons, of course, but again, since the semantic element is an aggregate construct, the force of the analogy is uncertain and the procedure may better be regarded as a pure convention.

Interactions between the Executive and the Active Semantic Network

The signal system. – One of the main channels for interaction between the executive and the semantic network is a system of signals and signal cells based on that used in G.P.S. During a step, signals may be set for any of several reasons.

The occurrence of a cognitive conflict anywhere in the semantic network is one of the several kinds of spontaneous events taking place there which may be noticed by the executive and which thus may have an effect on its subsequent behavior. Specifically, whenever the activation and inhibition levels for an element both exceed an arbitrary limit, a conflict signal is entered in the main signal cell and the name of the element is recorded elsewhere in the signal system as the immediate locus of the conflict. Now the executive is in a position to notice this conflict upon completion of the current step. What the executive does at that point will depend among other things upon the characteristics of the current subject and current strategy. Some people are easily distracted from a line of thought by such conflicts. Others may attend to them selectively, depending upon the locus of the conflict and what they are doing at the time. Still others may ignore them, or perhaps not even be aware of them. The use of separate activation and inhibition parameters permits us to represent such conflicts about a semantic focus, and it will make possible detailed exploration of the problem-solving consequences of individual differences in strategies for reacting to them.

Similarly, whenever an element fires as a result of increments in activation propagated from related elements, a signal is entered in the main signal cell and the name of the spontaneously firing element is recorded in an ancillary cell. Once again, any of a variety of responses may be made to such an event once the current step is completed.

The main signal cell is a pushdown list and thus may accumulate any number of such signals in the course of a step. In addition to those initiated by cognitive conflict or spontaneous activity, it may contain signals set with or by the strategies, and by other sources as well.

The executive cycle. – Once a step has been completed, responsibility for decisions about further action passes back up to the executive. The executive checks the main signal cell and then makes its decision in the light of the signals it finds there and the dictates of its current strategy. Thus the signal system makes possible a quite general decision based upon the state of the organism as a whole, including some aspects of activity in the cognitive structure for which the executive is not in any direct sense responsible.

This generalized decision is achieved by means of the executive cycle, depicted in slightly simplified form in figure 2. Though not at all complex in itself, the executive cycle makes possible a very high degree of flexibility for the Argus system as a whole. Specifically, as figure 2 indicates, once a step is executed, if no answer has been obtained to the current problem, the executive checks the signal cell. If there are no signals, it simply continues with the next step of the current strategy. If one or more signals are present, however, the executive's next action is taken from a current signal table, and its behavior is thus a joint function of the signals present and the particular subject and strategy under which the executive is operating. As alternatives to continuing to the next step in the current strategy, the executive may choose to jump to a non-sequential step in the strategy, or to another strategy altogether. The housekeeping routines associated with the system place no limitations on the executive's choice at this point.

This indirect mode of operation through the signal system means that actions need not be invariant with particular signals. Furthermore, there is a general reset routine which modifies the table of signal-action pairs as a function of information taken from the description lists associated with the current subject and the current strategy. In fact, one of the actions open to the executive in response to certain signals is just such a resetting of elements of the signal table.

It is very difficult to communicate the possibilities that an arrangement as flexible as this opens up. Certainly it should be clear, however, that the execution of a strategy, even one as rudimentary as the one depicted in figure 1, is in no sense a cut-and-dried affair. The modulation of behavior in response to

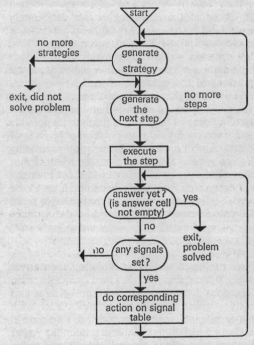

Figure 2   Executive cycle (slightly simplified). Subject and problem are specified beforehand. This gives the executive a set of strategies and rules for their use. The signal-action pairs in the signal table at any given time are a function of the rules.

signals permits events in the semantic network to exert a pervasive influence upon the over-all sequential control of the system. As a result, Argus now manifests something approaching the distractability and interruptability discussed at the beginning of this paper.

Executive controls over activity in the semantic network. – [. . .] There are two principal means whereby the executive may effect events taking place in the semantic network. The first of these is by the set of search, interrogation, and generation procedures programmed into the strategies (see figure 1 for examples). In general, when Argus elements are stimulated as a consequence of such executive action, their activity levels and effects upon related elements increase. Some of the strategies in fact deliberately instigate such activity in order to observe the subsequent firing.

A second means of control is possible in current Argus programs, though none of the strategies written so far make use of it. This would involve manipulation of the activation or inhibition levels generally or in portions of the semantic network. There is excellent experimental evidence that such level-changes take place in humans, and the experiences of relaxation and concentration might be interpreted in terms of them. In addition to its possible psychological significance, such local manipulation of levels is of interest as a potential control device for information-processing in artificial intelligence systems. In either case, the result is that Argus has at its command a probe of variable width and intensity which is capable of everything from gross discriminations to the finest and most precise effects, very much like that variable beam of light with which consciousness and attention have sometimes been compared.

Current Developments

Several reasons were presented earlier for exploring alternatives to strictly sequential systems such as G.P.S. These included human sensitivity to distractions from without and from within, and human ability to re-establish appropriate contexts after such interruptions, often despite intervening loss of detail. Two general methods have stood out which might enable a system like Argus to restore or rediscover context without explicitly preparing for context changes as G.P.S. does. The first of these is a time line; the second is a system for generating and using internal sentences. [. . .]

The time line. – The basic idea for the time line comes from Penfield and Roberts (1959), whose experimental stimulation of human cortex *in vivo* produced results which they interpret as suggesting that humans lay down a temporally-ordered cortical record of their experiences. Several Argus programs also lay down such a record. In later versions of Argus, this sequence of semantic elements corresponding to a sequence of experiential events will serve several important purposes. First, though incomplete cues may by themselves be inadequate as a context for problem-solving, when stimulated they may propagate activity to (and fire) the time-line record to which they refer. With such an entry to a relevant point in the time line, the problem-solver may have access to enough information on the original context at that point in the time line to be able to restore or reconstruct the balance.

The use of a time line also makes possible a rather straightforward and quite general treatment of forgetting. Since the time-line entries are themselves semantic elements, and since all associations among elements decay with time, no specific erasure of information is necessary to account for the loss of transitional objects created during information-processing, or for the forgetting of previous events in general. The only time-line entries which will continue to be retrievable will be those strongly tied in with other elements in the cognitive structure, e.g., as a result of frequent reference. As their fore and aft connexions within the time line decay to a low level, these individual entries will in effect come to be ordinary semantic elements, representations of the significant experience of the system. As such, they continue like other elements to be available to the executive, perhaps to be retrieved, for example, in the course of a search for specified concrete instances to use in deriving or testing some generalization or abstraction. In this way, moreover, the time line becomes an important source of new lexicographic units for the system, units which may enter into new attributes employed to describe still other objects (Reitman, 1964a). Thus, at least one kind of learning will be made a continuous and integral response of Argus, in keeping with the guiding aspirations described at the beginning of this paper.

The studies of Penfield and his associates, a number of psychoanalytic studies, and certain investigations utilizing hypnotic techniques all quite strongly suggest that the details of many experiences which no longer can be retrieved by strategies normally available to the executive nonetheless remain intact in memory and may be evoked by suitable techniques. In Argus, such a phenomenon could be reproduced by means of the time-line device with a very simple adjustment of the decay curve for associations. Alternately, since this phenomenon is not expected to be of practical significance for the sort of problem-solving behavior in which Argus will engage, the system may include an infrequent sweep through memory which returns linking cells to available space when the association between elements falls below some minimal strength.

Exploration of the time-line device suggests interesting alternative ways of looking at a number of traditional information-processing questions in psychology. To cite just one example, the lines between recalling, reconstructing, and re-creating information become much less clear. Suppose that the organism executive has gained access to one event in the time line and tries by direct stimulation to activate records of immediately subsequent events (i.e., 'tries to remember what happened after that'). Should that fail, the executive might switch strategies and try instead to reconstruct what might have happened next, from its knowledge of the goals and status of the situation at the event in the time line accessible to it. Suppose, furthermore, that now an immediately subsequent entry in the time line fires, due to activation propagated to it from elements stimulated during the executive's attempts at reconstruction. It examines the newly retrieved element, tests for its relation to the previously available event record, just as it would have done had an event record fired under the direct recall strategy, and concludes something equivalent to 'Oh yes, I remember'. But in this view, the main difference is at the strategy level, at the level of intent. In terms of the pattern of activation, it might well be impossible to separate those contributions to activity pattern changes due to 'recollection' from those due to 'reconstruction' or 'imagination'.

Internal sentences. – One need only overhear a snatch from a conversation – e.g., 'Mantle hit four runs. . . .' to realize how quickly humans can sometimes establish an appropriate context. Although the means whereby humans achieve the result remain unclear, such programs as Lindsay's (1963) provide some quite useful concrete suggestions. Current efforts toward an internal sentence mechanism for Argus are predicated on the assumption that the power to reproduce an appropriate context from a sketchy sequence of clues accessible in memory may very well depend on the same mechanisms that enable humans to understand equally sketchy external sentences, presumably by calling forth a context into which the information they convey is fitted. In conjunction with the time-line device, such a mechanism might provide an inexpensive and yet extremely powerful means of accounting for our insensitivity to loss of detail and ability to restore or reconstruct context.

Anyone who has had occasion to compare the comprehensibility of his lecture notes after a day, a week, and a year is familiar with the way in which such material grows cold. Archivists experience a somewhat similar phenomenon on a longer time scale. The design of library retrieval systems is complicated by a tendency for key terms to change in meaning over the years. Older classification schemes lose relevance to current usage, and it becomes increasingly difficult to retrieve pertinent older material unless one knows the meanings the category labels carried at the time the material was classified and stored. It is to be expected that a system built around time-line entries and internal sentences will show these same effects as some lexicographic units decay out of reach or are replaced by others, and as the relation-association-strength pairs change values with time. Such a result might perhaps be a drawback for some artificial intelligence applications, but it seems a clear advantage for a model of human information-processing which aims to derive such phenomena as learning and forgetting from a small number of simple and universally applicable system axioms.

Generalizing the cognitive structure. – Perhaps we may conclude by noting one other longer-range aspiration. As things stand now, a certain amount of the 'intelligence' of the system is encoded in special formats, notably the signal table and the strategies themselves. We would like to experiment with having the functions these components serve taken over by the general cognitive structure, so that all that remains of the executive is an organizational focus, something insuring the 'modicum of order' we were unable to account for with the Hebbian model. Like the Marxian state, the sequential executive may prove resistant to attempts to let it wither away, but the possibility has a theoretical simplicity and parsimony about it that make it very attractive.

References

BROADBENT, D. E. (1958), *Perception and communication*, Pergamon.
BROADBENT, D. E. (1962), 'Attention and the perception of speech', *Sci. Amer.*, vol. 206, pp. 143–51.
FEIGENBAUM, E. A., and FELDMAN, J. (1963) (eds.), *Computers and thought*, McGraw-Hill.
GELERNTER, H. (1960), 'Realization of a geometry-theorem-proving machine', *Proc. int. conf. on information processing*, UNESCO, Paris, pp. 273–82.
HEBB, D. O. (1949), *Organization of behavior*, Wiley.
HUNT, E. B. (1962), *Concept learning: an information processing problem*, Wiley.

HUNT, J. McV. (1961), *Intelligence and experience*, Ronald Press.

LINDSAY, R. K. (1963), 'Inferential memory as the basis of machines which understand natural language', in Feigenbaum, E. A., and Feldman, J. (eds.), *Computers and thought*, McGraw-Hill, pp. 217–33.

MILLER, G. A. (1956), 'The magical number seven, plus or minus two', *Psychol Rev.*, vol. 63, pp. 81–97.

MILLER, G. A., GALANTER, E., and PRIBRAM, K. H. (1960), *Plans and the structure of behavior*, Holt.

NEISSER, U. (1963), 'The imitation of man by machine' *Science*, vol. 139, pp. 193–7.

NEWELL, A. (1962a), 'A guide to GPS-2-2 program', Carnegie Institute of Technology, Pittsburgh.

NEWELL, A. (1962b), 'Some problems of basic organization in problem-solving programs', in Yovits, M. C., Jacobi, G. T., and Goldstein, G. D. (eds.), *Self-organizing systems*, Spartan Books, pp. 393–423.

NEWELL, A. (1964) (ed.), *Information processing language-V manual*, Prentice-Hall.

NEWELL, A., SHAW, J. C., and SIMON, H. A. (1958), 'Elements of a theory of human problem solving', *Psychol. Rev.*, vol. 65, pp. 151–66.

NEWELL, A., SHAW, J. C., and SIMON, H. A. (1960), 'Report on a general problem-solving program', *Proc. int. conf. on information processing*, UNESCO, Paris, pp. 256–64.

NEWELL, A., and SIMON, H. A. (1961), 'Computer simulation of human thinking', *Science*, vol. 134, pp. 2011–17.

PENFIELD, W., and ROBERTS, L. (1959), *Speech and brain mechanisms*, Princeton U.P.

REITMAN, W. R. (1964a), 'Heuristic decision procedures, open constraints, and the structure of ill-defined problems', in Shelly, M. W., and Bryan, G. L. (eds.), *Optimality and human judgement*, Wiley.

REITMAN, W. R. (1964b), 'Information processing models in psychology', *Science*, vol. 144, pp. 1192–8.

REITMAN, W. R. (1965), *Cognition and thought*, Wiley.

ROCHESTER, N., HOLLAND, J. H., HAIBT, L. H., and DUDA, W. L. (1956), 'Tests on a cell assembly theory of the action of the brain, using a large digital computer', *IRE Transactions on Information Theory*, PGIT-2, no. 3, pp. 80–93.

TOMKINS, S., and MESSICK, S. (1963), *Computer simulation of personality*, Wiley.

25 I. M. L. Hunter

Mental Calculation

Excerpt from I. M. L. Hunter, original English version of 'Kopfrechnen und Kopfrechner', *Bild der Wissenschaft*, April 1966, pp. 296–303.

During 1961, I had the rare privilege of studying a man with exceptional ability in rapid mental calculation. He is the distinguished mathematician, Professor A. C. Aitken (born 1895) of Edinburgh University. His unusual powers may be illustrated by two examples. He is asked to express as a decimal the fraction 4/47. He is silent for four seconds, then begins to speak the answer at a nearly uniform rate of one digit every three-quarters of a second. 'Point 08510638297872340425531914, that's about as far as I can carry it.' The total time between the presentation of the problem and this moment is twenty-four seconds. He discusses the problem for one minute and then continues the answer at the same rate as before. 'Yes, 191489, I can get that.' He pauses for five seconds. '361702127659574458, now that is the repeating point. It starts again at 085. So if that is forty-six places, I am right.' The second example concerns a more difficult problem. He is asked to give the square root of 851. After a short silence, he gives 29·17. Then, at irregular intervals, he supplies further digits of the answer. By the time fifteen seconds have elapsed, he has given 29·17190429. His ability is clearly remarkable. Indeed, he is probably the most expert mental calculator of whom detailed records exist. [. . .]

Professor Aitken solves any given numerical problem in a sequence of steps. First, he examines the problem and decides the plan or method by which he will calculate the answer: in doing this, he typically recasts the problem into a form which he can more easily handle. Then he implements his chosen method and, step by step, generates the answer. This step-sequence pattern is evident in the following report. He has just solved the problem of expressing the fraction 1/851 as a decimal.

The instant observation was that 851 is 23 times 37. I use this fact as follows. 1/37 is 0·027027027, and so on repeated. This I divide mentally by 23. 23 into 0·027 is 0·001 with remainder 4. In a flash I can get that 23 into 4027 is 175 with remainder 2, and into 2027 is 88 with remainder 3, and into 3027 is 131 with remainder 14, and even into 14,027 is 609 with remainder 20. And so on like that. Also, before I ever start this,

I know how far it is necessary to go before reaching the end of the recurring period: for 1/37 recurs at three places and 1/23 recurs at twenty-two places, and the lowest common multiple of 3 and 22 is 66, whence I know that there is a recurring period of 66 places.

This report suggests the analogy of a traveller who undertakes a cross-country journey on foot. First, he surveys the ground to be covered and plans a route which will involve the smallest number of manageable steps; then he follows the route, step by step. The report also illustrates two of the most basic features of Aitken's ability, namely, his large repertoire of number facts, and his repertoire of ingenious calculative plans.

For most people, there is a limited repertoire of numerical questions which they can answer rapidly and without any awareness of having to work anything out. What is twelve divided by two? The answer comes automatically. For people who do a lot of number work, say accountants or teachers of mathematics, the repertoire of such questions is larger. For Aitken, the repertoire is vastly more extensive than normal. For example, if he is given any number up to 1,500, he can automatically say whether it is a prime number or, if it is not prime, state its factors. Once, during discussion, the year 1961 was mentioned and he immediately commented that this is 37 times 53, or alternatively 44 squared plus 5 squared, or alternatively 40 squared plus 19 squared. So, he is able automatically to recognize many properties of numbers and to answer many numerical questions. Furthermore, he is able to recognize, and to think of, quite large numbers as distinctive, unitary items: this is comparable to the ability of literate people to deal with a word as a unit rather than as an unwieldy collection of letters or sounds. In solving a problem, this extensive repertoire of number facts is deployed to advantage. It enables him to recognize useful properties of the problem, for example, that 851 is 23 times 37, and that 1/37 is 0·027027 repeated. It also enables him to pursue his chosen method in a succession of large steps, to leap rather than walk. His extensive repertoire of number facts is clearly advantageous. However, it is also necessary that, during calculation, only the appropriate facts should be produced, and, furthermore, that they should be produced in appropriate sequence. The production of these facts must be governed by an overall plan of calculation.

Most, perhaps all, skilled activities involve step-sequences. Ability to carry out the component steps is necessary for skill, but it is not sufficient. The expert typist requires more than ability to strike any required key on the board; the master violinist requires more than ability to produce any required note from his violin; the fluent orator requires more than a large vocabulary. In all cases, it is necessary to organize component steps into an appropriate sequence. So also in calculating. When Aitken tackles a problem, his first priority is to decide a calculative plan. This is the key decision for it governs everything else which follows, and final success depends heavily on it. It is true that his activities at each successive moment will have to adapt to the changing circumstances of the moment, that the accuracy of his working will have to be assured and occasionally verified, and that advantage may be taken of some minor short-cut in working. But all this is subordinated to the plan decided at the outset. This plan preselects what is to be done at each step: it also ensures that each step will follow smoothly out of the steps which have gone before, and will lead smoothly into the steps which are to follow. It sometimes happens that, after he has selected and launched a plan, he becomes aware of another and better plan: but he does not change to this other plan because such a change would greatly disrupt his working. This fact, that one plan cannot easily be changed for another in mid-course, is further evidence for the central, and continuing, role of the plan in governing calculation.

Aitken has a large variety of calculative plans at his disposal, and he can solve the same problem in several different ways. So why should he choose one plan rather than another? The answer is: economy of effort. He searches for that plan which will carry him to the solution in the shortest time and with least difficulty. This may be illustrated by considering two problems which have already been mentioned. The problems are to express as decimals the fractions 4/47 and 1/851. Both problems could be done by straight division. But, for Aitken, there are other and more economical ways of working. In the case of 1/851, he factorizes 851 into 23 times 37, then expresses 1/37 as 0·027027027 repeated, and then divides this by 23 in a succession of large steps. The main economy here is that he can now divide by 23 instead of 851. In the case of 4/47, there is a similar economy. He transforms the problem so that he can divide by 8 instead of 47. He first recognizes that, since 47 is prime, he cannot proceed by factorizing. So he transforms 4/47 into 68/799, and this enables him to launch a plan which is familiar to him. He divides 68 by 800, in effect by 8, and makes certain corrections to allow for the fact that if he divides by 800 instead of 799 his answer will be in error by an 800th. The steps of this plan are represented in figure 1. These two examples illustrate that an appropriate plan can economize effort by reducing the difficulty and/or the number of steps required to solve a problem. A more familiar example of such economic planning occurs when a person is asked to divide a number by 25, and proceeds to multiply the number by 4 and then divide the outcome by 100.

Dividend	Answer	Remainder	Next Dividend
680 ÷ 8	0·085	none	85
85 ÷ 8	10	5	510
510 ÷ 8	63	6	663
663 ÷ 8	82	7	782
782 ÷ 8	97	6	697
697 ÷ 8	87	1	187
187 ÷ 8	23	3	323
323 ÷ 8	40	3	340
340 ÷ 8	42	4	442
442 ÷ 8	55	2	255
255 ÷ 8	31	7	731
731 ÷ 8	91	3	391
391 ÷ 8	48	7	748
748 ÷ 8	93	4	493
493 ÷ 8	61	5	561
561 ÷ 8	70	1	170
170 ÷ 8	21	2	221
221 ÷ 8	27	5	527
527 ÷ 8	65	7	765
765 ÷ 8	95	5	595
595 ÷ 8	74	3	374
374 ÷ 8	46	6	646
646 ÷ 8	80	6	680

680 which is the original dividend

Figure 1   A representation of the unconventional step-sequence followed by an expert calculator. The problem is to express the fraction 4/47 as a decimal. First, he transforms 4/47 into 68/799. Then he proceeds to divide 68 by 800 (in effect, by 8) with a recurring correction to allow for the difference between 799 and 800. Each line represents the same cycle of events. The dividend is divided by 8 to give two digits of the answer and a remainder; then the next dividend is formed by combining this answer and this remainder, e.g., from answer 10 and remainder 5, the next dividend is 510. Repetition of this cycle generates the answer to 4/47, two digits at a time.

Economy of effort is centrally important for Aitken's calculating, as it is for a great many human accomplishments. He, like anyone else, can only do so much at any one time. Within any period of time, there are limits to the amount which anyone can observe or say or think or remember. In brief, it is a universal property of human beings that they have limited capacity for concurrent activities. One consequence of this central fact is that many tasks must be done in a succession of steps rather than all at once. Another consequence is that, in carrying through any task, speed can be gained by excluding any activities which are not strictly necessary for the task in hand. Aitken does just this: he concentrates on minimum essentials. Some exclusions concern obvious irrelevances, such as reacting to events in his surroundings or thinking about other matters: when calculating, he is physically relaxed and inattentive to everything but the calculation. Other exclusions are made possible by his large repertoire of number facts and by his use of ingenious calculative plans. His ability to take large steps reduces the total number of steps required, and adherence to a chosen plan reduces his moment-by-moment activities of deciding what he should do next. Yet other exclusions concern speech movements and imaging. Just as people can learn to read silently instead of speaking or mouthing words, so Aitken calculates without speaking numbers or muttering instructions to himself. Likewise, he need not think of numbers in terms of visual or auditory symbols or, indeed, of any form of clearly conscious awareness. In brief, Aitken is able to exclude from calculating many activities which, for most people, are indispensable. He solves a problem with concentrated and streamlined effort. [. . .]

Let us leave Aitken for the moment, and consider a general question. What happens whenever a person, by whatever means, increases his calculative ability? Broadly, the answer seems always to be the same. He acquires a system of calculative techniques which has two general properties. First, when he solves problems in terms of this system, he saves effort. So he can solve in less time, and solve problems which were previously beyond his ability. Second, this effort-saving system can only be acquired through effort, that is, work must be expended to establish the system which saves him work. These two aspects of increased ability are of such general importance that they merit a few examples. Consider a person who increases his calculative ability by learning to use a slide-rule, or a table of logarithms, or an electric calculating machine. He has now mastered a calculative system. He translates numerical problems into this system and works them in terms of this system so as to generate the solution. And the system enables him to solve these problems with reduced effort. In such cases, part of the system is external to himself, embodied in the apparatus he has learned to use; and most of the work of establishing the system was done by the men who invented and made this apparatus. Consider the person who increases his skill in mental calculation. Again, he has mastered a calculative system which enables him to solve problems with reduced effort. But this system is entirely within himself and has no physical existence outside his own body. Further, almost all the work of establishing the system was done by the individual himself. [. . .]

Throughout history, there have been reports of people with exceptional ability in mental calculation. What can be learned from these reports? Perhaps the most striking thing is that they concern such a diversity of people with such widely different accomplishments. There are reports of young children, of gifted mathematicians such as Gauss and Ampère, of illiterates, and of people who are almost mentally defective. Some of those people solve a wide range of numerical problems by highly ingenious procedures and with great rapidity; others are specialists who excel only in some limited range of problems; others tackle only fairly simple problems by slow and conventional techniques, and are remarkable merely for their willingness to work without external aids; others show modest calculative accomplishments which would be unremarkable except for the person's lack of ability in any other direction. Even among those with moderately high calculative ability, there is diversity. Some rely heavily on visual imaging, some on auditory imaging, and some use little imaging of any kind. They also vary in their characteristic speed of working and in their techniques. For example, at the end of last century, the French psychologist Binet examined two men who had some renown as mental calculators. He gave each of them the same problems, written on paper, and required them to write the answer but nothing else. One problem was: multiply 58,927 by 61,408. One calculator (Inaudi) completed the answer in 40 seconds, the other (Diamandi) in 275 seconds; and I have recently met a professional accountant who completed this problem in 55 seconds. Inaudi produced the digits of his answer in the left-to-right order, whereas Diamandi produced these digits in the right-to-left order; my accountant also produced the digits in right-to-left order, but he used a calculative plan quite different from that used either by Inaudi or by Diamandi. Different calculators clearly have very different calculative systems.

Reports on mental calculators also show that these different calculative systems are, in every case, built up by experience with calculating. Exceptionally able calculators have usually had years of intensive practice and some have commented that, with lack of practice, their skill deteriorates. For example, Aitken has described how he became interested in numerical problems at the age of thirteen and how, until his mid-thirties, he continued to explore increasingly complex problems with intense fascination. In doing this, some routine of calculation would be evolved; this would be extended to further examples and, thereby, give rise to the discovery of new numerical relationships which, in their turn, would provide fresh problems for exploration and new plans for calculating. Through these cumulative achievements, he learned to solve hitherto unmanageable problems and to solve old problems in more economical and rapid ways. Even after his mid-thirties, his experiences of calculating were considerable, partly because of their utility in his mathematical work and partly because of their intrinsic interest. [. . .]

From all the fascinating details contained in reports on mental calculators, we can draw two general conclusions. The first has already been mentioned: each individual builds up, through his own numerical experience, a distinctive calculative system which enables him to solve this or that type of problem with reduced effort. The second conclusion, to which we now turn, is this: the accomplishments of mental calculators are restricted by limitations of temporary memory.

Consider the problem of multiplying 234 by 567. When asked to solve this, most people reach for paper and pencil, and pursue a calculative plan which they learned at school (figure 2). The person

		2	3	4
		5	6	7
	1	6	3	8
1	4	0	4	
1	7	0		
1	3	2	6	7	8

Figure 2   A representation of a conventional paper-and-pencil calculation. The problem is to multiply 234 by 567. The two numbers are written as shown. Then 234 is multiplied by 7, then by 6, and then by 5, to give three products. These products are then added to generate the final answer in right-to-left sequence. In this way, the working is decomposed into a sequence of small steps and, because of the written record, nothing much needs to be remembered at any one time. However, if the answer is to be written, but nothing else, this procedure is not feasible because there is too much data to be held in temporary memory.

writes the two numbers and progresses through an ordered succession of steps: 7 times 4 is 28, write 8, carry 2; 7 times 3 is 21, add the carried 2 to the 1, write 3, carry 2; and so on. In this way, he obtains three written products, and then he adds these products together to generate the answer in right-to-left order. Now, suppose we ask the person to solve this problem without writing anything except the final answer. If he pursues the same plan as before, but without jotting down the intermediate steps, he soon finds that there is too much to hold in temporary memory. He must remember the four digits of the first product, the four digits of the second product, and the four digits of the third; then he must recall these digits, in a different order, so as to add the three products; and all this must be done at the same time as he carries out the component calculative steps. Most people cannot complete this calculation, and the main reason is the limited amount of data which can be held in temporary memory.

Any mental calculator, however accomplished, has this difficulty of limited temporary memory. The difficulty becomes especially acute when he is required, at any one time, to hold a large amount of data in temporary storage. This restricts the range of numerical problems which he can profitably solve without external aids. In particular, it excludes most multiplication and division problems which contain large numbers. This restriction was clearly stated in 1856 by G. P. Bidder, a well-documented English calculator of considerable accomplishment.

The exercise of (temporary) memory is the only real strain on the mind, and which limits the extent to which mental calculation can be carried. . . . In proportion as the numbers increase, so the (temporary) registration by the mind becomes more and more difficult, until at last the process becomes as slow as registration upon paper. When that point is arrived at, it is clear that the utility of mental calculation ceases, and the process ought to be carried upon paper.

This restriction is all the more evident nowadays with the advent of powerful electronic computers. For example, Aitken reports that when, in 1923, he first used a calculating machine, even of the antiquated kind then available, he

saw at once how useless it was to carry out for myself any mental multiplication of large numbers. Almost automatically, I cut down my ability in that direction, though I still kept up squaring and reciprocating and square-rooting, which have a more algebraic basis and a statistical use. But I am convinced that my ability deteriorated after that first encounter.

So, the utility of mental calculation is restricted to problems which can be done without, at any juncture, having to hold a large amount of data in temporary memory.

Despite what has just been said, many mental calculators give the appearance of being able to hold an impressively large amount of data in temporary memory. In Aitken's case, there is little doubt that he has a greater than normal capacity for holding data in temporary store, whether the data is numerical or verbal or musical or diagrammatic. This may also be the case with some other calculators. However, quite apart from such above-normal capacity, there are two general ways in which calculators can reduce the amount which they need to hold in temporary memory. The first way is to devise calculative plans which lighten the required memory load. The objective here is, as Bidder said, 'to bring all calculations, as far as it may be practicable, into one result, and to have that one result alone, at a time, registered upon the mind.' The literature refers to a variety of such plans. One is exhibited (figure 3): this plan was much used by Bidder and by Inaudi, and gives the digits of the answer in left-to-right order. Another plan is shown (figure 4): this gives the digits of the answer in right-to-left order and was often used by Diamandi. This plan is especially interesting when we ask how it differs from the plan represented in figure 2. The multiplication steps are identical; what differs is the sequence in which these steps are taken. This altered sequence greatly reduces the amount which needs to be held in temporary memory at any one time.

$$200 \times 500 = 100,000$$
$$200 \times \ 60 = \ 12,000: \quad 12,000 + 100,000 = 112,000$$
$$200 \times \ \ 7 = \ \ 1,400: \quad \ 1,400 + 112,000 = 113,400$$
$$\ 30 \times 500 = \ 15,000: \quad 15,000 + 113,400 = 128,400$$
$$\ 30 \times \ 60 = \ \ 1,800: \quad \ 1,800 + 128,400 = 130,200$$
$$\ 30 \times \ \ 7 = \ \ \ \ 210: \quad \ \ \ 210 + 130,200 = 130,410$$
$$\ \ 4 \times 500 = \ \ 2,000: \quad \ 2,000 + 130,410 = 132,410$$
$$\ \ 4 \times \ 60 = \ \ \ \ 240: \quad \ \ \ 240 + 132,410 = 132,650$$
$$\ \ 4 \times \ \ 7 = \ \ \ \ \ 28: \quad \ \ \ \ 28 + 132,650 = 132,678$$

Figure 3   A representation of a step-sequence which reduces the strain on temporary memory. The problem is to multiply 234 by 567. The problem is treated as (200 + 30 + 4) (500 + 60 + 7) and the nine multiplication steps are taken in the order shown. The answer from each multiplication is added to the cumulative product obtained so far. This cumulative product is all that needs to be carried forward into the next line: all previous results can be forgotten. In this way, the cumulative product is built up, step by step, until it becomes the final answer. Note that the digits of the answer are generated in left-to-right order.

Problem: 234 multiplied by 567

Sub-problem		*Write*	*Remember·*
$7 \times 4 = 28$		8	2
$6 \times 4 = 24$:	$24 + 2 = 26$		
$7 \times 3 = 21$:	$21 + 26 = 47$	7	4
$5 \times 4 = 20$:	$20 + 4 = 24$		
$6 \times 3 = 18$:	$18 + 24 = 42$		
$7 \times 2 = 14$:	$14 + 42 = 56$	6	5
$5 \times 3 = 15$:	$15 + 5 = 20$		
$6 \times 2 = 12$:	$12 + 20 = 32$	2	3
$5 \times 2 = 10$:	$10 + 3 = 13$	13	

Figure 4   A representation of another step-sequence which reduces the strain on temporary memory. The problem is to multiply 234 by 567 and, usually, these numbers would be written down. However, the calculator writes nothing else except the final answer. Each digit of one number is multiplied by each digit of the other number and these multiplicative steps are taken in the order shown. Note that the digits of the answer are generated in right-to-left order.

The second general way in which calculators reduce the memory load derives from their economic ways of detailed working. Consider the working shown in figure 3 as it would be carried through by Bidder. For him, the strain on temporary memory is less than might be supposed. For one thing, he is familiar with the step-sequence involved, and so he knows precisely what to do at each moment. Again, he can think of numbers as distinctive qualities. He tried to express this by saying that, for him, every number up to a thousand was but one idea, and every number between a thousand and a million was, to his regret, two ideas. So, he does not remember a six-digit number as a string of six digits but, rather as two items. This lightens the load because it reduces the amount to be remembered: to give a familiar example, it is easier to remember 'mental calculation' as two words than as a string of seventeen letters. Then again, the very rapidity of working reduces the memory load because whatever must be remembered has to be kept in store for a shorter time. A number which is laid aside for future use is brought into that use before much forgetting can take place. It is no accident that mental calculators work as rapidly as they can. In summary, there are various ways in which calculators are able to reduce both the amount of data which they need to keep in temporary memory and also the length of time during which they must hold it. However, there are limits beyond which this cannot be done. When these limits are reached, the mental calculator must admit the superiority of certain other calculative systems, notably those involving the use of an electronic computer.

The most important general conclusion to be drawn from the study of mental calculation is probably this. Increase in ability concerns the development of techniques which enable the person to make more effective and economic use of his basically limited capacities for handling information. This increasingly effective use of limited capacities is evident in the many qualitative changes which bring about more rapid and accurate working. It is most evident of all in the apparently simple fact that the person can solve problems, that is, he can answer questions correctly even though he has never learned the specific answers to these specific questions. Life is too brief to permit the rote learning of each particular answer to every possible question.

Nevertheless, a novel question can be answered if the person can decompose it into several familiar questions and answer these in an appropriate sequence. Such problem-solving activity is a class of technique which makes vividly effective use of limited resources.

Within recent years an increasing amount of detailed study has been devoted to the techniques by which people acquire their many and varied abilities. What are the characteristics of such techniques in this or that sphere of accomplishment? How are they acquired? How can their development be facilitated? These are intriguing questions for scientific research, and their answers have significance for human well-being.

References

BARTLETT, F. C., *Thinking*, Allen & Unwin, 1958.
HUNTER, I. M. L., 'An exceptional talent for calculative thinking',
    Brit. J. Psychol., vol. 53 (1962), pp. 243–58.
HUNTER, I. M. L., *Memory*, Penguin Books, 1964.

Part Six COGNITIVE DEVELOPMENT

The study of the child's developing powers of reasoning has been pioneered by Jean Piaget. This research, and that of his colleagues at Geneva, has already become classical, but it is still in a process of vigorous development. We have selected one paper by Piaget himself (26) dealing with the theoretical aspects of his research, and another by his collaborators, Bärbel Inhelder and B. Matalon (27), which conveys something of the richness, ingenuity and range of his experimental approach. Two basic points in Piaget's recent theorizing are that thought is essentially internalized action and that the organization of both action and thought can be described in terms of logical structures.

Jerome Bruner and his colleagues at Harvard have carried out an intensive experimental investigation of cognitive growth which in some ways complements Piaget's research. Bruner's first paper (28) outlines the different types of internal representations of the environment which the child acquires, and the second one (29), by Bruner and Kenney, reports on a revolutionary method of teaching mathematical *concepts* to children. The dialogue between Harvard and Geneva has immense implications for education. The reader is referred to Bruner's own book, *Studies in cognitive growth*, Wiley, 1966, for a more detailed account of his research.

The Stages of the Intellectual Development of the Child

J. Piaget, 'The stages of the intellectual development of the child', *Bulletin of the Menninger Clinic*, vol. 26 (1962), pp. 120–8.

A consideration of the stages of the development of intelligence should be preceded by asking the question, what is intelligence? Unfortunately, we find ourselves confronted by a great number of definitions. For Claparède, intelligence is an adaptation to new situations. When a situation is new, when there are no reflexes, when there are no habits to rely on, then the subject is obliged to search for something new. That is to say, Claparède defines intelligence as groping, as feeling one's way, trial-and-error behavior. We find this trial-and-error behavior in all levels of intelligence, even at the superior level, in the form of hypothesis testing. As far as I am concerned, this definition is too vague, because trial and error occurs in the formation of habits, and also in the earliest established reflexes: when a newborn baby learns to suck.

Karl Bühler defines intelligence as an act of immediate comprehension; that is to say, an insight. Bühler's definition is also very precise, but it seems to me too narrow. I know that when a mathematician solves a problem, he ends by having an insight, but up to that moment he feels, or gropes for, his way; and to say that the trial-and-error behavior is not intelligent and that intelligence starts only when he finds the solution to the problem, seems a very narrow definition. I would, therefore, propose to define intelligence not by a static criterion, as in previous definitions, but by the direction that intelligence follows in its evolution, and then I would define intelligence as a form of equilibration, or forms of equilibration, toward which all cognitive functions lead.

But I must first define equilibration. Equilibration in my vocabulary is not an exact and automatic balance, as it would be in Gestalt theory; I define equilibration principally as a compensation for an external disturbance.

When there is an external disturbance, the subject succeeds in compensating for this by an activity. The maximum equilibration is thus the maximum of activity, and not a state of rest. It is a mobile equilibrium, and not an immobile one. So equilibration is defined as compensation; compensation is the annulling of a transformation by an inverse transformation. The compensation which intervenes in equilibration implies the fundamental idea of reversibility, and this reversibility is precisely what characterizes the operations of intelligence. An operation is an internalized action, but it is also a reversible action. But an operation is never isolated; it is always subordinated to other operations; it is part of a more inclusive structure. Consequently, we define intelligence in terms of operations, co-ordination of operations.

Take, for example, an operation like addition: addition is a material action, the action of reuniting. On the other hand, it is a reversible action, because addition may be compensated by subtraction. Yet addition leads to a structure-of-a-whole. In the case of numbers, it will be the structure that the mathematicians call a 'group'. In the case of addition of classes which intervene in the logical structure it will be a more simple structure that we will call a grouping, and so on.

Consequently, the study of the stages of intelligence is first a study of the formation of operational structures. I shall define every stage by a structure-of-a-whole, with the possibility of its integration into succeeding stages, just as it was prepared by preceding stages. Thus, I shall distinguish four great stages, or four great periods, in the development of intelligence: first, the sensorimotor period before the appearance of language; second, the period from about two to seven years of age, the preoperational period which precedes real operations; third, the period from seven to twelve years of age, a period of concrete operations (which refer to concrete objects); and finally after twelve years of age, the period of formal operations, or propositional operations.

Sensori-Motor Stage

Before language develops, there is behavior that we can call intelligent. For example, when a baby of twelve months or more wants an object which is too far from him, but which rests on a carpet or blanket, and he pulls it to get to the object, this behavior is an act of intelligence. The child uses an intermediary, a means to get to his goal. Also, getting to an object by means of pulling a string when the object is tied to the string, or when the child uses a stick to get the object, are acts of intelligence. They demonstrate in the sensori-motor period a certain number of stages, which go from simple reflexes, from the formation of the first habits, up to the co-ordination of means and goals.

It is remarkable that in this sensori-motor stage of intelligence there are already structures. Sensori-motor intelligence rests mainly on actions, on movements and perceptions without language, but these actions are co-ordinated in a relatively stable way. They are co-ordinated under what we may call schemata of action. These schemata can be generalized and are applicable to new situations. For example, pulling a carpet to bring an object within reach constitutes a schema which can be generalized to other situations when another object rests on a support. In other words, a schema supposes an incorporation of new situations into the previous schemata, a sort of continuous assimilation of new objects or new situations to the actions already schematized. For example, I presented to one of my children an object completely new to him – a box of cigarettes, which is not a usual toy for a baby. The child took the object, looked at it, put it in his mouth, shook it, then took it with one hand and hit it with the other hand, then rubbed it on the edge of the crib, then shook it again, and gave the impression of trying to see if there were noise. This behavior is a way of exploring the object, of trying to understand it by assimilating it to schemata already known. The child behaves in this situation as he will later in Binet's famous vocabulary test, when he defines by usage, saying, for instance, that a spoon is for eating, and so on.

But in the presence of a new object, even without knowing how to talk, the child knows how to assimilate, to incorporate this new object into each of his already developed schemata which function as practical concepts. Here is a structuring of intelligence. Most important in this structuring is the base, the point of departure of all subsequent operational constructions. At the sensori-motor level, the child constructs the schema of the permanent object.

The knowledge of the permanent object starts at this stage. The child is not convinced at the beginning that when an object disappears from view, he can find it again. One can verify by tests that object permanence is not yet developed. But there is the beginning of this subsequently fundamental idea which starts being constructed at the sensori-motor level. This is also true of the construction of the ideas of space, time, and causality. What happens during the sensori-motor level concerning all the foregoing ideas will constitute the substructure of the subsequent, fully achieved ideas of permanent objects, space, time, and causality.

In the formation of these substructures at the sensori-motor level, it is very interesting to note the beginning of *reversibility*, not in thought, since there is not yet representation in thought, but in action itself. For example, the formation of the concept of space at the sensori-motor stage leads to an amazing *decentration* if one compares the concept of space at the first weeks of development with that at one-and-a-half to two years of age. In the beginning there is not one space which contains all objects, including the child's body itself; there is a multitude of spaces which are not co-ordinated: there are the buccal space, the tactilokinesthetic space, the visual and auditory spaces; each is separate and each is centered essentially on the body of the subject and on his actions. After a few months, however, after a kind of Copernican evolution, there is a total reversal, a decentration such that space becomes homogenous, a one-and-only space that envelops the others. Then space becomes a container that envelops all objects, including the body itself; and after that, space is mainly co-ordinated in a structure, a co-ordination of positions and displacements, which constitute what the geometricians call a 'group'; that is to say, precisely a reversible system. One may move from A to B, and may come back from B to A; there is the possibility of returning, of reversibility. There is also the possibility of making detours and combinations which give a clue to what the subsequent operations will be when thought supersedes action alone.

Pre-Operational Stage

From one-and-a-half to two years of age, a fundamental transformation in the evolution of intelligence takes place in the appearance of symbolic functions. Every act of intelligence consists in manipulating significations (or meanings) and whenever (or wherever) there are significations, there are on the one hand the 'significants' and on the other the 'significates'. This is true in the sensori-motor level, but the only significants that intervene there are perceptual signs or signals (as in conditioning) which are undifferentiated in regard to the significate; for example, a perceptual cue, like distance, which will be a cue for the size of the distant object, or the apparent size of an object, which will be the cue for the distance of the object. There, perhaps, both indices are different aspects of the same reality, but they are not yet differentiated significants. At the age of one-and-a-half to two years a new class of significants arises, and these are differentiated in regard to their significates. These differentiations can be called symbolic functions. The appearance of symbols in a children's game is an example of the appearance of new significants. At the sensori-motor level games are nothing but exercises; now they become symbolic play, a play of fiction; these games consist in representing something by means of something else. Another example is the beginning of delayed imitation, an imitation that takes place not in the presence of the original object but in its absence, and which consequently constitutes a kind of symbolization or mental image.

At the same time that symbols appear, the child acquires language; that is to say, there is the acquisition of another phase of differentiated significants, verbal signals, or collective signals. This symbolic function then brings great flexibility into the field of intelligence. Intelligence up to this point refers to the immediate space which surrounds the child and to the present perceptual situation; thanks to language, and to symbolic functions, it becomes possible to invoke objects which are not present perceptually, to reconstruct the past, or to make projects, plans for the future, to think of objects not present but very distant in space – in short, to span spatio-temporal distances much greater than before.

But this new stage, the stage of representation of thought which is superimposed on the sensori-motor stage, is not a simple extension of what was referred to at the previous level. Before being able to prolong, one must in fact reconstruct, because behavior in words is a different thing from representing something in thought. When a child knows how to move around in his house or garden by following the different successive cues around him, it does not mean that he is capable of representing or reproducing the total configuration of his house or his garden. To be able to represent, to reproduce something, one must be capable of reconstructing this group of displacements, but at a new level, that of the representation of the thought.

I recently made an amusing test with Nel Szeminska. We took children of four to five years of age who went to school by themselves and came back home by themselves, and asked them if they could trace the way to school and back for us, not diagrammatically, which would be too difficult, but in a construction game with concrete objects. We found that the children were not capable of representation; there was a kind of motor-memory, but it was not yet a representation of a whole – the group of displacements had not yet been constructed. In other words, operations have not yet been formed. There are representations which are internalized actions, but these actions are still centered on the body itself. These representations do not allow the objective combinations that operations permit. I used to call the situation when actions are still centered on the body egocentrism; but it is better thought of as lack of reversibility of action.

359

At this level, the most certain sign of the absence of operations (which appear at the next stage) is the absence of the knowledge of conservation. In fact, an operation refers to the transformation of reality. The transformation is not of the whole, however; something constant is always untransformed. If you pour a liquid from one glass to another there is transformation; the liquid changes form, but its liquid property stays constant. So at the pre-operational level, it is significant from the point of view of the operations of intelligence that the child has not yet a knowledge of conservation. For example, in the case of liquid, when the child pours it from one bottle to the other, he thinks that the quantity of the liquid has changed. When the level of the liquid changes, the child thinks the quantity has changed – there is more or less in the second glass than in the first. And if you ask the child where the larger quantity came from, he does not answer this question. What is important for the child is that perceptually it is not the same thing any more. We find this absence of conservation in all the properties of objects, in the length, area, quantity, and weight of things.

This absence of conservation indicates that at this stage the child reasons from configuration. Confronted with a transformation, he does not reason from the transformation itself; he starts from the initial configuration, then sees the final configuration, compares the two but forgets the transformation because he does not know how to reason about it. At this stage the child is still reasoning on the basis of what he sees because there is no conservation. He is able to master this problem only when operations are formed and these operations, which we have already sensed at the sensorimotor level, are not formed until around seven to eight years of age. At that age the elementary problems of conservation are solved, because the child reasons on the basis of the transformation *per se*, and this requires a manipulation of the operation. The ability to pass from one point to another and be able to come back to the point of departure, to manipulate the reversible operations, appears around seven to eight years of age. It is limited when compared with the operations of the superior level only in the sense that they are concrete. That is to say, the child can manipulate the operations only when he manipulates the object concretely.

Stage of Concrete Operations

The first operations of the manipulation of objects, the concrete operations, deal with logical classes and with logical relations or number. But these operations do not deal yet with propositions or hypotheses, which do not appear until the last stage.

Let me exemplify these concrete operations: the simplest operation is concerned with classifying objects according to their similarity and their difference. This is accomplished by including subclasses within larger and more general classes, a process which implies logical inclusion. Such a classification, which seems very simple at first, is not acquired until around seven or eight years of age. Before that, at the pre-operational level, we do not find logical inclusion. For example, if you show a child at the pre-operational level a bouquet of flowers of which one half is daisies and the other half other flowers, and you ask him if there are more flowers or more daisies, you are confronted with this answer which seems extraordinary until it is analyzed: the child cannot tell you whether there are more flowers than daisies; he reasons either on the basis of the whole or the part. He cannot understand that the part is complementary to the rest, and he says there are more daisies than flowers or as many daisies as flowers. He does not understand the inclusion of the subclass of daisies in the class of flowers. It is only around seven or eight years of age that a child is capable of solving a problem of inclusion.

Another system of operations which appears around seven or eight years of age is the operation of serializing; that is, the arrangement of objects according to their size, or their progressive weight. This is also a structure-of-the-whole, like classification, which rests on concrete operations since it consists of manipulating concrete objects. At this stage, there is also the construction of numbers, which involves a synthesis of classification and seriation. In numbers there is inclusion – as in classes, and serial order – as in serializing. These elementary operations constitute structures-of-wholes. There is no class without classification; there is no symmetrical relation without serialization; there is no number without the series of numbers. But these structures-of-wholes are simple: groupings in the case of classes and relations, and groups in the case of numbers. They are very elementary structures compared to subsequent structures.

Stage of Formal Operations

The last stage of the development of intelligence is the stage of formal operations or propositional operations. At about eleven or twelve years of age we see great progress: the child becomes capable of reasoning not only about objects, but also about hypotheses or propositions.

An example which neatly shows the difference between reasoning about propositions and reasoning about concrete objects comes from Burt's tests. Burt asked children of different ages to compare the colours of the hair of three girls: Edith is fairer than Susan, Edith is darker than Sally; who is the darkest of the three? In this problem there is seriation, not of concrete objects, but of verbal statements. This requires a more complicated mental manipulation, and the problem is rarely solved before the age of twelve.

At this stage a new class of operations appears – propositional operations, and this class is superimposed on the operations of class and number. Here, compared to the previous stage, there are fundamental changes. It is not simply that these operations refer to language, and then to operations with concrete objects, but that these operations have much richer structures.

The first novelty is a combinative structure; like mathematical structures, it is a structure-of-a-system which is superimposed on the structure of simple classifications or seriations which are not themselves systems, because they do not involve a combinative system. A combinative system permits the grouping, in flexible combinations, of each element of the system with any other element of the system. The logic of propositions supposes such a combinative system. If children of different ages are shown a number of coloured discs and asked to combine each colour with each other, two by two or three by three, we find these combinative operations are not available to the child at the stage of concrete operations. The child is capable of some combination, but not of all the possible combinations. After the age of twelve, the child can find some method that enables him to make all the possible combinations. At the same time, he acquires both the logic of mathematics and the logic of propositions, which also supposes a method of combining. A second novelty in the propositional operations is the appearance of a structure which constitutes a group of four transformations. Hitherto there were two reversibilities: reversibility by inversion, which consists of annulling, cancelling, or negating and reversibility *via* reciprocity, leading not to cancellation, but to another combination. Reciprocity arises in connexion with relations. If A equals B, by reciprocity B equals A. If A is smaller than B, by reciprocity B is larger than A. At the level of propositional operations a new system envelops these two forms of reversibility. Here the structure combines inversion and reversibility in one single but larger and more complicated structure. It allows the acquisition of a series of fundamental operational schemata for the development of intelligence, which schemata are not possible before the construction of this structure.

It is around the age of twelve that the child, for example, starts to understand in mathematics the knowledge of proportions, and becomes capable of reasoning by using two systems of reference at the same time. For example, if you advance the position of a board and a car moving in opposite directions, in order to understand the movement of the board in relation to the movement of the car and to other movement, you need a system of four transformations. The same is true in regard to proportions, to problems in mathematics or physics, or to other logical problems.

The four principal stages of the development of intelligence of the child progress from one stage to the other by the construction of new operational structures, and these structures constitute the fundamental instrument of the intelligence of the adult.

27 B. Inhelder and B. Matalon

The Study of Problem Solving and Thinking[1]

Excerpts from B. Inhelder and B. Matalon, 'The study of problem
solving and thinking', in Mussen, P. H. (ed.), *Handbook of research
methods in child development*, Wiley, 1960, pp. 421–52.

Sensori-Motor Intelligence

Ever since the work of Preyer (1882) on the beginning of mental
activity in the child, the psychology of early infancy has constantly
been enriched by collections of observations. Three methods have
been used:

1. The monograph, which contains information concerning the
outstanding facts about one child.
2. The inventory or atlas, which records the presence of a
behavior pattern at a given stage of the development in a sampling
of children.
3. The longitudinal study, which observes the same child at
regular intervals in characteristic situations whose symptomatic
value has previously been shown by the first two methods, especially the second.

Although these methods have greatly contributed to our knowledge of the development of motor and emotional functions or of
the over-all course of mental development, they give us little
information about the formation of cognitive functions or, in
particular, about the acts of intelligence involved in problem
solving.

It is true that several scales of mental development include
problem-solving items for the preverbal period. The 'baby tests'
of Bühler-Hetzer (1932/1935), among others, make use of tests
such as K. Bühler's (1918) string problem. This test consists of
placing a toy with a string outside the child's immediate reach but
in such a way that the end of the string is accessible to him. It has
been shown that at first infants do not know what to do with the
string, whereas 75 per cent of babies eleven months or older are
able to make use of it to obtain the toy. These methods give us

1. This paper has been extensively edited in order to convey to the reader
a concise account of the experimental work of Piaget and his collaborators.
(Eds.)

information only about the presence or absence of problem-solving behavior, not about its formation. The important question that arises is this: did this behavior appear abruptly without antecedent, or did it develop progressively out of a more elementary pattern of behavior – grasping an object, for instance?

This 'genetic' approach to problem solving is characteristic of Piaget's investigations and of his method, which we will call 'developmental'. In fact, Piaget has studied the question – whose bearing is as much epistemological as psychological – of the formation of one of the first invariants in the child's knowledge of the external world: the schema of the permanent object. In his two monographs (1936/1953, 1937/1954) devoted to the development of the first acts of intelligence in his three children he made use of a mixture of observation and experiment, a sort of functional exploration in which experiments are suggested by previous observations.

For instance, Piaget was intrigued by a curious observation: a thirteen-month-old child was playing with a ball, which first rolled under an armchair where he could easily find it, then under a couch where he could not reach it. After a short unsuccessful search under the couch, the child went back to look for his ball under the armchair. This observation led Piaget to create experimental situations in which he could observe systematically the behavior of children towards objects disappearing from the visual field or moving about within it:

1. An object of interest (in this case a watch) is taken away from the child while he is handling it and is placed within his sight, a slight distance away.

2. The object is hidden under a pillow.

3. It is hidden under pillow A, to the left of the child, then brought out again within his sight and hidden under pillow B, to his right.

4. The same procedure as in 3, but with the difference that when it is moved from A to B the object is wrapped in a cloth so that the displacement is visible but not the object itself.

Between six and eighteen months, the three children who were observed succeeded in solving progressively, in order of increasing complexity, all the items of the experiment, although they had failed them all at first. Their behavior toward the missing object changed completely. Although they were already capable of coordinating the movements of their eyes and hands to grasp objects, nevertheless they made no effort at first to find an object when it disappeared from their visual field, and behaved as if it were no longer available. A few months later, they were able to locate an object whose position had been changed in any of the ways described above.

This experiment was followed by one involving the rotation of an object: at feeding time, the experimenter turned the baby's bottle 180 degrees and presented it the wrong way round. If the child did not spontaneously try to turn the bottle around, or show other signs of recognition, the bottle was presented in such a way that the nipple was still visible. The infants who at first refused the bottle the wrong way round, or who even tried to suck at the opposite end, were able a few weeks later to turn it around, in whatever position it was presented. In addition, the experiment with the watch was repeated with the bottle, with the same results.

It is evident that in these experiments certain rules must be observed: the object must be familiar and sufficiently interesting to the child. The experiments should not be done too frequently in order to keep the child interested in the relatively novel situation and to elicit in him genuine discoveries. The different types of behavior are recorded by means of protocols, which note movements, gestures, facial expressions, cries, and phonemes of the child and which take into account the functional context of the experimental situation.

The originality of Piaget's 'developmental' method consists not so much in observational and experimental procedures but, on the one hand, in the search for affiliations (developmental transitions) between different levels of behavior; and, on the other hand, in the demonstration of a whole network of related behaviors, which can be regarded as the elementary structures of sensori-motor intelligence.

These affiliations seem to be ensured by so-called schemata, which, for Piaget, constitute the unities of behavior. A schema is a mode of action elaborated by the subject, a mode of action capable of conservation, of transformation by generalization, and of coordination with other schemata. The functional aspects of these schemata appear as 'patterns of behavior'. From this perspective, it is possible to note a continuous series of schemata, from the grasping reflex to the recognition of permanent objects and their changes of position in space. This series, continuous from the point of view of functional activity (which does not necessarily imply continuity in the underlying neuromuscular maturation), culminates in a profound transformation of behavior. Whereas at the beginning of cognitive development objects have no meaning except in the functioning of the infant's own subjective activity (e.g., being touched, fed, or looked at), they progressively acquire an objective and independent meaning and form the first invariants of his physical and spatial world – that is, permanent objects that continue to exist even when they are not seen, and can be recognized no matter what their position.

The observations concerning this particular genetic affiliation, based on such a limited number of cases, would certainly be lacking in substance if they did not fit into a whole network of cognitive behavior described by Piaget. Thus, for example, he has been able to show that the schema of the permanent object is bound up with behavior related to its displacements (changes of position in space). Being able to order the positions of objects in space will later allow the child to order his own displacements in space; for instance, to make detours or to return to a starting point. Completing this progressive coordination of schemata of activity, the child will be able to achieve a certain reversibility in his own displacements, as well as in those of objects, canceling a movement in one direction with one in the opposite direction. This reversibility of sensori-motor and mental activity, which Piaget sees as the essential characteristic of intelligence, seems to be the culmination of a true process of development whose final structure is somewhat isomorphic with Poincaré's 'mathematical group of displacements'. It has likewise been found in investigations of the formation of the first intellectual instruments, namely intermediaries and tools.

Like all monographs, these are limited by their non-normative character. But they are, nevertheless, an ensemble of original facts, which have enabled Piaget to show that the invariants of logical thought are based on such sensori-motor invariants. [. . .]

Thought Contents of the Child

The long-standing interest in the beliefs and explanations of children had received renewed impetus from the field of anthropology in the study of the so-called primitive mentality of certain societies, characterized by collective animism, realism, and magic. In addition, the exploration of the unconscious in civilized adults had revealed a system of projective mechanisms, which foster, among other things, a belief in causality through participation. The question then arose whether such beliefs and explanations, which are also found in children, were due to social and emotional factors alone or whether cognitive factors were involved as well, the conceptions in this case being the authentic expression of a general, though transitory, stage in human thinking.

This was the state of the problem when Piaget (1926/1929, 1927/1930) undertook to study systematically the development of the different ways in which children represent and explain, in situations not involving conflict, a number of everyday phenomena.

His investigations dealt with the workings of simple machines, such as the bicycle, as well as with more complex notions derived from physical and psychological experience, such as the origins of names and their relation to the objects they name, the movements of stars and clouds, and the attribution of consciousness and life to living beings or to objects. It is of much less importance to know what significance the child attributes to one specific event than to know the common characteristics of his conceptions of the world. The psychological study of the development of children's beliefs has an epistemological bearing; it sheds light on the relations between the subject and the object. Thus the exploration of the successive types of explanation offered by children brought out new data to support the hypothesis that the traditional distinction between the two poles of knowledge – the subject with his thoughts, desires, and intentions and the object obeying physical laws – far from being primitive, is, on the contrary, the result of a long process of development, based on experimentation and socialization. In elementary forms of thought the two appear undifferentiated, thus giving rise to confusions comparable to the adualism of the ego and the nonego postulated by Baldwin.

This research, which was carried out quite some time ago, inspired a number of similar studies and raised a series of criticisms regarding the method and the validity of its results. Perhaps it is worthwhile to specify the characteristics of the 'clinical' method used by Piaget in exploring the beliefs of children. However, let us point out that the procedures used in his more recent (and more analytical) studies bear a closer resemblance to experimental methods.

It is important to keep in mind the aims of the method: (a) to establish an inventory of children's beliefs and explanations; (b) to evaluate their authenticity; (c) to distinguish the trends followed by changes in children's conceptions of the world in the course of their development.

The plan for each of the investigations originated in spontaneous remarks of children. In the case of the relation between a name and its object, for instance, the point of departure was a conversation between two 6·6-year-olds as they were playing at building, a conversation that seemed to reveal a tendency toward nominal realism.

X: And when there weren't any names . . .

Y: If there weren't any names you'd be in trouble. You couldn't make anything. How would you make things (if there weren't any names)?

Certain authors, for example, Isaacs (1930), have confined themselves to pure observation. Certainly, this method has the advantage that the reflections remain in their natural context, and it avoids the risk of influencing them unnaturally by questions that do not always correspond to the thoughts with which the child is concerned at the moment. However, pure observation does not enable us to form an exhaustive picture of all the possible ways of solving a particular problem. Children do not generally express their beliefs because they think that everyone believes as they do, because they are afraid of making mistakes or, finally, because the ideas are not sufficiently systematized to be formulated.

The clinical approach seeks not only to record beliefs that are already formulated but also to make explicit those that direct the child's reasoning more or less implicitly. It provokes reflection with a set of questions that complete and supplement one another. The interrogation on nominal realism, for instance, is built around the following questions:

1. What is a name?
2. How did names start?
3. How did we know the sun's name?
4. Where is the sun's name?
5. Do things know their names?
6. Did the sun always have its name, or was it there without a name at first and got its name afterward?
7. Why do we call the sun 'the sun'?
8. Your name is *X* and your friend's name is *Y*. Could we have called the sun 'moon' and the moon 'sun'?

Several experimenters took up Piaget's research into the mentality of the child, particularly in reference to animism and magic, but using a set of standard questions based on Piaget's, and without permitting themselves to follow up the answers in an exploratory fashion. This procedure makes it easier for the results to be scaled and for several judges to evaluate them; it also neutralizes the individual differences between interviewers. However, although it introduced important controls in areas that had already been explored, this technique proved to be inadequate for exploring new ground with as many unknowns as the domain of children's beliefs. In the rigid application of a pre-established schema, we run the risk of imposing on the child an orientation that is not

T – T.R. – O

his own. Moreover, without a knowledge of their context, the raw results are often unintelligible, and there is no way of estimating the amount of confabulation, a frequent factor at that age.

Piaget, aware of the disadvantages of pure observation on the one hand and standardized tests on the other, adopted an intermediate method inspired by the one used by psychiatrists. It consists in conducting a free conversation with the child, and directing it toward the nonexplicit regions of his thought. By exploring the context of each of the child's reflections, and asking control questions, the interviewer tries to verify their authenticity. If a child believes that the names of things are part of the things themselves and that, for example, it is sufficient to stare hard at the moon in order to find its name, one can only ask how is it that a child speaking another language would use another word. The art of the 'clinical' or, better, 'critical' method consists in letting the child talk and at the same time checking the working hypotheses during the discussion itself and not only afterward. Clearly, the successful use of this delicate method requires both aptitude on the part of the diagnostician and a long period of training.

In Piaget's exploratory researches the results are evaluated qualitatively: first, they are classified according to the type of belief they reveal. Here, for example, are a few typical categories of replies that show the progressive elimination of nominal realism:

1. Names have always been a part of things; things know their names.

2. Names have always been a part of things; things do not know their names.

3. Names were given to things by men; it is sufficient to look at things to know their names. It is not possible to change the names of things.

4. It is not sufficient to look at things to know their names; one invents or learns names. One can change them if everyone agrees, for example, when one goes to another country.

Then these ideas are ordered as they gradually appear and disappear with age. Finding this order constant for each of the beliefs studied, Piaget was able to establish 'stages' in the conception of the world and of causality. The term 'stage' has often aroused dispute, since it suggests the erroneous idea of discontinuity in development. In actual fact the transitions between the successive types of conceptions of the world are gradual and continuous and reveal a trend in thought from nondifferentiation to differentiation of subject and object. (Names that are first located in things and are part of their essence are gradually understood to be of human invention and arbitrarily attached.) [. . .]

The Study of Word Meaning

To study the significance that the young child attributes to the first words of his vocabulary, the method of integral observation is recommended. It consists in recording the spontaneous vocabulary in its natural context and relating it to the child's activities as a whole.

Thanks to the systematic findings of C. and W. Stern (1927) and to the judicious observations of Bühler (1918) and Piaget (1945/1951), we have reliable data on the (developmental) filiation characterizing the formation of concepts. The first verbal expressions such as 'Mama' are still closely tied to desires and actions and cannot be understood independently of them. The naming function, which generally appears during the second year, is contemporaneous with the beginnings of symbolic activity. In fact, it is precisely when the child attributes various symbolic significances, first to his own gestures and then to any object whatever, that one can observe his increasing interest in the names of things. However, these first names are not yet concepts in the sense of logical classes. They are preconcepts, whose significance is rather elastic, like the symbols that children use in imaginative play. The onomatopoeia 'wow-wow', for instance, can refer sometimes to one dog in particular or sometimes to any number of different objects. What is missing in these preconcepts is the comprehension of the genus-species relationship and the differentiation of the logical quantifiers 'one', 'some', 'all'. One child of 2·6 years, out for a walk, came across two different snails, and each time her comment was 'There is *the* snail.' Even when she went back to see the first, she could not decide if they were two members of the class snail or the same member. In another case the reaction of a 3·6-year-old shows an astonished interest in the significance of the 'all' concept. She had just been told that all birds lay eggs, and for every bird she saw she asked, 'That one too? That one too?' A child of 6·7 years, sorting different species of mushrooms, asked, 'Is "mushrooms" the name of all of them?', thus showing the beginnings of an understanding of genus-species relationships.

Questions like 'Bob is a boy; are boys people?' appear about the same time. One five-year-old established spontaneously the distinction between the concepts 'all' and 'some' in the following remark, 'I'm not going to give you all my flowers, just some of them'; but the distinction is full of difficulties when it is presented in connexion with a system of class-inclusion, as the following test shows (Inhelder and Piaget, 1959): the child is asked: 'A boy gave me all his roses. I gave the bunch back to him and then I asked him, "Give me some of your flowers." He gave me the same bunch again. Was that right?' The solution of the problem assumes the understanding that all of a form some of b if a is included in b.

These few examples show that even if it is true that only spontaneous remarks can reveal the appearance and the significance of concepts, which change according to the context, nonetheless a systematic interrogation is necessary each time we want to determine when and how the concepts become stabilized as veritable instruments of logical thought.

After having noted the place of observation in the study of spontaneous vocabulary, let us refer once again to methods designed to analyse the child's understanding of adult language. There are two procedures capable of shedding light on this understanding, which becomes more and more adequate as the child grows older. One involves definition of words, and the other involves inference from cues given by the verbal context of the sentence.

The definition tests introduced by Binet (1903, 1908) in his mental development scales are presented in the following way: 'you have seen a chair; tell me what a chair is.' They have revealed that young children tend to define by use ('it is for . . .') before they can construct conceptual definitions. Since conceptual definitions are often formally taught, it is sometimes very difficult to dissociate the part played by schooling from the need the children themselves feel to define in terms of concepts. By means of a more clinical analysis, Piaget (1924/1926, 1951) was able to reveal some typical difficulties encountered by young children, not only in the matter of definition, but also in understanding concepts expressing reciprocal relations such as 'brother' or 'foreigner'. The intellectual egocentrism of young children, sometimes reinforced by emotional factors, creates an obstacle to the comprehension that they can themselves be brothers or foreigners from the point of view of other people. [. . .]

The Mechanisms of Classification

The particular problem taken up by Inhelder and Piaget (1959) was that of understanding why the organization of classificatory behavior takes the forms it does and why these successive forms tend toward logical structures. The following three methods have been combined in this study, but any one by itself is not sufficient: (1) spontaneous classifications of natural and geometrical objects; (2) the shifting from one criterion to another and the anticipation of visual classifications (for instance, the child is asked what would be the minimum number of envelopes needed to class geometrical figures, differing in form, size, and color, and presented to him in a random order); (3) the formation of the operational mechanisms themselves. Techniques were designed to bear on the problem of how the structure of inclusion is formed. This structure is certainly not present from the beginning, either hereditarily or as a Gestalt, and its development is much too laborious to permit of an explanation simply in terms of verbal learning.

One experiment already carried out (Piaget and Szeminska, 1941/1952), and standardized later but yet to be published, revealed the difficulty experienced by children of less than 6·6 years of age in understanding that there are more elements in the whole class B than in the sub-class A included in it (if $B=A+A'$). In this technique the child is presented with an open box containing a dozen beads, which he can easily see are made of wood. Most of the beads (ten) are brown, and two are white. He is asked, 'Are there more wooden beads or more brown beads in this box? Could we make a longer necklace with all the wooden beads or with all the brown beads?' (He is made to understand that after making the necklace of wooden beads he can take it apart again to make the one of the brown beads.) Finally he is asked, 'If I take all the wooden beads out of the box, will there be any beads left? If I take out all the brown beads, will there be any beads left?' Because of the immobility of his thought, the child younger than six years of age cannot conceive of the same beads as forming part of two collections.

He answers that there are more brown than wooden beads, 'because there are only two wooden ones.' Once the brown ones are included in one class, he cannot at the same time include them in a second class. He can compare subclass A (the brown beads) only to subclass A' (the white beads) and not to the total class B (all the beads).

It was discovered that the problem of inclusion, even when it was solved with material consisting of a collection of countable objects, continued to offer difficulties when applied to a hierarchy of concepts such as the system of classes of animals. Without entering into the details of the technique, let us remark that it involved organizing pictures of familiar animals into a hierarchy of three classes and that the concept of the hierarchy was concretized by means of transparent boxes that could fit one inside the other. In this particular case, the correct solution consisted in putting the ducks into the smallest box, A; the class of birds, composed of A and its complement A' (birds that are not ducks) into the second box, B; and the animals, $A+B+B'$ (B' being animals that are not birds) into the largest box, C. Once this hierarchy is concretely established by the child, he is asked questions of the same kind as those regarding the beads. Here, as in all the research on classification, it was seen that the logical mechanisms do not operate as completely developed structures, which are applied to any content, but that they are gradually developed in relation to the different contents to be conceptualized. The divergence among authors as to the age at which the first conceptual systems appear would seem, then, to be partly the result of observations that too often have been sporadic or of experimentation limited to a single context. [. . .]

Genetic Analysis of Intellectual Operations

Among the concepts that are formed during childhood, those that serve as a point of departure for scientific thought deserve special interest on the part of psychologists. Piaget and his colleagues have studied the formation of the notions of number, space, speed-time, and probabilistic causality from an original point of view. Having first analysed the operations that are fundamental to these concepts once they are acquired, they asked whether the concepts resulted only from socially transmitted learning or whether the individual had some active contribution to make in their formation. The following experiments were designed essentially to examine this intervention of the child's activity.

We can follow step by step this development in the child, from its origin in his sensori-motor activities, through the period when it is enriched by mental representations, and finally to its accomplishment in a genuine system of operations.

We can outline here only a few of the techniques used:

1. The principle of numerical invariance (Piaget and Szeminska, 1941/1952). This technique was designed to study the manner in which children from four to six come to establish two equivalent collections of objects and to discover that this equivalence is preserved no matter how the elements may be arranged. In one form of the technique the children were first asked to take from a small basket as many eggs as there were eggcups in a row before them.

The experimenter noted, in particular, the way in which the children established the correspondence between the two collections. (The youngest children, not yet having discovered one-to-one correspondence, tended to construct two rows of equal length, regardless of the number of objects.) Once the one-to-one correspondence was established, the experimenter increased the spacing of one of the rows. Then, to find out if the child still accepted the equivalence of the collections, he put a series of questions in the following vein: 'Are there the same number of eggs as eggcups?' 'Are there more or less eggs than eggcups?' 'Can we put each egg in an eggcup without there being any empty eggcups or any eggs left over?' In all the experiments of this kind they took care that neither the intonation of the voice nor the order of the questions was suggestive. The analysis of the children's behavior and replies revealed that under the conditions described here, and in this particular cultural environment, numerical conservation is absent in most four-year-olds and that it is acquired gradually between the ages of four and six, until most six-year-olds assert it with a feeling of logical evidence. This process of acquisition, which can, of course, be accelerated by training, corresponds to a general progress toward an 'operational' quality in the thought of the child. The qualitative analysis of the reasoning seems to show that little by little the transformations imposed on collections of objects come to be conceived operationally; that is, each transformation can be mentally cancelled by its inverse. This can be formulated by the child in the following way: 'I only have to put the eggs back opposite the eggcups and I know there is always the same number.'

2. The principle of conservation of quantity. The formation of invariant concepts has been followed systematically in different domains of the child's thought. Once attained, each of the concepts is based on a nucleus of operations comparable to mathematical group structures (but more limited than they are), which Piaget has named a semigroup or 'grouping' of concrete thought.

To study the physical invariants of matter, weight, and volume, as the ideas develop between the ages of four and eleven, one method involved two balls of plasticene, identical in shape, size, and weight. (Piaget and Inhelder, 1941). One of the balls was stretched into the shape of a sausage, broken into little bits, etc., and questions of the following sort were asked:

Is there the same amount of plasticene in the sausage as in the ball?

Is there more in one than in the other?

How do you know that there is always the same amount? How do you know that there is more? (Or how do you know there is less?)

Will the ball and the sausage weigh the same on the scale?

A similar experiment concerns the conservation of the weight of sugar when it is dissolved in water.

3. Spontaneous measurement (Piaget, Inhelder, and Szeminska, 1948). Of a number of experiments in the realm of spatial concepts, we shall single out the one dealing with spontaneous measurement. How do four-year-olds discover on their own the conditions necessary for measurement, such as the use of a common measure involving transitivity, the constancy of the measuring instrument when its position is changed, and the construction or breaking down of the instruments into units. The authors started with a situation familiar to the child: building a tower with wooden blocks. They asked the child to build the tower just as high as a model tower, made of a single piece of wood and standing on a table at a different height from the one on which the child was to build. Every measurement involves a transportation of the measuring instrument, and in this experiment it was possible to classify the different types which tend to follow one another as the child develops. The earliest are direct visual or manual comparisons of height from the floor. They do not make use of a common measure. Next come various attempts to use part of the body or a gesture as the common measure, neglecting the conservation of the 'transported' dimensions or distances. Finally, the child discovers the need for a common measure with stable dimensions. At first, this has to be the same size as the model; but it is replaced by measures that are first bigger, then smaller, and finally by repeatable units of any size. After this general experiment, a series of more specific studies was designed, with a view to examining one by one the conditions necessary for measurement in Euclidean space, and the application of measure to areas and volumes.

4. Speed (Piaget, 1946). The study of the complex of speed-time-space concepts has shown that the notion of 'passing', as a change in order, is both fundamental and relatively primitive. However, its development follows certain stages, which one can discern with the help of the following material: (a) two cars on two straight, parallel tracks, moving for equal periods of time at different speeds; (b) two cars, again moving for equal periods of time at different speeds but on two circular, concentric tracks. Although the starts and finishes are simultaneous, the distances traveled are unequal. The phenomena included in the experiment are passing,

catching up, gaining ground, and crossing. Each of the children is asked to say, after witnessing the phenomena, if the two cars moved at the same speed. The factors that the children take into account in comparing the speeds vary with their ages. Between the ages of five and nine, the following reactions are observed: first, they take account only of the passing of one car by another, then only of relative positions at the finish; gradually, they take account of the starting points, as well, and finally of the set of rectilinear and circular paths traversed. At the end of this development, they discover the elementary operations of the concept of speed and the establishment of correspondences between displacements of objects in a given time.

5. Chance and probability (Piaget and Inhelder, 1951). The formation of these concepts has been studied with the help of a number of games of chance of the roulette or progressive mixing type. The accidental character of chance as an interference between independent causal series is discovered by the child only through a system of logical or mathematical operations. For example, in the case of the progressive mixture of balls, the child first comes to understand the fortuitous character of the mixture as the interference of independent movements. Later, after he has dissociated in this way the certain from the possible, he is gradually able to quantify the latter and to make probability judgments. In terms of our example, he is now able to refer to a theoretical system of permutations to conceive of the quantitative aspect of the progressive mixing. [. . .]

Use of Theoretical Models

Logical Models

When the presentation of problems is essentially verbal, it is generally tempting to analyse the different stages of the solution in terms of formal logic and to describe the observed behavior in terms of logical operations. This has the advantage of reducing the qualitatively different performances found at different stages to a common language, thus enabling one to identify the operations of which children are capable at various ages.

Logical errors have been studied frequently enough in the adult. The numerous studies on the syllogism, particularly on 'atmosphere effects', emotional factors, etc., are well known (Woodworth and Sells, 1935). In each of these cases the assumption is that the subject (a normal adult) possesses the necessary logical instruments, and the aim of the research is to study the factors that prevent these instruments from functioning and which thus result in false reasoning.

In the child the logical analysis of behavior can take on a more profound significance: here we are actually trying to find out what logical tools a given subject possesses. The disturbing emotional variables, interesting as they are in the case of adults, must then be reduced as far as possible so that the child can give his maximum.

This is the kind of analysis that Piaget has undertaken. On the one hand he has tried to establish a formalized model of natural thought and its development (1949) and on the other to study this development concretely, using the logical model to describe it. [Inhelder and Piaget (1955/1958).] Their subjects (aged five to sixteen) are presented with apparatuses that exemplify simple physical laws (for instance, the equilibrium of a scale balance, the inclined plane, non-elastic reflection, and communicating jars), which they must discover by experimenting freely with the material. The level of organization of the experimentation, the conclusions that the subject draws from each new item of information, and the generalizations made are analysed in terms of the classical logic of propositions. In their latest work (1959) in which they analyse classification and seriation they make use of the logic of classes and relations for their description. The essential point of interest is that in both these cases the logical analysis treats the actions and not only the verbal behavior of the subject.

Apart from the work of Piaget and his school, no other attempts seem to have been made to examine the thought of the child from the point of view of mathematical logic.

Nevertheless, we may ask which type of logic can accomplish this study most satisfactorily. Piaget uses the logic of classes, with the qualification that his classes are serially inclusive, since this is the type of classification that seems to him especially adapted to natural thought. But perhaps it would be possible to take a weaker model, such as intuitionist logic, which rejects the principle of the excluded middle. Certain relationships that are erratic from the point of view of the logic of classes can be described in this form, and it would be interesting to see if thought could be considered consistent in terms of this weaker framework. [. . .]

References

BINET, A. (1903), *L'étude expérimentale de l'intelligence*, Schleicher Frères.

BINET, A., and SIMON, Th. (1908), 'La mesure du développement de l'intelligence chez les enfants', *Année psychol.*, vol. 14. pp. 1–94.

BÜHLER, Ch., and HETZER, H. (1932), *Kleinkindertest*, Barth. Trans. 1935, *Testing children's development from birth to school*, Rinehart.

BÜHLER, K. (1918), *Die geistige Entwicklung des kindes*, G. Fischer.

INHELDER, B., and PIAGET, J. (1955), *De la logique de l'enfant à la logique de l'adolescent*, P.U.F. Trans. 1958, *The growth of logical thinking*, Basic Books.

INHELDER, B., and PIAGET, J. (1959), *La genèse des structures logiques élémentaires*, Delachaux et Niestlé.

ISAACS, S. (1930), *The intellectual growth of young children*, Routledge & Kegan Paul.

PIAGET, J. (1924), *Le jugement et la raisonnement chez l'enfant*, Delachaux et Niestlé. Trans. 1926, *Judgment and reasoning in the child*, Harcourt, Brace.

PIAGET, J. (1926), *La représentation du monde chez l'enfant*, Alcan. Trans. 1929, *The conception of the world*, Harcourt, Brace.

PIAGET, J. (1927), *La causalité physique chez l'enfant*, Alcan. Trans. 1930, *The child's conception of physical causality*, Harcourt, Brace.

PIAGET, J. (1936), *La naissance de l'intelligence chez l'enfant*, Delachaux et Niestlé. Trans. 1952 and 1953, *The origin of intelligence in children*, International Univ. Press.

PIAGET, J. (1937), *La construction du réel chez l'enfant*, Delachaux et Niestlé. Trans. 1954, *The construction of reality in the child*, Basic Books.

PIAGET, J. (1945), *La formation du symbole chez l'enfant*, Delachaux et Niestlé. Trans. 1951, *Play, dream and imitation in childhood*, Norton.

PIAGET, J. (1946), *Les notions de mouvement et de vitesse chez l'enfant*, P.U.F.

PIAGET, J. (1949), *Traité de logique*, A. Collin.

PIAGET, J., and INHELDER, B. (1941), *Le développement des quantités chez l'enfant*, Delachaux et Niestlé.

PIAGET, J., and INHELDER, B. (1951), *La genèse de l'idée de hazard chez l'enfant*, P.U.F.

PIAGET, J., INHELDER, B., and SZEMINSKA, A. (1948), *La géométrie spontanée chez l'enfant*, P.U.F. Trans. 1959, Routledge & Kegan Paul.

PIAGET, J., and SZEMINSKA, A. (1941), *La genèse du nombre chez l'enfant*, Delachaux et Niestlé. Trans. 1952, *The child's conception of number*, Routledge & Kegan Paul.

PREYER, W. (1882), *Die Seele des Kindes*, Leipzig. Trans. 1881–9, *The mind of the child*, Appleton.

STERN, C., and W. (1927), *Die Kindersprache*, Barth.

WOODWORTH, R. S., and SELLS, S. B. (1935), 'An atmosphere effect in formal syllogistic reasoning', *J. exp. Psychol.*, vol. 18, p. 451–60.

The Course of Cognitive Growth

J. S. Bruner, 'The course of cognitive growth', *Amer. Psychologist*, vol. 19 (1964), pp. 1–15.

I shall take the view in what follows that the development of human intellectual functioning from infancy to such perfection as it may reach is shaped by a series of technological advances in the use of mind. Growth depends upon the mastery of techniques and cannot be understood without reference to such mastery. These techniques are not, in the main, inventions of the individuals who are 'growing up'; they are, rather, skills transmitted with varying efficiency and success by the culture – language being a prime example. Cognitive growth, then, is in a major way from the outside in as well as from the inside out.

Two matters will concern us. The first has to do with the techniques or technologies that aid growing human beings to represent in a manageable way the recurrent features of the complex environments in which they live. It is fruitful, I think, to distinguish three systems of processing information by which human beings construct models of their world: through action, through imagery, and through language. A second concern is with integration, the means whereby acts are organized into higher-order ensembles, making possible the use of larger and larger units of information for the solution of particular problems.

Let me first elucidate these two theoretical matters, and then turn to an examination of the research upon which they are based, much of it from the Center for Cognitive Studies at Harvard.

On the occasion of the One Hundredth Anniversary of the publication of Darwin's *The origin of species*, Washburn and Howell (1960) presented a paper at the Chicago Centennial celebration containing the following passage:

It would now appear ... that the large size of the brain of certain hominids was a relatively late development and that the brain evolved due to new selection pressures *after* bipedalism and consequent upon the use of tools. The tool-using, ground-living, hunting way of life created the large human brain rather than a large brained man discovering certain new ways of life. [We] believe this conclusion is the most important result of the recent fossil hominid discoveries and is one which carries far-reaching implications for the interpretation of human behavior and its origins. . . . The important point is that size of brain, insofar as it can be measured by cranial capacity, has increased some threefold subsequent to the use and manufacture of implements. . . . The uniqueness of modern man is seen as the result of a technical-social life which tripled the size of the brain, reduced the face, and modified many other structures of the body [p. 49 f.].

This implies that the principal change in man over a long period of years – perhaps 500,000 thousand – has been alloplastic rather than autoplastic. That is to say, he has changed by linking himself with new, external implementation systems rather than by any conspicuous change in morphology – 'evolution-by-prosthesis', as Weston La Barre (1954) puts it. The implement systems seem to have been of three general kinds – *amplifiers of human motor capacities* ranging from the cutting tool through the lever and wheel to the wide variety of modern devices; *amplifiers of sensory eapacities* that include primitive devices such as smoke signaling and modern ones such as magnification and radar sensing, but also likely to include such 'soft-ware' as those conventionalized perceptual short-cuts that can be applied to the redundant sensory environment; and finally *amplifiers of human ratiocinative capacities* of infinite variety ranging from language systems to myth and theory and explanation. All of these forms of amplification are in major or minor degree conventionalized and transmitted by the culture, the last of them probably the most since ratiocinative amplifiers involve symbol systems governed by rules that must, for effective use, be shared.

Any implement system, to be effective, must produce an appropriate internal counterpart, an appropriate skill necessary for organizing sensori-motor acts, for organizing percepts, and for organizing our thoughts in a way that matches them to the requirements of implement systems. These internal skills, represented genetically as capacities, are slowly selected in evolution. In the deepest sense, then, man can be described as a species that has become specialized by the use of technological implements. His selection and survival have depended upon a morphology and set of capacities that could be linked with the alloplastic devices that have made his later evolution possible. We move, perceive, and think in a fashion that depends upon techniques rather than upon wired-in arrangements in our nervous system.

Where representation of the environment is concerned, it too depends upon techniques that are learned – and these are precisely the techniques that serve to amplify our motor acts, our perceptions, and our ratiocinative activities. We know and respond to recurrent regularities in our environment by skilled and patterned acts, by conventionalized spatioqualitative imagery and selective perceptual organization, and through linguistic encoding which, as so many writers have remarked, places a selective lattice between us and the physical environment. In short, the capacities that have been shaped by our evolution as tool users are the ones that we rely upon in the primary task of representation – the nature of which we shall consider in more detail directly.

As for integration, it is a truism that there are very few single or simple adult acts that cannot be performed by a young child. In short, any more highly skilled activity can be decomposed into simpler components, each of which can be carried out by a less skilled operator. What higher skills require is that the component operations be combined. Maturation consists of an orchestration of these components into an integrated sequence. The 'distractability', so-called, of much early behavior may reflect each act's lack of imbeddedness in what Miller, Galanter, and Pribram (1960), speak of as 'plans'. These integrated plans, in turn, reflect the routines and subroutines that one learns in the course of mastering the patterned nature of a social environment. So that integration, too, depends upon patterns that come from the outside in – an internalization of what Roger Barker (1963) has called environmental 'behavior settings'.

If we are to benefit from contact with recurrent regularities in the environment, we must represent them in some manner. To dismiss this problem as 'mere memory' is to misunderstand it. For the most important thing about memory is not storage of past experience, but rather the retrieval of what is relevant in some usable form. This depends upon how past experience is coded and processed so that it may indeed be relevant and usable in the present when needed. The end product of such a system of coding and processing is what we may speak of as a representation.

I shall call the three modes of representation mentioned earlier enactive representation, iconic representation, and symbolic representation. Their appearance in the life of the child is in that order, each depending upon the previous one for its development, yet all of them remaining more or less intact throughout life – barring such early accidents as blindness or deafness or cortical injury. By enactive representation I mean a mode of representing past events through appropriate motor response. We cannot, for example, give an adequate description of familiar sidewalks or floors over which we habitually walk, nor do we have much of an image of what they are like. Yet we get about them without tripping or even looking much. Such segments of our environment – bicycle riding, tying knots, aspects of driving – get represented in our muscles, so to speak. Iconic representation summarizes events by the selective organization of percepts and of images, by the spatial, temporal, and qualitative structures of the perceptual field and their transformed images. Images 'stand for' perceptual events in the close but conventionally selective way that a picture stands for the object pictured. Finally, a symbol system represents things by design features that include remoteness and arbitrariness. A word neither points directly to its referent here and now, nor does it resemble it as a picture. The lexeme 'Philadelphia' looks no more like the city so designated than does a nonsense syllable. The other property of language that is crucial is its productiveness in combination, far beyond what can be done with images or acts. 'Philadelphia is a lavender sachet in Grandmother's linen closet', or $(x+2)^2 = x^2 + 4x + 4 = x(x+4) + 4$.

An example or two of enactive representation underlines its importance in infancy and in disturbed functioning, while illustrating its limitations. Piaget (1954) provides us with an observation from the closing weeks of the first year of life. The child is playing with a rattle in his crib. The rattle drops over the side. The child moves his clenched hand before his face, opens it, looks for the rattle. Not finding it there, he moves his hand, closed again, back to the edge of the crib, shakes it with movements like those he uses in shaking the rattle. Thereupon he moves his closed hand back toward his face, opens it, and looks. Again no rattle; and so he tries again. In several months, the child has benefited from experience to the degree that the rattle and action become separated. Whereas earlier he would not show signs of missing the rattle when it was removed unless he had begun reaching for it, now he cries and searches when the rattle is presented for a moment and hidden by a cover. He no longer repeats a movement to restore the rattle. In place of representation by action alone – where 'existence' is defined by the compass of present action – it is now defined by an image that persists autonomously.

A second example is provided by the results of injury to the occipital and temporal cortex in man (Hanfmann, Rickers-Ovsiankina and Goldstein, 1944). A patient is presented with a hard-boiled egg intact in its shell, and asked what it is. Holding it in his hand, he is embarrassed, for he cannot name it. He makes a motion as if to throw it and halts himself. Then he brings it to his mouth as if to bite it and stops before he gets there. He brings it to his ear and shakes it gently. He is puzzled. The experimenter takes the egg from him and cracks it on the table, handing it back. The patient then begins to peel the egg and announces what it is. He cannot identify objects without reference to the action he directs toward them.

The disadvantages of such a system are illustrated by Emerson's (1931) experiment in which children are told to place a ring on a board with seven rows and six columns of pegs, copying the position of a ring put on an identical board by the experimenter. Children ranging from three to twelve were examined in this experiment and in an extension of it carried out by Werner (1948). The child's board could be placed in various positions relative to the experimenter's: right next to it, 90 degrees rotated away from it, 180 degrees rotated, placed face to face with it so that the child has to turn full around to make his placement, etc. The older the child, the better his performance. But the younger children could do about as well as the oldest so long as they did not have to change their own position vis-à-vis the experimenter's board in order to make a match on their own board. The more they had to turn, the more difficult the task. They were clearly depending upon their bodily orientation toward the experimenter's board to guide them. When this orientation is disturbed by having to turn, they lose the position on the board. Older children succeed even when they must turn, either by the use of imagery that is invariant across bodily displacements, or, later, by specifying column and row of the experimenter's ring and carrying the symbolized self-instruction back to their own board. It is a limited world, the world of enactive representation.

We know little about the conditions necessary for the growth of imagery and iconic representation, or to what extent parental or environmental intervention affects it during the earliest years. In ordinary adult learning a certain amount of motoric skill and practice seems to be a necessary precondition for the development of a simultaneous image to represent the sequence of acts involved. If an adult subject is made to choose a path through a complex bank of toggle switches, he does not form an image of the path, according to Mandler (1962), until he has mastered and over-practiced the task by successive manipulation. Then, finally, he reports that an image of the path has developed and that he is now using it rather than groping his way through.

Our main concern in what follows is not with the growth of iconic representation, but with the transition from it to symbolic representation. For it is in the development of symbolic representation that one finds, perhaps, the greatest thicket of psychological problems. The puzzle begins when the child first achieves the use of productive grammar, usually late in the second year of life. Toward the end of the second year, the child is master of the single-word, agrammatical utterance, the so-called holophrase. In the months following, there occurs a profound change in the use of language. Two classes of words appear – a pivot class and an open class – and the child launches forth on his career in combinatorial talking and, perhaps, thinking. Whereas before, lexemes like *allgone* and *mummy* and *sticky* and *bye-bye* were used singly, now, for example, *allgone* becomes a pivot word and is used in combination. Mother washes jam off the child's hands; he says *allgone sticky*. In the next days, if his speech is carefully followed (Braine, 1963), it will be apparent that he is trying out the limits of the pivot combinations, and one will even find constructions that have an extraordinary capacity for representing complex sequences – like *allgone bye-bye* after a visitor has departed. A recent and ingenious observation by Weir (1962) on her $2\frac{1}{2}$-year-old son, recording his speech musings after he was in bed with lights out, indicates that at this stage there is a great deal of metalinguistic combinatorial play with words in which the child is exploring the limits of grammatical productiveness.

In effect, language provides a means, not only for representing experience, but also for transforming it. As Chomsky (1957) and Miller (1962) have both made clear in the last few years, the transformational rules of grammar provide a syntactic means of reworking the 'realities' one has encountered. Not only did the dog bite the man, but the man was bitten by the dog and perhaps the man was not bitten by the dog or was the man not bitten by the dog. The range of reworking that is made possible even by the three transformations of the passive, the negative, and the query is very striking indeed. Or the ordering device whereby the comparative mode makes it possible to connect what is *heavy* and what is *light* into the ordinal array of *heavy* and *less heavy* is again striking. Or, to take a final example, there is the discrimination that is made possible by the growth of attribute language such that the global dimension *big* and *little* can now be decomposed into *tall* and *short* on the one hand and *fat* and *skinny* on the other.

Once the child has succeeded in internalizing language as a cognitive instrument, it becomes possible for him to represent and systematically transform the regularities of experience with far greater flexibility and power than before. Interestingly enough, it is the recent Russian literature, particularly Vygotsky's (1962) book on language and thought, and the work of his disciple, Luria (1961), and his students (Abramyan, 1958; Martsinovskaya, undated) that has highlighted these phenomena by calling attention to the so-called second-signal system which replaces classical conditioning with an internalized linguistic system for shaping and transforming experience itself.

If all these matters were not of such complexity and human import, I would apologize for taking so much time in speculation. We turn now to some new experiments designed to shed some light on the nature of representation and particularly upon the transition from its iconic to its symbolic form.

Let me begin with an experiment by Bruner and Kenney (1966) on the manner in which children between five and seven handle a double classification matrix. The materials of the experiment are nine plastic glasses, arranged so that they vary in three degrees of diameter and three degrees of height. They are set before the child initially, as in figure 1, on a 3 × 3 grid marked on a large piece of cardboard. To acquaint the child with the matrix, we first remove one, then two, and then three glasses from the matrix, asking the child to replace them. We also ask the children to describe how the glasses in the columns and rows are alike and how they differ. Then the glasses are scrambled and we ask the child to make something like what was there before by placing the glasses on the same grid that was used when the task was introduced. Now we scramble the glasses once more, but this time we place the glass that was formerly in the southwest corner of the grid in the southeast corner (it is the shortest, thinnest glass) and ask the child if he can make something like what was there before, leaving the one glass where we have just put it. That is the experiment.

The results can be quickly told. To begin with, there is no difference between ages five, six, and seven either in terms of ability to replace glasses taken from the matrix or in building a matrix once it has been scrambled (but without the transposed glass). Virtually all the children succeed. Interestingly enough, *all* the children rebuild the matrix to match the original, almost as if they were copying what was there before. The only difference is that the older children are quicker.

Now compare the performance of the three ages in constructing the matrix with a single member transposed. Most of the seven-year-olds succeed in the transposed task, but hardly any of the youngest children. Figure 2 presents the results graphically. The youngest children seem to be dominated by an image of the original matrix. They try to put the transposed glass 'back where it belongs', to rotate the cardboard so that 'it will be like before', and sometimes they will start placing a few glasses neighboring the transposed glass correctly only to revert to the original arrangement. In several instances, five- or six-year-olds will simply try to reconstitute the old matrix, building right over the transposed glass.

0 1 2 3 4 5 6   scale in inches

Figure 1   Array of glasses used in study of matrix ordering
(*Bruner and Kenney, 1966*).

The seven-year-old, on the other hand, is more likely to pause, to treat the transposition as a problem, to talk to himself about 'where this should go'. The relation of place and size is for him a problem that requires reckoning, not simply copying.

Now consider the language children use for describing the dimensions of the matrix. Recall that the children were asked how glasses in a row and in a column were alike and how they differed. Children answered in three distinctive linguistic modes (see figure 3). One

387

was *dimensional*, singling out two ends of an attribute – for example, 'That one is higher, and that one is shorter.' A second was *global* in nature. Of glasses differing only in height the child says, 'That one is bigger and that one is little.' The same words could be used equally well for diameter or for nearly any other magnitude. Finally, there was *confounded* usage: 'That one is tall and that one is little,' where a dimensional term is used for one end of the continuum and a global term for the other. The children who used confounded descriptions had the most difficulty with the transposed matrix. Lumping all ages together, the children who used

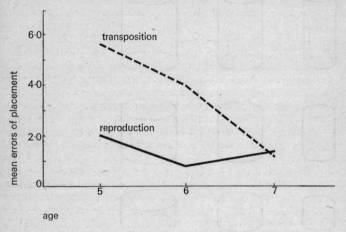

Figure 2   Mean number of errors made by children in reproducing and transposing a 3 × 3 matrix (Bruner and Kenney, 1966).

confounded descriptions were twice as likely to fail on the transposition task as those who used either dimensional or global terms. *But the language the children used had no relation whatsoever to their performance in reproducing the first untransposed matrix.* Inhelder and Sinclair[1] in a recent communication also report that confounded language of this kind is associated with failure on conservation tasks in children of the same age, a subject to which we shall turn shortly.

The findings of this experiment suggest two things. First, that children who use iconic representation are more highly sensitized

1. Bärbel Inhelder and Mimi Sinclair, personal communication, 1963.

to the spatial-qualitative organization of experience and less to the ordering principles governing such organization. They can recognize and reproduce, but cannot produce new structures based on rule. And second, there is a suspicion that the language they bring to bear on the task is insufficient as a tool for ordering. If these notions are correct, then certain things should follow. For one thing, *improvement* in language should aid this type of

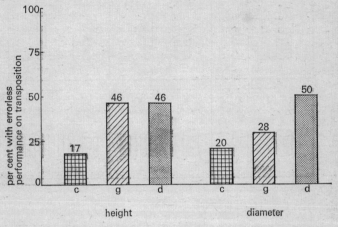

c – compounded
g – global
d – dimensional

Figure 3   Percentage of children (aged five to seven) using different language patterns who reproduced transposed matrix without error (Bruner and Kenney, 1966).

problem solving. This remains to be investigated. But it is also reasonable to suppose that *activation* of language habits that the child has already mastered might improve performance as well – a hypothesis already suggested by the findings of Luria's students (e.g., Abramyan, 1958). Now, activation can be achieved by two means: one is by having the child 'say' the description of something before him that he must deal with symbolically. The other is to take advantage of the remoteness of reference that is a feature of language, and have the child 'say' his description in the absence of the things to be described. In this way, there would be less likelihood of a perceptual-iconic representation becoming dominant and inhibiting the operation of symbolic processes. An experiment by Françoise Frank (1966) illustrates this latter approach – the effects of saying before seeing.

Piaget and Inhelder (1962) have shown that if children between ages four and seven are presented two identical beakers which they judge equally full of water, they will no longer consider the

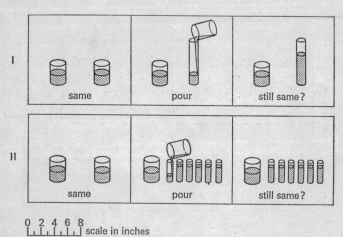

0 2 4 6 8
scale in inches

Figure 4   Two Geneva tests for conservation of liquid volume across transformations in its appearance (Piaget and Inhelder, 1962).

water equal if the contents of one of the beakers is now poured into a beaker that is either wider or thinner than the original. If the second beaker is thinner, they will say it has more to drink because the water is higher; if the second beaker is wider, they will say it has less because the water is lower. Comparable results can be obtained by pouring the contents of one glass into several smaller beakers. In Geneva terms, the child is not yet able to conserve liquid volume across transformations in its appearance.

Consider how this behavior can be altered. Françoise Frank first did the classic conservation tests to determine which children exhibited conservation and which did not. Her subjects were four, five, six, and seven years old. She then went on to other procedures, among which was the following. Two standard beakers are partly filled so that the child judges them to contain equal amounts of water. A wider beaker of the same height is introduced and the three beakers are now, except for their tops, hidden by a screen. The experimenter pours from a standard beaker into the wider beaker. The child, without seeing the water, is asked which has more to drink, or do they have the same amount, the standard or the wider beaker. The results are

screening prediction and feedback: part III

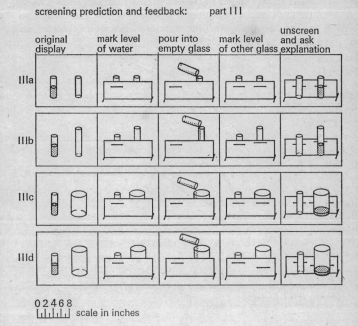

```
0 2 4 6 8
└┴┴┴┴┘ scale in inches
```

Figure 5   One procedure used in study of effect of language activation on conservation (Frank, 1966).

in figure 6. In comparison with the unscreened pretest, there is a striking increase in correct equality judgements. Correct responses jump from 0 per cent to 50 per cent among the fours, from 20 per cent to 90 per cent among the fives, and from 50 per cent to 100 per cent among the sixes. With the screen present, most children justify their correct judgment by noting that 'It's the same water', or 'You only poured it.'

Now the screen is removed. All the four-year-olds change

their minds. The perceptual display overwhelms them and they decide that the wider beaker has less water. But virtually all of the five-year-olds stick to their judgement, often invoking the difference between appearance and reality – 'It looks like more to drink, but it is only the same because it is the same water and it was only poured from there to there,' to quote one typical five-year-old. And all of the sixes and all the sevens stick to their judgement. Now, some minutes later, Frank does a post-test on the children using a tall thin beaker along with the standard ones, and no screen, of

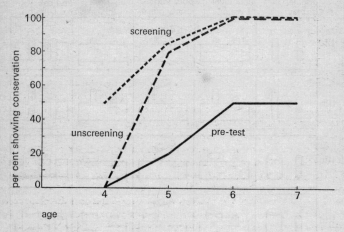

Figure 6   Percentage of children showing conservation of liquid volume before and during screening and upon unscreening of the displays (Frank, 1966).

course. The fours are unaffected by their prior experience: none of them is able to grasp the idea of invariant quantity in the new task. With the fives, instead of 20 per cent showing conservation, as in the pretest, 70 per cent do. With both sixes and sevens, conservation increases from 50 per cent to 90 per cent (see figure 7). I should mention that control groups doing just a pretest and post-test show no significant improvement in performance.

A related experiment of Nair's (1963) explores the arguments children use when they solve a conservation task correctly and when they do not. Her subjects were all five-year-olds. She transferred water from one rectangular clear plastic tank to another that was both longer and wider than the first. Ordinarily, a five-

year-old will say there is less water in the second tank. The water
is, of course, lower in the second tank. She had a toy duck swim-
ming in the first container, and when the water was poured into
the new container, she told the child that 'The duck was taking
his water with him.'

Three kinds of arguments were set forth by the children to
support their judgements. One is perceptual – having to do with
the height, width, or apparent 'bigness' of the water. A second

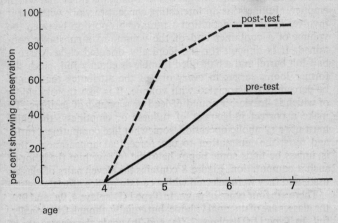

Figure 7 *Percentage of children showing conservation of liquid volume in
identical pre-test and post-test run after completion of experiment
(Frank, 1966).*

type has to do with action: the duck took the water along, or the
water was only poured. A third one, 'transformational' argument,
invokes the reversibility principle: if you poured the water back
into the first container, it would look the same again.[2] Of the
children who thought the water was not equal in amount after
pouring, 15 per cent used nonperceptual arguments to justify
their judgement. Of those who recognized the equality of the
water, two-thirds used nonperceptual arguments. It is plain that if
a child is to succeed in the conservation task, he must have some

2. Not one of the forty children who participated in this experiment used
the compensation argument – that though the water was lower it was
correspondingly wider and was, therefore, the same amount of water. This
type of reasoning by compensation is said by Piaget and Inhelder (1962)
to be the basis of conservation.

internalized verbal formula that shields him from the overpowering appearance of the visual displays much as in the Frank experiment. The explanations of the children who lacked conservation suggest how strongly oriented they were to the visual appearance of the displays they had to deal with.

Consider now another experiment by Bruner and Kenney (1966) also designed to explore the border between iconic and symbolic representation. Children aged five, six, and seven were asked to say which of two glasses in a pair was fuller and which emptier. 'Fullness' is an interesting concept to work with, for it involves in its very definition a ratio or proportion between the volume of a container and of the volume of a substance contained. It is difficult for the iconically oriented child to see a half-full barrel and a half-filled thimble as equally full, since the former looms larger in every one of the attributes that might be perceptually associated with volume. It is like the old riddle of which is heavier, a pound of lead or a pound of feathers. To make a correct judgement of fullness or emptiness, the child must use a symbolic operation, somewhat like computing a ratio, and resist the temptation to use perceptual appearance – that is, unless he finds some happy heuristic to save him the labor of such a computation. Figure 8 contains the eleven pairs of glasses used, and they were selected with a certain malice aforethought.

There are four types of pairs. In Type I (Displays 4, 9a, and 9b), the glasses are of unequal volume, but equally, though fractionally, full. In Type II (Displays, 2, 7a, and 7b) again the glasses are of unequal volume, but they are completely full. Type III (Displays 3, 8a, and 8b) consists of two glasses of unequal volume, one filled and the other part filled. Type IV consists of identical glasses, in one case equally filled, in another unequally (Displays 1 and 5).

All the children in the age range we have studied use pretty much the same criteria for judging *fullness*, and these criteria are based on directly observable sensory indices rather than upon proportion. That glass is judged fuller that has the greater apparent volume of water, and the favored indication of greater volume is water level; or where that is equated, then width of glass will do; and when width and water level are the same, then height of glass will prevail. But now consider the judgements made by the three age groups with respect to which glass in each pair is *emptier*. The older children have developed an interesting consistency based on an appreciation of the complementary relation of filled and empty space – albeit an incorrect one. For them 'emptier' means the glass that has the largest apparent volume of unfilled space

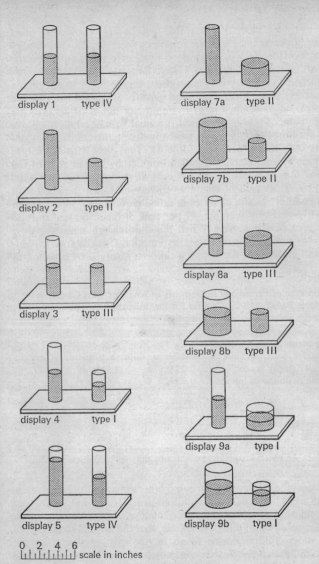

display 1   type IV

display 2   type II

display 3   type III

display 4   type I

display 5   type IV

display 7a   type II

display 7b   type II

display 8a   type III

display 8b   type III

display 9a   type I

display 9b   type I

0   2   4   6   scale in inches

Figure 8   Eleven pairs of glasses to be judged in terms of which glass is fuller and which emptier (Bruner and Kenney, 1966).

just as 'fuller' meant the glass that had the largest volume of filled space. In consequence, their responses seem logically contradictory. For the glass that is judged fuller also turns out to be the glass that is judged emptier – given a large glass and a small glass, both half full. The younger children, on the other hand, equate emptiness with 'littleness': that glass is emptier that gives the impression of being smaller in volume of liquid. If we take the three pairs of glasses of Type I (unequal volumes, half filled) we can see how the judgements typically distribute themselves. Consider only the errors (see Table 1). The glass with the larger volume of empty space is called emptier by 27 per cent of the erring five-year-olds, by 53 per cent of the erring six-year-olds, and by 72 per cent of erring seven-year-olds. But the glass with the smallest volume of water is called emptier by 73 per cent of the five-year-olds who err, 47 per cent of the sixes, and only 28 per cent of the sevens. When the children are asked for their reasons for judging one glass as emptier, there is further confirmation: most of the younger children justify it by pointing to

Table 1

Percentage of Erroneous Judgements of which of Two Glasses is Emptier Based on Two Criteria for Defining the Concept

Criterion for 'emptier' judgement	Age		
	5	6	7
Greater empty space	27%	53%	72%
Smaller volume of liquid	73%	47%	28%
	100%	100%	100%
Percentage correct	9%	8%	17%
N =	30	30	30

Note. – Criteria are greater volume of empty space and lesser volume of water.

'littleness' or 'less water' or some other aspect of diminutiveness. And most of the older children justify their judgements of emptiness by reference to the amount of empty space in the vessel.

The result of all this is, of course, that the 'logical structure' of the older children seems to go increasingly awry. But surely, though figure 9 shows that contradictory errors steadily increase with age (calling the same glass fuller and emptier or equally full but not equally empty or vice versa), the contradiction is a by-product of the method of dealing with attributes. How shall we interpret these findings? Let me suggest that what is involved is a translation difficulty in going from the perceptual or iconic realm to the symbolic. If you ask children of this age whether something can be fuller and also emptier, they will smile and think that you are playing riddles. They are aware of the contrastive nature of the two terms. Indeed, even the very young child has a good working language for the two poles of the contrast: 'all gone' for

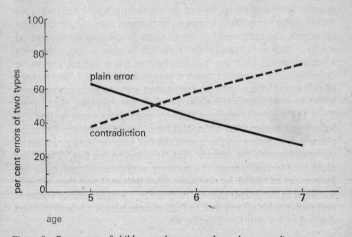

Figure 9   *Percentage of children at three ages who make contradictory and plain errors in judging which of two glasses is fuller and which emptier. (A contradictory error is calling the same glass both fuller or emptier or calling them equally full but not equally empty or vice versa. A plain error calling one glass fuller and the other emptier, but incorrectly. From Bruner and Kenney, 1966.)*

completely empty and 'spill' or 'tippy top' for completely full. Recall too that from five to seven, there is perfect performance in judging which of two identical beakers is fuller and emptier. The difference between the younger and the older child is in the number of attributes that are being attended to in situations involving fullness and emptiness: the younger child is attending to one – the volume of water; the older to two – the volume of filled space and the volume of empty space (see Table 2). The young child is applying a single contrast pair – full–empty – to a single feature of the situation. The older child can attend to two features, but he does not yet

397

have the means for relating them to a third, the volume of the container *per se*. To do so involves being able to deal with a relation in the perceptual field that does not have a 'point-at-able' or ostensive definition. Once the third term is introduced – the volume of the glass – then the symbolic concept of proportion can come to 'stand for' something that is not present perceptually. The older child is on the way to achieving the insight, in spite of his contradictions. And, interestingly enough, if we count the number of children who justify their judgements of fuller and emptier by pointing to *several* rather than a single attribute, we find that the porportion triples in both cases between age five and age seven. The older child, it would seem, is ordering his perceptual world in such a way that, shortly, he will be able to apply concepts of relationship that are not dependent upon simple ostensive definition. As he moves toward this more powerful 'technology of reckoning', he is led into errors that seem to be contradictory. What is particularly telltale is the fact, for example, that in the Type III displays, younger children sometimes seem to find the judgement easier than older children – pointing to the fuller by placing their finger on the rim of the full member and pointing to the emptier with the remark that 'It is not to the top.' The older child (and virtually never the younger one) gets all involved in the judgement of 'fuller by apparent filled volume' and then equally involved in the judgement of 'emptier by apparent empty volume' and such are his efforts that he fails to note his contradiction when dealing with a pair like Display 8b.

Table 2

Percentage of Children who Justify Judgements of 'Fuller' and 'Emptier' by Mentioning More than a Single Attribute

Age	'Fuller' judgements	'Emptier' judgements	N
5	7·2%	4·1%	30
6	15·6%	9·3%	30
7	22·2%	15·6%	30

Turn now to a quite different experimental procedure that deals with the related concept of equivalence – how seemingly different objects are grouped into equivalence classes. In the two experiments to be cited, one by Olver (1961), the other by Rigney (1962), children are given words or pictures to sort into groups or to characterize in terms of how they are alike. The two sets of results, one for words, the other for pictures, obtained for children between six and fourteen, can be summarized together. One may distinguish two aspects of grouping – the first has to do with the features or attributes that children use as a criterion for grouping objects: *perceptual features* (the color, size, pattern, etc.), *arbitrary functional features* (what I can do with the objects regardless of their usual use: you can make noise with a newspaper by crumpling it and with a book by slamming it shut, etc.), *appropriate functional features* (potato, peach, banana, and milk are characterized 'You can eat them'). But grouping behavior can also be characterized in terms of the syntactical structure of the equivalence sets that the child develops. There are, first, what Vygotsky (1962) has called *heaps*: collections put together in an arbitrary way simply because the child has decided to put them together that way. Then there are *complexes*: the various members of a complex are included in the class in accordance with a rule that does not account uniformly for the inclusion of all the members. Edge matching is one such rule: each object is grouped into a class on the basis of its similarity with a neighboring object. Yet no two neighboring pieces may be joined by the same similarity. Another type of complexive grouping is thematic: here objects are put together by virtue of participating in a sentence or a little story. More sophisticated is a key ring in which one organizing object is related to all others but none of those to each other. And finally, considerably more sophisticated than heaps and complexes, there are *superordinate concepts*, in which one universal rule of inclusion accounts for all the objects in the set – all men and women over twenty-one are included in the class of voters provided they meet certain residence requirements.

The pattern of growth is revealing of many of the trends we have already discussed, and provides in addition a new clue. Consider first the attributes or features of objects that children at different ages use as a basis for forming equivalence groups. As figure 10 indicates, the youngest children rely more heavily on perceptual attributes than do the others. As they grow older. grouping comes to depend increasingly upon the functional properties of things – but the transitional phase is worth some attention, for it raises anew the issue of the significance of egocentrism. For the first functional groupings to appear are of an arbitrary type – what 'I' or 'you' can do to objects that renders them alike, rather than what is the conventional use or function to which objects can be put. During this stage of 'egocentric functionalism', there is a corresponding rise in the use of first- and second-person personal pronouns: 'I can do thus and so to this object; I can do the same to this one,' etc. Gradually, with increasing maturity the child shifts to an appropriate and less egocentric form of using functional groupings. The shift from perceptual to functional groupings is accompanied by a corresponding shift in the syntactical structure of the groups formed.

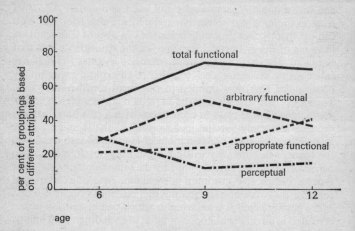

Figure 10   Features of objects used by children of different ages as a basis for placing the objects in equivalence groups (Olver, 1961).

Complexive groupings steadily dwindle; superordinate groupings rise, until the latter almost replace the former in late adolescence (see figure 11). It is difficult to tell which is the pacemaker in this growth – syntax or the semantic basis of grouping.

Rigney reports one other matter of some interest. Her young subjects formed groups of any size they wished, choosing pictures from a display board of several dozen little water colors. She observed that the most perceptually based groups and the ones most often based on complexive grouping principles were pairs. A count of these revealed that 61 per cent of all the groups made by six-year-olds were such pairs, 36 per cent of those made by eight-year-olds, and only 25 per cent of the groupings of eleven-year-olds.

On the surface, this set of findings – Olver's and Rigney's alike – seems to point more to the decline of a preference for perceptual and iconic ways of dealing with objects and events, particularly with their grouping. But closer inspection suggests still another factor that is operating. In both cases, there is evidence of the development of hierarchical structure and rules for including objects in super-ordinate hierarchies. Hierarchical classification is surely one of the most evident properties of the structure of language – hierarchical grouping that goes beyond mere perceptual inclusion. Complexive structures of the kind described earlier are much more dominated by the sorts of associative principles by

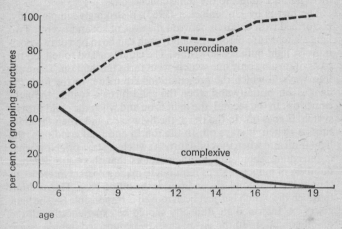

Figure 11 The use of two rules of equivalence grouping found in children of different ages (Olver, 1961).

which the appearance of objects leads to their spontaneous grouping in terms of similarity or contiguity. As language becomes more internalized, more guiding as a set of rules for organizing events, there is a shift from the associative principles that operate in classical perceptual organization to the increasingly abstract rules for grouping events by the principles of inclusion, exclusion, and overlap, the most basic characteristics of any hierarchical system.

We have said that cognitive growth consists in part in the development of systems of representation as means for dealing with information. The growing child begins with a strong reliance upon learned action patterns to represent the world around him. In time, there is added to this technology a means for simultanizing regularities in experience into images that stand for events in the way that pictures do. And to this is finally added a technology of translating experience into a symbol system that can be operated upon by rules of transformation that greatly increase the possible range of problem solving. One of the effects of this development, or possibly one of its causes, is the power for organizing acts of information processing into more integrated and long-range problem-solving efforts. To this matter we turn next.

Consider in rapid succession three related experiments. All of them point, I think, to the same conclusion.

The first is by Huttenlocher (1963), a strikingly simple study, performed with children between the ages of six and twelve. Two light switches are before the child; each can be in one of two positions. A light bulb is also visible. The child is asked to tell, on the basis of turning only one switch, what turns the light on. There are four ways in which the presentations are made. In the first, the light is off initially and when the child turns a switch, the light comes on. In the second, the light is on and when the child turns a switch, it goes off. In the third, the light is on and when the child turns a switch, it stays on. In the fourth and final condition, the light is off and when the child turns a switch, it stays off. Now what is intriguing about this arrangement is that there are different numbers of inductive steps required to make a correct inference in each task. The simplest condition is the off-on case. The position to which the switch has just been moved is responsible for the light going on. Intermediate difficulty should be experienced with the on-off condition. In the on-off case, two connected inferences are required: the present position achieved is rejected and the original position of the switch that has been turned is responsible for lighting the bulb. An even larger number of consecutive acts is required for success in the on-on case: the present position of the turned switch is rejected, the original position as well and the present position of the *other* switch is responsible. The off-off case requires four steps: rejecting the present position of the turned switch, its original position, and the present position of the other switch, finally accepting the alternative position of the unturned switch. The natures of the individual steps are all the same. Success in the more complex cases depends upon being able to integrate them consecutively.

Huttenlocher's results show that the six-year-olds are just as capable as their elders of performing the elementary operation involved in the one-step case: the on-off display. They, like the nines and twelves, make nearly perfect scores. But in general, the more inferential steps the six-year-old must make, the poorer his performance. By age twelve, on the other hand, there is an insignificant difference between the tasks requiring one, two, three, or four connected inferences.

An experiment by Mosher (1962) underlines the same point. He was concerned with the strategies used by children from six to eleven for getting information in the game of Twenty Questions. They were to find out by 'yes-no' questions what caused a car to go off the road and hit a tree. One may distinguish between connected constraint-locating questions ('Was it night-time?'

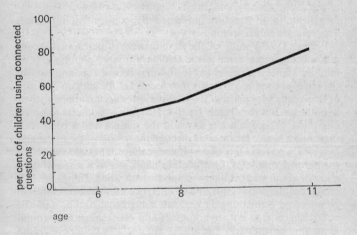

Figure 12   The proportion of children at different ages who use connected questions in a Twenty Questions game (Mosher, 1962).

followed up appropriately) and direct hypothesis-testing questions ('Did a bee fly in the window and sting the man on the eye and make him go off the road and hit the tree?') From six to eleven, more and more children use constraint-locating, connected questioning (see figure 12). Let me quote from Mosher's account.

We have asked children . . . after they have played their games, to tell us which of two questions they would rather have the answer to, if they were playing the games again – one of them a typical constraint-seeking question ('Was there anything wrong with the man?') and the other a typical discrete test of an hypothesis ('Did the man have a heart attack?'). All the eleven-year-olds and all the eight-year-olds choose the constraint-seeking question, but only 29 per cent of the six-year-olds do [p. 6].

The questions of the younger children are all one-step substitutes for direct sense experience. They are looking for knowledge by single questions that provide the answer in a finished form. When they succeed they do so by a lucky question that hits an immediate, perceptible cause. When the older child receives a 'yes' answer to one of his constraint-locating questions, he most often follows up by asking another. When, on the rare occasions that a younger child asks a constraint question and it is answered 'yes', he almost invariably follows it up with a specific question to test a concrete hypothesis. The older child can accrete his information in a structure governed by consecutive inference. The younger child cannot.

Potter's (1966) study of the development of perceptual recognition bears on the same point. Ordinary colored photographs of familiar scenes are presented to children between six and twelve, the pictures coming gradually into focus. Let me sum up one part of the results very briefly. Six-year-olds produce an abundance of hypotheses. But they rarely try to match new hypotheses to previous ones. 'There is a big tower in the middle and a road over there and a big ice cream cone through the middle of the tower and a pumpkin on top.' It is like a random collage. The nine-year-old's torrent of hypotheses, on the other hand, shows a sense of consistency about what is likely to appear with what. Things are in a context of likelihood, a frame of reference that demands internal consistency. Something is seen as a merry-go-round, and the child then restricts later hypotheses to the other things to be found in an amusement park. The adolescent operates under even more highly organized sequential constraints: he occasionally develops his initial hypotheses from what is implied by the properties of the picture, almost by intersection – 'It is red and shiny and metallic: it must be a coffee-pot.' Once such constraints are established, the order of hypotheses reflects even more the need to build up a consistent world of objects – even to the point of failing to recognize things that do not fit it.

What shall we make of these three sets of findings – that older children are able to cumulate information by asking questions in a directed sequence leading to a final goal, and that they are capable of recognizing visual displays in a manner governed by a dominating frame of reference that transcends momentary and isolated bits of information? Several points seem apparent. The first is that as children mature, they are able to use indirect information based on forms of information processing other than the act of pointing to what is immediately present. They seem, in short, to make remote reference to states and constraints that are not given by the immediate situation, to go beyond the information given. Second, and this is a matter that has already been discussed, they seem to be able to cumulate information into a structure that can be operated upon by rules that transcend simple association by similarity and contiguity. In the case of Twenty Questions, the rule is best described as implication – that knowing one thing implies certain other things and eliminates still others. In the experiments with the light switches, it is that if the present state does not produce the effect, then there is a system for tracing back to the other states that cause the light to go on. Where perceptual recognition is concerned, the rule is that a piece of information from one part of the display implies what other parts might be. The child, in sum, is translating redundancy into a manipulable model of the environment that is governed by rules of implication. It is this model of the environment that permits him to go beyond the information before him. I would suggest that it is this new array of cognitive equipment that permits the child to transcend momentaneity, to integrate longer sequences of events.

Let me urge, moreover, that such a system of processing environmental events depends upon the translation of experience into symbolic form. Such a translation is necessary in order for there to be the kind of remoteness of reference as is required when one deals with indirect information. To transcend the immediately perceptual, to get beyond what is vividly present to a more extended model of the environment, the child needs a system that permits him to deal with the nonpresent, with things that are remote in space, qualitative similarity, and time, from the present situation. Hockett (1959), in describing the design features of language includes this feature as crucial. He is referring to human speech as a system of communication. The same point can be made about language as an instrument of thought. That humans have the *capacity* for using speech in this way is only part of the point. What is critical is that the capacity is *not* used until it is coupled with the technology of language in the cognitive operations of the child.

The same can be said for the models of the environment that the child constructs to go beyond present information. This is not to say that non-verbal animals cannot make inferences that go beyond the present stimulus: anticipatory activity is the rule in vertebrates. But the models that the growing child constructs seem not to be anticipatory, or inferential, or probabilistic-frequency models. They seem to be governed by rules that can more properly be called syntactical rather than associative.

My major concern has been to examine afresh the nature of intellectual growth. The account has surely done violence to the richness of the subject. It seems to me that growth depends upon the emergence of two forms of competence. Children, as they grow, must acquire ways of representing the recurrent regularities in their environment, and they must transcend the momentary by developing ways of linking past to present to future – representation and integration. I have suggested that we can conceive of growth in both of these domains as the emergence of new technologies for the unlocking and amplification of human intellectual powers. Like the growth of technology, the growth of intellect is not smoothly monotonic. Rather, it moves forward in spurts as innovations are adopted. Most of the innovations are transmitted to the child in some prototypic form by agents of the culture: ways of responding, ways of looking and imaging, and most important, ways of translating what one has encountered into language.

I have relied heavily in this account on the successive emergence of action, image, and word as the vehicles of representation, a reliance based both upon our observations and upon modern readings of man's alloplastic evolution. Our attention has been directed largely to the transition between iconic and symbolic representation.

In children between four and twelve language comes to play an increasingly powerful role as an implement of knowing. Through simple experiments, I have tried to show how language shapes, augments, and even supersedes the child's earlier modes of processing information. Translation of experience into symbolic form, with its attendant means of achieving remote reference transformation, and combination, opens up realms of intellectual possibility that are orders of magnitude beyond the most powerful image forming system.

What of the integration of intellectual activity into more coherent and interconnected acts? It has been the fashion, since Freud, to see delay of gratification as the principal dynamism behind this development – from primary process to secondary process, or from assimilation to accommodation, as Piaget would put it today. Without intending to question the depth of this insight, let me suggest that delay of immediate gratification, the ability to go beyond the moment, also depends upon techniques, and again they are techniques of representation. Perhaps representation exclusively by imagery and perceptual organization has built into it one basic operation that ties it to the immediate present. It is the operation of pointing – ostensiveness, as logicians call it. (This is not to say that highly evolved images do not go beyond immediate time and given place. Maps and flow charts are iconic in nature, but they are images that translate prior linguistic and mathematical renderings into a visual form.) Iconic representation, in the beginning, is built upon a perceptual organization that is tied to the 'point-at-able' spatioqualitative properties of events. I have suggested that, for all its limitations, such representation is an achievement beyond the earlier stage where percepts are not autonomous of action. But so long as perceptual representation dominates, it is difficult to develop higher-order techniques for processing information by consecutive inferential steps that take one beyond what can be pointed at.

Once language becomes a medium for the translation of experience, there is a progressive release from immediacy. For language, as we have commented, has the new and powerful features of remoteness and arbitrariness: it permits productive, combinatorial operations in the *absence* of what is represented. With this achievement, the child can delay gratification by virtue of representing to himself what lies beyond the present, what other possibilities exist beyond the clue that is under his nose. The child may be *ready* for delay of gratification, but he is no more able to bring it off than somebody ready to build a house, save that he has not yet heard of tools.

The discussion leaves two obvious questions begging. What of the integration of behavior in organisms without language? And how does language become internalized as a vehicle for organizing experience? The first question has to be answered briefly and somewhat cryptically. Wherever integrated behavior has been studied – as in Lehrman's (1955) careful work on integrated instinctive patterns in the ringdove, it has turned out that a sustaining external stimulus was needed to keep the highly integrated behavior going. The best way to control behavior in subhuman species is to control the stimulus situation. Surely this is the lesson of Lashley's (1938) classic account of instinctive behavior. Where animal learning is concerned, particularly in the primates, there is, to be sure, considerable plasticity. But it too depends upon the development of complex forms of stimulus substitution and organization – as in Klüver's (1933) work on equivalence reactions in monkeys. If it should seem that I am urging that the growth of symbolic functioning links a unique set of powers to man's capacity, the appearance is quite as it should be.

As for how language becomes internalized as a program for ordering experience, I join those who despair for an answer. My speculation, for whatever it is worth, is that the process of internalization depends upon interaction with others, upon the need to develop corresponding categories and transformations for communal action. It is the need for cognitive coin that can be exchanged with those on whom we depend. What Roger Brown (1958) has called the Original Word Game ends up by being the Human Thinking Game.

If I have seemed to under-emphasize the importance of inner capacities – for example, the capacity *for* language or *for* imagery – it is because I believe that this part of the story is given by the nature of man's evolution. What is significant about the growth of mind in the child is to what degree it depends not upon capacity but upon the unlocking of capacity by techniques that come from exposure to the specialized environment of a culture. Romantic clichés, like 'the veneer of culture' or 'natural man', are as misleading if not as damaging as the view that the course of human development can be viewed independently of the educational process we arrange to make that development possible.

References

ABRAMYAN, L. A. (1958), *Organization of the voluntary activity of the child with the help of verbal instructions*, Unpublished diploma thesis, Moscow University. Cited in Luria, A. R. (1961), *The role of speech in the regulation of normal and abnormal behavior*, Liveright.

BARKER, R. G. (1963), 'On the nature of the environment', Kurt Lewin Memorial Address presented at American Psychological Association, Philadelphia.

BRAINE, M. D. (1963), 'On learning the grammatical order of words, *Psychol. Rev.*, vol. 70, pp. 323–48.

BROWN, R. (1958), *Words and things*, Free Press.

BRUNER, J. S., and KENNEY, H. (1966), 'The development of the concepts of order and proportion in children', in Bruner, J. S., *Studies in cognitive growth*, Wiley.

CHOMSKY, N. (1957), *Syntactic structures*, Mouton.

EMERSON, L. L. (1931), 'The effect of bodily orientation upon the young child's memory for position of objects', *Child Develpm.*, vol. 2, pp. 125–42.

FRANK, F. (1966), 'Perception and language in conservation', in Bruner, J. S., *Studies in cognitive growth*, Wiley.

HANFMANN, E., RICKERS-OVSIANKINA, M., and GOLDSTEIN, K.

(1944), 'Case Lanuti: extreme concretization of behavior due to damage of the brain cortex', *Psychol. Monogr.*, vol. 57, whole no. 264.

HOCKETT, C. F. (1959), 'Animal "languages" and human language', in Spuhler, J. N., *The evolution of man's capacity for culture*, Wayne State U.P., pp. 32–9.

HUTTENLOCHER, J. (1963), 'Growth and the organization of inference', in Center for Cognitive Studies, *Annual Report*, Cambridge, Mass.

KLÜVER, H. (1933), *Behavior mechanisms in monkeys*, Univer. Chicago Press.

LA BARRE, W. (1954), *The human animal*, Univer. Chicago Press.

LASHLEY, K. S. (1938), 'Experimental analysis of instinctive behavior', *Psychol. Rev.*, vol. 45, pp. 445–72.

LEHRMAN, D. S. (1955), 'The physiological basis of parental feeding behavior in the ring dove (*Streptopelia risoria*)', *Behavior*, vol. 7, pp. 241–86.

LURIA, A. R. (1961), *The role of speech in the regulation of normal and abnormal behavior*, Liveright.

MANDLER, G. (1962), 'From association to structure', *Psychol. Rev.*, vol. 69, pp. 415–27.

MARTSINOVSKAYA, E. N. (undated), 'Research into the reflective and regulatory role of the second signalling system of pre-school age', Collected papers of the Department of Psychology, Moscow University. Cited by Luria, A. R. (1961), *The role of speech in the regulation of normal and abnormal behavior*, Liveright.

MILLER, G. A. (1962), 'Some psychological studies of grammar', *Amer. Psychologist*, vol. 17, pp. 748–62.

MILLER, G. A., GALANTER, E., and PRIBRAM, K. H. (1960), *Plans and the structure of behavior*, Holt.

MOSHER, F. A. (1962), 'Strategies for information gathering', Paper read at Eastern Psychological Association, Atlantic City, N.J.

NAIR, P. (1963), 'An experiment in conservation', in Center for Cognitive Studies, *Annual Report*, Cambridge, Mass.

OLVER, R. R. (1961), *A development study of cognitive equivalence*, Unpublished doctoral dissertation, Radcliffe College.

PIAGET, J. (1954), *The construction of reality in the child* (trans. Margaret Cook), Basic Books.

PIAGET, J., and INHELDER, B. (1962), *Le développement des quantités physiques chez l'enfant*, Delachaux et Niestlé. (2nd rev. edn.)

POTTER, M. C. (1966), 'The growth of perceptual recognition', in Bruner J. S., *Studies in cognitive growth*, Wiley.

RIGNEY, J. C. (1962), *A developmental study of cognitive equivalence transformations and their use in the acquisition and processing of information*, Unpublished honors thesis, Radcliffe College, Department of Social Relations.

VYGOTSKY, L. S. (1962), *Thought and language* (ed. and trans. by E. Hanfmann and G. Vahar), Wiley.

WASHBURN, S. L., and HOWELL, F. C. (1960), 'Human evolution and culture', in Tax, S., *The evolution of man*, vol. 2, Univer. Chicago Press.

WEIR, R. H. (1962), *Language in the crib*, Mouton.

WERNER, H. (1948), *Comparative psychology of mental development*, Follett. (Rev. edn.)

Representation and Mathematics Learning

J. S. Bruner and H. J. Kenney, 'Representation and mathematics learning',
in *Mathematics Learning*, Monograph of the Society for Research in
Child Development, vol. 30 (1965), serial no. 99, pp. 50–9.

The central concern of the present study is the psychological
processes involved in the learning of mathematics by children
who, in Piaget's sense, are in the stage of 'concrete operations'
and are not, presumably, yet able to deal readily with formal
propositions. Better to understand how mathematics learning of
a highly symbolized type might occur, we worked with a small
number of children, observing them in minute detail to determine
the steps involved in grasping mathematical ideas. Such an
approach is, in our opinion, most pressingly needed at this stage
of development of new mathematical instruction. It is closely akin
to the detailed study of the naturalist and clinician. Perhaps such
study can serve to aid more large-scale psychometric testing or,
indeed, to elucidate the nature of instruction. It would be disin-
genuous to say that we (or any naturalist, for that matter) worked
without due regard to some theory. Our theoretical predilections
were, we should say, far clearer when we finished than when we
started. They will also be plain to the reader as our account
progresses.

The observations to be reported were made on four eight-year-
old children, two boys and two girls, who were given an hour of
daily instruction in mathematics four times a week for six weeks.
The children were in the I.Q. range of 120–130 and were enrolled
in the third grade of a private school that emphasized instruction
designed to foster independent problem solving. They were from
middle-class professional homes. The 'teacher' of the class was a
well known research mathematician (Z. P. Dienes); his assistant
was a professor of psychology at Harvard who has worked long
and hard on human thought processes.

Each child worked at a corner table in a generously sized room.
Next to each child sat a tutor-observer trained in psychology and
with sufficient background in college mathematics to understand
the underlying mathematics being taught. In the middle of the
room was a large table with a supply of the blocks and balance
beams and cups and beans and chalk that served as instructional

aids. In the course of the six weeks, the children were given instruction in factoring, the distributive and commutative properties of addition and multiplication, and, finally, in quadratic functions.

Each child had available a series of graded problem cards to go through at his own pace. The cards gave directions for different kinds of exercises, using the materials described above. The instructor and his assistant circulated from table to table, helping as needed, and each observer-tutor similarly assisted as needed. The problem sequences were designed to provide, first, an appreciation of mathematical ideas through concrete constructions using materials of various kinds for these constructions. From such constructions, the child was encouraged to form perceptual images of the mathematical idea in terms of the forms that had been constructed. The child was then further encouraged to develop or adopt a notation to describe his construction. After such a cycle, a child moved on to the construction of a further embodiment of the idea on which he was working, one that was mathematically isomorphic with what he had learned although expressed in different materials and with altered appearance. When such a new topic was introduced, the children were given a chance to discover its connexion with what had gone before and were shown how to extend the notational system used before. Careful minute-by-minute records were kept of the proceedings, along with photographs of the children's constructions.

In no sense can the children, the teachers, the classroom, or the mathematics be said to be typical of what normally occurs in third grade. Four children rarely have six teachers nor do eight-year-olds ordinarily get into quadratic functions. But our concern is with the processes involved in mathematical learning and not with typicality. We would be foolish to claim that the achievements of the children were typical. But it seems quite reasonable to suppose that the thought processes going on in the children were quite ordinary among eight-year-old human beings.

As we have noted, the instruction emphasized concrete construction and embodiment of mathematical concepts. It could have been more axiomatic, less dependent upon visual intuition of forms. It is highly unlikely that there is one optimum procedure for teaching or learning mathematics. The observations obviously reflect the approach of the study as well as the nature of mathematical learning.

Four aspects of the learning seem worth special comment: the role of construction, the uses of notation, the place of contrast and variation, and the character of 'insight'.

The Role of Construction

In mathematical factoring, to start with an example, the concept of prime numbers appears to be more readily grasped when the child, through construction, discovers that certain handfuls of beans cannot be laid out in completed multiple rows and columns. Such quantities have either to be laid out in a single file or in an incomplete row-column design in which there is always one extra or one too few to fill the pattern. These patterns, the child learns, happen to be called 'prime' or they could be called 'unarrangeable'. It is easy for the child to go from this step to the recognition that a multiplication table, so called, is a record sheet of quantities in *completed* multiple rows and columns. Here is factoring, multiplication, and primes in a construction that can

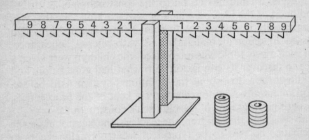

Figure 1   Balance beam and rings used on quadratic construction.

also be visualized. Take the matter of factoring in another physical embodiment: a balance beam with hooks placed equi-distant from a central fulcrum is the construction vehicle this time (figure 1). Contrast this with factoring as the usual computational exercise – as in the problem, 'what are the factors of 18?' Conventionally, the child parrots the correct set of factors with the usual uncertainty about whether 9 and 2 are different from 2 and 9, or 6 and 3 from 3 and 6. On the balance beam, we place 2 rings on hook 9; the child is encouraged to find and write down every combination of rings on hooks on the opposite side that will balance it. It is a beautiful discovery that 2 rings on hook 9 balances 9 rings on hook 2 – and an introduction to the idea of commutativity. Note again that the construction produces a basis for imagery. And before long some startlingly abstract principles couched in elegant terms emerge: 'You can exchange rings for hooks if you want.' Factors are now events. When notation is applied now, there is a referent.

Note that constructions can be 'unconstructed and reconstructed' even when the child does not yet have a ready symbol system for doing so abstractly. In short, construction, unconstruction, and reconstruction provides reversibility in *overt* operations until the child, in Piaget's sense, can internalize such operations in symbolized form.

Now consider quadratic functions. Each child was provided with building materials. These were large flat squares made of wood whose dimensions were unspecified and described simply as 'unknown or x long and x wide' (figure 2). There were also a large number of strips of wood that were as long as the sides of

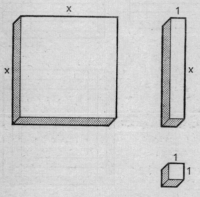

Figure 2   Three components for quadratic constructions.

the square and described arbitrarily as having a width of '1' or simply '1 by x'. And there was a supply of little squares with sides equal to the width '1' of the strips, thus '1 by 1'. The reader should be warned that the presentation of these materials is not as simple as all that. To begin with, it is necessary to convince the children that we really do not know and do not *care* what is the metric size of the big squares, that rulers are of no interest. A certain humor helps establish in the pupils a proper contempt for measuring in this context, and the snob appeal of simply calling an unknown by the name 'x' is very great. From there on, the children readily discover for themselves that the long strips are x long – by correspondence. They take on faith (as they should) that the narrow

413

dimension is '1', but that they grasp its arbitrariness is clear from one child's declaration of the number of such '1' lengths that make an x. As for '1 by 1' little squares, that too is established by simple correspondence with the narrow dimension of the '1 by x' strips. It is horseback method but quite good mathematics.

The child is asked whether he can make a square bigger than the x by x square, using the materials at hand. He very quickly builds squares with designs like those in figure 3. We ask him to record

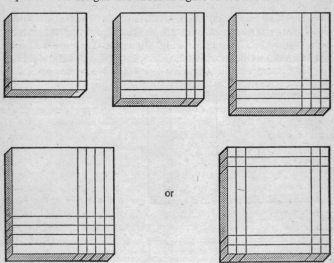

Figure 3   Squares of ever increasing size constructed with components.

how much wood is needed for each larger square and how long and wide each square is.

The Use of Notation

He describes one of his constructed squares; very concretely the pieces are counted out: 'an x-square, two x-strips, and a one square' or, 'an x-square, four x-strips, and four ones', or 'an x-square, six x-strips and nine ones', etc. We help him with language and show him a way to write it down. The big square is an '$x^\square$', the long strips are '1 x' or simply 'x', and the little squares are 'one squares' or 'one by one' or better still simply '1'. And the expression 'and' can be shortened to '$+$'. And so he can write out the recipe for a constructed square as '$x^\square +4x+4$'. At this stage, these are merely names put together in little sentences. How wide and long is the square in question? This the child can readily measure off – an x and 2 or $x+2$ – and so the whole thing is $(x+2)^\square$. Brackets are not so easily grasped. And so the child is able to put down his first equality: $(x+2)^\square = x^\square +4x+4$. Virtually everything has a referent that can be pointed to with a finger. He has a notational system into which he can translate the image he has constructed.

Now we go on to making bigger squares, and each square the child makes he describes in terms of what wood went into it and how wide and how long it is. It takes some ruled sheets to get the child to keep his record so that he can go back and inspect it for what it may reveal, and he is encouraged to go back and look at the record and at the constructions they stand for.

Imagine now a list such as the following, again a product of the child's own construction:

$x + 2x + \ \ 1$ is $x + 1$ by $x + 1$
$x + 4x + \ \ 4$ is $x + 2$ by $x + 2$
$x + 6x + \ \ 9$ is $x + 3$ by $x + 3$
$x + 8x + 16$ is $x + 4$ by $x + 4$

It is almost impossible for him not to make some discoveries about the numbers: that the x values go up 2, 4, 6, 8 . . . and the unit values go up 1, 4, 9, 16 . . . and the dimensions increase by additions to x of 1, 2, 3, 4. . . . The syntactical insights about regularity in notation are matched by perceptual-manipulative insights about the material referents.

After a while, some new manipulations occur that provide the child with a further basis for notational progress. He takes the square, $(x+2)^2$, and reconstructs it in a new way (figure 4). One may ask whether this is constructive manipulation or whether it is proper factoring. But the child is learning that the same amount of wood can build quite strikingly different patterns and remain the same amount of wood – although it also has a different notational expression. Where does the language begin and the manipulation of materials stop? The interplay is continuous. We shall return to this same example in a later section.

But the problem now is how to 'detach' the notation that the child has learned from the concrete, visible, manipulable embodiment to which it refers – the wood. For if the child is to deal with mathematical properties he will have to deal with symbols *per se*, else he will be limited to the narrow and rather trivial range of symbolism that can be given direct (and only partial) visual embodiment. Concepts such as x^2 and x^3 may be given a visualizable referent, but what of x^u?

Why do children wean themselves from the perceptual embodiment to the symbolic notation? Perhaps it is partly explained in the nature of variation and contrast.

Variation and Contrast

The child is shown the balance beam again and told, 'Choose any hook on one side and put the same number of rings on it as the number the hook is away from the middle. Now balance it with

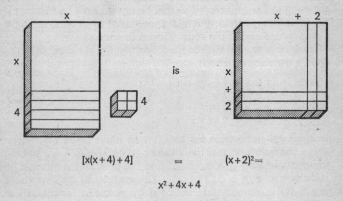

$$[x(x+4)+4] \quad = \quad (x+2)^2 =$$
$$x^2+4x+4$$

Figure 4   Syntactic exercise supported by construction.

rings placed on the other side. Keep a record.' Recall that the balance beam is familiar from work on factoring and that the child knows that 2 rings on 9 balances 9 on 2 or m rings on n balances n on m. He is back to construction. Can anything be constructed on the balance beam that is like the squares? With little effort, the following translation is made. Suppose x is 5. Then 5 rings on hook 5 is x^2, five rings on hook 4 is $4x$, and 4 rings on hook 1 is 4: x^2+4x+4. How can we find whether this is like a square that is $x+2$ wide by $x+2$ long as before? Well, if x is 5, then $x+2$ is 7, and so 7 rings on hook 7. And nature obliges – the beam balances. One notation works for two strikingly different constructions and perceptual events. Notation, with its broader equivalency, is clearly more economical than reference to embodiments. There is little resistance to using this more convenient language. And now construction can begin – commutative and distributive properties of equations can be explored: $x(x+4)+4 = x^2+4x+4$ or $x+4$ rings on hook x and 4 rings on hook 1 will balance. The child, if he wishes, can also go back to the wood and find that the same materials can make the design in figure 4.

Contrast is the vehicle by which the obvious that is too obvious to be appreciated can be made noticeable again. The discovery of an eight-year-old girl illustrates the matter. 'Yes, 4×6 equals 6×4 in numbers, like in one way six eskimos in four igloos is the same as four in six igloos. But a venetian blind *isn't* the same as a blind Venetian.' By recognizing the non-commutative property of ordinary language, the commutative property of a mathematical language can be partly grasped. But it is still only a partial insight into commutativity and noncommutativity. Had we wished to develop the distinction more deeply we might have proceeded concretely to a contrast between sets of operations that can be carried out in any sequence – like the order of eating courses at a dinner or of going to different movies – and operations that have a noncommutative order – like putting on shoes and socks – where one must precede the other. Then the child could be taken from there to a more general idea of commutative and noncommutative cases and ways of dealing with a notation, perhaps by identical sets and ordered identical sets.

Insight and Development

What was so striking in the performance of the children was their *initial* inability to represent things to themselves in a way that transcended immediate perceptual grasp. The achievement of more comprehensive insight requires, we think, the building of a mediating representational structure that transcends such immediate imagery, that renders a *sequence* of acts and images unitary and simultaneous. The children always began by constructing an embodiment of some concept, building a concrete form of operational definition. The fruit of the construction was an image and some operations that 'stood for' the concept. From there on, the task was to provide means of representation that were free of particular manipulations and specific images. Only symbolic operations provide the means of representing an idea in this way. But consider this matter for a moment.

We have already commented upon the fact that by giving the child multiple embodiments of the same general idea expressed in a common notation we lead him to 'empty' the concept of specific sensory properties until he is able to grasp its abstract properties. But surely this is not the best way of describing the child's increasing development of insight. The growth of such abstractions is important. But what struck us about the children, as we observed them, is that they had not only understood the abstractions they had learned but also had a store of concrete images that served to exemplify the abstractions. When they searched for a way to deal with new problems, the task was usually carried out not simply by abstract means but also by 'matching up' images. An example will help here. In going from the wood-blocks embodiment of the quadratic to the balance-beam embodiment, it was interesting that the children 'equated' *concrete* features of one with *concrete* features of another. One side of the balance beam 'stood for' the amount of wood, the other side for the sides of the square. These were important concrete props on which they leaned. We have been told by research mathematicians that the same use of props – heuristics – holds for them, that they have preferred ways of imagining certain problems while other problems are handled silently or in terms of an imagery of the symbolism on a page.

We reached the tentative conclusion that it was probably necessary for a child learning mathematics not only to have as firm a sense of the abstraction underlying what he was working on but, also, a good stock of visual images for embodying them. For without the latter, it is difficult to track correspondences and to check what one is doing symbolically. Here an example will help again. We had occasion, again with the help of Dr Dienes, of teaching a group of ten nine-year-olds the elements of group theory. To embody the idea of a mathematical group initially, we gave them the example of a four-group made up of the following four maneuvers (a book was the vehicle, a book with an arrow up the middle of its front cover): rotating the book a quarter turn to the left, rotating it a quarter turn to the right, rotating it a half-turn (without regard to direction of rotation), and letting it stay in the position it was in. They were quick to grasp the important property of such a mathematical group: that any sequence of maneuvers made could be reproduced from the starting position by a single move. This is not the usual way in which this property is described mathematically, but it served well for the children. We contrasted this elegant property with a series of our moves that did *not* constitute a mathematical group – indeed, they provided the counter-example themselves by proposing the one-third turn left, one-third turn right, half-turn either way, and stay. It was soon apparent that it did not work. We set the children the task of making games of four maneuvers, six maneuvers, etc., that had the property of a 'closed' game, as we called it. They were, of course, highly ingenious. But what soon became apparent was that they needed some aid in imagery – in this case an imagery notation – that would allow them to keep track and then to discover whether some new game was an isomorph of one they had already developed. The prop in this case was, of course, the matrix, listing the moves possible across the top and then listing them down the side, thus making it easily possible to check whether each combination of pairs of moves could be reproduced by a single move. The matrix in this case is a crutch or heuristic and as such has nothing to do with the abstraction of the mathematical group, yet it was enormously useful to them not only for keeping track but also for comparing one group with another for correspondence. Thus the matrix with which they started had the property of:

	s	a	b	c
s	s	a	b	c
a	a	c	s	b
b	b	s	c	a
c	c	b	a	s

Are there any four groups with a different structure? It is extremely difficult to deal with such a question without the aid of this housekeeping matrix as a vehicle for spotting correspondence.

A still better example is provided by a colleague, Dr Richard Hays, pointing to the role of imagery in dealing with certain formal properties. Suppose we specify the permissible moves in a finite state structure consisting of the states A, B, C, D, E. One may list the permissible transitions between states as follows:

$$AB$$
$$AD$$
$$BC$$
$$BE$$
$$CE$$
$$DD$$
$$ED$$
$$EA$$

Suppose we now ask of someone who has this set of rules for moving among the five states what is the shortest path from A to E that moves through C. Even with the ordered information in the list, it takes a moment to figure it out. How much easier the task becomes when one produces an image to carry the information, such as,

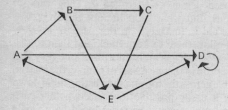

or better, the following:

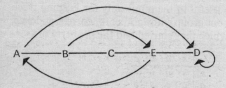

Much of mathematics is carried out with just such 'less-than-rigorous' technique, and it is likely to be important as abstraction in the actual *doing* of mathematical problems. One can use highly concrete embodiments to serve such uses. The building blocks used in teaching quadratic functions can serve as a 'source image' for checking and rethinking just as readily as the diagramming of finite state structures noted directly above.

In sum, then, while the development of insight into mathematics in our group of children depended upon their development of 'example-free' abstractions, this did not lead them to give up their imagery. Quite to the contrary, we had the impression that their enriched imagery was very useful to them in dealing with new problems.

We would suggest that learning mathematics may be viewed as a microcosm of intellectual development. It begins with instrumental activity, a kind of definition of things by doing. Such operations become represented and summarized in the form of particular images. Finally, and with the help of a symbolic notation that remains invariant across transformations in imagery, the learner comes to grasp the formal or abstract properties of the things he is dealing with. But while, once abstraction is achieved, the learner becomes free in a certain measure of the surface appearance of things, he nonetheless continues to rely upon the stock of imagery he has built en route to abstract mastery. It is this stock of imagery that permits him to work at the level of heuristic, through convenient and non-rigorous, means of exploring problems and relating them to problems already mastered.

Further Reading

General

BERLYNE, D. E., *Structure and direction in thinking*, Wiley, 1965.
BRUNER, J. S., GOODNOW, J. J., and AUSTIN, G. A., *A study of thinking*, Wiley, 1956.
HADAMARD, J., *The psychology of invention in the mathematical field*, Princeton U.P., 1945.
HUMPHREY, G., *Thinking*, Wiley Science Editions, 1963. Originally published 1951.
JOHNSON, D. M., *The psychology of thought and judgement*, Harper, 1955.
MANDLER, J. M., and G., *Thinking: from Association to Gestalt*, Wiley, 1964.
VINACKE, W. E., *The psychology of thinking*, McGraw-Hill, 1952.
WASON, P. C., 'Reasoning', in Foss, B.M. (ed.), *New horizons in psychology*, Penguin Books, 1966.

Problem solving

JUDSON, A. J., COFER, C. N., and GELFAND, S., 'Reasoning as an associative process. II. "Direction" in problem solving as a function of prior reinforcement of relevant responses', *Psychol. Reports*, vol. 2 (1956), pp. 501–7.
LUCHINS, A. S., 'Mechanization in problem solving', *Psychol. Monogr.*, vol. 54 (1942), whole no. 248.
MAIER, N. R. F., 'Reasoning in humans. I. On direction', *J. comp. Psychol.*, vol. 10 (1930), pp. 115–43.
MAIER, N. R. F., 'An aspect of human reasoning', *Brit. J. Psychol.*, vol. 24 (1933), pp. 144–55.
MAIER, N. R. F., 'The behaviour mechanisms concerned with problemsolving', *Psychol. Rev.*, vol. 47 (1940), pp. 43–58.
SCHEERER, M., 'Problem solving', *Sci. Amer.*, vol. 208 (April 1963), pp. 118–28.
WERTHEIMER, M., *Productive thinking*, Tavistock, 1959. (Enlarged edn).

Deductive reasoning

HUNTER, I. M. L., 'The solving of three term series problems', *Brit. J. Psychol.*, vol. 48 (1957), pp. 286–98.
SELLS, S. B., 'The atmosphere effect: an experimental study of reasoning', *Arch. Psychol.*, vol. 29 (1936), pp. 3–72.
WILKINS, M. C., 'The effect of changed material on ability to do formal syllogistic reasoning', *Arch. Psychol.*, *N.Y.*, 1928, no. 102.
WOODWORTH, R. B., and SELLS, S. B., 'An atmosphere effect in formal syllogistic reasoning', *J. exp. Psychol.*, vol. 18 (1935), pp. 451–60.

Inductive reasoning, matching problems and conceptual thinking

BOURNE, L. E., Jr, *Human conceptual behaviour*, Allyn & Bacon, 1966.
EIFERMANN, R., 'Negation: a linguistic variable', *Acta Psychol.*, vol. 18 (1961), pp. 258–73.
HOVLAND, C. I., and WEISS, W., 'Transmission of information concerning concepts through positive and negative instances', *J. exp. Psychol.*, vol. 45 (1953), pp. 157–82.
HUNT, E. B., *Concept learning: an information processing problem*, Wiley, 1962.
HUTTENLOCHER, J., 'Some effects of negative instances on the formation of simple concepts', *Psychol. Reports*, vol. 11 (1962), pp. 35–42.
SMOKE, K. L., 'An objective study of concept formation', *Psychol. Monogr.*, vol. 42 (1932), no. 4.
SMOKE, K. L., 'Negative instances in concept learning', *J. exp. Psychol.*, vol. 16 (1933), pp. 583–8.

WASON, P. C., 'Processing of positive and negative information', *Quart. J. exp. Psychol.*, vol. 11 (1959), pp. 92–107.

WASON, P. C., 'On the failure to eliminate hypotheses in a conceptual task', *Quart. J. exp. Psychol.*, vol. 12 (1960), pp. 129–40.

Information processing and computer simulation

BIDDER, G. P., 'On mental calculation', *Minutes of proceedings, Institution of Civil Engineers*, vol. 15 (1856), pp. 251–80

FEIGENBAUM, E. A., and FELDMAN, J. (eds.), *Computers and thought*, McGraw-Hill, 1963.

MENNINGER, K., *Calculator's cunning*, Bell, 1964.

NEWELL, A., and SIMON, H. A., 'G.P.S.: a program that simulates human thought', in Feigenbaum, E. A., and Feldman, J. (eds), *Computers and thought*, McGraw-Hill, 1963.

REITMAN, W. R., *Cognition and thought*, Wiley, 1965.

TURING, A. M., 'Computing machinery and intelligence', *Mind*, vol. 59 (1950), pp. 433–60. Reprinted in Feigenbaum, E. A., and Feldman, J. (eds.), *Computers and thought*, McGraw-Hill, 1963.

Cognitive development

FLAVELL, J. H., *The developmental psychology of Jean Piaget*, Van Nostrand, 1963.

INHELDER, B., and PIAGET, J., *The early growth of logic in the child*, Routledge & Kegan Paul, 1964.

HUNT, J. McV., *Intelligence and experience*, Ronald Press, 1961.

PIAGET, J., 'How children form mathematical concepts', *Sci. Amer.*, vol. 189 (November 1953), p. 74.

PIAGET, J., 'The child and modern physics', *Sci. Amer.*, vol. 196 (March 1957) pp. 46–51.

VYGOTSKY, L. S., *Thought and language*, M.I.T. Press, 1962.

Acknowledgements

Acknowledgements are due to the following for permission to publish extracts in this volume:

AMERICAN PSYCHOLOGICAL ASSOCIATION

R. E. Adamson, 'Functional fixedness as related to problem solving: a repetition of three experiments'. *J. exp. Psychol.*, vol. 44 (1952), pp. 288–91.

H. G. Birch and H. S. Rabinowitz, 'The negative effect of previous experience on productive thinking', *J. exp. Psychol*, vol. 41 (1951), pp. 121–5.

J. S. Bruner, 'The course of cognitive growth', *American Psychologist*, vol. 19 (1964), pp. 1–15.

L. J. Chapman and J. F. Chapman, 'Atmosphere effect re-examined', *J. exp. Psychol.*, vol. 58 (1959), pp. 220–26.

C. B. De Soto, M. London and S. Handel, 'Social reasoning and spatial paralogic', *J. Pers. soc. Psychol.*, vol. 2 (1965), pp. 513–21.

K. Duncker, 'On problem solving', *Psychol. Monogr.*, vol. 58 (1945), whole no. 270, chapters 1 and 3.

C. Gilson and R. P. Abelson, 'The subjective use of inductive evidence', *J. Pers. soc. Psychol.*, vol. 2 (1965), pp. 301–10.

R. C. Haygood and L. E. Bourne, Jr, 'Attribute- and rule-learning aspects of conceptual behaviour', *Psychol. Rev.*, vol. 72 (1965), pp. 175–95.

M. Henle, 'On the relation between logic and thinking', *Psychol. Rev.*, vol. 69 (1962), pp. 366–78.

E. I. Shipstone, 'Some variables affecting pattern conception', *Psychol. Monogr.*, vol. 74 (1960), whole no. 504.

AUTHOR INDEX

BEHAVIORAL SCIENCE
W. R. Reitman, R. B. Grove and R. G. Shoup, 'Argus: an information processing model of thinking', *Behav. Sci.*, vol. 9 (1964), pp. 270–81.

BILD DER WISSENSCHAFT
I. M. Hunter, 'Kopfrechnen and Kopfrechner', April 1966, pp. 296–303.

BRITISH PSYCHOLOGICAL SOCIETY
A. C. Campbell, 'On the solving of code items demanding the use of indirect procedures', *Brit. J. Psychol.*, vol. 56 (1965), pp. 45–57.
M. Donaldson, 'Positive and negative information in matching', *Brit. J. Psychol.*, vol. 50 (1959), pp. 235–62.
U. Neisser, 'The multiplicity of thought', *Brit. J. Psychol.*, vol. 54 (1963), pp. 1–14.
P. Sangstad and K. Raaheim, 'Problem-solving, past experience and availability of functions', *Brit. J. Psychol.*, vol. 51 (1960), pp. 97–104.

CAMBRIDGE UNIVERSITY PRESS
K. J. W. Craik, *The nature of explanation*, 1943, chapter 5.

GEORGE ALLEN AND UNWIN LTD
F. Bartlett, *Thinking*, 1958, chapter 6.

HOLT, RINEHART AND WINSTON, INC.
G. A. Miller, E. Galanter and K. H. Pribram, *Plans and the structure of behavior*, 1960, chapter 13.

JEAN PIAGET
'The stages of intellectual development of the child', *Bulletin of the Menninger Clinic*, vol. 26 (1962), pp. 120–28.

JOHN WILEY AND SONS, INC.
B. Inhelder and B. Matalon, 'The study of problem solving and thinking', in P. H. Mussen (ed.), *Handbook of research methods of child development*, 1960, pp. 421–52.

THE JOURNAL PRESS
A. S. Luchins and E. H. Luchins, 'New experimental attempts at preventing mechanization in problem solving', *J. gen. Psychol.*, vol. 42 (1950), pp. 279–97.

MOUTON AND CO, N.V.
A. D. de Groot, *Thought and choice in chess*, 1965, sections 58 and 62.

QUARTERLY JOURNAL OF EXPERIMENTAL PSYCHOLOGY
E. H. Rayner, 'A study of evaluative problem solving, Part 1', vol. 10 (1958), pp. 155–65.
P. C. Wason, 'The effect of self-contradiction on fallacious reasoning', vol. 16 (1964) pp. 30–34.
J. W. Whitfield, 'An experiment in problem solving', vol. 3 (1951), pp. 188–97.

SOCIETY FOR RESEARCH IN CHILD DEVELOPMENT
J. S. Bruner and H. J. Kenney, 'Representation and mathematics learning', *Mathematics Learning*, vol. 30 (1965), pp. 50–59.

Author Index

Subject Index